Tobacco Capitalism

Tobacco Capitalism

GROWERS, MIGRANT WORKERS, AND THE
CHANGING FACE OF A GLOBAL INDUSTRY

Peter Benson

FOREWORD BY
Allan M. Brandt

PRINCETON UNIVERSITY PRESS · PRINCETON AND OXFORD

Published by Princeton University Press, 41 William Street,
Princeton, New Jersey 08540

In the United Kingdom: Princeton University Press, 6 Oxford Street,
Woodstock, Oxfordshire OX20 1TW

press.princeton.edu

An earlier version of Chapter 4 was published as "Good Clean Tobacco:
Philip Morris, Biocapitalism, and the Social Course of Stigma in North Carolina."
American Ethnologist 35 (3): 357–79 and is reprinted with permission.

An earlier version of Chapter 5 was published as "El Campo: Faciality and Structural
Violence in Farm Labor Camps." *Cultural Anthropology* 23 (4): 589–629 and
is reprinted with permission.

Library of Congress Cataloging-in-Publication Data

Benson, Peter, 1979–
Tobacco capitalism : growers, migrant workers, and the changing face of a
global industry / Peter Benson ; foreword by Allan M. Brandt.
p.   cm.
Includes bibliographical references and index.
ISBN-13: 978-0-691-14919-6 (alk. paper)
ISBN-10: 0-691-14919-4 (alk. paper)
ISBN-13: 978-0-691-14920-2 (pbk. : alk. paper)
ISBN-10: 0-691-14920-8 (pbk. : alk. paper) 1. Tobacco workers—North Carolina—
Social conditions. 2. Migrant agricultural laborers—North Carolina—Social conditions.
3. Tobacco farmers—North Carolina—Social conditions. 4. Tobacco industry—
Social aspects—North Carolina. 5. Antismoking movement—Social aspects—
North Carolina. I. Title.
HD8039.T62U625 2012
331.7'6337109756—dc23

2011017665

British Library Cataloging-in-Publication Data is available

This book has been composed in Sabon

Printed on acid-free paper. ∞

Printed in the United States of America

10 9 8 7 6 5 4 3 2 1

Contents

Illustrations

Foreword

Allan M. Brandt

IN THE SANDY LOAM OF WILSON COUNTY, North Carolina, tobacco farming remains a dominant economic and cultural trade. Peter Benson, a gifted ethnographer and social analyst, worked the tobacco fields side by side with undocumented migrants and African Americans who labor on these family farms, eager to understand both the meaning of this work and its context in a complex and highly contentious global market for tobacco products. There was a time—in the not too distant past—when growing tobacco was equated with national pride and public identity, a critical link between the early nation and its agrarian ideals, economy, and culture. Tobacco growing has never been easy work, but in those heady days of the colonies and the new republic it would have been impossible to anticipate the predicament in which tobacco farmers today find themselves, deeply implicated in powerful historical forces that often feel to be no more controllable than the rains of spring, so crucial to the crop.

Today, as Benson so clearly shows us, tobacco farmers see themselves as besieged, under attack from all quarters, diligently working to defend their farms, their product, and their deeply held moral values. In this remarkable book, Benson enters their world committed to understanding precisely how they come to terms with the difficult economic and moral questions they face. He treats these farmers with great respect, but at the same time, he is able to see their words and their actions in a dense global context. How do they justify their role (often exploiting vulnerable workers) in producing a crop that leads inevitably to such extensive disease and death?

There is a disturbing message here about how deep cultural processes and social dynamics allow people to rationalize what they do. Benson finds a common "script" carefully authored and promoted by the tobacco industry and spoken confidently and fluently by the farmers it so aggressively exploits. According to this logic, the diseases associated with the tobacco plants farmers grow and harvest are explicitly the responsibility of smokers themselves who have "decided" to take this risk. And besides, they argue, there are far more serious problems than those associated with this historic legal product. These aggrieved farmers utilize a set of arguments to defend their identities against the government and public health bureaucrats whom they now view as threatening their livelihood

and their way of life. At the same time, Benson shows how in seeking government support they fashion an appeal for special and qualified needs.
Is this identity of tobacco farmers as victims merely self-deception or
the expression of a deeply internalized rationalization that facilitates the
mundane moral choices of the family farm?

Benson demonstrates that notions of responsibility are central to the
moral world of tobacco farmers. The only way to avoid complicity in
the chain of human action that produces tobacco-related disease is to
locate responsibility somewhere else for someone else. He shows that
American individualism provides a powerful context for dissociating
these aggrieved farmers from the profound health effects of smoking in
their communities and around the world.

Benson runs these farmers' grievances to ground in the pages that
follow. In doing so, he demonstrates how the relationship of the local to
the global connects powerful processes of economy and consumption,
of exploitation and governmental inaction. Benson is able to recover the
world of these farmers at the same time that he places them in the intricate chain of a predatory industry that disregards the health of its own
consumers in a global system that trades health for profit.

All too often, those most deeply committed to alleviating the destruction caused by tobacco have focused simply on consumption; they have
failed to trace the problems of tobacco-related disease back to the agricultural system and the massive structures of agribusiness interests and
activity. *Tobacco Capitalism* navigates the complex and contested relationships between the local and the global, between the sandy soil of
the Tidewater and the international trade agreements that shape the demands of farming the golden tobacco leaf.

This insightful and passionate study offers new opportunities to re-
consider the control of a deadly product that cannot be uncoupled from
the labor that produces the tobacco crop—despite the best efforts of tobacco company executives and farm owners. But equally important, it
offers a humane strategy for considering the most difficult and important
moral dilemmas of a global economy in which all of us are implicated.

Never Reject Anything Human

TOBACCO GROWERS IN NORTH CAROLINA and workers on the farms let me into their lives when they didn't need to. I'm deeply grateful for this hospitality and trust. Riding around in pickup trucks, hauling and heaving the tobacco, and wasting time in labor camps are truly some of the most fulfilling times of my life. To protect the identities of the growers and the workers with whom I spent my time, I must refrain from thanking individuals here. Except for historical references, all names used in this book are pseudonyms. Also, at the request of growers, I did not include any photographs of them or their farm operations.

My hope is that those folks who let me into their lives and left an enduring mark on me will read this book. Yet, this is not the entirely positive picture of tobacco agriculture that is found in museums or in other history books, or espoused and embraced in many tobacco households and communities. This fact is something that I will always struggle with. Writing this book has often been morally and emotionally difficult for me as a result. Several farm families in North Carolina are now like family to me. A key personal and scholarly problem in my work has been balancing a sympathetic and sensitive account of these folks with the reality of how tobacco agribusiness works.

"Never reject anything human" is what my graduate advisor, the anthropologist and physician Arthur Kleinman, told me when we discussed this challenging goal. The multinational tobacco industry, in its decision to maximize profits at the expense of so much that is human, also threatens the dignity and security of the people who work on tobacco farms, some of them more vulnerable than others. It's very easy to blame growers for the serious problems that are part of this business, or tell a simple story about hypocrisy and exploitation on tobacco farms, which essentially rejects their humanity. Instead, I've tried to heed this admonition to be careful about all that is human by writing about the contexts and concrete processes that inform how growers see themselves and relate to others, as I take this proscription as a call to contextualize and contextualize again, to make sense of attitudes and actions that may, from an outside perspective, seem contradictory or even unethical.

The growers with whom I studied knew me and my background, the goals of my project, my position at an elite university, and my political inclinations. Part of why they let me into their lives, I believe, was because they saw me as a sensitive, easygoing, clean-cut white guy from a working-class background who asked lots of stupid questions to learn everything I could about tobacco farming, who was eager to get my hands dirty and actually do the work, and who smoked cigarettes on occasion because it was enjoyable and because I was not an undercover antismoking advocate. The growers knew this and we got along well, so it pains me to surmise that many growers might read this book and become defensive or disappointed, perhaps hoping that I would uphold that pristine portrait of tobacco agriculture given by museums, history books, and tobacco companies.

Sugarcoating and whitewashing reality for the sake of a pleasing story is, I believe, disrespectful, condescending, and part of the process of rejecting something human, because our lives and the work that we do—and our efforts to make meaning and live together or apart—are often complex and compromising. It is because I have great respect for tobacco farm families that I feel impelled to place them in the context of realities that are perhaps not so pleasing, and to take for granted rather than obviate the fact that these are people who, like all of us, contend with difficulties and dangers.

I'm as sorry as the next person. "That's us," writes Cornel West, a preeminent philosopher and scholar of religion, "born between urine and feces" (2008: 28). My intention in wanting to tell an honest story that emphasizes the fraught dignity of ordinary people, the precariousness of contemporary life, and the power of big forces like industry, government, and social movements to make things better or worse comes out of my belief that in spite of the sanitation of history and reality that goes on, and expressions of pride, mastery, and control, life is not altogether pleasant, and humility and vulnerability are what we have in common.

Thanks and Dedication

This book comes out of research that I conducted for my doctoral dissertation at the Department of Anthropology at Harvard University and was funded primarily by the Wenner-Gren Foundation. I'm most thankful for the truly unmatched mentorship of my advisors, Arthur Kleinman and Woody Watson. I also want to thank others from my graduate school days, including Ajantha Subramanian, Allan Brandt, David Rodowick, Homi Bhabha, Kay Warren, Marilyn Goodrich, Mary Steedly, Michael Fischer, Michael Herzfeld, Paul Farmer, Peter Gordon, Randy Matory, Steve Caton, and Ted Bestor, all of whom inspired me in classrooms and conversations. I'm indebted to the graduate students at Harvard who made my time there stimulating, and sometimes infuriating, in a good way, especially Akin Hubbard, Angela Garcia, Gant Asbury, Joon Choi, Juno Parreñas, Linda Ellison, Noelle Stout, Omar al-Dewachi, Tim Smith, and Will Day.

I completed major revisions for this book as a postdoctoral fellow in the Program for Agrarian Studies at Yale University, where I want to thank the program directors, Jim Scott and Kalyanakrishnan Sivarama-krishnan, the program administrator, Kay Mansfield, and my co-fellows for a singular opportunity and invaluable support and guidance.

My deep gratitude goes to all of the people who have provided crucial advice, intellectual engagement and encouragement, friendship and sus-tenance, or the hard work of reading drafts and providing comments, in-cluding my colleagues at Washington University in St. Louis and at many other places, especially Anna Tsing, Archana Sridhar, Barbara Koenig, Bob Canfield, Brad Stoner, Bret Gustafson, Bruce Knauft, Caitlin Zaloom, Carolyn Sargent, Derek Pardue, Don Donham, Glenn Stone, Graham Colditz, Jim Ferguson, João Biehl, Joaquin Barnoya, John Bowen, Kath-ryn Dudley, Katie Hejtmanek, Kaushik Sunder Rajan, Kevin O'Neill, Kim Fortun, Lois Beck, Mark Nichter, Matthew Kohrman, Maury Steigman, Michael Frachetti, Mike Fortun, Peter Brown, Priscilla Song, Quetzil Castañeda, Rebecca Lester, Roland Moore, Scott Lacy, Shanti Parikh, Stephanie Larchanche, Virginia Dominguez, and Walt Little. There is also a set of people who I do not know personally but whose scholarship has had a significant impact on me, and I want to express my respect for their work and sincere thanks, namely, Alphonso Lingis, George Lip-sitz, and Kathleen Stewart. I greatly appreciate the assistance of Keith Barnes of Wilson, North Carolina, and Kim Cumber of the North Caro-lina State Archives, who helped me compile images for this book. Finally, I acknowledge Princeton University Press for superior assistance and a most rewarding experience, especially Fred Appel, Kathleen Cioffi, Karen Fortgang, and Diana Goovaerts, copyeditor Cathy Slovensky, and the anonymous reviewers of the manuscript.

It's common to say of a completed project that it would not have been possible without the support of certain people. This is definitely true in my case, and I want to conclude by expressing my deepest thanks to them. I thank Ted Fischer for helping to propel me into anthropology and providing invaluable guidance and opportunities in the early stages of my work. Arthur Kleinman has taught me so much and influenced me in so many ways, personally and professionally. His mentorship has eas-ily been the most enriching intellectual engagement that I've experienced, and I hope that I'm not overstepping in writing that it has also been a fa-therly relationship for me. My friend Stuart Kirsch, who was a co-fellow at Yale, has helped me to think in more critical ways about the world and to maintain a spirit of hope in the face of personal doubt and societal resignation. Without these individuals, there is truthfully no way that I would be doing what I'm doing in life, and this book would not exist.

Kedron Thomas, my spouse, is my coauthor in everything, and if it were not for a gut feeling that pulls me to do otherwise, I'd have dedicated this book to her and her late father, whose fateful, hard work in the tobacco fields and on the tractor was the inspiration for this work.

But there is someone else, a friend in graduate school, who challenged me in ways that I had never been challenged before nor have been since. Our time together in what for me was an intense intellectual and social relationship is something that I think about always and for which I am irredeemably grateful. This book is dedicated to Joon Choi.

Tobacco Capitalism

Introduction _____

SINCE SMOKING PREVALENCE has waned in the United States, it is often presumed that tobacco farming has gone by the wayside. North Carolina has long been the country's leading producer of tobacco. Now the state has a new economy of biomedical and pharmaceutical research to brag about. There is the Research Triangle near Raleigh, and Durham, once a premier tobacco town and headquarters of James B. Duke's global cigarette monopoly, is now home to Brightleaf Square, a converted tobacco warehouse district that offers an array of restaurants and shops in the downtown area and is close by one of the great medical care and research complexes in the world.

The fact is that tobacco remains the seventh most valuable agricultural commodity in the United States. Each year's crop is worth about $1.5 billion. Although lacking any nutritional value, tobacco is worth far more as a commodity than most vegetables produced in the United States. Tobacco's market value is triple the value of the country's sweet potatoes, about the same as the value of the orange crop, and slightly more than tomatoes. It is worth six times as much as the cucumber crop. It is more valuable than artichokes, asparagus, cauliflower, cabbage, spinach, and squash combined. The tobacco cultivated in the United States is worth twice as much as the country's entire onion crop.[1]

Tobacco can be terrifically profitable, with growers netting several hundred dollars per acre. Tobacco's intensive managerial and labor requirements mean that this remains a crop where small farms sit beside large operations, although major changes in tobacco agriculture in the United States in the past few decades have promoted waves of consolidation and mechanization. In spite of this industrialization process, tobacco is produced in North Carolina on farm operations that are considered to be family businesses. Nearly all growers trace their farms back at least a few generations. This is important for them. But to satisfactorily appreciate what the growers and families have at stake in these businesses, the story must go beyond a simple notion of heritage or a basic economic calculus. An explanation of why growers cling to and defend tobacco amid thinned profits, thickened clouds of ethical suspicion, and intensified industry power requires a fuller historical and anthropological account of what it means to be a successful tobacco farm business owner and operator. This includes what growers stand to gain or lose, their efforts

---

[1] These data are taken from regularly updated reports of the National Agricultural Statistics Service, United States Department of Agriculture.

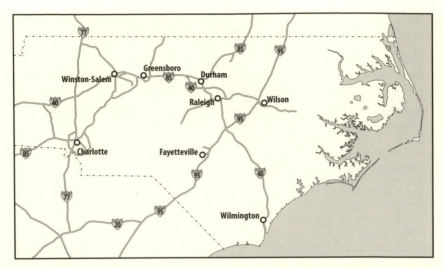

Map I.1. Map of North Carolina

to mechanize and expand factory farms in order to remain profitable in the present—which may be motivated by a mixture of both ambition and need—and the process of how potent meanings of citizenship and patterns of social and political affiliation have been produced on North Carolina tobacco farms alongside billions and billions of pounds of leaf.

Tobacco was cultivated by large numbers of African American families in the past. Tobacco farms are now owned and operated by white men in all but a few cases. As tobacco farms have become like factories, what growers do and their relationships to employees have also changed, with the workforce rescaled to an international level. Traditional work relations involving tenancy, debt peonage, swapping help, and family labor have been replaced by a system of seasonal labor that involves mostly undocumented migrant workers from Mexico and Central America who now do the bulk of the grueling manual work and live in notoriously squalid labor camps. Migrant workers sit at the bottom rungs of this harmful industry. Meanwhile, growers with lots of pride and emotion bundled up with tobacco leaf face intense levels of economic competition and uncertainty, not to mention looming ethical and political questions about the dependence of their agribusiness operations on a vulnerable workforce, decades of special government protectionism and financial assistance, and a cash crop that contains the addictive chemical nicotine and many carcinogens. The vast majority of growers employ undocumented workers in businesses that produce the main ingredient in cigarettes, and smoking is the leading cause of preventable

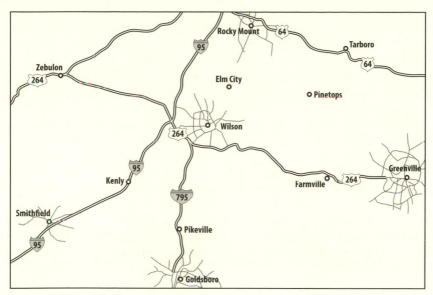

Map I.2. Map of Wilson County

disease and death in the United States and worldwide. Consequently, these growers experience the stress of a long economic downturn in a context where they are already primed to feel somewhat defensive about their livelihood.

This book examines decades of social change and industrial decline in North Carolina, where I have conducted years of research with tobacco growers and workers, farm labor and immigrant rights advocates, union organizers, and public health groups. My study of tobacco agriculture and the tobacco industry has been centered in Wilson County, the largest and most active tobacco-producing region in the country, and is set against the backdrop of the antitobacco movement, the globalization and industrialization of farm and food chains, and the intense political struggles over immigration. This book scrutinizes what public health policies related to smoking and tobacco industry strategies look like in rural North Carolina and their impact on communities that have long been dependent on tobacco revenues and structured around distinctive racial meanings and social and economic disparities linked to tobacco production. Based on twenty months of anthropological field study and archival research conducted from 2002 to 2010, my goal has been to produce an account of the production and supply side of the tobacco industry that is richly informed by historical understanding, critically attendant to political economy, and deeply appreciative of subjective experience.

In the process of narrating broad stories about industry power, agrarian change, and the science and politics of public health, I zoom in on everyday life and social relations in tobacco farm workplaces and households, migrant labor camps, and erstwhile tobacco communities. I am especially interested in how and why structural transformations in the international tobacco leaf trade have tended to yield intensely antagonistic and divided social conditions in this region. International market shifts driven by the pursuit of cheap foreign leaf by tobacco companies have posed and continue to pose a serious threat to the financial solvency of North Carolina tobacco farms. Growers experience changing business conditions as a challenge not just to their financial situation but more holistically to the social, cultural, and historical conditions that are bound up with their livelihoods. Aspects of farm livelihood that may be threatened include the masculinity that over time has become embedded in tobacco farm management, the idea that this livelihood is the foundation of families that are icons of normalcy and part of an imagined mainstream, the material signs of being middle-class and the way that tobacco money permits access to things like new trucks and brick houses, and the values of heritage and tradition having to do with the longevity of family tobacco businesses. The racial division of labor, which for centuries has marked those who own and manage tobacco operations as distinct from subordinated groups of tobacco workers, may also be threatened. The lens through which I apprehend the impact of the international tobacco trade in North Carolina focuses on the subjective experiences and social lives of growers, who sometimes respond in ways that aim to maintain social boundaries, hold on to class status and cultural distinctions, and reassert existing power relations.

Apart from the antagonized relations that I document on farms, a major component of the moral experience of tobacco growers—how they feel threatened and how they respond—has been the more public articulation of a politics of "plighted citizenship," where growers claim to be or are said to be the victims of undue hardship. They commonly feel that various outside forces conspire to attack and undermine their life and work. By virtue of involvement in a harmful industry, tobacco growers sometimes feel compelled to wrestle with society's changing attitudes about tobacco in ways that are often deeply personal and difficult. This moral and emotional experience is not the automatic result of the fact that antitobacco sentiment exists at the national level or that tobacco farming involves increasing levels of financial instability and failure. Negligent local newspaper reporting and tobacco industry propaganda have goaded the grower ranks into a collective feeling of being conspired against, even though there isn't any evidence of a concerted attack on tobacco livelihoods waged by the government and public health groups.

This way of thinking is similar to that of religious groups who say that Christianity is under attack in the United States, which rouses political and social defensiveness among adherents. Fantastical scandals of lost privilege, where victimhood is claimed by relatively advantaged constituencies who now feel negatively marked or valued, provoke sometimes dangerous responses and policy perspectives (Berlant 1997).

As tobacco growers experienced increased levels of hardship since the 1980s, they pursued more government assistance, and cultural resources were used to convert the economic and ethical paradoxes that define this business into contexts of injury and unfair treatment. Growers adopted a particular kind of Face and used it to pursue entitlements. A public discourse heavily influenced by the tobacco industry lit a fire under cultural issues and matters of citizenship, like welfare and the composition of families, coaching growers to see themselves as model citizens, victims of the state and aggrieved racial minorities, plighted citizens, an inherently innocent company of people deserving of a kind of social assistance that is not stigmatized, not a handout, not special treatment, and not what stereotyped others receive; in other words, a kind of social assistance that is legitimate, what national icons have earned. This cultural politics of citizenship was promoted by the tobacco industry to foment the allegiance of southern growers as a strategy to help contain the reach of public health regulation in the United States and deflect attention from the powerful role of corporations in offshoring the tobacco economy of states like North Carolina.

At a more general level, this book is about racial power and racial projects, and the meaning and politics of innocence and responsibility in the United States. I hone in on the vernacular use of the word "sorry" and seek to understand the values and meanings that are invoked when white tobacco growers refer to each other as sorry farmers, especially when the aging black men and women and the Mexican and Latino migrants who do the bulk of the manual tobacco labor are routinely called sorry. While being in the company of innocence has been most at stake for white tobacco farm families in past decades, I develop a broader analysis of white claims to victimhood and struggles over entitlement and justice given the nation's historical burdens. As a way of setting an ethnographic stage for these discussions, this introduction describes my research on tobacco farms and develops the concept of plighted citizenship.

The Triangle

In North Carolina, tobacco accounts for nearly one-third of the economic value of agriculture. This most harmful crop continues to be produced with vigor just a couple of highway exits outside of the Research Triangle. But the residential gentrification and forms of remembering that have occurred there tend to make tobacco history into something consumable and ornamental.

The public Face of North Carolina has a little white devil on one shoulder and a little white angel on the other. The devil is holding a lit cigarette and coughing, his chest cavity exposed, as in an anatomical atlas, to reveal blackened lungs and a strangled heart. Maybe he wears coveralls and rides around a tobacco patch in a junky pickup truck surrounded by faceless workers. This scene is in black and white, and it is recessed into the background. The eyes of the big, stately public face are happily staring ahead into the foreground at the high-definition scene of an angel wearing a lab coat, a little rendition of pharmaceutical research backlit by other scenes from the suburban lifestyle that symbolizes the Triangle. There are office buildings, a man with a stethoscope, families on their way to the Whole Foods Market, a dinner party at Brightleaf Square— all ethical consumers and investors who would not dare step foot on a tobacco farm. People from all kinds of backgrounds are in these scenes, including lots of northerners who like the fact that there are four seasons but no severe winter and who work in pharmaceuticals, where they perhaps design nicotine patches; youngsters on a fieldtrip at the Duke Homestead and Tobacco Museum located in Durham, who look lethargically at a diorama of an old-timey tobacco farm scene; and college students unpacking SUVs, moving into dorms, and practicing on the sports fields at Duke University in the August heat.

The state of North Carolina hires public relations firms to design brochures (placed at highway rest stops) that promote economic investment and residential relocation, but what these brochures disclose of the actual history of tobacco and its part in creating North Carolina is, of course, excruciatingly narrow. They do not depict a professional tobacco grower or a migrant worker as "the Face." On their way down Interstate 95 from New Jersey, Duke students do not receive brochures that tell them that just a few exits from their dormitories and athletic fields are neighborhoods that were built up and then gutted by the tobacco industry, and further still that there are active tobacco farms where some of the most grueling kind of work on the planet is being done. Their first-year orientation does not go beyond the trivial fact that the university namesake was the great tobacco magnate, much less describe how the state's and the nation's economy were from the beginning soaked with blood spilled for the sake of tobacco. The brochures for the Duke Homestead and Tobacco Museum attract motorists from the highway and give them the impression that tobacco is gone with the wind. Not entirely out of the picture, tobacco is carefully packaged so that the stark racial order built on segregation and violence, which tobacco production (and Duke) helped make, seems aeons from the sparkling scenes of life in brochures for the Triangle and the university. Attending a university like Duke can instill in the student critical reflection about who gets to attend, how disparities are made and reproduced, and the uneven distribution of material resources, access to education, and health, safety, and security in a society where there are people who are working hard or slouching in every strata. But it does not necessarily, perhaps not usually, have this effect.

Things get lost in the Triangle. There is so much that the placards with white lettering that indicate what lies off the exits mask. Loblolly pines and sound barriers also mask empirical realities that many people would just as soon overlook anyway. If it were my tobacco road, I'd put up a sign that indicates that right there in the Triangle, as elsewhere in the United States, a disproportionate number of racial minorities smoke cigarettes, have higher rates of cardiovascular disease and cancer incidence and mortality, and have worse access to the healthcare advances being pioneered around the corner. Instead of celebrating the presence of unskilled workers in North Carolina as a lure for investors and businesses, my brochures would discuss the history of how labor surpluses and socioeconomic disparities have been made and the role of international free trade agreements, like the North American Free Trade Agreement (NAFTA), in inducing economic instability and change in the United States and south of the border. Highway signs that point motorists to the museum do not point them to active tobacco operations where dependence on foreign labor mixes with anxieties about the changing composition of rural communities. Highway signs are anti-ethnography machines that could point in many directions, indicate critical information, and provide a different tour of history and place than the tourist traps.

There is no sign that indicates that North Carolina has much lower tobacco-control funding than other states and one of the highest smoking rates in the country. Off these exits 12,200 people die each year from smoking. Off these exits 200,000 children and adolescents currently living in North Carolina will one day die from smoking diseases. Whereas $2.5 billion is spent each year in North Carolina on the treatment of diseases caused by tobacco use, the state government spends a paltry $18.5 million on public health programs to limit tobacco use (only one-sixth of the amount of money that is recommended by the Centers for Disease Control for the state's population). No highway signs indicate that almost all smokers begin smoking when they are adolescents, that the tobacco industry continues to aggressively and strategically market to youths, or that the federal government collects about $7 billion per year from cigarette excise taxes but annually spends more than $50 billion through its healthcare programs on the treatment of smoking disease.

No highway signs indicate that the financial burden of tobacco-caused health costs for governments in the United States amounts to $600 in taxes per household, smoking-related mortality results in $100 billion in lost productivity in the national economy each year, and the tobacco industry contributes more than $2 million annually to federal political candidates and political parties and spends $25 million on congressional lobbying.[2] For that matter, no highway signs indicate that in 2004 Republican politicians in North Carolina and tobacco companies worked in conjunction to undermine federal efforts to infuse money into the state to help communities to transition away from tobacco livelihoods and develop a more diverse and stable economy. No sign states the fact that they kept literally billions of dollars in federal funds from reaching tobacco-dependent communities because the industry had an interest in keeping rural people tied to a livelihood that is increasingly unpredictable and, like it or not, harmful.

Motorists driving eastward from the Triangle probably consume the rural expanse of North Carolina's flat coastal plain as a string of convenient stopping places for home-cooking cafeterias, gas stations, and gift shops. Professionals who live and work in the Triangle see the sandy loam that stretches out to the Atlantic Ocean not as soil in which exceedingly high-quality tobacco is still grown but as a smoking section of red-state reactionary politics bypassed on an air-conditioned getaway to the Outer Banks. When motorists pull off to fill their tanks, a phenomenology of perception, bent on commodity fetishism, envisions the cigarette packs behind the counter as nothing more than a consumer product. They do not see the cigarettes, or the bags of chips and soft drinks, as products that come from actual places, or that they are designed and marketed to induce further consumption, processes relegated and legitimized by a pervasive and misleading ideology of informed adult choice when it comes to terribly harmful and costly behavioral health issues. Cigarette packaging conceals the fact that tobacco and profit are not all that is produced on tobacco farms, but that identities and relationships are produced, too. There is no book on tape that describes how over centuries tobacco agriculture has been the basis for the formation of a cultural ideal of legitimate personhood, or, more specifically, legitimate white manhood, in rural North Carolina. No book on tape tells motorists how this model of the human arose within a steep division of labor, or that the positive ideals about the livelihood and hard work to which tobacco farmers have dedicated themselves encode ideas about racialized blackness and whiteness and the tacit assertion that tobacco farm livelihoods are white heritage.

---

[2] National Institute for Tobacco-Free Kids (2007, 2010b, 2011).

Highway signs function as "anti-politics machines" (Ferguson 1994) that make places seem natural and timeless. Exits are places with food, gas, and lodging (and perhaps something quaint like a museum) and towns where people go about their lives. Motorists do not realize that the product in front of them at the gas station is related to botanical ancestors that helped to make the Atlantic system and plantation slavery, and that these towns have long been connected to distant places largely through the medium of tobacco exchange and labor migration. Motorists do not think about the complex relationships that are stuffed into, say, a bag of chips. The subsidized price of corn for midwestern farm operations makes the chips too affordable, while international free trade agreements displaced many Mexican farmers who are now forced to compete with cheap U.S. grain. The ensuing northward migration has helped sustain the tobacco farms in North Carolina that contribute leaf to the cigarettes behind the counter, minimizing the labor cost associated with tobacco products and making cigarettes only that much more affordable. In the meantime, out on the highway, motorists snacking on their corn chips do not smoke and believe they have no relationship to tobacco, the harm it causes, or the histories and structures that surround tobacco products. Not venturing beyond the gas pump, where they would see the dangerous and depraved labor camps, motorists stay out of old tobacco boomtowns where there is unseemly unemployment, poverty, and housing problems. They do not realize that tobacco products are linked to forms of human and environmental harm even before being smoked. The mileage markers that lie between Richmond, Virginia, and Wilson, North Carolina, are not accompanied by signs indicating that decisions made up there, at Philip Morris headquarters, have a complexly adverse impact on farmers and farmworkers down here. There are no signs that describe the intricate ripple effects of the intense corporate power that rains down on North Carolina farms and communities. Mileage markers quantify distance, while a qualitative understanding of the histories that make places and the practices that unmake histories seems way too complicated to include on highway signs. How many books on tape are not lulling machines that facilitate a mode of travel geared toward using the highway as the most direct path, even though it is not the most interesting one? Getting to the beach no longer means driving through every little tobacco town on the way. Forget the nostalgia about all the cozy diners that dotted the state roads—much more is now bypassed than quaint eateries. Billboards convert the existential surge of wanting to enter rather than exit, wanting to get to know "a place on the side of the road" (K. Stewart 1996), into a consumer impulse to stop and buy something. Places seem connected to other places in terms of mileage and the marked distance between consumption options and rest stops. Predicaments of place and personhood in this smoking section are not advertised as phenomena that might interest motorists. They are not entirely pleasant, and their intricacies make them unavailable to being diagrammed in a museum, blurbed on a billboard, or sold in a gift shop.

Residents of the Triangle who may never want to enter a labor camp nonetheless feel compelled to join boycott efforts that seek to improve working conditions for farmworkers. Right now activists in the Triangle are working to ameliorate historical burdens. Farm labor advocates are in camps and communities, attempting to raise awareness of the vulnerable workforce on which tobacco corporations depend. Scholars are doing the important historical analytical work of connecting dots, discrediting the facile idea that the world that tobacco helped make is left in the dust, and reflecting on the precarious position of populations that have been affected by and remain dependent on the tobacco industry. Motorists are feeling the ethnographic surge of being on the road, which is to say, getting the heck off the highway. They want to understand themes and topics having to do with politics and the economy in terms of lived effects and experiences out in the actual community, not just what they have learned in classrooms. They go to local libraries and are swallowed up by microfilm machines and books about the history of the tobacco industry, the history of the South, and the politics of entitlement. They find work on farms and hang out in labor camps, attend all kinds of church services (because this is a good way to get to know people), and smoke cigarettes to break the ice. They make friends with people who grow a harmful product and doubly break the law when they house undocumented workers in substandard camps because it is cheap. They scrap their idea of recording a book on tape called *When Good People Do Bad Things* because there are already lots of other books with similar titles. Month after month spent working on tobacco farms, the motorists meet no devils and angels, only humans who wrestle with particular ideas about what it means to be human in the context of broad relationships that are sustaining or threatening. Time spent on tobacco farms and at the microfilm machine leads the motorists to sense that the book ought to be about responsibility in a complicated world, what it means to live a moral life and claim to be worth something, and a unique politics of race, innocence, and citizenship that is implicit in everyday economic and moral pursuits and social relationships off these exact exits.

Almost all tobacco research is focused on consumption. In the United States, policy makers and healthcare professionals have historically paid little attention to tobacco growers and lacked cultural knowledge about their communities (Altman et al. 1998: 381).[3] However, production and

---

[3] I want to acknowledge other recent anthropological studies of tobacco agriculture, especially Ann Kingsolver's study (2011) of Kentucky farms and David Griffith's work (2009) in North Carolina.

supply issues, as much as health behavior, are important public health matters. The tobacco industry does not want signs posted along the highway that detail occupational health and safety problems related to industrialized tobacco production, the problem of farm livelihood loss and fragility, or the exploitation of immigrant workers. This book expands tobacco's public health picture beyond a focus on smoking to include critical perspectives on the global tobacco industry and the social and health issues and forms of structural violence that are related to industrial agriculture and labor migration. Historical and ethnographic research on tobacco farming broadens and sharpens the critical understanding of the tobacco industry's impact on humans and the environment. As is beginning to happen in some parts of the world, the traditional public health focus on the regulation of smoking behavior finds a useful complement in research and advocacy concerning labor conditions, farm livelihoods, and industry strategy and propaganda. Attention to these issues enables a critique of the structural foundations and capitalist dynamics of the tobacco industry and must be a central part of a comprehensive tobacco-control agenda.

Negotiations and Love Songs

I first pulled off the highway in North Carolina tobacco country in the summer of 2004. I drove an old red pickup truck to a tobacco farm in Wilson County, where I moved into a tenant house that the farmer rented to my wife and me for a few hundred bucks each month. My wife, who is also an anthropologist and comes from a tobacco farm background, assisted with aspects of the fieldwork, while working part-time for a local nonprofit organization. Her late father was a small-scale tobacco and cattle producer in Appalachia on a farm that had been in their family for several generations and that utilized mostly family labor. During visits there, I was comfortable helping with the farmwork, baling hay and working cattle mostly, although I really had no choice (the suitor's obligation). In my suburban New England upbringing, I imagined that this—riding on a shaky wagon pulled by an old tractor, blisters busting my hands open as I heaved hay bale after hay bale into the cold, hardened fields for the cattle to feed on—was what farm life ought to be like. It was small, family-oriented, and hands-on, and we would go out, my wife's father and I, and castrate the young calves, jumping off the four-wheeler and plunging a hard knee into their throats to restrain them, tossing the testicles to the side for the farm dogs. Later we would get into the chute to bolt tags into the ears of calves pissing and shitting all over a uniform of rubber coveralls. This way of life appealed a great deal to my sense of what is decent and virtuous in a certain kind of agriculture.

At the farm, everyone pitched in with the tobacco. We stripped gummy leaves off stalks and ordered them by color, stalk position, and texture to make bales, an artisanal aspect of tobacco agriculture that has historically been an important basis of pride among tobacco farm families. Meanwhile, I was thinking, *Who really cares which leaf goes where and what the grade is? What does quality mean when it comes to tobacco? And was this really happening? Was tobacco really being manufactured there in the winter months on holiday visits with a family where only one man is allowed to smoke?* Lots of things go into thinking about a romantic relationship, and there were fleeting thoughts about whether the family's involvement in tobacco should have any impact on my feelings about my future wife. But I was in love, and I also felt some guilty pleasure, a legitimate way to have my hands all over a product that my parents (and my wife's parents) would never want me to consume. There, in a small metal-sided farm shop heated by a wood-burning furnace, no one talked about where the product wound up. We willed commodity fetishism. Tobacco's social life was never discussed. These were not cigarettes that we were helping to make at Christmastime.

Her father smoked and I daydreamed, riding about with him on the farm, of bumming a cigarette, smoking together, like Marlboro Men. In itching for nicotine I wanted to have something in common in a fantastical rural scenario, but also to just light a cigarette and demand to know how this familial politics of prudish behavior was not hypocritical. *It's okay for other people and other people's kids to smoke?* But the eager scholar and suitor in me kept quiet.

It was in the context of coming to know my wife's family that my research project began. I was interested in learning about how tobacco farmers like my wife's folks, who see themselves as good and decent people, think about the ethics of what they do for a living. I had just gone through graduate seminars where we read about the social life of things (Appadurai 1986) and ethics in a globalized world (Ong and Collier 2005). The expansion of media influence in the modern world has heightened the visibility of problems and amplified the public nature of ethics. There are "fundamental disjunctures" between local worlds and larger regulatory systems and ethical frameworks (Appadurai 1996: 32–33). Such disjunctures affect how people see themselves as part of larger social constellations. Broadscale political and ethical impulses often challenge the social norms and identities that have taken shape in particular locations or networks.

Now I realize that my interest in tobacco stems from my personal experience in coming to grips with the rather common dilemma of how we justify doing something we know is bad. We make excuses, provide rationales and reasons, or claim that it's temporary. And yet there is also the recognition that people's actions are so constrained by political economy and other pressures that they are unlikely to do right, as in the complicity of raising a family of nonsmokers by raising tobacco leaf, exploiting a migrant worker while railing against the threat of illegal immigration, or, in my case, sneaking off to light a cigarette at an academic conference. My study of tobacco has the flavor of being closely involved with tobacco growers, but also the critical recognition that powerful inducements and constraints affect what one does, what one can do, and how one feels about it, so that ambivalence, coping, defensiveness, and strategy are defining tensions and dangers of moral life rather than its aberrations.

Fieldwork

Tobacco grower Frank Warren was skeptical of my motives for wanting to interview him. Over the phone I introduced myself as an anthropologist interested in the history and culture of tobacco in North Carolina.

"Too busy; find somebody else," he replied, and hung up the phone.

Later I met Frank at a wintertime farm meeting. Another grower whom I already knew introduced us. Doing his friend a favor, Frank agreed to talk with me for "five minutes only." Frank produces roughly one hundred acres of tobacco, a typical, medium-size operation for the region, as well as rotational fields in corn and soybeans. He lives in a modest house, where he was finishing his morning coffee when I arrived. We wound up talking for a full hour. He spoke about how neighboring farmers had gone out of business and his contentions with reduced tobacco leaf prices and intensified competition. Owned and operated for decades by his parents and grandparents and the handful of tenant families they employed, his family farm business is less stable than ever. Media accounts and tobacco growers tend to blame the public health tobacco-control movement for conditions of economic hardship and uncertainty. In fact, these conditions are the direct result of the international trade dynamics and tobacco industry strategies described later in this book.

"That five-minute rule was a bluff," Frank admitted to me as our interview wound down. "I was expecting a journalist. They just care about smoking. The interview begins: 'Do you smoke?' Question two is: 'Do you want your kids to smoke?' When you say 'nope' each time, they get around to it: 'Well, isn't that hypocritical?'"

The "critical medical anthropology" perspective, focused on industries and the global trade regime as vectors of disease, is a dominant paradigm in studies of many harmful commodities, including tobacco (Baer et al. 2004; Stebbins 2001). My goal has been to balance the critical consideration of industry power and government neglect with an apprehension for local experience and the sociocultural context of tobacco dependency (Nichter 2003). During interviews I often found myself wanting to interject my ideas about what is disturbing about the tobacco industry and the contributions of industrial agriculture to significant public health problems. But I listened to growers and let them lead the way. Beyond appearances (including skin color, gender, and other forms of embodiment that have allowed me to socialize felicitously with tobacco grower families as if I were not completely suspect or strange), my rapport involved the openness that defines ethnography. I asked how they got into farming, how and why they have continued, and the major changes that farm families have faced, only to have them start talking about the contentious ethical and health issues without me even bringing it up.

The anthropologist Matthew Kohrman's (2004, 2008) ethnography of Chinese physicians who smoke offers striking similarities with my study. These are people who struggle to come to grips with a coherent and decent subjectivity at the crossroads of competing value systems and regimes that define what is normal and acceptable. What results, according to Kohrman, is a social and personal struggle to negotiate a "fraught identity." The content of how these different groups reflect on their tobacco dependencies and what is at stake differ completely, but in both cases the public health approach to tobacco is experienced in terms of a potential loss of national belonging and the feeling that antitobacco regulatory impulses jeopardize not only a livelihood, but also a sense of personal worth and a level of social standing that is deserved because one feels responsible, professional, and acceptable. "The perception is that just because you grow tobacco you are prosmoking," Frank tells me, insisting on his own normalcy and mainstream morality. "That's not how it works. You can grow tobacco and be sensible about smoking." When growers talk about tobacco, they are also talking about other values and relationships that are at stake for them. This book is about the active construction of morality in a historical context influenced by industry, which ends up looking a lot like a dominant model of consumer citizenship and familial politics in the United States at large.

Few studies have examined what tobacco growers believe about their participation in the industry given its public health toll. Here is what Frank says, as we leave the house and ride in his pickup truck to scope out his summer crop:

> Tobacco farmers are the most despised people around. You'd think we were drug dealers. Every day there's an article in the newspaper about a new study that says that smoking is bad for you. We get the message. It's not like I disagree with that. But I'm proud of what I do. I'm not going to apologize for growing tobacco. It's legal and it's up to adults,

if they want to smoke or not. I don't want my kids to smoke and I talk to them about it. I feel like other people might think I'm the worst person in the world because I grow tobacco. But they should look at my family and the business that I've grown. I've got two kids in college. And there are more serious problems in society and things that are illegal that are being done. I wonder where the focus on those things is.

He pulls up beside a field where tobacco harvesters run and the truck idles. This is what he does most of the day: driving, sitting, and supervising. A cassette tape of country music hits has probably been playing on a loop in this truck for a decade. I wonder what part of his comments (the pride in tobacco, the no apologies, the claim to be a victim, and the contrast with other social types) reflects real emotional turmoil versus a strategic appropriation of victimhood to mask relative advantage—all that the chasm between this air-conditioned pickup truck and manual field labor symbolizes and entails—or the influence of tobacco industry propaganda. My interviews with tobacco farmers involved lots of this talk. There is the hypocrisy of a government that promotes public health and collects taxes on cigarette sales. There is the bias of media sources that "pay no attention to how tobacco helped make this country, I mean look at Duke University," Frank tells me. There is the misguided focus on tobacco farms when "just look at the inner cities." The decent and hardworking families take all the heat, it seems, and what really threatens the nation is the illegitimacy of so many families and social groups, not the aggressive industrial efforts to get people hooked on harmful and useless products.

My goal is not to quantify what degree of this discourse about disrespect and unfairness, which is also amped on the conservative talk radio, reflects actual feelings of disrespect versus a strategic politics of victimhood. My point is exactly that the experiential context of real farm loss, foreclosure, and going out of business has been coproduced alongside stories and images of plight that nudged growers to adopt a language of victimization and envision the state and public health as enemies because a harmful industry sought to cultivate loyalty and fantasy at the grass roots.

Tobacco-state newspapers and politicians were of little help, usually functioning as nothing more than public relations vehicles for the tobacco industry. As part of my research, apart from working on tobacco farms and conducting interviews, I read every edition of the *Wilson Daily Times* since its inception in the late nineteenth century. Perhaps thousands of articles and editorials were published in this newspaper and other tobacco-state newspapers in past decades, where the government is depicted as the enemy of tobacco farmers. In 1971, the *Wilson Daily Times* ran the following editorial:

[T]he mystery remains as to why the relentless attack on tobacco continues. There is insufficient evidence pertaining to the health aspects of bright leaf and in view of the traumatic effect its extinction would have on the economy nationally when that is in a pitiful condition is unbelievable. Tobacco has suffered a crippling blow at the hands of those who would protect us from ourselves. (Graham 1971: 15)

The public health approach to tobacco control has been depicted as a "relentless attack," a misleading notion—largely promulgated by the tobacco industry itself—that frames government regulation as the cause of the hardships experienced by farm families and masks the impacts of international market forces and the ambition of multinational tobacco companies to globalize their operations. This contrived image of an attack also contradicts the fact that the public health regulation of smoking in the United States has actually been woefully underdeveloped given the massive epidemiological toll caused by tobacco consumption. And yet another editorial published in this newspaper in 1983 suggested that the public health focus on tobacco is unnecessary because smoking risks are "already known" and "the public has been informed of its dangers." Leadingly entitled "Another Tobacco Fight," the editorial argued that more legislation concerning the "health aspect" is "harmful" to the "economic factor" (*Wilson Daily Times* 1983a), thus reiterating the deceptively false argument that tobacco control directly hurts tobacco farm families. There was no mention of the role of international market forces and the globalization of industry that decimated tobacco as much as textiles in the old confederacy.

To Washington

On March 17, 2003, an individual identified as a white male drove a John Deere tractor into the shallow pond at Constitution Avenue Gardens on the National Mall. He squatted between the Washington Monument and the Lincoln Memorial for two days. Decked out in olive drab fatigues, "tractor man," as the press called him, flew an upside-down American flag (a conventional distress signal) and another flag depicting golden tobacco leaves (Copeland 2003; Nakamura and Lengel 2003a).

Dwight Watson, fifty years old, wore an ill-fitting military helmet, like the one he wore decades earlier while deployed as a marine in Vietnam. He had driven up the interstate from his home in North Carolina where he was the owner-operator of a family tobacco farm. Like thousands of other growers, he had recently gone under. In Washington, he sought to publicize what he called the "plight" of tobacco growers and the government's failure to respond with relief and assistance (Fahrenthold and Lengel 2003; Nakamura 2003).

Watson claimed to possess chemical fertilizer, enough to "bring D.C. to its knees" and "leave a mark on the Mall never to be forgotten." The Mall was evacuated, federal buildings, concession stands, and monuments shut down (Nakamura and Lengel 2003a).[4] Watson did all he could to intensify fears, driving out to an island in the pond where he "moved the bucket on the tractor up and down, smashing it into the island," official reports note.[5] He alluded to incidents in Ruby Ridge and Waco (Nakamura 2003: A6). He told reporters, "They can blow my ass out of the water. I'm ready to go to Heaven" (Nakamura and Lengel 2003b: A1). He claimed to have deposited explosive "Easter eggs" at Philip Morris headquarters in Richmond that would detonate if dampened by an early spring rain. He also claimed to have mailed hazardous materials to the offices of each state's attorney general, the offices from which the major public health litigation against the tobacco industry in the 1990s was spearheaded.

After three days, he finally surrendered. No explosives or hazardous materials were found (Fahrenthold and Lengel 2003: B1). In custody, Watson "erupted into an angry tirade against the government and its policy toward tobacco farmers," according to the presiding judge in his trial:

> [Watson's] rage was palpable and he displayed absolutely no ability to control himself. It is clear to me that his crusade against the government has overwhelmed his judgment and self-control. After witnessing such an outburst, and appreciating the crime charged and his apparent willingness to destroy himself and others to make his point, I find that the defendant is a danger . . . to any community.[6]

Watson was convicted for threatening false information concerning the use of an explosive and destruction of government property. He was sentenced to six years' imprisonment, a punishment that was reduced after Watson offered a formal apology to the court (Leonnig and Lengel 2004).

Stiffed

The social critic Susan Faludi (1999) would probably argue that Dwight Watson went to Washington because he felt "stiffed" or "betrayed," and that his protest exemplifies the backlash of white men who feel disre-

---

[4] *United States v. Watson* 253 F. Supp. 2d 1 (2003).
[5] *United States v. Watson* 376 U.S. App. D.C. 22; 483 F.3d 828 (2007).
[6] *United States v. Watson* 253 F. Supp. 2d 1 (2003).

spected and victimized. Her book *Stiffed* is a journalistic study of what she calls the "betrayal of the American man" in the last several decades. Interviews conducted with all sorts of disgruntled men—former dockworkers, chauvinist gang members, weepy born-again Christians, and many other groups—led Faludi to argue that being uncertain about who one is and where one is going is the definitive problem in the lives of the majority of white men in the United States.

All that these men wanted in life was "to be dutiful, belong, and adhere to the roles society had set out for them as men," Faludi writes of the "peculiarly modern American perception that to be a man means to be at the controls and at all times to feel yourself in control" (9). Promised were the far reaches of space, the glories of combat and the heroism of coming home, and the distinctive feelings of power and independence that defined the Marlboro Man and John Wayne. Alas, things did not work out. The civil rights movement, the demands of feminism, waves of industrial decline, the historical and moral failures of war and imperialism, and the end of cold war certitude undercut the symbolic foundations of white manhood. Men not only lost their "jobs, homes, cars, families," Faludi writes, but also "lost their compass in the world" (9). The backlash against women and minorities often exhibited by white men of different backgrounds is explained as a response to fraught masculinity and unrealized expectations of modernity.

This argument is onto something empirical in linking social conflict to broadscale societal and structural transformations. Decades of neoliberal economic policies have meant major changes in nearly every facet of American life (Holland et al. 2007: 5). Social welfare safety nets have been eroded, farm programs altered to benefit agribusiness, including in tobacco, collapsed industries replaced by impermanent employment, and labor markets rescaled to an international level. These processes have left lots of people with less control over life chances, including new and unprecedented levels of downward mobility in the middle classes (Newman 1988, 1993; Storper 2000). However, there are several important limitations to this account. Faludi walks a fine line between social analysis and naturalizing stereotypes. Her discussion of the historical inflation of a gender ideal at times participates in this inflation, romanticizing the masculinity of great expectations and space travel and the silver screen at the expense of a more intricate account of how engendering discourses have intersected with race and class structures in different locales. Tobacco farmers like Watson probably came of age looking up to ideals embodied in the Marlboro Man advertisements and the cowboys of black-and-white television programs. But this level of analysis skims over rich historical and cultural details of how manhood has been defined in places like rural North Carolina and leaves us feeling somewhat stiffed in terms of how to comprehend what was at stake for the tractor man on the National Mall. While similarities may exist in terms of what defines conservative backlash at a general level, I am interested in the specific ethnographic and industrial conditions in which such a politics becomes preferable and widespread. For example, the sociologist Michele Lamont (2000) argues that dignity is often what is at stake for working- and middle-class Americans who face job loss as a result of industrial restructuring. As a sense of pride and self-worth related to doing a particular kind of work and belonging to a vocational group is threatened, so too are the racial boundaries and senses of social distinction that are traced around class affiliation and employment. The white men that Lamont studied have tended to respond to industrial restructuring by blaming foreign workers as the cause of job displacement. Narratives of victimhood among white men are powerful constructions of fundamental "differences between themselves and others," Lamont writes, explaining the impacts of structural adjustment and the international economy in terms of cultural problems and felt disrespect (2).

A major limitation in Faludi's account of betrayal is the lack of attention paid to the politics of victimhood. Her account lumps many historical and societal processes together as the cause of white male disgruntlement, an argument that seems appealing on a general level but leads to confusion about the dynamics of social conflict. The civil rights movement did not cause feelings of betrayal. Rather, the discourse of betrayal itself emerged as part of a conservative cultural politics that has sought to contain civil rights claims and has appealed to white men who may be experiencing real adversity. Whereas Faludi takes the subjective experience of feeling betrayed at face value, my strategy is to more fully assess these claims to victimhood, disrespect, and betrayal as part of a political project. Many people who presently claim to be victims are not "stereotyped peoples burdened by a national history but icons who have only recently lost the protections of their national iconicity," the literary scholar and social theorist Lauren Berlant writes. They are, she continues, "white and male and heterosexual people of all classes who are said to sense that they have lost the respect of their culture, and with it the freedom to feel unmarked" (1997: 2). This politics of what Berlant calls "imperiled privilege" reflects a social strategy of reasserting and maintaining structures of comparative advantage and discrediting policies that aim to bring about a more equitable and just society as excessive concessions to undeserving constituencies and grave threats to the tacitly white family as the national icon (Lipsitz 2006: 454–56; Berlant 1997: 6). Watson's protest involved these assertions of power and entitlement at the same time as it was fueled by farm loss and the feeling that power is slipping away.

Plighted Citizenship

The central concern of the modern state is to foster the life and growth of the population, what the historian Michel Foucault calls "biopower" (1980: 143). This partly means providing social assistance to disadvantaged constituencies. However, the provision of assistance has often been linked to the skeptical idea that if you just give money to people, they will use it in unproductive ways (Barry et al. 1996; Gordon 1991; Foucault 1991; Hall and Held 1989). That citizenship is a legal right guaranteed by law does not mean that in practice all citizens receive equal treatment and have equal access to government or community support. Anthropologists understand citizenship as a context of group membership that is configured in terms of social norms, cultural values, and political strategies (Greenhouse et al. 1994; Rosaldo 1997). The kinds of citizenship that are deemed valuable to the nation reflect "underlying assumptions about the relative moral worthiness of different categories of subjects" (Ong 2003: 9–10). One of the most important aspects of Foucault's work was to demonstrate how the universal, even unconditional precept of social assistance that defines a formal social contract has been actualized in more narrow ways that involve the moral classification and evaluation of social groups. With relief or assistance guaranteed by moral evaluation rather than legal right, questions of normalcy and the social construction of citizenship have become the basis for economical distribution and political recognition (Petryna 1999).

Foucault refers to the "duty of man in society" in discussing the need for citizens to be certain kinds of people in order to seem deserving and valuable to the nation. He writes that the distribution of assistance is guided by the "semi-moral, semi-psychological analysis" of the morality of citizens, rather than "a definition of contractual obligations" (cited in Gordon 1991: 23–24). It is thus not surprising that the media is chockfull of stories about the appropriate reach of compassion, the limits of pity, the kinds of people who are deserving and undeserving, and the kinds of sympathy and solidarity, as well as indifference and apathy, that are considered acceptable or preferential.

A dominant model of citizenship in the contemporary United States casts citizenship as a "condition of social membership produced by personal acts and values, especially acts originating in or directed toward the family" (Berlant 1997: 1, 5). The relative worth of citizens to the nation and their ethical responsibilities are measured in terms of parenthood, participation in lawful activities, and the social stability and mobility of families. One broad political effect of this modal citizenship is to contain the scale of civic engagement. Although played out in public, spectacles like Watson's protest are symptomatic of the domestication of American politics (K. Stewart 2005). It was symbolically important that Watson stylized the national dream gone awry in terms of the family farm under attack. His claim was not that structural adjustment policies have made life precarious for all kinds of people or that the federal government has failed to meet contractual obligations to whole swaths of citizens. He was asking to be recognized as someone who is due recompense on the basis of who he is, what his family and lifestyle are like, and the news that these bedrocks of the nation are jeopardized.

This model of the ideal citizen as a family member who is inherently worthy and unfairly damaged is what I mean by "plighted citizenship," a vernacular form of the politics of imperiled privilege and backlash that is so evident on a societal level. Plight is an explanatory model and cultural model of citizenship that became dominant in the vocabulary of tobacco farm politics in the last several decades, although it embeds meanings going back to the plantation period, and even further. As a social construction, plight refers to a situation of misfortune and disadvantage where these conditions absolutely do not index personal or familial blameworthiness. The plighted citizen is an innocent citizen and others are to blame. The plighted citizen is a hardworking person who is "said to feel that they have lost access to the American Dream" (Berlant 1997: 2). Look at the juxtaposition of stylized agrarian family values and urban moral decline in Frank's language. Tobacco farm families seem harangued by public health, which instead ought to be thankful that such families exist because "look over the other shoulder at the more serious problems in society," he says. Then look at the burden of disease attributable to smoking as compared to illicit drug use (see figure I.1).

Tobacco farmers have turned to a familiar agrarian politics, focused on the imperiled family farm, to mitigate public disapproval of what they do for a living and advance the ideology that illicit drugs, not tobacco, are the most dangerous threat to public health. They define the value of their livelihood and their citizenship in terms of parenthood and punch their ticket as part of an imagined mainstream of middle-class families with shared values. But what are understandable ways to rationalize a problematic business in positive terms also embed political assertions about what different categories of people are worth to the nation, why relatively advantaged families like tobacco households but not stereotyped others deserve assistance in the face of misfortune, and who rightfully ought to be under attack in America. What began for the motorist as curiosity about how growers reconcile the ethical ambiguities of their businesses turned out to reflect a common story about conservative backlash amid economic pains that span the social ladder and the ability of industry to encourage stressed people to fear that the threat is cultural or racial in

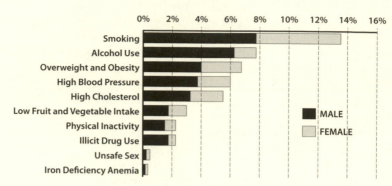

% TOTAL DISEASE BURDEN

Figure I.1. Burden of disease attributable to the ten leading risk factors in North America.
Source: Figure 7 in "Eight Americas: Investigating Mortality Disparities across Races, Counties, and Race-Counties in the United States," by C. J. L. Murray et al. 2006, PLoS Medicine 3 (9): e260.

nature, to seek to further circumscribe the scope of biopower and state assistance, and to resist progressive policy responses even though they might entail concrete benefits for them and their families.

The Politics of Plight

In the federal case brought against Watson, the process of sentencing converted an occasion to explore the widely felt problems that drove him to Washington into an assessment of individual character, a "semi-moral, semi-psychological analysis" of the "duty of man in society," returning to Foucault's terms. The media reporting and public discourse focused on what kind of person he is rather than what kind of society cultivates domestic terrorism.

"I hope you will give Mr. Watson's years as a *good citizen* as much weight as possible as you deliver the sentence," Bob Etheridge, a congressman from North Carolina, wrote in a letter to the judge asking for leniency (Leonnig 2004a: B1; my italics). Watson's family and community members sent many letters to the judge attesting to his "honesty and integrity." Perhaps as a result of these petitions, the already lenient sentence was eventually reduced to little more than a year (Leonnig 2004b; Leonnig and Tucker 2004).

A focus on the family and the supposedly independent business as the proper arenas of citizenship and political identification, and the morally evaluative structure of the empirical welfare state, can encourage citizens to understand themselves as having no relationship to and no responsibility for problems that affect other people. Beltway commuters yawned at Watson's protest and were late for a happy hour. They sat in traffic and listened to radio hacks make fun of the tractor man. They smoked cigarettes or planned a family vacation to the Outer Banks. They called him a "redneck" (Copeland 2003: C1; Pulliam 2003). Meanwhile, Watson sat alone in his cab, not supported by other growers back in North Carolina, many of whom disparaged his extremism as a sign of personal weakness, nor by farm labor advocates, who work hard to improve the lives of migrant farmworkers but tend to personally blame farmers like Watson for the depraved living and working conditions of workers, nor by an antitobacco movement that has largely been distant from farms. Social distress and economic decline were reduced to the interiority of the tractor, indeed, the interiority of the person. The capital city's congressional delegate said, "Incidents like this bring out nuts." The county commissioner in Watson's hometown explained the protest in terms of psychological "problems of which we are not aware." Struggling to make sense of what had become an embarrassing national spectacle, Watson's neighbors in North Carolina told reporters that he was "pushed to the edge" and was not a "crazy person" or "deviant from the social norm" (Nakamura 2003: A6; Nakamura and Lengel 2003a: B1).

The tobacco industry has propagated this dominant ethics of individualism—live and let live (or die), to each their own—to pin risk assumption on smokers. Although there is a strong antitobacco movement in the United States, large segments of the general population are not mobilized around an intense desire to eradicate smoking disease, though this would lead to major improvements in the quality of life for smokers and their families, minimize nonsmoker exposure to secondhand smoke, and massively reduce healthcare costs and tobacco's burden on taxpayers. The main impediment to a broader politics of indignation about tobacco is a belief that has been strategically cultivated and disseminated by the tobacco industry for decades: the tendency to "identify the smoker as the one responsible for his *sorry* fate," in the words of historian Allan M. Brandt (2007: 444; my italics). While the tobacco industry benefits from this individualization of risk and harm put onto consumers, there is a striking parallel to how other social problems are likewise circumscribed, localized, and pinned. The dilemmas of poverty, joblessness, homelessness, drug abuse, a lack of health insurance, and violent crime all have very clear and well understood social determinants. But the common societal and governmental responses to these problems are often rationalized in terms of the individuals and populations affected being "responsible," to quote Brandt, for their "sorry fate." They are seen as inherently sorry, in the sense of being blameworthy, and also worthless, personally or collectively guilty for conditions. The ideology of individual responsibility that has been largely constructed by industries like tobacco (think also of beer commercials that instruct consumers to "drink responsibly" as another of the countless examples) combines with increasing levels of corporate philanthropy to further underwrite the notion that harm and misfortune are basically personal or domestic problems, not fundamentally linked to efforts on the part of industries and comparatively advantaged groups to evade being responsible for historical, social, and medical burdens.

Watson's protest, like many other kinds of violent public spectacle, was made to seem idiosyncratic, a personal problem, and he utilized the language of family and heritage to pursue recognition and relief. The structural changes that underpinned his protest and the role of tobacco capital in stressing growers and destabilizing family farms remained causes never scrutinized as causes. They were domesticated as a family's sorry fate, and character was made into the moral of the story. Nowhere did reporters attempt to analyze the real predicaments of livelihood and personhood behind Watson's direct action. Law enforcement officials even told reporters it was "unclear why he was there and what he wanted," apparently overlooking the fact that Watson had received an official permit to demonstrate with a tractor on the grounds of the National Mall to provide information about tobacco farming issues (Fahrenthold and Lengel 2003: B1; Nakamura and Lengel 2003a: B1). Reporters did not adequately discuss the feasibility of alternative sources of livelihood in rural communities in North Carolina. They did not critically analyze the industrial restructuring that has made it harder for some tobacco growers to stay afloat. While the newspaper coverage tended to erroneously equate farm loss with the decline of smoking, there was little coverage of the fact that tobacco growers (and workers, for that matter) receive a much smaller portion of the revenues from tobacco sales compared to the recent past, and that tobacco companies have continued to profit at home and abroad in spite of social awareness about health risks (Capehart 2004a).

Just a few years after September 11, 2001, this was the most serious threat of terror in the United States: the homegrown terrorism of a tobacco grower who impotently promised to cause a more visible and spectacular kind of damage and destruction than the crop that used to come off his family farm. But the title *terrorist* was not used in the media reports.[7] That it plainly would have been if he were from a different background is evidence of a cultural and racial politics at work in structuring which forms of protest and political engagement seem legitimate and which categories of subjects seem inherently worthy in spite of perhaps

---

[7] In the trials, Justice Department attorneys called Watson a "domestic terrorist" (Leonnig and Lengel 2004: B1), and a judge called Watson a "one-man weapon of mass destruction" (Leonnig and Tucker 2004: A1).

crossing a legal threshold. Watson was partly taken with a grain of salt in the media coverage and among beltway commuters. His performance escaped the more pronounced forms of interrogation and punishment that are predictable for other people who threaten to explode the nation's capital. All of this is evidence of the cultural and moral force of plighted citizenship as a tacitly white kind of damaged citizenship that seems legitimate and harmless, and the romantic image of a family farmer and military veteran staked out in a John Deere on the National Mall. Imagine a Muslim individual parked in a vehicle on the Mall claiming to possess heaps of explosives. Imagine reservoirs of federal funding and think tanks mobilized to explain and respond to the event. Imagine the public outcry about a clash of civilizations and the dangerous media reporting and political responses that would likely ensue but that never occurred around the tractor man.

Reporters did note the irony that "on the eve of war with Iraq and a heightened terrorism alert," it was a "lone farmer from North Carolina" who "could so easily disrupt life in the capital," the *Washington Post* stated. What is "to stop an international terrorist organization armed with advanced technology," the editorial goes on, "let alone weapons of mass destruction? We're giving Saddam Hussein 48 hours to leave Iraq. How much longer are we going to give Dwight in the pond?" (Sandalow 2003: A1). Another reporter cynically celebrated Watson's protest as "a reminder of what makes this country unique," by which she apparently meant the right of public demonstration, stereotyping the Muslim world as inherently backward in this regard (Jacoby 2003: A12). This double-standard discourse portrayed Watson as an icon of patriotism, assimilated into a prefabricated image of what farmers are like. Tom Ridge, then secretary of Homeland Security, said the protest was not "in any way connected with the kind of terrorism" authorities "expect" from Islamic militants. At the very instant that Watson was on the Mall, Ridge announced a plan, "Operation Liberty Shield," to enhance national security by requiring mandatory detention of asylum applicants from many Muslim countries and the interrogation of Arab Americans. "We want to make absolutely certain," Ridge said, "[that] you are who you say you are" (Jacoby 2003: A12).

The media was correct in emphasizing Watson's deep personal troubles. He had recently gone through a divorce that had perhaps been influenced by financial difficulties. Leading up to the protest he exhibited signs of serious distress and was contemplating suicide (Collins 2003; Jubera 2003; Nakamura and Shear 2003).[8] Psychology was no doubt part of

---

[8] Watson was deemed competent to stand trial. A clinical psychologist with the D.C. Department of Mental Health interviewed Watson prior to his hearing and found he did not "behave in a manner typical of people who are mentally ill. . . . His judgment appeared adequate, but unsophisticated and somewhat naive" (Tucker 2003: B3).

why Watson drove to Washington and risked his own life while threaten-ing others. However, an anthropological emphasis on historical and so-cietal contexts that influence psychological and emotional life (Kleinman 1986) deepens an appreciation of the motivations behind the protest. Rather than being guided by a concern "with finding a psychological origin" of distress, anthropologists attempt to understand, to borrow the words of João Biehl, a "sense of psychological interiority as ethnological, as the whole of the individual's behavior in relation to her environment and to measures that define boundaries, be they legal, medical, relational, or affective" (2004: 481).

Watson's commute to Washington, about a seven-hour drive from North Carolina, was made into a spectacle of familial plight, largely as a result of his own festooned performance of this appealing image. His commute to a federal prison punished the public and threaten-ing manner in which he conveyed an experience of personal loss and jeopardy that affects people from many vocations and social positions. Meanwhile, the romantic discourse about family farms encourages a desire to commute his sentence, to pardon him. Here is what Congress-man Etheridge said: "I obviously wish he had not chosen to make the statement in the way he did, but it really is an example of the *plight* we see in rural America today. Tobacco farmers see a way of life vanishing, a way of life they've lived all their life, not just a generation or two, but back to the Colonial days" (Nakamura and Shear 2003: B1; my italics).

This language of plight is a condescending discourse that limits an ad-equate understanding of the role of changing economic conditions, driven by the reorganization of multinational capital, in inducing hardship and difficulties in rural regions and the different impacts of these processes for differently positioned individuals, families, and groups. Reference to the plight of tobacco farmers seems congenial, as in the congressman's words, but there is a political valence that is linked to the depiction of economic crisis and hard times as a uniform, national condition, the con-cealment of race and class stratification, and the appropriation of victim-hood and discrimination for the benefit of white constituencies. Plight is a big word on a highway billboard that packages the complex and uneven conditions of life that exist off exits as phenomena that can be consumed on the fly. It makes the stress and worry that people like Watson experi-ence seem hapless rather than directly induced by a particular political economy; the precariousness of declining fortunes seem urgent and un-warranted, even though hardship is, in fact, the common predicament for most people on the planet; and their claims and responses, which are sometimes quite dangerous and tendentious and often have clear strategic value, seem innocent.

Reporters did not wonder about where the idea that tobacco farm families are hapless victims originated anyway. My interest is in historicizing and contextualizing how plighted citizenship became a vernacular mode of damaged citizenship and the political and corporate interests it has served. This goal entails apprehending plight both as a set of real conditions confronting farmers and the set of ideological meanings grafted onto those conditions in order to minimize a popular sense of the determinate role of industry in making them. What I have in mind is an account of North Carolina's tobacco region as a "transitioning political and economic world," to cite the anthropologist Adriana Petryna, where the public health response to smoking disease, the government's failure to stabilize and diversify the economy of tobacco regions, and the growth of international markets have worked in tandem to bring about substantial challenges to tobacco farm livelihoods and how farmers understand themselves. By looking at how these broadscale forces are complexly realized in "human conditions and conditions of citizenship" (Petryna 1999: 6–7), I aim to explain the cultural politics of response in this agrarian setting and the extent to which meanings and acts of citizenship reflect strategies to pursue entitlements, diagram social boundaries, and articulate belonging at the farm level and the national level. Eschewing the easy narrative—good people doing bad things—requires acknowledgment of the vast social disparities that tobacco farming helps to reproduce and the fact that, however well intentioned, growers are complicit in and derive some advantage from human conditions and conditions of citizenship that adversely affect the farm labor workforce. At the same time, there is the need to remain aware that these growers are themselves at the mercy of multinational corporations, and that limiting the analysis of culture and politics to a local level misses an important chance to implicate tobacco companies in forms of suffering for which growers are often personally blamed and to locate growers as part of the larger conservative backlash that defines a volatile moment in American history. To scrutinize the language of plight is to stay close to the vernacular meanings and relationships that are at stake in a local politics of citizenship and moral worthiness, while acquiescing to the urge to get broader and broader, opening up the context of accountability for domestic terrorism, and finding that much of the backlash that Faludi attempts to explain has less to do with a generic threat to manhood than with the complex ways that industrial restructuring simultaneously destabilizes where people sit in their communities and organizes particular kinds of ideologies about the causes of instability. Scrutinizing plight reflects a desire to convert the anomie that comes out of the massive social restructuring that intensified in the Reagan era from the private property of automobile commuters mired in a tractor or in traffic into a social fact and a basis for solidarities. Given what this anomie can do to people—driving Watson to domestic terrorism, prompting more mundane antagonisms at workplaces and in communities, or coalescing into conservative extremism—it seems just as relevant to a discussion of national security as the singular targeting of the nature and culture of Islamic fundamentalism.

To Not Be Sorry

Motorists who nestle up to the early-morning counter at the country store where farmers munch on ham biscuits and slug down cups of strong rural coffee might hear one particular word used in unexpected ways. This word might start to seem like a central thread that needs to be unwound as part of a complex account of the history and ethnography of tobacco farms. Accumulated entanglements of power and prestige are there in its utterance.

People in North Carolina regularly call people "sorry," and tobacco growers do so in patterned ways. Workers are "sorry workers." Marginal and failed farmers are "sorry farmers." The people who sit idle on their porches because they do not want to work for the meager wages paid out in *el campo* (the field) are "sorry people." The word colloquially means "no-good," "good for nothing," "worthless," and "blameworthy." It combines the idea that a person is not successful with the indication that said misfortune is that person's fault. As a result, financial success in farming (or at least its display), maintenance of a clean and modern operation, an ability to expand production and upgrade equipment, and maintenance of a good working relationship with tobacco companies are all signs that a farmer is not sorry. Farmers work hard to produce quality tobacco, fetch high grades, and grow successful businesses, but also to exhibit public signs as evidence that these pursuits stem from a personal commitment.

My wife's father helped my project in many ways. Tobacco agriculture in Appalachia looks a lot different than it does in North Carolina, where the farms are bigger and economic dependence on tobacco is usually more intense. But we had long conversations about the production process and major challenges facing people who own and operate tobacco farm businesses. He told me that a sorry person is a person who does not do a good job. It is a farmer who does not practice weed control so things get out of hand. The fields are messy and the farm shop is unkempt. These are sometimes the older farmers who did not go to university to study modern agricultural techniques and best practices in farm management and conservation like he did, but there are also active farmers who could care less about how their farm looks and the quality of the job they do. Sorry people are essentially people who do not live up to the Protestant work ethic. Whether the fields are clean and orderly is taken as a reflection of the moral fabric of the grower, and so one aspect of the language of sorriness is about self-worth, a claim to possess real skills, and pride in doing something well and in a way that does not cut corners.

My wife's father died attempting to not be sorry, just a couple of years after I had completed my fieldwork in North Carolina. He was mowing tall grass on a hillside next to a small tobacco patch and got close to the bank where the hillside falls down into the patch. This is something he had done a thousand times, but on this occasion the wheel slipped and the tractor flipped over the bank, landing on top of him. How he died says a lot about how he lived. He did not need to mow that close to the edge. There was no impact in terms of the quality of the tobacco leaf. But it was a thing of pride. Maintaining immaculate fields was important to him—no, that is an understatement—it was an act that was part of an entire way of being, an existential act, not a means to an end but the way he did things as a matter of course. He got close to the edge because tall grass around the field would mean neglect, implying that a choice had been made to not do this extra work.

His death was horrible, coming suddenly. My wife and I rented a car and immediately drove back down the highway from Boston. Family members struggled to make sense of the accident. Why did this happen to such a good man? At the funeral, everyone talked about what a meticulous farmer he was and how his fields were the neatest and cleanest, his tobacco the prettiest in the area, and he was such a good husband, father, and friend to so many. Everyone knew this was the proper eulogy, and they did not have to use the word sorry to say that he was definitely not that.

The cause of death was trauma related to the off chance that the hillside was slippery that day. But that's just one explanation. The concept of "moral experience," as developed by the anthropologist Arthur Kleinman, has been central to my approach. This concept refers to "what is locally at stake" for a given population. It refers to the local meaning of such values as "status, relationships, resources, ultimate meanings, [and] one's being-in-the-world" and the experience that they are being threatened or transformed for one reason or another (1999: 360–62). Moral experience refers not to a universal morality but to the immense diversity of values across social locations. It refers to the process whereby particular values, relationships, and meanings come to matter deeply and where there is a great deal at stake in maintaining or losing them.

What was at stake for Dwight Watson on the National Mall? What model of the human was he attempting to convey, inhabit, or uphold in his own sorry way? What model of the human is worth dying for because doing a good job matters? I am convinced that the appropriate historical and ethnographic context for understanding what is at stake for tobacco farmers and what has them often on edge is sorriness. This does not mean that my father-in-law's death was not an accident—just that an active investment in a value that makes mowing a field more than just mowing a field, the value of not being sorry, linking the aesthetics of farm tidiness to the "duty of man in society," was part of what made the accident happen. The little things, like mowing each and every blade of grass, like throwing oneself into the shoot to tag the calves—these acts reflect commitments to household and family, and to models of the moral person that are irreducible to but often bound up in political strategies.

Sorriness is multivalent. The whole analysis becomes trivial unless the multiple layers are held together. There is the positive side to sorriness, where not being sorry is an expression of self-worth and pride. The presentation of a hardworking self is an important moral defense for farmers given the uncertainties of the weather and market volatility, the ups and downs of fuel and other input costs, and the possibility that despite heaps of effort no rain (or too much) will leave a farmer with what is called a "sorry crop of tobacco." Tactical displays of hard work and industry help secure a social reputation and mitigate the moral hazard that the sorriness of a crop will be taken as evidence of the sorriness of the grower. However, leaving the language of sorriness there, as positive terms for talking about work, misses the important political valences. "From an ethnographic perspective," Kleinman writes, "what is at stake, what morally defines a local world, may be, when viewed in comparative perspective, corrupt, grotesque, even downright inhuman. That is to say, the moral may be unethical" (1999: 365–66).

Not all farmers have equal access to these values or their public display, owing to differences of farm size, market access, and the race and class disparities in the tobacco farm landscape that government rural modernization efforts did nothing to challenge. The word is used to denigrate vulnerable people like farm laborers, farmers with limited finances and limited access to the newest and best equipment, the handful of active black tobacco farmers, and failed farmers reluctantly forced out of business. The word designates that these groups are culpable for and deserving of their comparative disadvantages and vulnerabilities. In rural North Carolina, the language of sorriness is also deleteriously racialized, sometimes equated with blackness.

Some farmers, like my wife's father, a decent man, take pride in expressing pride through work, out on the tractor, and not in huddled circles at the farm shop or the tobacco warehouse. Their ability to not be sorry hinges less on the attribution of negative qualities to other people in the intimate recesses of whiteness. But for many farmers, positive displays of self-worth are the flip side of talking shit. My sense is that things are different in Appalachia, where my wife's father farmed. In rural North Carolina where I did my fieldwork, perhaps reflecting deeper historical linkages to plantation slavery and more visible and intense realities of and political struggles around racial disparities, sorriness is the everyday white discourse used to naturalize inequalities in terms of the essential moral decrepitude of racialized populations and the innate work ethic and national value of the person who uses the word in this way. It is heard in passing conversations at the corner store, in the complaints of the farmer who comes home from the farm and sits down to a stack of bills, and in my interviews. One of the central arguments of this book is that white farmers call black people sorry to reroute blame onto them and justify illegal but economical dependence on undocumented migrant labor. This dependence is said to be necessary because black people are "sorry," meaning indolent. As blame shifts onto black people, the white people who are breaking laws do not have to say, "I'm sorry," because they seem victimized by a government that is said to unfairly sanction the sorriness of racial minorities, while their own pursuit of largesse and their lawbreaking are rationalized in terms of the flaws of these others. It is as if the sorrier other people are, the more the self seems innocent and valuable, capable of discerning and discrediting the sorry sorts said to threaten the nation and claiming to be plighted by the added burden of having to employ and manage them. As is seen across the United States, the cultural politics of imperiled privilege and backlash often takes the form of "rage at the stereotyped peoples who have appeared to change the political rules of social membership" and "a desperate desire to return to an order of things deemed normal" (Berlant 1997: 2).

Media accounts assimilated Watson as a generic figure of rural disgruntlement at the same time as they made him seem truly idiosyncratic: clinging to a dying way of life and completely off his rocker. The time I spent in Watson's stomping grounds—he farmed just a couple of exits from Wilson County—pushes me to challenge these facile accounts. His protest originated in a particular historical and sociological context of accountability where relationships to the government, the tobacco industry, and the farm labor workforce have been sustaining but have also implied blame or dependence. Heritage and a vague notion of plight understandably seem like what is at stake when the media solicits sound bites for the sake of a consumable story like a driver eager to get where they are going and so only stopping to get gas and snacks. In praising and ridiculing Watson at the same time, the media never took him seriously. What if he drove to Washington to not be sorry because this feat matters back home? What if what it means back home has a great deal to do with the overtones of having done something wrong, being a sorry person, perhaps needing to apologize for something, representing, like the other stereotyped groups, a threat to the nation and no longer national iconicity? Perhaps this is why Watson called the *San Francisco Chronicle* a year before his protest to voice discontent about predicaments affecting tobacco farmers but also a claim about innocence. "If you grow tobacco, everybody thinks you're evil," he said. "I'm not down here manipulating nicotine. I'm following the laws of the federal and state government" (Ryan 2002: D4).

What if he were not so much protesting as insisting that he was hard-working, a good farmer, and a good person who did not have to apologize for anything? Maybe he was claiming to not be sorry. Maybe this is why his neighbors stressed to reporters, "He is a meticulous farmer. His fields are immaculate" (Nakamura 2003: A6). This claim to not be sorry involves both these local diacritics of industry and management and a larger claim about national belonging and iconicity. For people facing the real possibility of failure and status loss, a claim to not be sorry, a claim to be worth something, which sometimes comes at the expense of others and targets them, can be a deeply moral act. When farmers told me that they would never apologize for growing tobacco, and then when I heard frequent attributions of sorriness around the workplace, I came to understand that these are two sides of a broken record. Growers are also unlikely to apologize for illegal labor recruitment, dependence on government largesse, or the sometimes hostile treatment shown to workers. Contrition is difficult when vernacular idioms that subtend ideals of legitimate national and local belonging make the phrase "I'm sorry" a personal indictment more than a mere apology.

This book tracks the politics of innocence on multiple levels of the tobacco industry, including the abdications of accountability that are part of corporate strategies, the new kinds of consumer responsibilities that are built into the expanded federal regulation of tobacco products, the serious issues raised by farm labor advocates about noncompliant agricultural employers and a neglectful government, and the ways that growers wrestle with but mainly take distance from the moral ambiguities of producing a harmful product and being part of a farm labor system built on vulnerability and exploitation. Rather than converting the ambiguity that defines the subjective experiences of cultivating tobacco into a billboard, where there is only room enough for a simple story about good people doing a bad thing, a focus on sorriness forces a more sweeping format that places the ethnographic present of farm loss, contentious racial politics and tensions, the public debate about immigration, and the conservative backlash against the backdrop of historical trajectories in the rural South and the influence of the tobacco industry in making many rural residents at once economically dependent and socially defensive.

This book is comprised of interrelated sections, the first having to do with the history of the tobacco industry and public health politics, and the second having to do with farm life and labor. The story of the rise and fall of tobacco agriculture in this region provides an important set of reference points for thinking about the structures of race and class and engendering discourses that have all along been produced alongside tobacco. Only by looking at the historical trajectory of tobacco agriculture over centuries is an adequate understanding of the politics of plight and entitlement possible, since this politics builds heavily on values—especially those having to do with race and innocence—that have considerable historical depth. This combination of materials discourages a view of tobacco grower defensiveness as parochial, generic, or natural, encouraging instead a thorough historical explanation of how a preference for claiming victimhood came to define the relationship of growers to their governments. Sorriness is multivalent and puts transverse force relations into play, a keyword where realities and representations are enveloped, the ideological imagery of farm loss and agrarian decline pulsing with the felt plight of financial duress, social power steeped in anxiety. The claim to not be sorry and that others are sorry is a claim to self-worth that is linked to gendered and racialized notions of deservedness buttressed by powerful mythologies of agrarianism ensconced at the Jefferson Memorial, just a short walk from where Watson was camped.

PART I

THE TOBACCO INDUSTRY, PUBLIC HEALTH, AND AGRARIAN CHANGE

Chapter 1

Most Admired Company

TOBACCO HAS BEEN A VISIBLE PART of daily life in large parts of the world for hundreds of years. Profound changes in tobacco's prevalence and effects occurred in the twentieth century. The modern commercial cigarette and multinational tobacco corporations proliferated. Smoking is now the single greatest cause of preventable disease and death worldwide. In the last century, there were one hundred million tobacco-related deaths. Although smoking declined and tobacco-control measures took hold in several countries over the past few decades, it is now widely recognized that the unabated global demand for cigarettes will kill 1 billion people in the current century (Proctor 2001). The majority of these deaths will be in developing countries, where the industry continues to infuse smoking with positive social meanings, recruit adolescent smokers, maintain free-market environments for this harmful product, and leverage political influence to limit public health efforts, including implementation of the international Framework Convention on Tobacco Control of the World Health Organization (World Health Organization 2008a).

In the United States, however, the tobacco industry now engages with public health critique and policy through different strategies. Leading the way is Philip Morris USA, which adopted a corporate social responsibility platform in the last decade. Its company website boldly claims, "There is no safe cigarette" (Philip Morris USA 2007b). The website is part of a broader media campaign, including television and print ads aimed at publicizing information about smoking risks. Why would the biggest of Big Tobacco, the world's largest, most powerful cigarette maker, insist to the public that its product is unsafe?

On one level, this insistence is about public image, Philip Morris's makeover into a "responsible corporate citizen" (Brandt 2007: 444). Hence, the website also attests, "Our goal is to be the most responsible . . . manufacturer and marketer of consumer products" (Philip Morris USA 2007a). The firm is pursuing image-enhancement strategies to overturn decades of delegitimization and deception that have made the tobacco industry a symbol of corporate wrongdoing (Hirschhorn 2004). But this image-control strategy is also a means of limiting corporate liability and deflecting risk assumption for smoking disease and death onto consumers. Philip Morris has also aligned itself with the leading public health groups (e.g., National Campaign for Tobacco-Free Kids, American Lung Association, American Heart Association, and American Cancer Society) in the United States in supporting sweeping tobacco-control measures, namely, legislation granting the Food and Drug Administration (FDA) authority to regulate cigarettes and other tobacco products.

In this chapter I explore some of the economic and ethical paradoxes that define this contentious policy change and Philip Morris's newfound commitment to corporate social responsibility. I am interested in what these transformations reflect about contemporary capitalism and the effects of corporate power and strategy on public policy and on populations of consumers and producers. Whereas later chapters explore these phenomena from the standpoint of tobacco farms and migrant farm labor, here I discuss the politics around the FDA legislation, highlighting the dangerous role of a particular corporate oxymoron—the safe cigarette—in Philip Morris's strategic engagement with public health and consumer markets. Although Philip Morris admits on its website that there is "no safe cigarette," the firm is banking on the expectation that FDA regulation will inadvertently sustain the continued promotion of the profitable illusion of a "safer" cigarette. Like many other multinational corporations, the firm paradoxically capitalizes on health problems to bolster corporate image and boost the bottom line, strategically merging economic, ethical, and political interests in an exemplary case of what anthropologists theorize as "biocapitalism" (Sunder Rajan 2006). Analysis of the tobacco industry's evolving biocapitalist trends enhances understanding of social and cultural dynamics on tobacco farms, and, as later chapters will show, tobacco farming provides fruitful ground for theorizing the consequences of the involvement of corporations in regulatory politics.

Motorists driving up and down Interstate 95 pass Philip Morris's headquarters outside Richmond. I passed the behemoth corporate campus on my drive from Boston, where I was a graduate student at the time, to North Carolina to do my fieldwork. Between the highway shoulder and the parking lots there is a tall metal obelisk (it looks like a giant cigarette) wrapped with the logos of the company's most popular cigarette brands: Marlboro, Virginia Slims, Parliament, L&M, and Basic. Many motorists probably roll their eyes, thinking about this company's public relations they've seen in print or on television and the perversity of Philip Morris now fashioning itself as something of a public health advocate.

But the company's image has improved, according to internal and independent polls. In the mid-1990s, Americans had a highly negative view of Philip Morris, giving it an average favorability rating of about 33 percent (only slightly higher than the smoking rate at the time). By 2004, nearly 60 percent of all Americans (more in the young adult age-group) said Philip Morris was acting more responsibly than in the past, and they distinguished it as more responsible than other tobacco companies (McDaniel et al. 2006: 219–20).

In 2008, *Fortune* magazine ranked Philip Morris the tobacco industry's "most admired" company. The company's overall "admiration" ranking (8.4 out of 10) reflected the magazine's evaluation of such factors as social responsibility, people management, financial soundness, global competitiveness, and product quality. I scanned the lists in each industry and, incredibly, this rating is higher than the score of any other company. Philip Morris is apparently the most admired company in the world. The magazine offers no explanation for why Philip Morris is therefore not included in its published list of the Top 50 most admired companies, alongside such icons as Apple, Berkshire Hathaway, Google, Johnson & Johnson, Coca-Cola, Walt Disney, and McDonald's. Nor in the case of Philip Morris does *Fortune* provide an extended commentary about "Why It's Admired," a blurb included for all nontobacco companies. The company does appear, however, in the alphabetized list of the Top 363 most admired companies, and quite near the top, as one of Philip Morris's strategic responses to critique was to change its name to the Altria Group.[1] My preference is to use the name Philip Morris here so as to not validate the pernicious notion that a new day has dawned in the tobacco industry, which, as I show later in the chapter, was precisely the goal of the name change.

Problematization

The science of smoking-related disease that arose in the early twentieth century did not identify a problem never before recognized as requiring sociopolitical intervention. In his famous "A Counterblaste to Tobacco," published in 1604, King James I admonished that tobacco is "a custom loathsome to the eye, hateful to the nose, harmful to the brain, dangerous to the lung." Subsequent centuries saw various social movements critique tobacco consumption and seek prohibition. Perhaps the most forceful was the temperance movement in the early twentieth-century United States, which placed tobacco alongside alcohol as the main source of moral ruination in modern society (Brandt 2007: 45–48).

[1] The rankings for each year are contained at http://money.cnn.com/magazines/fortune/mostadmired. For 2010, the rankings changed, with the Altria Group slipping to third in the tobacco industry, and Philip Morris International assuming the top slot, probably because of the continued spread of smoking around the world.

In the last half century, antitobacco politics were radically amplified and distinctively transformed in parts of the world. These changes certainly have to do with the biosciences' mounting interrogation of smoking and the new alliances between science, government, and civil society, as well as the sheer magnitude of the public health catastrophe that was increasingly being linked to tobacco consumption. A watershed here was the landmark 1964 U.S. Surgeon General's Report, which helped publicly solidify the scientific and medical consensus about smoking and health. The tobacco industry responded with various strategies, including redoubling marketing campaigns to legitimize the smoking habit and secretly funding pseudoscience to foment public debate and doubts about even the most basic facts of tobacco's toxicity (Benson and Kirsch 2010; Kohrman and Benson 2011; Brandt 2007).

It is tempting to narrate the history of tobacco's changing social meaning as a shift from a "sacred" period to a "profane" period (Kohrman and Benson 2011). Tobacco was once glamorized on the silver screen and recommended to patients by doctors in advertisements and office visits. Then all of a sudden things changed. The smoking rate declined. The industry was vilified, and the antitobacco movement linked medical and public health research to policy development.

This is a too simple story. Things did not change with one fell swoop. Smoking underwent a process of "problematization" (Foucault 1985, 1997a; Deacon 2000).[2] In historical perspective, there are many ways that society might respond to health problems related to smoking. The concept of problematization encourages a study of the concrete historical processes through which this particular phenomenon came to be regarded in a very public way as a problem. Analysis of this ethical and epistemological classification, what it means for tobacco to be a problem today, entails apprehending, among many other things, the forms of political calculation and intervention that have evolved in relation to tobacco; the development of official government approaches, as well as criticism and advocacy work; and the responses and engagements of the tobacco industry and its political supporters. More than the increase in scientific evidence linking smoking to disease, or the simple fact that government regulation of tobacco has increased in the last half century, Foucault's concept of problematization refers especially to the organization of new and different kinds of institutional and societal arrangements for defining and acting upon a problem (Foucault 1985: 115).

The anthropologist Aihwa Ong (2003: 6) uses the phrase "problem-space" to refer to a sociopolitical context that is sculpted over time as

---

[2] The anthropologist Matthew Kohrman (2008) refers to the concept of problematization in his study of smoking in China.

a given phenomenon becomes the object of ethical deliberation, political calculation, and technoscientific endeavors. A problem like tobacco comes to occupy the philosophical and intellectual space of public and private thinking about what is right or wrong, proper or improper, and normal or abnormal in a society, and also the physical space of the institutional environments and intervention strategies that link up with the industries and populations that are affected. The concept of problematization encourages a view of the tobacco industry as being actively involved in configuring the philosophy and practice of public health and the government of health behavior, while Ong's concept of problem-space reiterates the need to analyze the historical construction of problems and the ethics and politics that define responses to them.

Instead of setting out with the belief that public health and industry are opposed, I examine how corporations respond to critique or increased public awareness about the environmental and health problems that are related to their business. Far from being opposed to governments, corporations are often actively involved in shaping regulation as both an intellectual space linked to normalized ethical and cultural values and an institutional space defined by dominant approaches and concerns. This focus is amenable to the way Foucault conceived of power as a field of strategies and relationships (Lazzarato 2002). This perspective is broadly appropriate to the study of other health problems because claims to corporate social responsibility are evident across many industries, including among the food and beverage companies that market products that significantly contribute to chronic disease conditions. My goal is to open up the crucial role of corporations in modern public health to more rigorous analysis and to develop critical reflection about the inadequacies of contemporary public health approaches that do not attend to the harm caused by industry and the role of corporations in the social management of harm. To avoid an uncomplicated account of antitobacco sentiment arising overnight and in defiance of the tobacco industry, I document how the modern tobacco problem emerged and continues to evolve in the middle of interests that are superficially understood as being opposed. Tobacco companies never simply responded to a problem that existed apart from their involvement in shaping what that problem looked like exactly. The tobacco problem was constructed out of the dialectical relationship between the intensified criticism of the industry in the last half century and the responses and justifications provided by the industry.

In contrast to the temperance movement's somewhat religious focus, the regulatory approaches of the postwar decades were more secular. The emphasis on sin and moral ruination shifted to a concern with health. Not health in the vague sense referenced by early monarchs and the temperance movement, who were of course aware of smoking-related ailments, but rather a scientific understanding of health in terms of epidemiological risk factors (Brandt 1990). Regarding smoking as gravely threatening to the nation would not have been an implausible response to the scientific evidence about smoking and health in the 1950s. But this is not what happened. Tobacco's legitimacy and legality were not questioned, even though tobacco killed more Americans in the last century than all of the country's military operations combined. The federal government was not going to take bold action with tobacco products ubiquitous throughout the culture. The surgeon general's report did not lead to a call for prohibition or even the wholesale restructuring and regulation of the tobacco industry. The report instead led to new government interventions designed to enhance public awareness of risk and improve individual decisions, mainly by mandating warning labels on cigarette packs and beginning to regulate tobacco advertisements. The project of eliminating tobacco from society, an approach characteristic of the prohibition movement, was replaced by the biopolitical goal of enhancing "probabilities of life," to use Foucault's phrase (1984: 264). The overarching aim was to link accumulated knowledge about smoking risk to the development of techniques for managing risk at the population level and promoting behavior management and modification at the individual level. Hence, the modern antitobacco movement has been and remains premised on the idea that more and more scientific information about smoking risk is essential to improving the public health. This epistemological and organizational framework of tobacco control determined in large measure how other chronic disease problems like obesity would be conceptualized and managed. Prevention has been part of the official public health response to the epidemiological transition, characterized by an increased chronic disease burden and disease problems linked to consumption and lifestyle issues. But the dominant approach has favored health promotion over prevention, making consumers the locus of intervention (as in the case of warning labels) and upholding distinctive American beliefs in individual autonomy and responsibility and the cultural framing of freedom in terms of the marketplace (Brandt 2007: 442–45).

A public health agenda that focused on the management of risk and harm as individual medical problems rather than essential industrial problems and the pursuit of risk reduction through technological development were two means of reconciling health values and market values as the tobacco problem took shape. In the 1960s and 1970s, the tobacco industry and the federal government worked collaboratively to develop potentially reduced-risk tobacco products. The U.S. Department of Agriculture funded studies in search of less toxic tobacco leaf varieties. The American Cancer Society and the American Heart Association pushed for the removal of "high-tar" cigarettes from the market, believing that "low-tar" products would reduce disease prevalence. Leading public health officials formed the Less Hazardous Cigarette Working Group (later renamed the Tobacco Working Group to appease the industry) and contracted with scientific laboratories and industry scientists to develop less risky products. Meanwhile, the federal Public Health Service cautioned that the promotion of supposedly reduced-risk products "might lull the consumer into believing that he could smoke this kind of cigarette without *any* accompanying risk" (Fairchild and Colgrove 2004: 193–95; original italics). The relationship of government and industry is not so starkly posed if one considers the institutional complicities that influenced how tobacco was reckoned a problem and that drove responses that were frankly quite nonchalant given the public health impact.

Tobacco Industry Strategies

Powerful events have spurred public outrage against industry, for example, the release of the 1964 surgeon general's report on smoking and cancer, or the publication of Rachel Carson's watershed *Silent Spring*, which catalyzed a broadscale critique of the industrialized food system. These tipping points have the potential to galvanize social activism, what sociologist Ulrich Beck (1992: 78) calls the "enabling power of catastrophes." However, tobacco is a good example of how these events are not always or fully threatening to corporations, which push back by proliferating doubt and fragmenting social movements and forms of critique that coalesce around tipping points, leading to policy changes that are focused on reforms rather than wholesale restructuring of society and economy (Benson and Kirsch 2010: 465).

In an article on the anthropology of capitalism, Stuart Kirsch and I proposed to reorient the study of power in anthropology to more fully assess the tactics and strategies corporations use to respond to their critics (Benson and Kirsch 2010). In case studies of the tobacco and mining industries, we identified a model in which corporations move through three phases in response to social and government critique. Phase 1 corporate response involves denial that the critique is valid or that a legitimate problem exists. The objective of this response is to limit liability for externalities. Phase 2 involves the acknowledgment that a problem exists, that something is defective or harmful, and that the basis of critique has some scientific or ethical validity. However, phase 2 responses are primarily limited to symbolic gestures of recompense or amelioration. The goal at this stage is to avoid paying the full costs of solving the problems that corporations have caused. Phase 3 response entails crisis management. It is defined by the risk that the problems facing a particular corporation

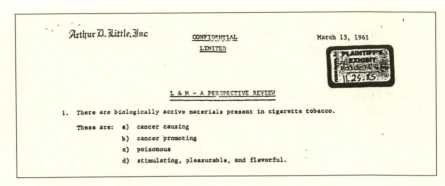

Figure 1.1. Memo entitled "Confidential Limited: L&M—A Prospective Review,"
March 15, 1961.
   Source: Tobacco Documents Online. Anne Landman Collection, Bates no.
2021382496/2498. http://tobaccodocuments.org/landman/
176632.html.

or industry will become financially and socially too great to manage. The
threat of catastrophic loss, bankruptcy, industry collapse, or complete loss
of legitimacy motivates corporations to shift their strategies. As Kirsch
and I describe, this can involve the appropriation of the discourse and
strategies of oppositional movements, the development of certification
programs that enshroud production and consumption processes with a
stamp of public approval, or the strategic promotion of an ideology of
"harmony," including such values as compromise and responsibility, with
the aim of portraying critics as troublemakers and justifying limited rather
than wholesale reforms (Nader 1997). Corporations may also envision
the possibility for competitive gain and the achievement of a new kind
of legitimacy through their participation in regulatory processes, as seen
below in my case study of the world's most admired company.
   The tobacco industry is illustrative of how corporations and industries
effectively engage with criticism or public awareness about harms in order to sustain marketability, limit government intervention, and maintain
some legitimacy. One way to understand this process is to analyze the series of shifting justifications or rationales that the industry has presented
for why tobacco products ought to remain not only legal but relatively
underregulated compared to other harmful products. Through a variety of shrewd responses, the tobacco industry was able to raise doubts
about the relationship between smoking and disease, reassuring smokers
and sustaining tobacco consumption. Clear knowledge of the dangers of
smoking, as in the excerpt in figure 1.1 from an internal tobacco company document, was sequestered.

In its phase 1 response, the tobacco industry sponsored its own scientific studies and funded nongovernmental organizations, most infamously the Tobacco Institute, to disseminate favorable reports presented as though they were the product of neutral scientific research. The proliferation of doubt as a key phase 1 strategy was pioneered by the tobacco industry (Brandt 2007) and has since become standard practice across a range of industries. As recently as the 1990s, the tobacco industry continued to deny that there is a direct causal link between smoking and disease and that nicotine is a powerfully addictive drug. The industry has also used marketing campaigns to discourage smokers from being concerned about health issues, most notably in Philip Morris's Marlboro Man campaign, which linked smoking to images of individual autonomy and defiance about risk and government (Brandt 2007: 263–64).

This phase 1 response overlapped with phase 2 efforts to address specific concerns about risk and harm. During the 1950s and 1960s, the tobacco industry introduced a series of products, such as filtered cigarettes, that were purported to be safer than conventional cigarettes. These new products were marketed as a form of what one company called "health protection" (Brandt 2007: 244), implicitly acknowledging that tobacco products were causing harm. Subsequent advertising used misleading product descriptors like "light" or "low-tar" to allay consumer anxieties (Pollay and Dewhirst 2002). However, it was well known within the industry that these new products provided a false sense of security. Tobacco companies chose not to divulge their knowledge that these products delivered as much tar and nicotine as conventional cigarettes. Aggressive marketing perpetuated dependence on tobacco as smokers switched to the new products en masse in the mistaken belief that they were less risky (Fairchild and Colgrove 2004). The market share for light cigarettes increased from 4 percent in 1970 to 50 percent in 1990 and, with aggressive advertising campaigns, to 80 percent in 1998. People "believed, and still do, that these products pose less risk to health than other cigarettes" (Institute of Medicine 2001: 26), a testament to the power of the phase 2 response of the tobacco industry.

Another core element of the industry's phase 2 response was a protectionist economic argument. The industry and its political supporters in tobacco-farming states claimed that tobacco ought to remain legal and that tobacco-control measures ought to be restrained because rural farming communities and tobacco-manufacturing towns were dependent on tobacco revenues. The use of this justification intensified during the 1980s and 1990s as the industry faced increasing scrutiny from the national anti-tobacco movement and extensive litigation. The tobacco industry used tobacco farmers' support as a way to secure its own legitimacy, discounting the fact that government programs could have reduced tobacco use while assisting farmers to transition away from their dependency on tobacco revenues. This justification also covered over the contradiction that the globalization of tobacco production, driven by the major tobacco companies, undermined the small-scale family farm units promoted as the rationale for protecting the industry (discussed in detail in chapter 3).

In the late 1980s and 1990s, the threat of litigation against the tobacco industry in the United States intensified. These lawsuits are an example of a tipping point, when the problems faced by an industry become potentially unmanageable, raising questions about its continued existence. It became clear that the cost of defending themselves against simultaneous class action lawsuits in multiple municipalities in the United States would cripple tobacco companies. At the same time, their chances of success in court were greatly diminished because previous suits of internal industry documents revealed a history of deception about the dangers of smoking. Industry consultants began to speak of a "litigation time bomb" (Smith and Malone 2003b: 208). Institutions such as universities divested from tobacco stock. Public image and legal liability were impacting the market value of tobacco companies (208), while tobacco control was gaining as a movement, with several strong national organizations, a widespread network of public health activists and researchers, and an approach that now included the more forceful strategies of litigation, excise taxes on cigarettes, clean air ordinances, and other public health regulation (McDaniel et al. 2006: 216). These factors combined to push the industry into phase 3, in which denial is no longer a feasible response to criticism.

Project Sunrise

In the late 1980s, Philip Morris considered quitting the cigarette business because mounting legal pressures threatened the company's food and beverage subsidiaries, namely, Kraft, General Foods, and Nabisco. Certain executives wanted to gradually move away from tobacco by focusing on immediate profits from cigarette sales rather than long-term growth or strategic political engagement. They believed that this "controlled retreat" would probably accelerate "into an abrupt end" and suggested that "fighting back" was not preferential since a large proportion of the corporation's revenues came from the other businesses. "I think we all believe that our future lies outside tobacco," an executive said in the late 1980s, "I certainly believe this" (Smith and Malone 2003b).

After analyzing public opinion data, inspecting lessons from historical cases of industry collapse and holding numerous executive planning sessions, the company's management decided to engage with public health and subsequently created a legal shelter by incorporating its tobacco businesses as separate entities (Smith and Malone 2003a, 2003b). The international tobacco operations now go by the name Philip Morris International. The domestic tobacco business has been renamed the Altria Group, which is basically a code word for Philip Morris USA and some smaller domestic alcohol and tobacco companies. The Altria Group is ranked 61 on the Fortune 500 list. It owns Marlboro, the premium cigarette brand that controls more than 40 percent of the domestic market (Altria Group 2009a).

According to corporate officials, the purpose of the name change was to "reduce the drag on the company's reputation that association with the world's most famous cigarette maker has caused" (Smith and Malone 2003b: 210). Philip Morris seems modernist and passé compared to the futuristic and seemingly pharmaceutical Altria brand. The word means "high" in Latin and has semantic associations with concepts like reputability and trustworthiness. Along with the new name came new positioning concepts. Philip Morris conducted focus groups to test the focal points that would guide its repositioning, finding that standard concepts like size and power, which work well inside the company, are not as appealing to tobacco consumers or the general public as concepts like trustworthiness and caring about consumer health. Focus groups also showed that notions of community commitment and providing choice worked particularly well, boosting company likability by 30 percentage points (Smith and Malone 2003b: 210).

The company hired public relations experts to create a media campaign to publicly associate these values with the Altria Group. The resulting campaign, called "Project Sunrise," also known as "PM21," meaning "Philip Morris in the 21st Century," was launched in 1995. Most of what the public has seen involves positive images of corporate social responsibility and the corporation's investments in certain public health issues like youth smoking prevention. But the archived company documents make it clear that management's goal all along was to "ensure the social acceptability of smoking" (McDaniel et al. 2006: 215). The company openly acknowledges on its website that tobacco products are inherently unsafe, but behind the scenes corporate officials created a public relations campaign designed to maintain consumption and limit liability. Specifically, the standard public relations fare of media spots to gain visibility for the company were complimented by targeted efforts to reach smokers with prosmoking messages and coupons and special offers to maintain brand loyalty and thwart the development of a culture of smoking cessation. The company conducted social research on smoking and smokers with the aim of tailoring products and programs to promote social acceptability and reinforce smoking rituals. The multisided campaign also involved an "accommodation" strategy, namely, efforts to assure that smoking remained permitted in public places. Here the company invested in cigarette butt litter reduction programs; research to promote the use of ventilation systems in restaurants, bars, and other public places as an alternative to smoking bans; and the design of cigarettes said to be less toxic or emit less secondhand smoke. Last, Project Sunrise involved what the company called the "Fair Play" strategy, involving research on tobacco-control advocates and organizations with the aim of using this information to gain leverage within the public health community and promote a moderate agenda for tobacco control as a putatively fair and balanced approach (McDaniel et al. 2006: 215–16).

The company has been involved in amassing a database on the composition and objectives of different tobacco-control groups, as well as their relationships to one another and to funding sources. According to internal documents, company executives believed that this "competitive intelligence" would improve the company's ability to respond in "proactive" and "offensive" ways to the tobacco-control movement. The identification of more "moderate" groups would facilitate efforts to "disrupt" the movement's "cohesion," executives stated. From the beginning the database was imagined as a political resource for shaping public health intervention and regulation, forging partnerships with groups deemed moderate, and using collected information to demonize other tobacco-control perspectives as, in the words of the internal memos, "extreme" and "prohibitionist." Through this kind of engagement, the memos disclose, managers aimed to reposition Philip Morris as "reasonable," acknowledging some element of risk or harm while claiming to work with the public health to "expand the debate over tolerance for lifestyle choices and freedoms." The company determined through focus groups that this message is effective with younger generations and taps into a larger "pro-choice/ tolerance" ethos in the culture (McDaniel et al. 2006: 217–18).

Motorists might think that Philip Morris has been headquartered in Richmond forever. The building does blend in nicely with the brickwork of the old tobacco warehouses and cigarette factories that are now either boarded up or redeveloped there. In fact, it was only in 2004 that Philip Morris decided to relocate from a posh Manhattan tower—the Philip Morris Building at 120 Park Avenue—that had been its main office for decades. The company publicly described its relocation as a cost-cutting measure, the somewhat less metropolitan but more tobacco-friendly southern town having offered millions in tax incentives. The explanation was a neat way to make this enormously profitable company seem strapped, victimized by the financial fallout of lawsuits and tobacco-control efforts. But the move may have also been a strategic retreat to a place where its operations would receive more favorable media coverage.

In addition, around the time of the move, New York City required all buildings to be smoke-free. The behemoth that motorists pass on the Virginia highway has a powerful ventilation system to accommodate smokers, a more "reasonable" public health approach, the company claims.

Not only are ventilation systems costly for the hospitality industry, but they are ineffective in completely eliminating nicotine and other toxins from environments or protecting against secondhand smoke exposure. Besides, the health benefits of legislation prohibiting smoking in public places are well documented. Such legislation dramatically reduces smoking prevalence in populations and reduces exposure to secondhand smoke, whereas the point of the accommodation strategy is to maintain the acceptability of smoking in workplaces and other public spaces (Barnoya and Glantz 2006a). Although many municipalities in the United States have legislated smoke-free policies, there continues to be strong opposition in many areas because of the tobacco industry's financial support of legislators and sideways lobbying through the chambers of commerce and trade associations that it supports. For example, as part of Project Sunrise's accommodation aspect, Philip Morris provides free consulting services to the hospitality industry, emphasizing ventilation systems and separate seating sections in restaurants and bars. These options are promoted by hospitality trade organizations who argue that smoke-free legislation threatens their economic interests, even though public health research finds just the opposite, that smoking bans actually increase the consumer market for the hospitality sector (National Institute for Tobacco-Free Kids 2010a).

The tobacco industry also works hard to instill public doubt about the adverse health consequences of exposure to secondhand smoke. Beginning in the late 1980s, Philip Morris began systematic efforts to undermine smoke-free legislation around the world by paying scientists and consultants who are usually affiliated with academic institutions and who conduct research on secondhand smoke to attend international symposia without acknowledging their corporate sponsorship. These researchers and consultants are hired to disseminate "accurate" (pro-industry) information concerning smoking regulation in public places, with the goal of influencing policy makers, media, and the public (Barnoya and Glantz 2006b). Only a handful of countries have passed comprehensive smoke-free legislation in spite of the fact that such legislation has long been recommended by the World Health Organization and other major public health groups.

Along with its opposition to smoke-free legislation, Philip Morris vigorously opposes the other truly effective means of reducing smoking prevalence: taxation. It opposes public health measures—smoke-free environment laws and excise taxes on tobacco products—that have been proven time and again to reduce the size of the smoking population.[3] Meanwhile, as part of its repositioning, the company supports public health endeavors where the outcomes are more ambiguous, if not ineffective.

Since the 1990s, for example, Philip Morris has invested $1 billion in an internal Youth Smoking Prevention department, which creates communications and resources aimed at encouraging parents to "talk to their kids about not using tobacco products," as the company's website states. The department provides schools and youth organizations with grants to support the development of "healthy lifestyles" and funds programs to inform tobacco product retailers about smoking laws (Philip Morris USA 2010). This selective public health focus is strategic. Internal company documents reveal that Philip Morris executives have long believed that philanthropic engagement with youth health issues is an especially effective way of demonstrating that the company "is acting reasonably and responsibly," one memo states, while shaping the public debate about health behaviors to focus on parents and kids rather than industry (McDaniel et al. 2006: 217). In one memo from the early 1990s, corporate officials strategized about how to tilt the balance of "youth smoking versus prohibition" trends in public health (217). They sought to reconfigure the smoking problem as a problem of law enforcement related to age limits and youth access. The narrowing of tobacco governance to focus on adult choice, law enforcement, and family matters are choreographed effects of what appear on the surface simply to be noble investments in public health on the part of a responsible corporate citizen. Why should corporations be held accountable for smoking disease when the task lies with law enforcement officers, convenience store clerks, high school educators, and parents?

The $100 million television campaign launched by the Youth Smoking Prevention department in the early 2000s, called "Think. Don't smoke," is the largest antitobacco campaign ever undertaken by the tobacco industry. Apart from the fact that youth education programs are a less impactful means of controlling tobacco use than regulatory measures, public health research finds that effective youth smoking prevention programs must include comprehensive information about smoking disease and the nature of addiction, and also critical anti-industry perspectives that discuss the ways tobacco companies market products to underage popula-

[3] The Philip Morris USA home page frequently features a link that brings surfers to tobaccoissues.com, which is a website that is funded by the company and provides an "online community of activists" with information about cigarettes taxes and other tobacco-related policy issues. It is essentially a means for the Altria Group (i.e., Philip Morris) to marshal political support around policy positions that are beneficial to the company, such as opposition to increased excise taxes for cigarettes and other tobacco-control measures.

tions and prey upon young people in order to turn a profit (Thrasher et al. 2004). Not surprisingly, Philip Morris's television and print media steer clear of these issues and favor an emphasis on parenthood. According to a scathing review of the campaign in the *New York Times* (2006), the ads convey the "fuzzy-warm," upbeat idea that smoking is for adults, which may instigate smoking behavior. The ads are not meant to denounce or contain the problematization of tobacco. The campaign aims to bend an ongoing process of problematization toward the private domains of the family and the individual consumer, actively inciting viewers to "Think," and thereby domesticating in a very public way the meaning of responsibility and the management of risk. Sociological studies of how viewers respond arrive at the same conclusion. Regular viewers of this campaign believe that tobacco companies are "more responsible" socially than in the past and are not culpable for smoking harms (Biener 2002; Farrelly et al. 2002; Friedman 2007; Szczypka et al. 2007; Wakefield et al. 2003).

FDA Regulation

By the 1980s, public health groups were seeking to include cigarettes under the FDA's regulatory mandate, which covers foods, drugs, pharmaceuticals, and cosmetic products, partly to control the tobacco industry's deceptive marketing practices. The introduction of products said to be "safer" than unfiltered, conventional cigarettes implied corporate acknowledgment that cigarettes are inherently unsafe, and government regulation seemed warranted given the industry's use of relative product safety as a marketing tool (Fairchild and Colgrove 2004: 197). In 1996, the FDA autonomously claimed authority to regulate nicotine as a drug and tobacco products as medical or drug delivery devices (Kessler 2001). With the FDA set to restrict and regulate tobacco advertising, Philip Morris and four other U.S. tobacco companies filed a federal lawsuit claiming the FDA could not exert such authority. In 2000, the U.S. Supreme Court ruled that Congress never intended to grant the FDA such regulative authority under the agency's original mandate, thus shifting the political battle to Congress, where a new bill would be needed (Brandt 2007).

Interestingly, the FDA had already been regulating nicotine since the mid-1980s, when nicotine gum and other medicinal therapies were approved as short-term treatments for nicotine dependence. The FDA approval of such products for over-the-counter sale in 1996 signaled a shift in the medical meaning of nicotine dependence. The first clinical care guidelines, developed that same year, classified nicotine dependence and withdrawal as disorders and included the use of medicinal nicotine as a recommended treatment. Then, in 2000, a Public Health Service report

framed nicotine dependence as a "chronic condition that warrants repeated treatment until long-term or permanent abstinence is achieved,"
equating nicotine dependence with other "chronic conditions" such as
high blood pressure, high cholesterol, diabetes, and major depression
(Faircloth and Colgrove 2004: 198–99). Medicinal nicotine products
have wide support in medical and public health communities, where
there is growing concern that significant populations of smokers either
do not want to quit, or believe they are unable to quit smoking. Even
with the most advanced clinical therapies (e.g., medicinal nicotine products, psychological counseling), smoking cessation is difficult, and most
people who attempt fail (Bolliger 2000). Medicinal nicotine products can
potentially benefit large numbers of smokers, even if complete cessation
is not achieved. Harm reduction strategies that promote chronic use of
medicinal nicotine to reduce smoking levels and minimize toxin exposure
in smokers now complement the primary public health focus on cessation
(Hatsukami et al. 2004).

Harm reduction has been widely supported for a variety of health and
behavior issues, such as infectious disease control through the promotion
of safe sex or needle exchange programs to make intravenous drug use
less risky. When it comes to cigarette smoking, harm reduction remains a
controversial precept in medical and public health communities because
it can either refer to harm reduction through the use of these pharmaceutical therapies or those therapies in addition to tobacco products (Benson 2010b). Tobacco companies have introduced a spate of new tobacco
products that claim to reduce risk for consumers who do not want to
or cannot quit. There are products that supposedly yield less risk of secondhand smoke exposure, products with a modified tobacco or nicotine
content, and "smokeless" cigarettes that use chambers to scorch rather
than burn tobacco as a way of reducing some toxins. Tobacco companies
have also become aggressive in marketing new oral tobacco products.
Because these are smokeless products, there is the tacit suggestion that
they are safer than cigarettes, even though all tobacco products entail
health risks. In contrast to the plain packaging of older varieties of spit
or chewing tobacco, the new oral products are marketed as clean and
refreshing, with colorful packaging and the use of flavors, which makes
them seem more like bubblegum or candy. Public health critics argue that
these approaches seek to make tobacco use more acceptable and that the
new products reflect enduring myths of safe tobacco products. This seems
like a familiar strategy of using product design to provide consumer re-
assurance about habitual tobacco use. The availability of tobacco products that are said to lessen the risks of secondhand smoke might also be
used by the tobacco industry to undermine the political impetus to pass
smoke-free legislation in municipalities and countries.

Skepticism about harm reduction in the tobacco-control movement reflects serious concerns about the tobacco industry's interests in shaping what this approach entails and not necessarily opposition to harm reduction as a reasonable precept for public health. What worries many antitobacco researchers and advocates is that the tobacco industry would like the tobacco-control movement to adopt a harm reduction strategy that "the industry could use to promote its alternative nicotine delivery systems," writes one critic (Pierce 2002: 53). In seeking to compete with pharmaceutical companies, the tobacco industry wants harm reduction to include not only medicinal nicotine but also its potentially reduced-risk cigarettes and new smokeless products. Members of the tobacco-control movement fear that this expanded concept will help sustain existing tobacco markets and facilitate new ones, and that it is really a project of "harm maintenance" (53). Whereas gums, patches, and inhalers deliver controlled levels of nicotine and their efficacy and safety as replacement products are basically understood, there has been very little verified or replicated scientific data about the new tobacco products (Shiffman et al. 2001). The inclusion of tobacco products as part of a harm reduction strategy would require a significant amount of independent research on their impact on individual and population levels (Hatsukami et al. 2004; Institute of Medicine 2001).[4]

In 2000, Philip Morris reversed its position on FDA regulative authority and began to support "meaningful tobacco regulation." Rather than opposing enhanced government oversight, Philip Morris decided its financial and legal interests were best served by participating in the development of such regulation. The firm said that regulation creates better-informed consumers because of ingredient disclosures, enables the development of safer cigarettes and tobacco products, and strengthens age limits on tobacco purchases and youth anti-access laws (McDaniel and Malone 2005; Philip Morris USA 2008). Beginning in 2000, there were several efforts to pass FDA legislation in Congress. Philip Morris played an active role in crafting the public debate and the legislation's exact

---

[4] The Alliance for Health, Economic, and Agriculture Development (AHEAD), an informal organization based in Washington, D.C., has produced several interesting white papers on harm reduction and tobacco, which are available at tobaccoatacrossroads.com. The group's main objective, stated on this website, is to "educate, stimulate, and facilitate discussions with and between public health advocates, growers, the scientific community, tobacco manufacturers, consumers, pharmaceutical and biotech interests about a spectrum of issues related to the production, processing, manufacture, distribution, labeling, marketing and use of tobacco and tobacco products." While the group supports some goals of the tobacco-control movement, such as applying smoking restrictions, on the topic of harm reduction it endorses the controversial precept that both medicinal nicotine and potentially reduced-risk tobacco products should be more widely available to consumers (Ballin 2010).

language. The FDA's standard litmus test to approve products is reasonable assurance of safety and efficacy. Because tobacco products can never be reasonably safe, their regulation required an alternative standard, involving the FDA's capacity to take actions to protect the public health by controlling tobacco toxicity and marketing. "The bill is not perfect," the *New York Times* (2009) editorialized. "It will not allow the [FDA] to ban cigarettes or nicotine—a concession made years ago to avoid drawing intense opposition from smokers and free-market advocates. But the agency will still have far-reaching powers."

The legislation passed overwhelmingly in Congress in June 2009 and was signed by President Obama, a decision trumpeted by public health groups and Philip Morris. It empowered the FDA to approve products that make exposure and risk-reduction claims and ban the sale and distribution of any product not preapproved by the agency. It also authorized new, larger package warning labels, allows the FDA to restrict advertising and promotions that appeal to children, requires the publication of an annual list indicating harmful constituents in each brand, and prevents manufacturers from using terms such as "low-tar" and "light" without advance agency approval (Shatenstein 2004: 438; Layton 2009).

Throughout the debate over FDA regulation, major public health groups supporting tobacco regulation have insisted that in the absence of strong governmental authority, the tobacco industry will continue to pursue deceptive marketing practices that target youths and withhold important information about cigarette content that could be vital to public health scientists (Myers 2004: 441). However, less moderate segments of the public health community raised several critical questions about the legislation. They emphasized that the bill forbids the FDA from banning tobacco sales to adults ages eighteen and older or requiring that nicotine yields be reduced to zero, and suggested that the bill's language will make it difficult for the FDA to substantially reduce nicotine levels at all (Siegel 2004: 440). Critics also emphasized the vivid economic interests behind Philip Morris's support. The bill may limit the industry's liability and strengthen its financial solvency at home and abroad. And unlike other firms, Philip Morris supported the bill because marketing restrictions would limit competition and guarantee its Marlboro brand's continued dominance in the domestic market. Other firms have called the bill a "Marlboro Monopoly Act" (Hsu 2001).

One of the most important points of criticism to arise among public health critics concerns harm reduction. The FDA bill takes bold steps in permitting federal regulators to stop the tobacco industry's pattern of "making false statements, suppressing evidence of harm, and manipulating the design of cigarettes to increase their addictiveness" (*New York Times* 2009). The industry's claims that modified tobacco products reduce toxin exposure will now be subject to federal oversight and will require scientific substantiation. However, there is inconclusive evidence about which ingredients in tobacco products are linked to particular morbidities and mortalities and at what level (Givel 2007: 217). The link between reduced toxin exposure and ingredient control and health outcomes remains extremely complex and poorly understood, and it is unclear exactly how the federal government will regulate claims about reduced risk. Critics worry that tobacco companies will be able to legitimately market products that make verified claims about reduced toxicity, even though there may not be scientific evidence to show that reducing particular toxins also reduces health risks. Far from clearing the air, critics worry that the FDA legislation might "institutionalize the problem of unsubstantiated health risk claims by cigarette marketers" (Siegel 2004: 439). It is possible that tobacco companies will be able to continue to treat risk as a selling point by promoting different products or improved product design, using anxieties about health to enhance the marketability of their products and encouraging smokers who are thinking about medicinal nicotine to instead purchase a modified tobacco product, thus protecting the company's share of the nicotine-dependence market from pharmaceutical companies. As Philip Morris recently commented, the FDA bill will "create a framework for the pursuit of tobacco products that are less harmful than conventional cigarettes" (Montopoli 2009).

Capitalism, Civic Virtue, and Public Health

Philip Morris's forging of a public-private alliance around health concerns is perhaps an exemplary case of "biocapitalism," a development in global business that, although not entirely new, has reached unprecedented proportions (Sunder Rajan 2006). The term refers to the coproduction of economic values and ethical values by corporations. For example, public relations that hype the positive health and social impact of corporate activity use the fact that certain conditions are publicly problematized as an opportunity to strengthen the corporation's financial position and take advantage of emergent markets. The increasing tendency to problematize dimensions of human biological life as urgent sociopolitical and ethical issues (Foucault 1980; Rose 2007) has dovetailed with the liberalization of national and international markets (Harvey 2005), allowing for increasingly efficient and flexible transactions between political economy and life politics. The "organizing principle" that defines biocapitalism, writes social theorist Nikolas Rose, is the corporate strategy of capturing "a value that is simultaneously that of human health and that of economic growth" (2007: 32–33). When it comes to the handling of the growing burden of chronic diseases, business plans and marketing strategies across various industries are developed in light of public health concerns and take advantage of a dominant governmental approach that emphasizes corporate and consumer agency rather than industry regulation. Multinational corporations like Philip Morris claim to operate for the public good and address problems of human life more efficiently and effectively than the state, and in adopting governmental rationales and goals they are perhaps working to hold back state power. Neoliberalism in such cases has not led to the waning of government but, rather, its capitalization and distribution to private firms (Ferguson 2006; Ong 2006; Ong and Collier 2005).

One well-studied example of biocapitalism is the pharmaceutical industry, which arose out of the liberalization of life sciences and medical research and the rise of direct-to-consumer advertising for prescription drugs (Sunder Rajan 2006). Companies use television ads to bypass health professionals, create a direct informational link to self-medicating consumers, and individualize health risk and management. This strategy is also about fostering consumer desires and cultivating corporate images (Applbaum 2006). On the surface, the tobacco and pharmaceutical industries appear fundamentally different. Tobacco harms people. Pharmaceuticals purport to enhance and save lives. Yet these industries overlap around shared strategies of biocapitalist production and marketing that include the pharmaceuticalization of public health problems as clinical problems best addressed through biotechnological innovation (Biehl 2007); the capitalization of chronic health conditions, such as nicotine dependence and high blood pressure, as markets for "drugs for life," products to be taken for a long time to maintain suboptimal health conditions (Dumit 2002); and shared reliance on the FDA as a product certification system. Warning labels, instructions for use, and ingredient disclosures are legal apparatuses that safeguard corporations from liabilities related to consumption and underwrite individual risk assumption, while corporations are strengthened through their development of and participation in what the anthropologist Paul Rabinow describes as "markets in civic virtue" (2003: 26). Corporations redefine their own value as actors and the value of their products in the process of molding the scope of an emergent problem or responding to a tipping point. Across multiple settings, multinational corporations have strategically turned to a language of social responsibility and civic virtue to legitimize corporate activities with negative human and environmental consequences.

Another example is that of Walmart making public claims about its efforts to maintain chronically low prices while improving the nutritional quality of its food products by pressuring its suppliers to reduce levels of fat, sodium, and sweeteners, an act of corporate social responsibility praised by the federal government in the United States (Stolberg 2011). This shift presumably arose in direct response to public health research that shows that Walmart's food sales alone account for 10 percent of the increase in obesity prevalence in the United States (Courtemanche and Carden 2011). Meanwhile, the retail giant's adoption of health values may also reflect a powerful economic strategy to foreshorten public criticism and further disadvantage competitor firms that will likely be less capable of simultaneously changing product offerings and containing costs within their more limited supply chains.

These trends in capitalism call for a broader definition of biocapitalism than is currently found in the literature. The narrowest definitions focus on the accumulation of capital through the corporate patenting of biological materials such as genes (Waldby 2000). Biocapitalism is also used to refer to the unprecedented levels of capital investment in life sciences research in the pharmaceutical and biotechnology industries and the hyping of how these industries and their products help to improve conditions of life (Sunder Rajan 2006). These views are useful for thinking about how corporate actors are reconfiguring scientific practice and objectives, the social meanings of human biology, and the cultural expectation that private businesses participate in public works. Biocapitalism seems to reflect the spirit of the times, what the anthropologist Kaushik Sunder Rajan describes as the "increasingly constitutive fact of biopolitics in processes of global capitalism" (2006: 34). However, there has been less attention paid to a comparative analysis of social responsibility claims across industries or to why particular corporations and industries attempt to reposition and remake their images when they do. These claims must be scrutinized in light of the backstage intentions of corporations that are revealed in internal documents and communications, and through anthropological research with the communities and stakeholders that are part of industries or impacted by them. There are likely to be important discrepancies between what companies say they are doing and what their activities actually do to populations and environments.

As the phrase "millennial capitalism" describes various features of contemporary capitalism (Comaroff and Comaroff 2000), my examination of tobacco capitalism also points to a broad process that is not just about what is happening in the cigarette business but also helps us to more fully understand the biopolitical aspects of capitalism. However well intentioned corporate actors may be or claim to be, their social responsibility agendas are beholden to their fiduciary responsibility to shareholders, requiring them to constantly maximize profits. This often entails continuously legitimizing and expanding industrial processes that are harmful in one way or another. Tobacco capitalism reveals the constitutive fact of harm and the politics of harm in processes of global capitalism. In many industries, such as mining and tobacco, corporate social responsibility has obviously been a means of "seizing control of the movement before it seized control over them" (Welker 2009: 145; Benson and Kirsch 2010). Anthropologists can scrutinize the exact ways that corporations claim to resolve health and human problems in light of alternative approaches, and they can explicate why companies choose to focus their humanitarian endeavors on certain issues while often opposing other efforts to improve life conditions, as seen in Philip Morris's focus on youth smoking and parenting. Not only is such research helpful for understanding how biopolitics shapes capitalism, but it also reveals the underappreciated role of corporations in shaping what the ethics and politics of life mean, how problem-spaces are strategically structured and governed, and how supply chains that bring harm to humans and environments are maintained even in the face of substantial criticism. Such investigation should be an indispensible part of future directions in the anthropology of capitalism.

Tobacco Haze

There are many reasons why modern tobacco control does not look like the temperance movement. An adequate account of the differences would really amount to a much fuller history of tobacco's problematization. This history would reveal layers of ethical and political valences that come to the fore or recede into the background from decade to decade. Traces of the moralizing dimension of earlier antitobacco movements have certainly persisted in contemporary public health and the wider culture, even as the goal of prohibition has all but disappeared. But the spirited political and even moral indignation and focus on industrial harm that drove decades of lawsuits and antitobacco advocacy in the last three decades is more and more being made to seem unreasonable. The Bush administration had always indicated its opposition to the FDA bill, claiming, with many tobacco companies, that it would overburden the FDA and would be difficult to implement. The power shift at the federal level in 2009 made its passage possible. Now, politicians of various persuasions, Philip Morris, and the major public health groups all tout the FDA bill as a significant step forward in public health. Emergent and enduring complicities, rather than a simple opposition between tobacco industry and public health, continue to define how tobacco is governed.

Prohibition would seem to be the only response that lives up to the government's constitutional mandate to protect the general welfare. Tobacco is the only legal consumer product that is harmful when used as intended. "In a perfect world, we'd ban all cigarettes," acknowledged Representative John D. Dingell, a Michigan Democrat, when speaking about the proposed FDA legislation. "But the hard fact of the matter is that there are a lot of jobs depending on this. And more importantly, there are a lot of people out there who are addicted to this and they've got to have their fix" (Saul 2008a: C3). The tacit acceptance of tobacco's legality is the direct result of decades of the tobacco industry's influence in the culture. Perhaps the most enduring of the tobacco industry's strategies has been the argument that individual consumers are aware of smoking risks and are therefore responsible agents, an ideology that is powerfully recapitulated when Philip Morris disseminates information about smoking and health in its public relations. Brandt writes:

> The companies successfully utilized a deeply traditional American cultural norm that held individuals uniquely responsible for their own death. As the knowledge of smoking's harms came to be widely disseminated, rather than drawing attention to the actions of the industry, many came to agree that individuals should either quit or bear the consequences. To hold the industry responsible for such individual failings seemed to violate core American values of individual agency. (2007: 5)

Rather than abandoning a risky product, Philip Morris has crafted a strategy that capitalizes on health risks to create an image of a caring and innocent company that promotes lawful behavior, respects consumer autonomy, and works with and for the public health. A dominant cultural model of the consumer as a rational chooser is central to the alignment of certain tobacco corporate interests and certain public health policy interests around the FDA bill. The National Campaign for Tobacco-Free Kids, a leading antitobacco advocacy group and the bill's most vocal proponent, emphasizes at the front of a fact sheet about the legislation:

> Adults are free to choose to use tobacco, which, despite the health risks involved, remains a legal product for adults to purchase and use. The bills advocated by the public health community . . . enhance adult choice by providing consumers with the information they currently do not have access to on what is in the tobacco products they use and the health risks associated with any of the ingredients in the product or the chemicals contained in tobacco smoke. As a result, under the bills advocated by the public health community, adult choice is an informed choice. (National Institute for Tobacco-Free Kids 2003a: 1)

As seen here, the prevailing assumption is that "given adequate product design, human users will be able to make responsible choices" (Lochlann Jain 2004: 299). FDA legislation does nothing to challenge and powerfully upholds this model.

This process is reflective of broad trends seen in the marketing of food and beverage products and many other products. Corporations use the very health problems that consumer products help to generate as a market opportunity for selling harm reduction products or therapies for medicalized conditions. As consumption practices lead to higher levels of chronic disease, there is an expanded market for pharmaceuticals that treat, for example, diabetes, high cholesterol, hypertension, and sleep disorders. Meanwhile, the use of misleading product descriptors such as "low fat" and "lite," pioneered by the tobacco industry, is more prevalent than ever for foods and beverages. Rather than developing a more robust system of public health prevention and economic regulation to contain the growth of chronic diseases, Western countries under the influence of powerful industries have largely left health promotion to the private sector of product marketing.

FDA regulation has been a major goal of many public health groups for years. It culminates the work of one strand of the tobacco-control movement in the United States that has promoted health education to improve health beliefs and behaviors. In some sense, Philip Morris's capitulation to the dominant public health positions represents a major victory for public health groups. "This has been a very long battle," said Senator Christopher Dodd, a Connecticut Democrat. "For the first time we're going to make a difference. The FDA is going to regulate the production, sale and marketing of these products. That is history" (Layton 2009). Clearly the regulation has many benefits. The Congressional Budget Office estimates that the legislation will reduce youth smoking by 10 percent in the 2010s and adult smoking by 2 percent (*New York Times* 2009). However, in historical perspective, the FDA legislation involves the reassertion of a particular model of harm reduction focused on making tobacco products safer, which may also end up benefiting tobacco corporate interests. Michael Siegel, a public health policy researcher, warns that the bill will "result in consumers perceiving that [the] FDA has given a stamp of approval to tobacco products, and the public's perceived level of the health risk posed by tobacco products will therefore decline." He continues, "[The] Bill will improve the public image and goodwill of tobacco companies because they will be able to use the fact of being regulated by [the] FDA to achieve improved public opinion" (2004: 439). Besides, the legislation has nothing to do with tobacco-control methods such as taxation and smoke-free legislation, which are proven to be most effective in reducing tobacco use. Critics warn that it might deflect government attention and resources away from these methods (Givel 2007; Siegel 2004).

The FDA legislation does nothing to address worldwide smoking trends or the international free-market environments in which tobacco companies operate. By potentially reducing the serious threat of litigation against the industry, it may actually help sustain the international market (Givel 2007; Siegel 2004). Although the new tobacco regulation is anticipated to have positive outcomes, it does not address certain questions about industry liability and does very little to attend to hidden structural costs, namely, the extent to which product certification can actually help stabilize harmful corporations. The legislation does not take into account many of the evidence-based recommendations that are found in the extensive public health and medical anthropology literatures on tobacco. These literatures suggest that a more comprehensive policy approach would complement the regulation of manufacturing and marketing with programs and policies that expand the scope of medical treatments available to smokers, prohibit smoking in public places, and build partnerships in tobacco-dependent rural and urban communities to facilitate transitions to alternative sources of livelihood. As the *New York Times* (2009) acknowledges, "clearly the regulators will still need help from strong anti-smoking campaigns." It is also crucial that tobacco-control regulation be a means of effectively discrediting rather than substantiating the industry's oxymoronic claims about cigarette safety.

In effect, Philip Morris is pursuing a strategic trade-off, accepting regulations at home in order to limit liability and ensure the company's long-term profitability and survival. These paradoxes are not news to the public health community. The bill is largely a case of pragmatic resignation: antitobacco groups were willing to broker the best deal possible, given the tacit acceptance of tobacco's legality. The *Wall Street Journal* (2009) went so far as to describe the bill as pure cynicism: "It lets the politicians claim to be punishing Big Tobacco while further cementing their financial partnership."

The government's own dependency on tobacco revenues is also a powerful factor constraining the political impetus to prohibit tobacco products. The Master Settlement Agreement of 1998 settled a large number of class action lawsuits brought by individual states against the industry to recoup public medical expenditures. It was the largest civil settlement in U.S. history, with the industry agreeing to pay more than $200 billion to cover medical costs and public health initiatives over a twenty-five-year period in return for protection from future litigation brought by public entities, although it did not affect the rights of private citizens to pursue their own legal claims. The settlement was controversial: much of the public health community was opposed to it because it included only modest restrictions on cigarette marketing and would not be sufficient to cover the full cost to the public of smoking-related disease. The money from the settlement has rarely been used by states as intended (Brandt 2007: 420–34). Many states even sold bonds against future funds from the settlement, creating an immediate cash flow that discounted the overall value of the tobacco payments and was easily diverted to unrelated projects. Consequently, states have a vested interest in protecting the tobacco industry. Some states have even sought to set caps on pending tort claims, since unrestricted payments to individuals would also threaten public spending. In what Brandt calls a "remarkable turnabout," some state governments are now "*defending* the industry and its economic well-being" (original italics). Far from toppling tobacco, the settlement has proven to be "one of the industry's most surprising victories in its long history of combat with the public health forces" (Brandt 2007: 435–36).

Perhaps the resignation and appeasement that surround tobacco in the United States, where this most harmful substance remains legal amid a costly, ineffective, and violent war on drugs, are what the American poet Allen Ginsberg had in mind when he wrote of the "tobacco haze of Capitalism" in his famous poem "Howl" (1956). FDA regulation is a convenient way to reconcile the fact that tobacco ought to be banned with the recognition of widespread nicotine dependence and the need to balance state budgets with proceeds from litigation against the tobacco industry. We can understand why large segments of the public health community support FDA regulation, even though Philip Morris does, too. Yet FDA regulation of tobacco products also institutionalizes an ideology of adult choice that has long benefited the tobacco industry and spans all three phases of corporate response. Even though nearly all smokers begin smoking before reaching the legal age of consent, and nicotine is highly addictive, the problematization of tobacco has come to revolve around the idea that smoking is something that informed adults choose to do. Even though Philip Morris continues to aggressively pursue profits through cigarette manufacturing and to blame consumers and avoid accountability when faced with litigation related to smoking diseases, the public increasingly believes that the company is a responsible actor and toes the line when it comes to pinning blame on individual smokers. So smokers and the public are left with acceptance of tobacco's legality, which guides public policy and reproduces an obviously problematic status quo. As anthropologists increasingly study the new civic virtue capitalism, it is important that they also historicize the reasons behind why corporations and industries move to adopt the values of social responsibility and examine the strategies used to shape and constrain the responses of governments and the society.

Chapter 2 _____

The Jungle

MOTORISTS TEND NOT TO THINK of the North Carolina they drive through as part of the Atlantic system. The tobacco maturing in carefully managed fields with the straight rows of people who take pride in not being sorry seems either unfamiliar, like a vestige of the past, or like nothing more than a commodity. These fields do not seem to house the botanical progeny of plants that helped fuel the slave trade. Billboards rise from land on which blood has been spilled over tobacco, people whipped and warehoused, reputations made, an agrarian social order ordered, and immense takings taken on the backs of subordinated, laboring populations. Off one exit in Wilson County there is a neighborhood that was pejoratively called "Jungle Town" by local white people in the last century. The perception of the past and the present is often blind to the sordid facts of history. The highway shields motorists from historical burdens like the decimated neighborhoods of East Wilson where generations of black families have worked on the dusty floors of tobacco warehouses and cigarette factories. The media does all it can to cast historical legacies as the inherent social pathology of particular people and places. The chronic clustering of crime, unemployment, and depravity in Wilson's old tobacco district—it's the same thing in other tobacco towns, like Durham—is made to seem like an insular culture of poverty, conditions to be avoided rather than engaged, an irredeemably guilty place segregated and sensationalized so as not to sully what is tacitly innocent about the people and places classified as "normal." Predictable media reporting need not use the old racist euphemism for the neighborhoods to reinforce a similar kind of stereotype and legitimize abandonment and indifference as valid social responses. Together the highways and the headlines cleanse history and naturalize contingent realities that have been ever so willfully made, monikered, and maintained.

Wilson became the country's most important tobacco town in the late nineteenth century. Soil conditions were favorable to the cultivation of the new bright tobacco, the main ingredient in the modern commercial cigarette. The town's industrial infrastructure was also more developed than elsewhere in eastern North Carolina because there were existing railroad ties to the Atlantic coast (Valentine 2002; McAdams 1996). By the interwar period, there were dozens of tobacco warehouses downtown. These immense brick structures for auctioning and storing tobacco took

Figure 2.1. Tobacco delivery at the Carolina Warehouse in Wilson, 1946. Photograph by and reproduced with permission from Raines & Cox Photographers, Wilson, NC.

up whole city blocks, physical manifestations of the wealth and power of the local tobacco elite, the white families who owned land out in the countryside and controlled the markets in town. Tobacco town streets smelled dank and musty because of the millions of pounds of cured leaf in the warehouses come August and September. Local people still talk about that smell and what it signified: truckloads of tobacco delivered each week, round-the-clock labor of poor tenants in curing barns, the call of the auctioneer, the corruption and sideways dealings of the market, and, most of all, money.

Lots of cultural work went into making Wilson a clubby hub of tobacco. Every August there was the regionally famous annual tobacco festival: parades involving schoolchildren and the social clubs, speeches from regional and national dignitaries, a beauty contest, young white women dressed in bright tobacco leaf bikinis, and a whole culture of camaraderie. All of this coincided with the opening of the auctions. Local newspaper reporting touted Wilson as the best of the region's many tobacco market towns. Article after article about how Wilson's warehousemen were the most knowledgeable and the fairest in dealing with growers, and how the facilities themselves were the most modern—with details about the number of overhead lights, the floor space, and the storage capacities—blurred the line between journalism and boosterism. They reported it and

Figure 2.2. "Wearing bright leaf costumes, maids of the annual tobacco festival at Wilson adorn a giant corncob pipe." Photograph by J. Baylor Roberts/National Geographic Stock. *National Geographic*, July 1941. Reprinted with permission from the National Geographic Society.

helped to make it a reality. By World War Two, Wilson's tobacco market was the largest in the world, known regionally as the "World's Greatest Tobacco Market," hence the call sign of a local radio station, WGTM. The town's commodity culture was even profiled in a 1941 issue of *National Geographic*. Magnificent pictures of the festival, the warehouses, and tobacco farms left no room for any mention of the slave trade or the extremely uneven postbellum division of landownership and labor upon which this economy and social world were built.

The public face of the tobacco boom was a shared culture of prosperity and ritual. In reality the tobacco boom benefited some people more than others. It relied on labor control mechanisms that helped maintain the basic social order that came out of the Civil War (Flowers 1990). Racial categories and meanings pervaded every aspect of society, structuring the organization and distribution of resources, the division and meaning of labor, and the composition of power and privilege (Omi and Winant 1994). In this chapter, I draw on the historical literature to provide an overview of the development of tobacco agriculture and agrarian life in North Carolina. I also draw on my work in the archives of Wilson's local newspaper to analyze its coverage of tobacco issues and debates about farm policy in the Great Depression, the New Deal, and the Cold War.

While tobacco leaf was being made, race and class structures were, too. The institutional policies that governed the tobacco trade, including the New Deal reforms, reinforced these abiding divisions. Cultural meanings of belonging, entitlement, and modernity, which reflected and redoubled long-standing assumptions about race, class, gender, and geography, were also cultivated.

Tobacco and Slaves

Tobacco was used ubiquitously, with a range of everyday, medicinal, and ritual uses, by indigenous groups throughout the Americas in the pre-Columbian period. References to tobacco, including a sophisticated cosmology of tobacco smoke, were common in the diverse origin myths and oral traditions of indigenous peoples. This anthropological context of tobacco use differs greatly from the contemporary public health perspective. Tobacco can be used in diverse ways. That tobacco has caused so much disease and destruction is the result not of the plant itself but rather the political, cultural, and industrial systems that have colluded to promote habituating products and use patterns (Kohrman and Benson 2011).

In the 1600s, European merchants and political rulers realized that tobacco, like other colonial imports such as coffee, tea, and pepper, had vast market potential. Tobacco use crosscut European social classes long before other imported commodities, in part because European medical experts touted tobacco as a panacea (Brandt 2007). Increasing consumer demand made tobacco production incredibly profitable and drove colonial settlement. By 1640, tobacco was the main cash crop across the British colonies (Goodman 1993: 134–47).

The Chesapeake Bay region on the Atlantic coast provided the bulk of European tobacco. Its rich, dark soil was conducive to the cultivation of tobacco varieties used in the snuff and pipe tobaccos that dominated the early modern European market. The British Crown encouraged and enabled tobacco farming in the American colonies, banning domestic production and restricting imports from other nations and colonies to protect Chesapeake planters. Laws requiring colonial leaf to be marketed and manufactured domestically made London the primary world market and created a system of interdependence between the colony and the metropolis. In the absence of colonial credit sources or capital, Chesapeake planters depended on the "consignment system," in which London merchants fronted finances and supplies and managed the transatlantic transportation and marketing process. Colonial planters entrusted their tobacco to merchants who arranged its sale in London and furnished access to European consumer goods and house furnishings and whatever profits shook out after the marketing and accounting (Breen 1985).

As a plant, tobacco requires the scrupulous management of each and every acre. Contrasted with cotton, rice, or sugar, economies of scale in tobacco were limited. Yeomen farm families were thus able to coexist alongside plantations. Indentured servants at first provided the bulk of the manual field labor, commonly establishing credit sources and consignment contracts to transition into yeoman or small planter status. But by the late 1600s, the indentured servitude system had declined, and Chesapeake planters turned to African slaves. In the 1700s, the slave population in the Chesapeake ballooned from 100,000 to nearly 1 million (Kulikoff 1986). The average plantation size grew larger, new forms of labor control and field management developed, and the social stakes of being a planter, as compared to a yeoman farmer, intensified. The reputation and status of planters was increasingly linked to slaveholding and the display of gentility, which rested on and reinforced the mercantile contracts as a means of accumulating aristocratic sensibilities and European goods (Goodman 1993: 148–50, 158–62). Mercantile contracts were "a badge of class," writes a leading historian of the Chesapeake, "a means of distinguishing great planters from those of lesser status" (Breen 1985: 36).

Tobacco was never sold in the abstract; it was always separated into grades, so that leaf quality, not just yield, mattered greatly. Chesapeake slaves were divided into small work units. Moving "gangs," as they were called, from field to field enhanced leaf quality because planters and supervisors could focus collective labor efforts on fields requiring more pruning or weeding, ensure consistency, and closely supervise a production process involving handicraft care at each stage. Pest and weed control, the application of nutrients, the cultivation of the soil between tobacco rows, and the pruning of flowers and suckers to divert energy to leaf comprised the unending process of tobacco field labor. While some historians have argued that this "ganging" system created a more hospitable social climate for slaves because they worked in close proximity to one another and were part of units that were collectively responsible for crop quality, it is more accurate to understand ganging as an efficient mechanism of labor control that also involved the brutalization that existed across the slave states. Planters assigned the hardest-working slaves as pacesetters and employed trusted supervisors to use punishment to drive the work (Morgan 1998). At the same time, weapons of the weak, like foot-dragging, malingering, and shirking, were extensive on Chesapeake plantations because there was never respite, always more tobacco work, and thus "no incentive to work quickly." Planters and supervisors spoke and wrote about the "feckless, shiftless, and irresponsible character of their slaves" (191). A key part of the Chesapeake plantation system was this racial formation in which the necessities of tobacco cultivation and the predication of so much on planter reputation incentivized a feedback loop involving aggressive managerial strategies to maximize leaf quality and indigenous forms of resistance to the brutal work of ganging.

The Chesapeake's tobacco economy and social order were challenged in the 1760s when, amid worldwide economic depression, tobacco leaf prices declined, colonial liabilities mounted, and London merchants called in their debts. Even the largest and most powerful planters, including George Washington and Thomas Jefferson, were unable to repay the merchants, and Washington actually went out of business. As access to European markets and goods was now limited, the indexes of gentility for colonial planters were threatened. It is not surprising that the Chesapeake planters played a prominent role in the American Revolution. Schoolbook history says that a group of Founding Fathers was ignited by liberal idealism and democracy. In fact, the push for independence arose as a response to the collapse of the aristocratic social order and threats to the class and race standing that were underwritten by landholdings, slaveholdings, and mercantile contracts. The planters resorted to political resistance in large part to maintain rather than transform their world (Breen 1985). Meanwhile, as planters came under economic pressure, slaves were made to seem blameworthy. "Nothing can be conceived more inert than a slave," a Virginia planter said in the 1790s, going on to complain that "his unwilling labour is discovered in every step he takes; he moves not if he can avoid it; if the eyes of the overseer be off him, he sleeps; the ox and the horse, driven by the slave, appear to sleep also; all is listless inactivity; all motion is evidently compulsory" (Morgan 1998: 191).

By the 1800s, tobacco was deeply embedded in the commerce, labor organization, and social rituals of the United States and Europe, all before the cigarette came to predominate (Brandt 2007: 25). In "all the public places of America," Charles Dickens (1874: 130–31) observed the "filthy custom" of tobacco use on his tour of the new nation in the 1840s.[1] The availability of captive labor and the geographical expansion of tobacco agriculture westward into Appalachia allowed for significant increases in tobacco production to serve the continuously growing markets for tobacco products in mostly urban areas of North America and Europe (Goodman 1993: 159–61, 178, 205–6). As the modern cigarette became popular in the 1880s and 1890s, an important geographical shift occurred. Tobacco agriculture moved away from the Chesapeake and became the primary cash crop in the coastal plain of the Carolinas, as well as in the piedmont and mountain regions of the mid-South. Cultivating tobacco in lighter and sandier soils like those of the flatlands around Wilson County reduced the darkness of the leaf, while new flue-curing meth-

---

[1] Cited in Brandt (2007: 25).

Figure 2.3. Processing tobacco at James I. Miller Tobacco Company, a Wilson processing factory, during the 1940s. Photo by an unknown *Wilson Daily Times* photographer. Reproduced with permission from the *Wilson Daily Times*.

ods exacerbated leaf brightness and allowed for greater control of the curing process than traditional open-fire methods. The taste, aroma, and mildness of the new bright tobacco were also more conducive to inhalation and frequent smoking, the defining features of cigarette consumption (Brandt 2007: 24; Goodman 1993: 206; Tilley 1948).

Wide-Awake Wilson

The historical trajectory of Wilson County exemplifies broader patterns and themes in the history of the postbellum South. Understanding that history is essential for discerning why there is now a stark residential divide in the town of Wilson and unusually high poverty and unemployment levels both in the outlying rural parts and in the predominantly African American neighborhoods in East Wilson.

After the Civil War the migration of former slaves and the development of tobacco-manufacturing facilities led to urban growth in Wilson, which in turn gradually caused drainage problems and overcrowding. The city's white elite moved to higher ground on the municipality's western edge, where they built renowned manors and the magnificent townhouses of Nash Street, which remain a selling point to lure motorists off the highway. These families retained land in East Wilson, where they

Figure 2.4. Tenant farmers and tobacco barn in Granville County, North Carolina, 1939. Photograph by Dorothea Lange. Reproduced with permission from the Library of Congress.

rented to the African American families that provided the bulk of the manual labor for the tobacco facilities. Landlords and local tobacco barons developed densely packed lots with one room wide, two or three rooms deep shotgun houses to shelter this segregated labor force with limited mobility and few other life chances (Valentine 2002: 145–46). At the same time as the manual tobacco work of these former slaves and their descendents helped grow Wilson's economy, they were denied full citizenship. In 1896 the municipal border of the city itself was redrawn to exclude the "negro settlement on the lower side of the railroad" (*Wilson Advance* 1896). Compared to other parts of the South, where there was a northward migration after the Civil War, the availability of urban tobacco jobs, together with efforts to maintain labor surpluses for the benefit of the local tobacco elite, meant that Wilson County's black population increased, more than doubling from 1860 to 1890 and increasing another 64 percent from 1900 to 1920 (Valentine 2002: 154).

In the countryside residential segregation was less stark. Tobacco field labor involved both poor black and white families. The plantation model morphed into a model of landless families tied to small production parcels that were usually part of the consolidated landholdings of the gentry. The crop-lien, or "sharecropping," system was a paternalistic, political-economic arrangement linked to Jim Crow laws that bound poor tenants and sharecroppers to the land (Daniel 1986; Shifflett 1982). They typi-

Figure 2.5. Farmer fertilizing tobacco plants, early 1950s. Photo by an unknown *Wilson Daily Times* photographer. Reproduced with permission from the *Wilson Daily Times*.

cally had no other choice than to obtain credit from the landowner at bloated interest rates in exchange for a portion, or "share," of the crop or meager wages. Their contract was generally an oral agreement, which meant that landowners benefited from literacy and corrupt legal systems (Cobb 1992: 100–103; Billings 1979: 147). Unwritten laws discouraged competing landowners and farm employers from enticing tenants by offering higher wages or better contracts. Vagrancy statutes authorized the entrapment and forced labor of people who refused to work for whatever reason. The landed class wielded various kinds of force to bring about a process of agricultural proletarianization (Daniel 1972; Wood 1986), including influencing state and local legislatures, engaging in collusion, using physical violence, and supporting the rise of white supremacy as a backlash to Reconstruction, a process in which the political and economic powers of eastern North Carolina played a leading part (E. Anderson 1981). Whereas the Piedmont and Appalachia farm operations were always smaller, and the sharecropping system was not as prevalent, the early twentieth-century landscape of the coastal plain in North Carolina looked a lot like the plantation system. Labor and debt peonage, rather than freedom, replaced slavery in the region.

Given the intensive manual labor needs of tobacco, this peonage system was conducive to the interests of landowners because, as in the case of cotton, it established concentrated production on small parcels of land (Abrams 1992: 4). Although considerable supervision was exercised over tenants (Wood 1986: 26), the impermanent nature of the tenant arrangements, the existence of rural and urban labor surpluses, the dependence of tenants on landowner credit, and the time lag of the tobacco market, tenants going into debt in the spring and then being paid, if at all, after the fall harvest, were modes of discipline and control that helped to incentivize hard work among tenants and minimize managerial and supervisorial requirements for the landowners (Daniel 1986).

By 1925, North Carolina had the second-largest farm population and the fewest cultivated acres per farm in the country, a testament to the role of tobacco agriculture in shaping a steep agrarian social hierarchy and a particular kind of agrarian demography and geography (Abrams 1992: 4). From 1880 to 1935, the state's tenant population grew at the highest rate in the country, tripling to nearly 150,000 families (about 15 percent were then displaced in the Great Depression) and paralleling the rapid expansion of the cigarette market (Wood 1986: 27). North Carolina's tobacco boom was centered on the area around Wilson, with the highest tenancy rate in the state, much lower levels of yeomanry than in the Piedmont or Appalachia, the lowest level of black land ownership, and the most intensive tobacco monocropping. In 1900, only 12 percent of Wilson County's black farmers and 46 percent of its white farmers were landholders, compared to 32 percent and 67 percent statewide (Valentine 2002: 93–96; McAdams 1996: 24). Debt peonage and consolidated wealth and power were as developed and intense there as anywhere else in the South, including in the cotton belt of the Deep South.

If the colonial order ensured that London dominated the scene for a couple of centuries, by the 1900s towns like Wilson became the dominant players in the international tobacco trade. James B. Duke, taking advantage of North Carolina's leaf agriculture and the availability of labor surpluses, began to expand manufacturing capacities, thus building his tobacco empire. Histories of tobacco usually spend more time romancing Duke's novel advertising techniques than his influence on industrial organization and the unshakable control of his monopoly at tobacco auctions. It is true that the rise of the modern cigarette in the new century was spurred by his innovative marketing strategies. Duke pioneered corporate sponsorship, national branding, premiums and coupons, celebrity endorsements, and images of modernity, but technological developments and corporate power were also factors in his success. After assuming con-

trol of his father's Durham-based tobacco company in the 1880s, Duke
made the first substantial order of the revolutionary cigarette rolling machine, which produced as many cigarettes in a minute as hand laborers
could roll in an hour. He secured an exclusive contract with the manufacturer and eventually controlled the patent, an important shift in the
patent system from a legal framework that protected small inventors to
one that could substantially benefit monopolized capital. With this intellectual property, Duke achieved massive economies of scale and crippled
his competitors (Brandt 2007: 26–31). His main innovation was vertical integration. "Duke was the first to take steps," writes Brandt, "to establish a fully integrated industry." His company, the American Tobacco
Company, had an extensive raw materials sourcing operation known as
the Leaf Department, as well as a large sales and marketing team. Together these operations "assured the movement of cured tobacco from
warehouse to factory to sales," Brandt continues, a model that became
the ideal in other industries. Duke sought to eliminate inefficiencies at
every stage of production. With access to capital being more important
than proximity to agriculture, the trust was eventually headquartered in
New York City. One of the three largest corporations in the United States
before the federal government broke it up into a handful of smaller tobacco companies in 1911, Duke achieved a tobacco empire that controlled 90 percent of domestic sales and more than 60 percent worldwide,
with tentacles extending deep into Europe and Asia. Duke brashly said,
the "world is now our market for our product" (Brandt 2007: 25–39;
Goodman 1993: 100–101, 230–32).

Duke did not completely integrate farms. He did not own them because capital investment did not generate the same economies of scale on
farms as in factories. Labor management and response to weather and
other conditions remained local and were handled by the local landowners and tenant families. But Duke indirectly controlled the fortunes of
rural people. As his company bought or put other firms out of business, it
also began dictating prices at the tobacco auctions, where, until his trust
was busted, there was no competitive bidding and farmers and tenants
were forced to settle for stagnant leaf prices (Brandt 2007: 35). Farmers
did revolt, sometimes by forming cooperatives and sometimes by destroy-
ing fields, as in the famous case of the 1908 Kentucky tobacco strike, the
only major farmer strike in U.S. history. More often, the Leaf Department
used its immense purchasing power to undermine this kind of solidaristic
behavior and force farmers to perhaps grudgingly accept low prices. Because the major protests and most evidence of popular resistance to Duke
were in Appalachia where there was less tenancy, it is also likely that the
tenancy system limited agrarian opposition to the monopoly (Campbell
1992, 1993; Tilley 1947). Insofar as many rural landowners were also

Figure 2.6. Auction at Clark Warehouse, Wilson, mid-1950s. Photograph by
and reproduced with permission from Raines & Cox Photographers, Wilson,
NC.

principle investors in the tobacco warehouses and leaf-processing facilities in towns like Wilson, they perhaps shared a degree of class affiliation
with Duke, even though they were also beholden to the low prices offered
by the only buyer in town.

At the tobacco auctions, bales of tobacco were evaluated by supposedly "unbiased experts," graders who worked on behalf of the federal
agriculture department, and sales were governed by a system of grades to
ensure "uniform standards of quality" and "efficient and fair" marketing
(Womach 2004a: 4). In practice, auctions remained notoriously corrupt
throughout the twentieth century. Cultural solicitations of favoritism and
kickbacks (e.g., a pocket of cash or a bottle of liquor) ensured higher
grades or better floor position for some sellers. Bidding was greatly limited for tenants, many of whom were not permitted by their landlord
to attend the auction. Attending the auction in the stead of the tenant
who actually produced the crop in the field, landlords could benefit from
fudged arithmetic upon returning back to the farm, telling the tenant
that the prices just did not add up this year and that debt would there-

fore carry over. Since black farmers would routinely receive unfair treatment, worse floor position, and worse grades, or even be denied access
to some warehouses, they were at a disadvantage, and white landowners
had an incentive—an alibi really—to not permit black tenants to attend
the auctions. Tobacco buyers often underpaid black farmers in comparison to white farmers, which was permitted by collusion among buyers
and warehouse personnel (Gilbert et al. 2001). That two warehouses in
Wilson became known for fair dealings regardless of race is evidence that
the opposite was true across the market (McKinney 2003: 14).

The social world of the tobacco town and the surrounding countryside was completely infused with racial meanings and the tobacco business built on basic divisions. The majority of tenants in North Carolina
were white, but over time black labor became more important because a
growing and segregated textile industry, and other kinds of economic opportunity, provided an exit from this situation for white tenant families
(Wood 1986: 27). Although the tenancy system generally continued to
expand, the mobility of black families was constrained in deeper and different ways, with less market access, the constant threat and pressure of
discrimination, and more exploitative tenancy arrangements than what
white families faced. "Ownership and control of the crop and its marketing," writes a historian of the South, "in a context of widespread black
illiteracy and political powerlessness . . . effectively left the amount of the
cropper's [share] to the landlord's discretion" (Wood 1986: 24).

In 1896, the *Wilson Daily Times* published a fascinating editorial,
more promotional than empirical, that spoke to the evolving meanings
of class and race in the postbellum period. It diagrammed a model of the
ideal "farmer." The "farmer should be educated," they wrote. "The day is
gone by when the 'fool of the family,' who is not considered smart enough
to send to college, was considered smart enough to manage the farm."

In their view the ideal farmer must be "a man of broad education" (*Wilson Daily Times* 1896b: 7). The word *farmer* is a misleading term here.
Although it seems to suggest someone who works in the dirt, the editors
were in fact referring to landowners, a class of person that seems closer
to the antebellum planters than to manual laborers. The editorial goes on
to distinguish this class of person from other agriculturalists portrayed as
backward and less modern. "In a recent trip among our prosperous farmers," the editors wrote, "we noticed the difference in thrift of farms lying
side by side, and of the same natural advantage." Through interviews with
men called the "most successful farmers," the editors learned that, "the
difference consisted of this, that the one man had learned to farm according to the best and most approved methods, while the other man farmed
without system, just as his father had done thirty years ago" (*Wilson Daily Times* 1896a: 3). Essentially, the story that is told is one of equal oppor-

tunity and unequal merits and ambitions. This quintessentially American tale frames economic success as an individual achievement ("the one man ... the other man") that is reckoned innocent, starting from ground zero, not having benefited from some contrived form of advantage, such as a legacy of social power or a family inheritance, because an equal playing field ("the same natural advantage") is said to exist. The lesser class of rural person is depicted as ultimately ignorant and even helpless, although not worth helping, because they are irredeemably backward and bound by tradition. "The worst of his condition," the editors continued, "is that he will not now learn anything. He will not take a farm paper, nor does he care to read one if it is given to him." In contrast, the editors wrote, "our most successful farmers are readers of farm papers that they may learn the results of other men's experience, and get their advice as to the best methods of conducting the whole management of their farms" (3). Adding to this contrast of distinctive rural classes, including perhaps subtle racial notes, the editors ran another commentary piece one year later that spoke of economic growth in Wilson as being driven by "live, wide-awake, business men" and "those engaged in professional pursuits." They described rural people in truly belittling terms, as being, for example, the source of "annoying complaints, foolish proposals, and inexcusable ignorance," having "little intelligence," tending to "not value time," be "lazy and easy-going," and "remain at home too closely," not giving "time to study," having "no regard" for "quality" and "no aim to acquire the best by careful [management]," and being "careless and wasteful" (*Wilson Daily Times* 1897: 7).

The distinctions between "successful" and unsuccessful farmers, "wide-awake" and "lazy" classes of people, encouraged a view of the countryside as being essentially divided by different levels of merit and value, while associating those depicted as modern farmers with the urban professionals. The result was a dominant perspective that recognized distinctive groups of people as having inherent cultural traits and explained differences of economy in terms of these attributes. In general, the landowner no longer plays a role in farm management, and growers have direct contracts with tobacco companies. New levels of corporate integration are a powerful challenge to the tradition of more localized farm management in North Carolina. At the same time, the political economy of contemporary tobacco agriculture has built into it long-standing trajectories of social power and advantage that kept land in the hands of certain people, limited competition in the regional labor market, kept places and resources underdeveloped for the sake of tobacco capital, negatively valued manual work and venerated management, and ensured that, as the century wore on, a predictable division of labor and ownership not only continued to exist but defined evolving meanings of citizenship, moral worth, and livelihood at the bottom rungs of the tobacco business. The moral economy of cultural values that has developed in tandem with the political economy of leaf production positions the grower not just as having a different job than the racialized proletariat but also as belonging to a higher order of the human and being worth more to the community, the nation, and even the species.

Best Citizens

The social geography of tobacco tenancy mediated the impact of the Great Depression in North Carolina and the course that local politics and political lobbying took. In 1930 three-quarters of the state's population resided outside of towns (Abrams 1992: 4). This rural population was inauspiciously positioned for the national economic downturn because land had become scarce, credit sources were tight, and access usually went through landowners; and landowners, given their own economic interests, encouraged tenants to produce tobacco rather than have a more diverse economy, including subsistence crops. The underdeveloped education system and other public works in counties like Wilson, where there were few alternatives to tobacco work, also contributed to the downturn (Abrams 1992; Wright 1986; Daniel 1986).

In the 1920s, tobacco leaf sold above twenty cents per pound. Prices dipped to eight cents per pound by 1930. In that year alone, 150,000 pieces of farm property were forcibly sold in North Carolina. In Nash County, which lies just north of Wilson County, 3,500 of 5,250 farms were foreclosed. Thousands of tenant farmers faced extreme adversity. Tightened credit markets and low prices forced many landowners to release tenants, consolidate production where possible, and shift to seasonal wage labor rather than yearlong share arrangements (Daniel 1986: 119). In the eastern part of the state, where tobacco and tenancy were most concentrated, the eviction of tenants and the consolidation of tobacco leaf production led to unusually high levels of poverty, homelessness, underemployment, and forced labor migration. Compared to landholders, the laboring population of tenant families faired much worse during the Depression (Abrams 1992: 3–5).

The Wilson County government agricultural agent at the time, Clifton Tomlinson, claimed years later in an oral history interview that eviction was the result of a rational economic calculus. Some tenants, he stated, "could get better production out of the land, and if they were poor farmers, they had to go. You tried to get a farm family that was more productive. That way you could get better yields" (L. A. Jones 1986). But this explanation occludes as much as it explains. Why were particular farm families poor to begin with? If the sign of modern farming was indexed most of all in a will to improve the farm, as the editors of the *Wilson Daily Times* suggested decades prior, wouldn't the uneven distribution of citizenship and educational resources in the segregated South dictate which farmers were more capable of not being or seeming "poor"? Because he fails to mention the full context of social disparity, Tomlinson's explanation rehashes the inaccurate idea that all farmers have the same "natural advantage," to again cite the newspaper editorial, and that differences among farms reflect personal work ethic rather than collective forms of comparative advantage. In fact, the statistics on tenant eviction demonstrate that landowner decisions were not purely economical.

According to one government report from Wilson County, the three hundred tenant families that moved from outlying rural areas to the town of Wilson from 1931 to 1934 were mostly African American families, with high rates of illiteracy and high incidence of disease. Only fifty of these families came with some financial assistance from the evicting landowner (Daniel 1986: 119). In general, landowners showed white tenant families favoritism. Even though there was an overall decline in the tenant population, the proportion of white tenant families in Wilson County actually increased by 75 percent during the 1930s. Displaced black families greatly outnumbered displaced white families across North Carolina, creating a situation in which more black families became dependent on government social assistance (Blackwell 1934; Matthews 1999; Spellman 1947: 21, 56). This selective eviction pattern built on a tradition of social welfare rooted in plantation slavery, where limited resources were generally denied to black people. Now social assistance was increasingly associated with the stigma of indolence and unworthiness in the New Deal era (E. Green 1999; Katz 1986). Tomlinson's remark that "poor farmers . . . had to go" presents the image of a surgical procedure. The comment by another state official in 1934 that "a considerable amount of chiseling" was occurring on tobacco farms (Badger 1980) carries the subtle implication of social eugenics. Economical reasons and matters of productivity were no doubt part of landowner decisions. But these factors perhaps also functioned as alibis for a more morally and racially potent kind of judgment. Not just about agriculture, the decisions were apparently about dispensing with and chiseling away that which seemed—or had been made to seem—poor, an ambiguous term to say the least.

The segregated tobacco towns became further crowded. In 1934, a social worker involved in a local sanitation campaign described the living conditions in East Wilson where former tenants had relocated:

[They are] unimproved and unsanitary—houses poorly built and unat-tractive, water supply from open wells, no sewage system. [It is] so crowded you could hardly get into the place. Every house, every aban-doned shack in town, is filled . . . They're *not* all bums, either. They *haven't* come to town to get work in the mills or on CWA [Civil Works Administration]. They've come because there's no place for them to live in the country, every abandoned shack in the countryside is filled up. (cited in Lowitt and Beasely 1983: 188–89; original italics)

Would this official emphasize that not all displaced persons were "bums" if the countervailing attitude of blaming the victim (regarding the mostly black rural migrants as indolent and not hardworking) were not preva-lent in the dominant discourse? Would the official emphasize that their migration was forced if the idea that this displaced population was seek-ing government assistance and averting work were not common? This historical moment—the changing tenant system, its racial dimension, and the explanatory models that circulated to make sense of landowner deci-sions and urban resettlement—is a blip in the genealogy of morals that I discuss more deeply and broadly later in the book. Note here how the fact of white comparative advantage and the racial project of treating white farm families more hospitably are converted into a story about the inherent poverty of a vulnerable population and the legitimacy of racially patterned social engineering. This displacement of agency from the decision-making landowners, the stereotypes of the public culture, and the metaphors of surgery and pathology espoused by government of-ficials onto the exiled population itself is an important part of how class divisions and levels of participation in the tobacco industry were created.

Ironically, the structural cause of the extreme downturn in agricul-tural commodity prices in the Depression era, chronic overproduction, was partially the result of landowner pressure on tenants to maximize cash crop yields at the expense of a more sustainable model (Tilley 1948: 96–97). But in the official discourse, blame was routed down the social ladder, as in this excerpt from a 1934 academic textbook on farm man-agement in North Carolina:

The tenant, and especially a negro tenant, is easier to manage when confined to a few crops. Diversified farming would require more super-vision than the southern landlord, especially the absentee owner, is willing to give. The landlord favors a money crop that cannot be eaten or fed on the farm. The coastal plain counties, where the tenants grow a higher yield than do owner-operators [yeomen], show that more su-pervision does pay, however. A good deal more supervision is given in the coastal plain area than in the Piedmont. (Landon 1934: 251)

If supervision was already a definitive aspect of what it means to be a modern farmer, here it seems like a white man's burden. The idea that black farmers are like livestock or children, in needing to be confined and constantly monitored, reflects how planters talked about slaves. Agricultural knowledge and managerial authority seem like the natural propensities and properties of certain white people, and black people, while useful as labor, were a nuisance and a responsibility. Even though overproduction driven by landowner motives led to consistently low prices, this textbook provides a convenient excuse. Because a "negro tenant" must be confined to a few crops, and because these stereotyped tenants are said to pilfer subsistence crops, the landowner must conveniently encourage the tenant to produce the "money crop" year after year.

In 1933, the federal government passed the Agricultural Adjustment Act to resolve the dilemma of overproduction. Subsequent agrarian reforms were legislated throughout the decade, all part of the New Deal effort to stabilize prices for landowners, tenants, and farmers through the maintenance of consistent and rationalized production levels. Although lacking any clear use value, tobacco was eventually included in the law, which at first addressed only so-called "basic commodities" like cotton and wheat. Tobacco even received favoritism. Whereas the parity price for the other basic commodities was based on prices that existed several decades prior, tobacco state politicians pressured the U.S. Department of Agriculture (USDA) to use the higher prices of more recent years as the base price for leaf. Similar attempts by leaders from other geographical areas and for other commodities failed (Badger 1980: 40).

To implement the new crop control measures, to successfully get sometimes ornery, stubborn, and reluctant farmers to abide by federal production quotas, which established for each parcel of land the maximum amount of tobacco that could lawfully be produced, the federal government needed a massive rural outreach campaign. Farmers accustomed to overproducing now had to comply. The USDA recruited the Extension Service to administer this nationwide effort. The hierarchical structure of the Extension Service, with a central agency in each state and an office in each county, was amenable to this kind of outreach because the task of meeting with rural communities was devolved to the county level. County officials received more federal funding and reached more farmers in face-to-face meetings than ever before. In North Carolina alone, county agricultural agents signed up 150,000 cotton farmers in 1933 to participate in the crop control program. Farmers plowed up acres of cotton (Badger 1980: 43–44).

The USDA had prioritized control measures for crops such as corn and cotton, at first leaving the regulation of tobacco plantings to a later date. But that year tobacco-state politicians and large landowners from tobacco states demanded that attention be paid to their cash crop with the same degree of urgency. A vocal social movement calling for immediate intervention claimed to represent the true interests of the entire tobacco farmer population, using the language of "economic democracy" and insisting that farmers, not the federal government, should decide on the timetable for reforms. But such rhetoric was not at all reflective of the concerns and interests of the majority of farm families. Large growers and landowners, especially in eastern North Carolina, used their private money and power to publish pocket circulars and advertisements and sponsor rural rallies to whip up support for crop control. Their interest was maintaining the status quo and bringing about agrarian forms that continued to limit competition. Fixing an exact quota level to the land was precisely the way to accomplish this, freezing the geography of who could grow tobacco where, keeping the landlord as the gatekeeper of tobacco agriculture, and stymieing the possibility of accumulation or mobility for a tenant or yeoman family, while at the same time stabilizing prices for landowners and alleviating potential rural unrest and conflict.

Wilson was the site of several important rallies led by prominent farmers and specialists from the state's Department of Agriculture and Extension Service. In the words of the *Wilson Daily Times* editors, these "best citizens" warned the masses that there would be "deprivation, hardship, ruin and consequent dispossession of the tobacco farmers" without government intervention. This was true; the problem of chronic overproduction would remain if not for drastic changes in the production and marketing systems. But the question of what kind of government intervention or how to restructure agriculture in a more sustainable and perhaps also just way was left underdeveloped in favor of unilateral public promotion of a land-based quota mechanism. The Raleigh *News and Observer* ran a front-page editorial highlighting a rally in the state capital that about two thousand farmers attended. With no breakdown in terms of demography or socioeconomic background, the report described an "angry and excited crowd," some threatening violence and force, and cited this as evidence that "the farmers do want help" (Daniel 1986: 113; Badger 1980: 46–52). Farm policy was being driven by a contrived grassroots movement spearheaded by a core group of landed interests with disproportionate political and media influence. They demanded that all warehouses in North Carolina be closed under the exercise of martial law until the federal government intervened to increase tobacco leaf prices. The state governor ordered an immediate market holiday. On Labor Day 1933 the movement organizers went to Washington and staged a protest at the office of the USDA, demanding something similar to what the government was already imposing on cotton. The appeal worked. Federal agriculture leaders decided to reduce tobacco acreage for the following year and, in exchange, subsidize the price of the leaf already ready for market. The big growers of eastern North Carolina had gotten what they wanted: government price support and a mechanism for limiting competition in the future (Badger 1980: 50–54; Abrams 1992: 55–81).

The smallest producers, those with less than four acres of tobacco, were extremely hesitant. They saw the ruling to reduce acreage by a percentage as unfair since that kind of regressive cut makes a more noticeable dent on small operations, perhaps bringing them below a subsistence level. Nonetheless, by late September 1933, more than 95 percent of farmers were signed up for the acreage reduction program, partly because landowners prodded tenants to participate in spite of their reservations. The marketing holiday ended and North Carolina tobacco farmers (in large measure, the landowners) received $85.6 million for their product compared to $34.9 million the year prior. "Eastern North Carolina, a very large section devoted to agriculture has been prostrated for five years. This year the people are really prosperous," a North Carolina senator issued a public statement to President Roosevelt. "With one accord they give the credit to the President." Federal farm credit agencies in eastern North Carolina reported a 99 percent return on that year's farm loans, the best record for any region in the country (Badger 1980: 50–71). The value of farmland in North Carolina rose twice as fast as the national average from 1930 to 1948 as a result of the new quota system, but this had the unfortunate effect of limiting the ability of smallholders to expand production and freezing competition to maintain existing land use and ownership structures (199–220). Expanding branches of government enacted reforms that stabilized prices and resolved structural problems in the agriculture sector, at least for several decades, but also funneled government largesse through the hands of landowners and helped to sustain tenancy, essentially a feudal system based on highly consolidated landholdings.

Abuse in the distribution of federal price support payments for tobacco was common. Research at the time found that tenants in Wilson County widely believed that landowners were cheating them in various ways. Landlords might keep the transfer payment and continue to pay tenants a lower price or increase the amount they charged tenants for supplies and necessities. When problems surfaced, agricultural officials commonly blamed tenants themselves for not understanding how their contracts worked and attributed accusations of landowner misconduct to the ignorance and paranoia of a lower class of people. The local arbitration committees that were formed to settle disputes were populated with individuals who the *Wilson Daily Times* described as the "kind of men" who are "familiar with farming conditions in the country and community," "successful in their own farming operations," who have an "ability to assist in education," "keep themselves informed on the program generally," and, above all, are "capable of developing suggestions . . . for its betterment" (Thomas 1939: 7). These were already powerful individuals. The committees were the result of elections in which the voting rights of tenants and sharecroppers, especially black farmers, were greatly constrained by landowner pressure and the culture of Jim Crow. No black tenants or sharecroppers participated in the committees, and while about 90 percent of white landowners voted in a given election, only about 10 percent of rural black families did (Abrams 1992: 172; Badger 1980: 201–3).

Agrarian reforms helped to accelerate the descent of black farmers and sharecroppers down the socioeconomic ladder. At the same time, the major tobacco companies and manufacturers in North Carolina (principally the R. J. Reynolds Corporation and Brown and Williamson) resisted the new labor reforms that were also part of the New Deal. They successfully lobbied the federal government for the legislation of a minimum wage that was lower than for other industries, and yet they also mechanized their operations to reduce labor costs and worked hard to stymie unions. By 1940, only about 4 percent of the nonagricultural labor force in North Carolina was unionized, one of the lowest rates in the country. Along with industry opposition, unions in tobacco work faced all the traditional obstacles, including religious conservatism, employer paternalism, deference to authority, the seasonal nature of the work, and racial and sexual intimidation. From the 1930s to the 1940s, black workers as a percentage of the tobacco factory workforce decreased from 75 percent to 55 percent, and the number of white workers grew by 40 percent. Where unions did take hold in the tobacco industry, Jim Crow laws excluded black workers from them, and they had little political or legal recourse when companies replaced menial jobs generally performed by black workers with machines (Abrams 1992: 161–89; Korstad 2003). "For many North Carolina blacks the New Deal years brought more adversity than economic and social progress," to quote one historian (Abrams 1992: 189).

Even though the majority of tobacco farmers during the New Deal era were landless tenant families, tobacco interests held great clout as a political block capable of making special claims on the federal government and strategically articulating these petitions in a language of economic democracy and in a tone of crisis. The public cultural framing of the farmer as a deserving citizen who urgently needs intervention and assistance, a "best citizen" facing "deprivation," "hardship," and "ruin," to use the words of the local newspapers, was crucial for garnering special treatment, even though the hardship was not uniformly endured and the agrarian reform largely benefited already powerful interests. The public face of a unified tobacco constituency played an important ideological role amid industry restructuring, helping to conceal internal fault lines, confound potential cooperative behavior across rural and urban workers, and engender comparative and competitive advantage for landowners and manufacturing interests. The disproportionate release of black workers and families from farms and factories in the 1930s is only one context that helps to explain disproportionate patterns of social epidemiology and life chances. The seasonal nature of tobacco work, the political efforts to maintain low wages and limit alternative livelihoods in towns like Wilson, and the impact of racial segregation in all areas of life helped to maintain and extend disparities.

In the early twentieth century, as today, a particular public discourse helped to explain structural differences as the result of the constitution of different groups of people. Although it is not at all true that black people in Wilson do not want to work on farms (do white Wilsonians want to do manual field labor?), it is entirely appropriate to wonder why they would, given the meager wages, ubiquitous white ownership of farms, and racialized subordination and ostracism in southern agriculture. The history of violence and dispossession in North Carolina's tobacco industry still gets swallowed up in a black hole image: Jungle Town. The media does all it can to disconnect places that have long been connected and interdependent, to arouse fears and promote indifference and hostility as acceptable social attitudes, and to make it all seem so darn natural. In the ceaseless public refrain about who works hard and who doesn't, who deserves what and who doesn't, who is a best citizen and who is a pariah, historical facts dissolve into an ahistorical object, a Face, a stereotyped image or impression of whole swaths of people or circumscribed places and what they are like. Innocence in America has a lot do to with how populations are construed as being a burden or as carrying a burden.

By century's end, tobacco politics was once again centered on a romantic portrait of the tacitly white tobacco farmer as the bedrock citizen. This image likewise helped mask social divisions and convert special government treatment for an advantaged group into something that seems reasonable and equitable.

Marlboro Men

Philip Morris can say what it wants about corporate social responsibility. This is the company that created the Marlboro Man in the 1960s, when a generation of future tobacco growers—baby boomers like Dwight Watson—came of age. In 1962, the Marlboro Country campaign was launched with a jingle:

For a man's flavor come to Marlboro Country. My Country. Its [*sic*] big, open, makes a smoker feel ten feet tall. . . . This is my cigarette, Marlboro. It's like this country, has spirit. . . . Come to where the flavor is, come to Marlboro Country. (Brandt 2007: 263)

This campaign aimed to allay consumer anxieties about the health risks of tobacco use. It encouraged a defiant attitude about risk, science, and government, and shuttled potent meanings of gender and power along the way. "Rarely, if ever," Brandt writes, "had marketing so brilliantly combined American values, traditions, and symbols with a promotional message" (2007: 264).

The Marlboro Man campaign undoubtedly provided an important context of meaning for the current generation of active tobacco growers, those who, for the first time, came into the tobacco livelihood in the midst of an increasingly well-organized antitobacco movement. In the 1960s, these men were advancing through North Carolina's segregated school system, taking vocational agriculture classes, and sitting in the front row at Future Farmers of America meetings. As these farmers were taught to depend on and trust agricultural science, the Marlboro Man promoted an ideal masculinity that was not dependent on or defined by science and lived at a distance from government. Some tobacco growers perhaps felt groomed to become Marlboro Men themselves and identified with this image, although what it symbolized contrasted with the paradox that these growers came to rely on the government much more than previous cohorts. Even as the federal government now recognized the negative medical and public health consequences of tobacco use, the government did very little to try to diversify tobacco-dependent communities away from the harmful commodity. Researchers at land-grant institutions like North Carolina State University busily developed new tobacco seeds and production technologies and tested agronomic techniques. Extension agents worked directly with growers to improve, manage, and expand their tobacco farms. Growers benefited from federal farm loan and farm insurance programs. And the federal government continued to subsidize the price of domestic tobacco leaf through the price support system established in the New Deal.

In the 1960s, tobacco leaf production capacities significantly increased around the world as a result of direct foreign investment from tobacco companies and the involvement of the United States in promoting tobacco agriculture and other kinds of international market integration as an approach to fighting the Cold War. The primary tobacco market in Rhodesia (erstwhile Zimbabwe) overtook Wilson County as the single largest tobacco leaf market in the world, partly because of the tobacco-related

Figure 2.7. "Come to Marlboro Country," tobacco advertisement, 1967. From *Life* magazine 62 (8): February 24, 1967. Courtesy of http://tobacco documents.org./pollay_ads/Marl51.07.html.

Figure 2.8. Tobacco farmer in a tobacco field in Wilson County, North Carolina, 1960s. Photo by an unknown *Wilson Daily Times* photographer. Reproduced with permission from the *Wilson Daily Times*.

economic development projects that governments and companies were funding. The federal government used public resources to both grow tobacco agriculture around the world and incentivize competition among tobacco growers at home, benefiting tobacco companies on both fronts by making tobacco leaf more widely available and subsidizing the expansion of economies of scale and sourcing mechanisms (Finger 1981). "The responsibility of growing the kind of tobacco that puts extra dollars in the farmer's pocket," an agricultural scientist in North Carolina wrote in the 1960s, specifically discussing the need for domestic growers to improve their operations to maintain a competitive advantage, "has been put squarely on the shoulders of the grower himself" (*Wilson Daily Times* 1963). Although its main purpose was to communicate core messages to smokers, the social meanings encoded in the Marlboro Man image converged with this postwar push to get growers to embrace such values as individual accountability, ambitious expansionism, and the acceptance of risk. Of course, even though this intensification process shrunk the size of the tobacco grower population over time, the cultural portrayal of the grower as an entrepreneur helped to reconcile and recast dependence on the state in terms of the values of autonomy and cold war tobacco capitalism enshrined in the image of the Marlboro Man.

The widespread use of the tractor by the 1950s meant that a single farmer could tend acreage that previously supported a handful of tenant families. From 1954 to 1959, North Carolina lost one-quarter of its tobacco farms (nearly forty thousand farms), although acreage remained constant. Farmers sought to maximize the returns on the new equipment, and expanded credit sources in rural North Carolina, commonly subsidized by the federal government, allowed them to begin to rent and consolidate parcels of land. Tenant families were released, and nonproducing landowners now distanced themselves from farm management, renting their land to active producers with increasing debt loads and ambitions to expand production. In 1962, a major reform in the federal tobacco crop control program allowed farmers to further consolidate production. Since the New Deal, land had been affixed with an annual tobacco quota, and only that amount of tobacco could be produced on that given parcel of land. With the new "lease-and-transfer" reform, active farmers could lease these production rights from nonproducing landowners and then grow the tobacco on parcels of land closer to their home base of operations. The link between land and production, which was at the core of the New Deal crop control program, privileging landowners for some decades, was now loosened to the benefit of enterprising producers. Initially limited to a total of five acres, further reform in 1967 allowed for unlimited leases and transfers (Mann 1975).[2]

This was the main policy reform that led to farm consolidation in tobacco (Daniel 1986: 263; Hart and Chestang 1978). Tobacco growers now rented land and tobacco quota, managed multiple parcels and divisions, and financed production costs, not through a relationship to the landowner, as in the tenancy system, but rather through independent relationships to banks and lenders. A middle category between aristocracy and peonage, the grower was an owner-operator, usually a landholder, although some landless tenants came to own equipment and rent land. Tobacco growers were minor capitalists, "small businessmen," in the words of an article from the *Wilson Daily Times* (1961: 17). Whereas consolidation was slower in the foothills and the mountains, the flatland of eastern North Carolina was especially conducive. From 1954 to 1974, the number of tobacco operations east of Raleigh dropped by 76 percent, from about 25,000 to about 6,000 units, while average per-acre yield,

---

[2] For a comprehensive overview of tobacco farm policy changes from the New Deal through the 1960s, see Finger (1981).

benefiting from new mechanical technologies, increased from 1,340 to 2,084 pounds of tobacco (Hart and Chestang 1978: 453).

Government-sponsored rural modernization and farm assistance programs did nothing to challenge social disparities in rural communities. In fact, they exacerbated them and helped to determine the white racial composition of the emergent class of capitalist tobacco producers. For example, the North Carolina state government established the Challenge Program in 1954 to improve agricultural yields and modernize farms. The goal was to promote a model of modern farming through the organization of a contest among farmers and the public celebration of winning teams. The local newspaper encouraged growers to "increase the size of their farm units as rapidly as possible," "to use machinery," and to "improve their level of management" in order to transition into the kind of entrepreneurial farmer that the state's high-modernist vision idealized (Lamm 1955a). Each county organized a delegation of leading farmers to compete in Raleigh. In Wilson County, delegates were selected in preliminary competitions in their small rural communities, with jurors coming from local chapters of white farm groups such as the Farm Bureau, the Grange, and Home Demonstration clubs. The county's "colored farm families," the *Wilson Daily Times* states in a set of articles that report on the contest, competed before a separate panel of black community leaders. The white delegation from Wilson went on to win the state contest, where none of North Carolina's black farmers were permitted to compete (Lamm 1955b). The winning team received a $1,000 cash prize from the state, which the local daily promptly matched. Plus, the individual farmer who was judged to be the best farmer on the winning team received a $2,000 scholarship for his child to study agricultural sciences at North Carolina State University. Prizes in the local black competition were divided into two categories: tenant families and landowners. The highest-scoring tenant family received a $75 prize, the second family a $50 prize. For propertied black families there was only a first prize. The newspaper reckoned, "there are more than twice as many colored tenants as there are land owners" (Lamm 1955a; V. Martin 1955).

Is it surprising that when I did my fieldwork there were no active black tobacco farmers in Wilson County and only a handful in the surrounding area? The general trend in U.S. agriculture in the last half century was industrialization and land consolidation (D. Fitzgerald 2003). But below the surface there was a glaring process of uneven exodus. From 1920 to 1990, more than 97 percent of all black farmers exited farm production, compared to 63 percent of white farmers. By 1997, there were fewer than twenty thousand black farmers, about 1 percent of all farmers, compared to 14 percent in 1920. Several factors caused this disparity. The communal memory of slavery and sharecropping probably motivated against intergenerational farming in black families, and the civil rights movement created alternative economic opportunities for rural black people (Schweninger 1989). But other historical processes and human efforts went into making agriculture a white vocation. The segregated school systems meant black farmers obtained lower-quality and less-formal education. In 1964, the average black farmer completed five years of schooling, compared to almost ten years for white farmers. Teachers in black schools earned about half of what white teachers earned. Spending per black pupil was about 70 percent less. These facts are crucial because formal education has been shown to enhance economic efficiencies on farms and help operators manage resource constraints, market conditions, environmental variables, and new technologies (Huffman 1981).

Even though the legislative mandate of the Extension Service is to "serve the greatest number of farmers and to answer the greatest needs of the group" (Faris 1963), government funding for agricultural modernization projects was skewed. From 1925 to 1937, black farms comprised nearly one-third of all farms across the South but received 6 percent of all extension funding. In the 1930s, there was roughly one extension agent for every 1,500 white farmers in North Carolina, compared to a ratio of one to 3,500 for black farmers (Abrams 1992: 172). From 1945 to 1960, all federal appropriations and almost all state funds went to the white side of the extension institutions and services (Huffman 1981). County extension agents were also often participants in the widespread racial bias in the farmland real estate business in the South. Together with realtors, landowners, and lenders, many government officials worked to undermine black landowners, selling them worse-quality land, offering impossible interest rates, or helping to contrive tax code or other legal violations in order to free up black landholdings for purchase, a situation compounded by the low literacy and formal education levels in the black population (Mitchell 2000). A sociological case study of one North Carolina county found that these multiple factors combined to cut black landholdings in half in the 1950s and 1960s alone (Darling 1982). The steady decline of black land ownership in the postwar South resulted in greater dependence on social assistance, less ability to participate in political leadership, and worsened social epidemiology indicators (Gaventa 1998; Gilbert et al. 2001; Beauford et al. 1984). This cycle made rural black farm families less attractive to lenders, more sensitive to market changes, and less efficient producers (Gilbert et al. 2001).

The *Wilson Daily Times* wrote of the ideal white extension agent as a man "familiar with area people and their requirements" and the "needs of varying communities" (Faris 1963). On the ground, however, it was exceedingly rare for white county agents to provide services to black farmers. I interviewed Bill Lewis, Wilson County's head agent in the postwar decades, at length. Part of his job involved writing weekly articles in the local newspaper to inform area producers about new agronomic trends, knowledge, and strategies. Linking an existing emphasis on literacy and a will to improve to an emergent emphasis on technical rationality and entrepreneurial management, Lewis wrote articles on the use of commercial inputs, equipment upgrades, soil conservation techniques, labor management, farm and household budgets, and all other excruciatingly detailed aspects of commercial farm operation. He was writing to an audience that was tacitly white and literate, the readers of the local newspaper. In the other part of his job, working directly with growers to do field tests or give them advice, Lewis largely confined himself to a select group of white farmers (see Grim 1995, 1996).

Before meeting Lewis, I read lots about the uneven resources afforded black farmers across the South by the Extension Service. Lewis, who oversaw the county's segregated extension office, told me that his work with farmers was influenced and constrained by many factors. In describing a preference for working with a certain kind of farmer, he invokes issues of efficacy and practicality. "I tried to work with decision makers, people with clout and respect," Lewis told me. "The decision maker was not always a landowner. He might have been a tenant farmer, but he was influential enough with his landowner that if a farm became available the landowner could buy the farm and let him tend it. If you influenced him and if he thought well of what you were saying he could organize a meeting at the store and tell other farmers that you want to have a meeting. Then there would be a crowd and you could reach more people."

This kind of practical favoritism was a statewide phenomenon. In 1963, only two hundred of the tens of thousands of tobacco farmers in North Carolina participated in extension projects and worked closely with county agents to improve their farms and knowledge. Five of these participants were in Wilson County (Hyatt 1963: 6). A selective approach to extension, focusing all the resources on a small number of recipients, was common in colonial settings as well. In the British colonies in southern Africa, for example, it was known as the "focal-point approach," which developed as a direct response to a "brick wall of peasant conservatism," notes a 1956 document from the colonial Agriculture Department in British southern Africa. The traditional agronomic practices of most peasants, although perhaps embodying accumulated wisdom about sustainable production and subsistence needs, were seen as an impediment to the market-oriented interests of colonial administrators. Rural modernization programs in colonial settings involved the extension work of agents who promoted a model of scientific agriculture centered on rationalized farm management and enterprise. Agents focused their work on a select group of "progressive farmers who would then be mobilized to practice modern agriculture," the political scientist James C. Scott writes, while the promotion of cultural stereotypes of black farmers as stubborn, lazy, and uncooperative was a crucial means of underwriting these efforts (1998: 260). In Malawi, extension agents attempted to depopulate a rural area of all but those inhabitants designated as "master farmers." According to the anthropologist Pauline Peters (1993), the aim was to create a new ecology of "neatly-bounded, mixed-farming lot[s] based on rotation of single-stand crops which would replace the scattered, multi-cropped farming . . . considered backward."[3]

The meaning of reputation and the structure of promotion within the Extension Service probably added to the biases that were built into segregated institutional life throughout the South to incentivize a similar focal-point approach. If a field demonstration project worked, if a well-known and well-respected farmer (Lewis's "decision maker") put the extension agent's advice to work with positive results, this boosted the agent's reputation in the community and within the larger agronomical sciences and extension outreach fields. There was a context of accountability and achievement among white agents in which they were motivated to selectively focus on farmers who were already reputable, perhaps those working on the most fertile land or with access to the most competitive creditors, rather than to pay attention to the most vulnerable in the rural population. The rural modernization push was a government-sponsored means of making marginal farmers and black farmers more susceptible to failure in relation to the select bunch that received truly useful information and powerful public resources. Consequently, access to tobacco as a livelihood was available for an increasingly narrow slice of the rural population, and government employees, working with taxpayer dollars, were brokers in a larger network of socially emboldened and institutionally legitimized bias.

By the 1960s, Lewis was one of the most respected farm agents in North Carolina. He worked hard to make farms more efficient and helped consolidate operations, reduce the size of the rural labor force, and empower families that were not the most disadvantaged. It is easy to criticize this work. But, in the time that I spent with him, I came to understand that what Lewis did in Wilson County reflected a vision of farm policy that dominated at the national level, where the American farmer and American agriculture were publicly glorified and associated with values such as independence, enterprise, autonomy, and growth. The real-

---

[3] Cited in Scott (1998: 260).

ity was that the national restructuring of agriculture in line with Cold War politics and a corporate model of production involved layers of loss (Kirby 1987; Thompson 2002).

Tobacco farm modernization had many effects. Farms got bigger. The work shifted to seasonal wage labor. The rural neighborhood, or cluster of tenant families, as the social and organizational basis for tobacco farm labor, who engaged in "swapping help," came to an end, although workers continued to be called "help" by growers, perhaps reflecting the paternalism of earlier periods when labor was indeed unpaid. Lots of rural people were displaced, leading to increased dependency on social assistance between tobacco seasons and further migration into tobacco towns, where there was seasonal labor in tobacco facilities and impermanent jobs in the expanding service sector of the postindustrial era. Epochal changes in the nature of leaf production and tobacco labor need to be part of how the unusually high unemployment rate and reliance on state relief in present-day North Carolina are conceptualized. Aspects of life that are evident across rural America, and that are ordinarily understood in terms of individual failings or group stereotypes, reflect the powerful influence of historical forces.

The changing tobacco economy also involved social changes on tobacco farms. There was now a widening gap between the farm and the household. This gap marked economic modernity and bourgeois gender roles in an outwardly normative family unit. County agents loudly encouraged farmers to avoid using family labor under the assumption that the farm was a business, not part of the household economy. And in promoting the idea that the farmer is a manager, with the formal payroll as a key material token of this new role, they also helped to promote the common idea that family labor indexes financial troubles because it means the business cannot afford "help." "Family labor has always been part of tobacco," an active grower tells me in an interview. "But that's part of a tradition. The kids help a bit in the summer. Your wife might help a little, too. But if they're out there working full-time, then you're basically saying that they are worth minimum wage, that's what that right there says."

The Agricultural Extension Service and the Home Demonstration clubs were administered as county branches of the USDA in states across the South. These institutions were not just segregated along racial lines but just as select men were involved with the extension agent, select women were involved in the clubs. But these groups worked together in a social sense, both helping to normalize a particular model of the rural, middle-class household as the ideal to which families should aspire. Farm and family were now modern economies linked to expert knowledge and discourse. Home Demonstration clubs idealized the modern rural woman as a domestic counterpart whose contribution to the family came not through farm labor but rather through good housekeeping, food preservation and canning, the use of modern appliances, the application of scientific findings in the parenting role, and many other techniques and tidbits found in popular magazines and discussed at regular potlucks (L. A. Jones 2002).

The farm business was organized in terms of a stark division of labor that bore residues of the values and practices of earlier periods.

The importance of supervision as something that distinguishes the farmer from the manual worker, evident in the planter period and the tenancy system, endured. In one of his newspaper articles, Lewis admonished the grower "not to have a specific task so that he might keep the process moving smoothly" (1963a: 9; 1963b: 13). In interviews, Lewis told me that "pencil work" was essential to the new style of farming he promoted. As seen in this quote, the transition of the tobacco farmer into a category of professional knowledge worker was part of a larger transition into a middle-class identity characterized by other kinds of social practices and aspirations.

> The most important thing was to help people make enough money to have a good life and educate their children. I had no desire to see them make it without having to work. You have to be willing to work. Working to me is not just manual labor. I said a pencil then, but now it's with a computer. You should also assume community responsibilities. You should be active in the school system, farm organizations, in the political arena. All of these things are part of the life that I think is essential for a progressive farmer.

The mechanization of the tobacco economy involved the promotion and adoption of new signs and practices of sociality, which came to index individual achievement and normative family status, positive reflections on the duty of man and woman in society, the standing of the family unit within a local rural world, and a tacit affiliation with broader trends of the suburbanization and professionalization in American life.

Lewis wrote in 1963 that those who are "employed," meaning seasonal tobacco workers, "admire organization and efficiency on the part of the operator" (1963a: 9, 1963b: 8). Tobacco farm management was not regarded as a profession in this way in previous eras. In the colonial period and in the tenancy system, tobacco involved artistry, the idea that, look, if that barn catches fire, no amount of schooling is going to help you bring it under control, or, look, I know when the field is ready to harvest because of how the leaves look, smell, and feel. The postwar decades saw the remodeling of the tobacco grower as a technician and a professional. The citizenship of this group was defined in light of what capitalist agriculture (which was ironically dependent on and aided by massive government interventions) meant to cold war politics. The organized and market-oriented farmer as a best citizen to emulate was the image given to the public, while at the same time cultural models of the enterprising nuclear family covered over the paradoxical dependency of Marlboro Men on the state and on science. But there remains an important smidgen of the Hegelian idea that you cannot learn to swim by reading a book in how industrial tobacco growers talk about their pride in having achieved the skills to grow and cure tobacco through work and experience in fields.

Chapter 3

Enemies of Tobacco

AT ONE WILSON EXIT there is the financially strapped Tobacco Farm Life Museum, established by the R. J. Reynolds Corporation in the 1980s to espouse a positive view of tobacco as a heritage. Motorists learn interesting facts about old-fashioned production techniques of the Depression-era tenant world that have now been swept away by technological change. They browse among the handicrafts, lots of wooden farm equipment, and black-and-white photographs. For the tobacco industry this kind of cultural investment was strategic. The museum frames tobacco agriculture as an innocent pastime available to motorists and local growers alike. In favor of a wholly positive rather than complexly realistic view of tobacco, the museum does not describe the health risks associated with tobacco use. The public education that it provides avoids a conversation about where tobacco agriculture can legitimately and feasibly go, given the harmfulness of the plant.

The museum was one part of a public relations campaign launched by the tobacco industry in the Reagan era to portray growers, and motivate growers to reckon themselves, as a group of people whose culture and tradition have been disrespected, the victims of undue hardship caused by what Jesse Helms, a Republican senator from North Carolina, called "enemies of tobacco," namely, antismoking advocates and the political supporters of public health. This kind of fear-based public relations reflected the more general conservative politics of the day. A cultural politics of victimhood, which played so strategically on meanings of race, geography, and the family, helped foment the support of growers at the very same moment that tobacco companies were aggressively globalizing their operations and steadily moving to foreign tobacco leaf sources. At the museum there are no diagrams of how neoliberal trade policies, facilitating this market shift, demanded new levels of capitalization and debt financing in North Carolina tobacco farm households, drove their dependence on low-wage seasonal and migrant labor, and put the majority of these operations out of business. Amid the rise of the national antitobacco movement and pervasive sentimentality surrounding the tacitly white and middle-class nuclear family, in a simplified story of plighted heritage, tobacco companies found a handy cultural resource for deflecting attention from international, industrial restructuring and fomenting a valuable political alliance with the grower population.

Motorists work their way to the gift shop at a museum that is now tenuously supported by grants, the tobacco corporate backing gone, and their impulse buys. They purchase postcards, old-timey recipe books, and little wooden tractors. How the museum represents tobacco history by freezing an idealized image of the past to make tobacco agriculture quaint, with no mention of the slave trade or the subordination of sharecroppers and tenants—not to mention public health issues—remains amenable to the cultural politics of rural white victimhood and innocence. This condescending form of appreciation celebrates tobacco agriculture only because it gives the false impression of a people without history (Wolf 1982). A different museum would not shirk the realities of history or of the present. This book is in many ways my attempt to make a museum of tobacco agriculture. My wager is that by not appreciating the realities of the history of the tobacco business in North Carolina, we are also unable to fully apprehend the subjective experience of being a tobacco grower and what growers have had at stake in this business over time. The local moral world where tobacco and tobacco livelihoods have positive cultural meaning is a historical world where those meanings are completely tied into the division of labor and the changing relationship of rural communities to the wider society and the state. My museum mentions Dwight Watson and attempts to contextualize his protest not as a protest to preserve a dying heritage but as an effort to save face, while going into the history and ethnography of how faces have been made in this neck of the woods.

Politics of Friendship

The most notable feature of agriculture in the Reagan years was the farm crisis caused by rising input costs and decreased crop prices. It was never as extreme in North Carolina as in the Midwest and the Great Plains, where debt loads, farm foreclosures, and family breakdown and mental illness associated with farm loss were more widespread (Ramírez-Ferrero 2005; Dudley 2000). But, across the United States, the farm crisis accelerated a dualistic industrial structure where big operations used poor market conditions and government relief frameworks to expand and recover, while small operations usually faced more limited recovery options (Barlett 1993).

Tobacco's special ethical and health issues make those factors, not structural problems that were similar to elsewhere in the country, seem like the cause of the farm crisis in states like North Carolina. Tobacco farm businesses went under, it appears, because smoking is bad for you and the smoking level had declined. This is a misleading argument. Exported tobacco leaf historically comprised a large proportion of total U.S. tobacco production (Dohlman et al. 1999; Finger 1981; Womach 2003). However, the crop control system for tobacco eventually distorted the price of domestic leaf and limited the competitive position of U.S. growers. With the waning of the tenancy system (see chapter 2), most domestic tobacco by the 1970s was produced through rental agreements between a landowner and an active producer. The grower paid annual rent for use of the land. On top of that, there was an annual premium to lease the "quota" tied to that land, the franchise or right to produce tobacco established in the New Deal. This built the cost of leasing quota into the cost of tobacco leaf production. Domestic exports began to sharply decrease by the 1980s, even as smoking was rapidly increasing around the world. Currently, more than half of the tobacco content of cigarettes made in the United States comes from foreign countries, while it was once almost all grown at home (Womach 2003). As the smoking rate decreased in Western countries, and as the costs related to public health–related litigation in these countries mounted, tobacco companies worked hard to open new markets and uphold their responsibility to shareholders by more profitably sourcing leaf from around the world (Brandt 2007: 449–72).

As part of the New Deal crop control program, the federal government purchased any domestic leaf that went unsold at the auctions at a guaranteed minimum price. This served as a kind of safety net for growers in exchange for their participation in a system of regulated supply, but it also helped to inflate leaf prices. Grower-managed cooperatives were established by the federal government to act as the local buying agent in this process. The co-ops took out loans from the U.S. Treasury to pay farmers a minimum price, and then ideally resold inventories for a profit during a leaf shortage to repay the loans. This is not how the program worked in practice, however. Declining export levels and increasing import levels meant that the co-ops were using taxpayer dollars to purchase more and more domestic leaf by the 1980s. And these inventories of unsold (usually undesirable) leaf were being held over year after year, with the loans going unpaid and accruing massive amounts of interest (Lehman 1982a, 1982b; *Wilson Daily Times* 1981). Public health groups and fiscal conservatives called for the termination of the imploding New Deal program. "Let the tobacco farmer stand on his own two feet," said a Republican congressman from Oregon, "as we are asking the welfare recipients and the poor and the needy and the minorities and all others in America" (White 1988: 57). Tobacco-state newspapers, politicians, and tobacco farmer lobbies responded by claiming that the program had to be maintained. Eliminating the quota system would lead, they correctly admonished, to the immediate consolidation of the largest farms (Lehman 1982a; Welch 1981). Prices would plummet, putting the most mechanized and efficient operations at a distinct advantage, and, absent any geographical restriction on where tobacco could be grown, production would become concentrated on a handful of operations in the most competitive counties.

Defending the tobacco program from criticism and warding off its elimination became the pet issue of Jesse Helms, a Republican senator, and Charlie Rose, a Democratic congressman, both from North Carolina. They were the two most important politicians in the tobacco farm policy debates of the 1980s, with Helms becoming the most popular—but perhaps also the most controversial and ultimately destructive—politician among tobacco growers (White 1988).

Under the leadership of Helms and Rose, tobacco-state politicians reached a compromise with those who sought to eliminate the tobacco program. Starting with the 1982 crop season, the tobacco program would function at "no-net-cost" to the Treasury. Theoretically, tobacco farmers would finance the guaranteed minimum prices for their unsold leaf through a three-cent per-pound assessment on all leaf sold at auction. These funds would then go to the co-ops and enable a self-sustaining safety net system (White 1988: 58–59). But this compromise only worsened things. There were no incentives for tobacco companies to purchase more domestic leaf, much less a critical discussion of the international free trade arrangements that facilitated tobacco leaf globalization. Leaf imports soared to new levels in 1983. The co-ops took on more leaf, nearly 35 percent of the entire crop going unsold in some regions, borrowing more than $500 million in Treasury loans to finance these purchases. In contrast, the grower assessments collected that year totaled only $29 million, less than 6 percent of what the co-ops borrowed. Consequently, the federal government intervened, more than doubling the assessment on growers for the following crop season to seven cents per pound. Together with the familiar characteristics of the nationwide farm crisis, such as rising input costs, this increase pushed thousands of tobacco farmers out of business that year (Lehman 1982b, 1982c; G. Stewart 1983; *Wilson Daily Times* 1982).

Charlie Rose introduced legislation in late 1983 that sought to resolve these structural problems in the tobacco economy and satisfy common interests. As a concession to tobacco companies, his bill would have lowered the minimum prices that the government established for tobacco each year, making domestic leaf more attractive to buyers and boosting exports. As a concession to public health groups criticizing the dependency of tobacco agriculture on the Treasury, the bill called for a substantial increase in the federal cigarette tax. This revenue would then be used to eliminate the rising assessments on growers and fund the co-ops, therefore shifting the financial burden for crop control and price stabilization onto smokers. As head of the Senate Agriculture Committee, Jesse Helms undermined this comprehensive legislation, preventing it from even moving to the floor of the Congress for a full debate or vote. In public statements he justified opposition to what seemed like a sensible approach by cynically warning that any effort to pass tobacco farm–related reforms would lead critics, referring specifically to "Ted Kennedy and other enemies of the tobacco farmers of North Carolina," to reject the compromise legislation and demand that the government cease subsidizing tobacco agriculture in whatever fashion (*Wilson Daily Times* 1983b).

This rhetoric masked the fact that fiscal conservatives within his party were vocal critics of federal support for tobacco agriculture. His opposition to a bill that would have brought immediate benefits for farmers in his state was perhaps also related to the fact that his senate seat was up for grabs the following year, in the 1984 election, when he could offer his own proposal and strategically leverage the worsening tobacco economy to get reelected. In the meantime, realizing that the urgency with which Rose proposed the bill was real, Helms tried to work behind the scenes, writing a private letter to President Reagan requesting that the administration implement a temporary tariff on imported leaf. It would be "harmful to me and other Republicans in North Carolina" if the problem of foreign imports was "not resolved quickly," Helms wrote to the president, "and the momentum will have been established to take me out of the Senate." The letter was leaked, leading to a senate subcommittee investigation of Helms for possible ethical violations in making a direct appeal for special treatment. Helms publicly dismissed the inquiry as a case of "politics against tobacco," blaming antitobacco and public health advocates in language that became common and predictable. Never providing any critical analysis of Helms's ethics or his foot-dragging, the *Wilson Daily Times* ran the headline that Helms "was only trying to help." For his part, Rose stated publicly that just limiting imports for a year was not reflective of long-term thinking, evidence, Rose said, that Helms was "playing politics at the very highest level with the future of tobacco farms" (*Wilson Daily Times* 1983c, 1983d, 1983e).

That Helms worked against the comprehensive reforms likely also had to do with his close personal and political association with the R. J. Reynolds Corporation, one of his primary financial backers. In the 1970s and 1980s the company was a major corporate sponsor in North Carolina and the second-largest cigarette manufacturer behind Philip Morris. It helped finance the relocation of Wake Forest University, Helms's alma mater, from its original location north of Raleigh to Winston-Salem, where the company is headquartered. In his opposition to Rose's legislation, Helms played up the issue of taxes. He claimed that higher cigarette taxes ultimately hurt domestic tobacco farmers, even though, as already noted, the complexities of the global leaf market meant that there was not a one-to-one equation between the domestic smoking rate and the level of U.S. tobacco leaf production. Representing taxes as detrimental to rural communities was rather a strategy of the tobacco industry. Tobacco companies have always vigorously opposed excise taxes on tobacco products (because this measure does reduce demand) and have touted the need to protect industry jobs as a justification. For example, internal company documents from R. J. Reynolds reveal that in 1993 the company mailed a form letter to federal officials. Supposedly written by an employee at the company, the letter stated:

> *Dear Senator Helms:*
>
> *I realize that funds have to be raised through excise taxes to support programs designed for the general good of the nation. However, I am upset that tobacco taxes seem to be the only source of funding many people in Washington look to. Why is this? . . . All I ask is that you fairly tax all goods and not cripple any one industry. As I work for R. J. Reynolds Tobacco Company, I have a vested interest in the excise tax. My job is at risk now and will be even more so if tobacco has to carry its unfair burden of the new taxes . . .*
>
> *Thank you,*
>
> *Franklin A. Stump, Jr.[1]*

In 1983, Helms portrayed the proposed tax hike as being potentially harmful to tobacco constituencies, even though Rose intended the legislation to stabilize tobacco farm businesses and eliminate their controversial dependency on the Treasury. A year later, an R. J. Reynolds executive sent Helms a memo thanking him for his opposition to increased cigarette taxes. "Naturally we at Reynolds," the memo reads, "are relieved that the excise tax on cigarettes will [decrease]. I know that you played a very important part in the negotiations . . . and I want to express my appreciation."[2] Because of his support for cigarette tax increases, Rose was depicted in much of the regional media as a suspicious partner of the constituencies and politicians that Helms labeled "enemies." In spite of his corporate allegiance, Helms positioned himself as having the best interests of even the smallest farmer in mind, and played to an abiding spirit of regionalism and hesitation about taxes in the rural South (White

---

[1] Legacy Tobacco Documents, University of California, San Francisco, http://legacy .library.ucsf.edu/tid/hyj51c00.

[2] Ibid., http://legacy.library.ucsf.edu/tid/tvd88d00.

1988). Here is what one tobacco warehouse owner from Wilson County told me during an interview:

> You have some politicians in this area who genuinely have the farmer interests in hand. But the companies have also been strong allies of these politicians. Jesse Helms, for example, was thought of as a tobacco god. In the 1980s, I was at farm meetings where Jesse Helms walked in and it was as if Jesus had walked into the life of the American tobacco farmer. He was the great champion of their product. The first sincere proposals that I saw came from Charlie Rose, who was a Democrat, and that did not fit with where most farmers were in terms of party affiliation. Lots of farmers were scared. Who were they going to turn to? There were a lot of antitobacco politicians in the Congress, folks like Ted Kennedy. And Rose was in their political party. Where else would you go if you were a tobacco farmer than to Jesse Helms?

Both politicians spoke to the press of the plight of farmers, but Helms did it in a way that involved polarizing language and hyperbole and the notion, promoted by Reynolds (see below), that tobacco farmers were like a family, part of a common group under attack, not simply one part of a multifaceted industry with economic interests that differ from those of tobacco companies. "There was a sense that we were all in it together," an active grower, a white man in his fifties, tells me. "Everybody was against you. Everybody was against tobacco. Jesse Helms was the one person who was really for us tobacco farmers." As an unreconstructed southern Democrat—Helms switched parties in the 1970s as a response to federal involvement in integration and other civil rights issues—he also spoke of tobacco in the context of a broader set of cultural and political issues that were said to victimize southern white people and reflect a liberal urbanite agenda. He fervently opposed feminism, gay rights, affirmative action, government sponsorship of the arts, and civil rights. As an icon of the Christian right, the appeal of Helms among tobacco farmers must be understood both in terms of his personal rhetorical power and the broad appeal of conservative populism in the South in the past decades (Black and Black 2002).

Helms popularized the notion that "there is no tobacco subsidy" (White 1988; *Wilson Daily Times* 1981). This was a little white lie that he used to both defend the tobacco program from critics and play up hostilities and fears about welfare. While fiscal conservatives attacked the tobacco program for being an illegitimate government subsidy, Helms insisted that it was something altogether different. Whereas grain farmers have historically received a direct subsidy payment from the federal government to increase their income, tobacco growers never did. But in a roundabout way, the government did end up buoying tobacco leaf prices and ensuring that no leaf went unsold. Even when the program went to the "no-net-cost" mechanism, where, supposedly, growers would themselves finance the program, the result was only deeper dependency on the Treasury. Besides, even absent any government support to boost leaf prices, recall from the last chapter the vast public resources that went to tobacco regions in the postwar decades to improve farms, disseminate state-sponsored agricultural research, and selectively finance rural modernization. Helms's insistence that "there is no tobacco subsidy" erased the vivid race and class biases that went into that work, masked the indirect but no less real system whereby tobacco leaf prices depended on government funds, and distanced tobacco farming from the stereotypes and stigma that, amid Reagan's war on welfare, defined words like subsidy, assistance, relief, and welfare.

Distancing government support for tobacco agriculture from stigmatized forms of social assistance involved homogenizing tobacco farmers as a group, since divisions within their ranks might confound the image of the deserving yeoman. A front-page article in the *Wilson Daily Times* in 1985 had the headline, "Even the Best Farmers Are Having Difficulty Coping." The reporter described the farm crisis as haphazard, impacting farmers regardless of their natural or historical advantages. "[E]ven Wilson County's most successful farmers say they have been hit hard by the failing federal tobacco program," the article stated. "The problems farmers face are . . . based on uncertainty, not on a lack of business savvy. . . . Skill alone won't get a farmer through these problems." This reporting was important for casting tobacco farmers as people who legitimately deserved government assistance, while masking the reality of uneven farm loss, which ensured that a decreasing number of farmers would actually benefit from it. "I'm sure it sounds awkward to the taxpayers that I should think they should help bail me out," a Wilson County farmer told this reporter. "But when I look at the money they have made through the years on the commodity I have been producing, I don't mind asking them to help out. We can't do it by ourselves" (Kendall 1985b). For his part, President Reagan "strongly opposed" the idea that the government ought to continue supporting tobacco agriculture since it would "impose," he stated, "significant costs to the taxpayer" (*Wilson Daily Times* 1985g).

The cultural image of tobacco farmers as not "subsidized" was essential for converting the fact that they were collectively in debt into the idea that they deserved further special treatment, and also that such treatment ought not to be publically marked or stigmatized because this constituency was characterized by hard work, undue hardship, and other indexes of national iconicity. "The man that's working out there now is getting whipped," one farmer told the *Wilson Daily Times* in 1982 after going under. "Everything got too high and the labor got scarce and

I couldn't afford to go mechanized. Everybody's gotten now to where they didn't want to do nothing as long as they could sign up and get food stamps" (Lehman 1982c). This grower blamed the failure of his business on state welfare programs and the imputed indolence of poor people. The newspaper quoted him. It did not provide any analysis of why he might feel this way, why the labor force might have in fact contracted, or how downward pressure on farms in the context of an international market shift led to increased competition and a need to mechanize (his undoing), as well as stagnant farm labor wages. In quoting him and leaving it pat, the newspaper helped frame farm loss as something that lazy black people inflicted on hardworking white people, who, "working out there," were distinguished from the sensationalized problems of the inner city. With reference to food stamps, as well as this tacit geographical differentiation, and given that black people have historically provided the bulk of manual tobacco labor in North Carolina, this discourse pits the tobacco farmer as the opposite of an "underclass" that is styled as black and illegitimate. The pursuit of entitlement and protection by tobacco growers thus reflected the racial stereotypes that have been part of the war on welfare and debate about social disparities in the United States.

Under the Influence

Helms got reelected in 1984. Imports again soared, and the co-ops purchased lots more leaf. Their debt to the Treasury now totaled $1.7 billion (*Wilson Daily Times* 1985f). Consequently, the assessment on growers spiked to an astounding twenty-five cents per pound in order to at least partially fund ongoing Treasury loans. The assessment amounted to 15 percent of the total price of tobacco leaf. A grower who netted about $30,000 from tobacco production in 1983 now netted less than $10,000 (Jernigan 1985). Thousands more farmers went out of business. "[This was] the roughest year I've ever had," one of these farmers from Wilson County told the local newspaper. "There are a bunch of sad people around here, and they are all losing big money. The assessment got all the profits this year. I can't keep running with it. I've lost enough money this year to have lived several years without working" (Kendall 1985a). Economic effects rippled outward. Many local agricultural equipment and products suppliers shut down (LaFey 1986b).

At the start of the growing season in 1985, there was talk that come the harvest in the fall, assessments on growers would double again to fifty cents per pound. This would have been the end of the line for all but the most mechanized and largest producers. Charlie Rose again proposed a legislative solution, now with a more appealing concession for tobacco companies. There would be further reductions in the guaranteed minimum price of tobacco. Tobacco companies would in turn agree to purchase all the leaf inventories held by the co-ops at moderately discounted prices, allowing the co-ops to repay at least part of their massive public loans. Meanwhile, lower leaf prices would incentivize tobacco companies to purchase more domestic leaf going forward and also increase exports. In addition, a new regulatory mandate imposed by the government would require the tobacco companies to purchase a minimum amount of domestic leaf, ensuring that the glut of heaps of unsold tobacco having to be purchased by the co-op would be avoided in the future. Rose again included a cigarette tax increase as the funding mechanism for making this tobacco program—the co-op system and the price supports—sustainable (*Wilson Daily Times* 1985a, 1985c, 1985f, 1985b). The USDA and the leadership at the tobacco cooperatives, who had been elected by growers, supported this plan. However, the tobacco companies did not. R. J. Reynolds claimed that the discounted and decreased leaf prices were still too high (*Wilson Daily Times* 1985d).

This stated explanation masked the company's motivation in getting the tax hike out of the legislation, which Helms eventually helped do. He proposed a rival reform package that was friendly to the companies. Under his plan, the sale of co-op leaf inventories would involve a much deeper discount than what Rose proposed, which would allow tobacco companies to purchase that leftover leaf at a 90 percent reduction, in turn reducing the amount that the co-ops could repay the Treasury. There was no excise tax to help fund repayment or to stabilize the tobacco program in the future. Helms basically asked the Treasury to swallow the loss on its loans (White 1988: 62–64). "The only people I see excited" about the plan, Rose remarked, are "the cigarette company representatives." Indeed, the tobacco companies were public about their support for this reform package, as they were eager to swoop up cheap leaf and avoid the tax increase (*Wilson Daily Times* 1985e). But R. J. Reynolds was also careful to imply that it was not using its influence over Jesse Helms to pursue special interests. In a press release from the company, it stated that it would now start to purchase more domestic leaf, seemingly out of goodwill for growers. The press release gave Helms the credit for encouraging this commitment and insisted that the company was not narrowly motivated by assurance about taxes. Here is a fragment of the release:

> Helms said Monday the company would not base its import cuts on assurances that federal excise taxes on cigarettes will not be increased. "I did not agree to any quid pro quo," Helms said. But Helms said he was confident excise taxes on cigarettes would not be raised this year.

In a recent White House meeting, Helms said, congressional leaders received an "ironclad commitment" from President Reagan that he would veto any efforts to raise the cigarette tax.

"I am delighted that they are going to decrease their use of imports," Helms stated, as the release continued. "I think tobacco farmers should welcome this." Rose had a different sentiment. "It certainly doesn't excite me, and I doubt it will excite many tobacco-state congressmen," he said. The industry favored voluntary company responses rather than government mandates for obvious reasons: voluntary actions could easily (and would predictably) change course in a matter of years. Hence, the press release concludes with a statement from a Reynolds spokesperson: "It's very hard for us to say emphatically we would continue this [meaning a preference for domestic leaf] indefinitely. We are very uncertain about what our economic condition is going to be in five years."[3]

Growers were not unanimous in their support for the Helms proposal. In one article from 1985, a tobacco farmer told the *Wilson Daily Times* that he "voiced" his "concerns" with the major tobacco corporations, which, the farmer said, "appear indifferent to the plight of tobacco farmers." Not all tobacco farmers "believed" the "manufacturing interests" when they said "trust us," another farmer told the newspaper. In still another article, the *Wilson Daily Times* quoted the president of the North Carolina Farm Bureau, who admitted, "There's a lot of feeling that [Helms] is listening to the companies and not the farmers."

Congress passed the Helms proposal that fall. He took credit for salvaging what he simply allowed to breathe a tad longer. As chair of the Senate Agriculture Committee, he was empowered to bring his reform package to the full Congress, where, with help from Robert Dole, a Republican from Nebraska and head of the Senate Finance Committee, it was buried in a bloated budget bill that no one could oppose. "In the final analysis," Rose said, the "companies and the senators cut a poor deal for the growers" (*Wilson Daily Times* 1985g). Because the grower assessment was about to explode, Rose, not wanting to appear to be one more enemy of tobacco, was forced into compliance and saw this bill as a lesser evil (White 1988: 62–68). The only farmers involved in public hearings in the Senate Agriculture Committee, which was overseen by Helms, were leaders of the Tobacco Growers Association, a faux grassroots political advocacy group organized and funded by the tobacco industry. During the public hearings, the group did a mass mailing to every tobacco farmer in North Carolina, urging support for the Helms bill. Rose was never invited to participate in the hearings (62–68).

---

[3] Ibid., http://legacy.library.ucsf.edu/tid/unb99b00.

The proposal had a devastating impact on tobacco growers. It altered the formula used by the USDA to calculate quota levels. Traditionally based on domestic consumption and leaf exports, the formula was now based on the stated purchase intentions of the major tobacco companies. Under the influence of R. J. Reynolds, Helms tucked this neoliberal kicker into what seemed on the surface to be a bill that preserved the government protectionism framework. About the Helms plan, the North Carolina secretary of the state Department of Agriculture said, "While I feel that the tobacco producer did not come out as well . . . as I hoped he would, this legislation has at least preserved the tobacco program for our producers." The North Carolina chapter of the Grange, a major national farm group, offered a similarly cynical endorsement: "We have some points we don't like and the companies have some they don't like. But we can live with it, and we hope it's a package that can save the program." (*Wilson Daily Times* 1985h, 1985i).

The new legislation did away with the threat of overproduction, and the companies were restricted to reducing their domestic purchases by 6 percent per year for the decade. After that, however, the sourcing was unrestricted. Tobacco companies were effectively in charge of the government tobacco program. Helms had done nothing to address the underlying structural conditions of trade that negatively affected the North Carolina tobacco economy or to contain tobacco companies in their understandable goal of further integrating international distribution and production. Over the course of the 1990s, their intensified sourcing of foreign leaf drove the program into the ground while deepening economic competition and desperation among North Carolina growers. These conditions of distress became the phenomenological basis for embedding plight as a powerful ideology of undue hardship and lost privilege, and a keyword that the tobacco companies could use to marshal the political support of the very growers they were putting out of business. Doubletalk about agrarian plight was just as calculated and duplicitous as the industry's collusive burial of scientific evidence about smoking.

Fistful of Tobacco

Tobacco farmers talk about pride. They brag about leaf quality, high prices received, bad weather overcome, and the preponderance of local knowledge and skills honed over generations, even in an era of mechanized production. This bragging is sometimes collective in tone, articulated in the third person. "We produce the best quality leaf in the world," a grower tells me in an interview. "We're not fooling around out here. I'm really good at what I do, and I'm proud of that, because it's hard to grow tobacco. People think farming is easy. It's not, much less tobacco farming.

You've got to know when to plant, when to harvest, how to cure the leaf. There is so much that goes into the business. And you've got to be a good manager." That these men are proud of their businesses and know-how is not surprising. Ethnographic studies of U.S. agriculture everywhere find pride to be a defining part of moral life for farmers, shaping how they see themselves, understand the worth and purpose of their livelihood, and identify as part of a social group (Ramírez-Ferrero 2005; Dudley 2000).

Realizing the cultural and moral importance of this kind of pride, public relations wizards at R. J. Reynolds decided to objectify it. Right when antitobacco efforts were coming together at the national level, the company took hold of this historically vital emotion and source of identity, turned it into a slogan, infused it with a spirit of defensiveness, and plastered it on billboards.

The company's "Pride in Tobacco" campaign was launched in the late 1970s and peaked in the early 1980s (R. J. Reynolds 1978a, 1982; White 1988). Internal company documents clarify that the purpose of the campaign was to use a positive image of tobacco to counter antitobacco efforts, especially in tobacco-producing states. The explicit goal was to generate "wider and more favorable coverage than the tobacco industry has enjoyed in many years" (R. J. Reynolds 1978a: 2–8). Along with the characteristic "Pride in Tobacco" bumper stickers, placards, and billboards (figure 3.1), the campaign involved press conferences and rallies in major tobacco markets like Wilson. In 1978 alone, the campaign's first year, there were more than 1,300 stories referencing the campaign in about 700 newspapers. Internal documents from Reynolds reveal that the campaign's audience was imagined as "industry elements." Although the images and media coverage were public, the aim was to reach an internal constituency of people involved in the tobacco business, although not formally embedded as company men. This group included "manufacturers, farmers, warehousemen, wholesalers, retailers and their suppliers." The goal was to encourage "people whose way of life depends on this important commodity," a planning memo states, to see themselves as having a great deal at stake in political allegiance to tobacco companies (R. J. Reynolds 1978b: 11). The company seems to have been aware that growers and these other groups were perhaps feeling the negative pressure of antitobacco politics and, with something important at stake in tobacco policy, were perhaps ideally positioned to influence it. By "demonstrating the economic importance of tobacco," an internal memo states, the company would become "the primary friend of the grower" among manufacturers, and growers could become a key constituency "to influence legislative and regulatory bodies" (R. J. Reynolds 1982: 1).

At the same time, internal documents show that Reynolds was clearly aware of the contradictions and problems facing growers, including the company's own shift to purchase more foreign leaf. In one document from 1977, entitled "Tobacco Grower Relations," the company's director of Corporate Public Affairs notes the potential for friction due to "the market price of leaf tobacco" and increases in imported tobacco, as well as a history of grower suspicions about the motives and interests of buying companies. The memo cites the need to confront these potential tensions between Reynolds and tobacco growers by emphasizing through public relations a need for "complete industry unity" in the face of the "health scare." The memo recommends the formation of a Tobacco Growers Information Committee within Reynolds in order to "improve" relations with growers and "provide the Company and the Industry with a legislative defense mechanism" (cited in A. Jones et al. 2008). The committee was one part of the rural public relations campaign that was thus conceived, a memo from 1978 states, as an "industry-wide campaign to create support for the nation's oldest agricultural livelihood," stressing "the economic importance of the crop to everyone associated with tobacco" and seeking "to unite these interests into a cohesive force that will help ensure all viewpoints receive a fair hearing when the industry and its people are threatened by anti-tobacco activists" (R. J. Reynolds 1978b: 11). Across tobacco-producing states, the company distributed information kits and brochures that described the economic contribution of tobacco agriculture to rural communities. There was data on the tax contribution of tobacco products. Brochures included "suggestions on how tobacco people can combat anti-tobacco groups." One of the most effective ways, the brochures noted, was to tell antitobacco people about the economic and cultural value of tobacco agriculture (R. J. Reynolds 1978a: 8). Even though tobacco agriculture has indeed embedded distinctive cultural values in producer regions and has been of great economic importance, it is crucial to emphasize here that these facts were being politicized in subtle ways, and the public health was portrayed as the main threat to these realities. Growers were coached to get preachy, thereby contributing free public relations labor for the company that was relocating their livelihoods offshore. The logo proclaiming "Pride in Tobacco" featured a hand clenching tobacco leaves and giving a thumbs-up. Growers hung signs on farm trucks and in farm shops. The company placed 180 billboards sporting the campaign logo along North Carolina highways (1978a: 8). The cultivation of defensive pride through this campaign no doubt contributed to why Helms, the political minion of R. J. Reynolds, was so liked by growers.

The campaign also involved the "Tobacco Center Concept." R. J. Reynolds identified eight tobacco towns and focused promotions there, with the goal of "[h]eavy emphasis" on "'Pride' visibility in local tobacco markets." This concept took advantage of the presence of influential growers, extension workers, and agricultural lenders and suppliers in key towns, including Wilson. Local committees of farmers and businessmen

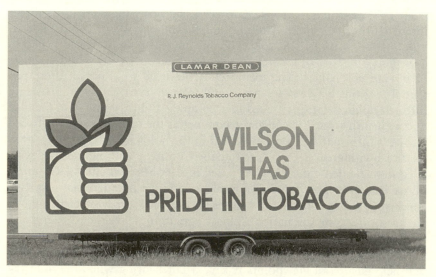

Figure 3.1. Billboard from the "Pride in Tobacco" campaign of the R. J. Reynolds Corporation, near Wilson, late 1970s. Photo by an unknown *Wilson Daily Times* photographer. Reproduced with permission from the *Wilson Daily Times*.

were established by Reynolds to administer company-sponsored community events like auction-hollering contests, essay-writing contests in public schools, tobacco festivals, animal and farm shows, local beauty contests, community barbecues, and historical reenactment activities (R. J. Reynolds 1982: 2–10). At free meals corporate reps made speeches that depicted the industry as a unified "tobacco family" (White 1988; R. J. Reynolds 1979). In the hands of Reynolds pride became a language game that tapped into popular sentiments and fears in rural regions and was linked to a strategic corporate agenda.

"The issues that surround smoking are so complex, and so emotional, it's hard to debate them objectively," a public newsletter circulated by the company in 1984 states, the "Pride" logo affixed at the bottom. It continues:

Over the years, you've heard so many negative reports about smoking and health . . . that you may assume the case against smoking is closed. . . . [We] think reasonable people who analyze it may come to see this issue not as a closed case, but as an open controversy. We know some of you may be suspicious of what we'll say, simply because we're a cigarette company. . . . But we have confidence in the ability of people to reason after they have been presented with all points of view. (R. J. Reynolds 1984: 1–2)

The campaign was an effective way to connect with growers. It organized growers into what the anthropologist Benedict Anderson (1983) calls an "imagined community," a fictive kinship among people who have no direct relationship but feel like a family. It was a vehicle for smuggling a strategic politics of public health and industry loyalty into what seemed simply to be congenial talk about pride and heritage. Use of the word *tobacco* played a key role. The campaign did not advocate pride in cigarette manufacturing. The logo's nondescript leaf clenched by a hand has farmers holding on for dear life, but, most important, clinging to something that is agricultural in nature, not industrial. The clenched hand is holding something good, a tradition, not a deadly product. Imagine a "Pride in Cigarettes" bumper sticker instead. The campaign created a constituency that was comfortable possessing a respectable and valuable heritage but that was led to respond to negative news reports about smoking and health as a personal attack.

The whole thing was ultimately tragic. An internal memo that circulated in 1978 among Reynolds brags about the success of the Pride campaign in fomenting loyalty among growers, while just a few pages later it mentions the company's favorable economic forecast given its massive expansion of leaf sourcing and tobacco-manufacturing capacities in the developing world (R. J. Reynolds 1978b). Reynolds was not the only company to connect with growers through public relations. Around the same time, Philip Morris launched a similar campaign that involved leadership training courses for select growers, company-sponsored retreats and vacations for growers and their families, and college scholarships for grower families. An internal Philip Morris memo from 1985 explains why they did this: "Assuming the deterioration of the grower-manufacturer alliance," the note states, "and there is good reason to believe that it has already begun, we must concentrate immediately and intensely on the necessity for building new coalitions and alliances." The note also states that reaching growers through positive public relations and corporate sponsorship was a viable means of "consolidating strength with congressional representatives" because of the power of senior southern politicians in the Congress (cited in A. Jones et al. 2008). In sum, internal documents from across the industry reveal that the tobacco companies were keenly aware of the structural problem of increased leaf imports and foreign production. Mounting evidence of the negative health effects of tobacco use added fuel to tobacco-control advocacy, although the tobacco companies used this evidence as an opportunity to divert blame for structural problems onto the public health and to foment deceptively gracious political alliances with growers. Factors intrinsic to tobacco agriculture, such as the cultural and economic value of the livelihood and limited diversification options for most growers, combined with the antigovernment ideology espoused in the tobacco company campaigns to create formidable challenges for tobacco control and allow the industry to increasingly move offshore without facing significant opposition at home (see A. Jones et al. 2008).

Farm Crisis

The next wave of farm crisis in tobacco regions started with Hurricanes Bertha and Fran, which devastated eastern North Carolina agriculture in 1996. Together with a worldwide leaf shortage, the weather-related reduction of domestic leaf precipitated a sharp increase in company purchases in 1997, a record year for North Carolina tobacco growers. To handle the bumper crop, there was an unprecedented wave of capital investment. Growers purchased bulk curing barns and automatic harvesters, costing thousands of dollars, to ready for higher production levels. It was as if tobacco companies were in cahoots with the weather to stage economic catastrophe, exaggerate expectations, and inflate farm debt, only to plummet purchase intentions in the years to come. From 1977 to 1997, the total share of world tobacco production in high-income countries fell from 30 percent to 15 percent, while it rose from 40 percent to 60 percent in Asia and from 4 percent to 6 percent in Africa (World Bank 1999: 58). The level of U.S. tobacco production was then cut in half from 1997 to 2004. Here I tell the story of how this happened, what the impact was, and why the responses to farm crisis, as in the previous decade, were limited and, to be sure, company friendly.

In 1998, North Carolina tobacco production dropped 16 percent, then another 18 percent in 1999 to the lowest level ever. In 2000, it declined by 19 percent, and then another 10 percent in 2003. All of this was the result of reduced company purchase intentions, which, remember, Helms had made the basis for putatively protecting grower businesses (E. Fitzgerald 1997a; *Wilson Daily Times* 2002). Leaf imports now accounted for an astounding 55 percent of the tobacco content of cigarettes manufactured in the United States (Capehart 2004c: 2). Tobacco growing just down the highway from North Carolina cigarette factories was more expensive to use than imported leaf, because free trade policies enabled global integration.

The international market shift stimulated intense competition among North Carolina growers. They depended on a stable production level to facilitate farm loan repayment and realize the full value of capital investment, ensuring that the new curing barns and harvesters purchased after the hurricanes, for example, did not idle. The still-existing New Deal program, which fixed minimum prices, disallowed farmers from competing with one another in terms of marginal cost and price points, so competition took place in the land and quota rental markets. Farmers scrambled to piece together more and more parcels of land, parcels carrying the franchise to produce more pounds of tobacco leaf. The rent price of land in tobacco states exploded (Brown et al. 1999: 11). More than 25 percent of the cost of production was going to nonproducing landowners in the form of rent, which substantially dented farm incomes. In 1996, tobacco farmers received an average profit of $667 per acre. By 2004, the average return to management dropped to a deficit of $750 per acre (Foreman 2006). Because of the combination of fixed costs and lower production levels, growers were now losing money on a crop that for decades far surpassed other crops in profitability. The operations most reliant on tobacco monocropping were the hardest hit. More diversified operations, which in eastern North Carolina have tended to be larger farm businesses that cultivate sweet potatoes and cucumbers alongside tobacco, leveraged cash flow from these other crops. Because large operations typically rent land from a larger number of landowners than do small operations, they were also able to maintain a lower average rental rate while nonetheless paying sometimes astronomical rent to certain landowners to take over quota that had been previously rented to struggling neighbors.

"Tobacco was the money crop for my family," David Vann, a small producer told me in an interview. "We didn't have sweet potatoes or cucumbers, just tobacco. When the quota got cut, everybody wanted to rent more land. Things snowballed. Farmers got like sharks in a bloody tank." David's tobacco output was cut from thirty acres to ten acres when a large grower outbid him on land that he had tended for decades. David was forced to auction his equipment and began to work for wages as the foreman on the farm that had outbid him. He makes a decent living, but he is no longer in charge, which affects him. He operates equipment, now works somewhat grudgingly, and complains that his neighbor was unfairly aggressive. "Friends were stealing each other's livelihood. I don't begrudge the landlord for taking the higher offer. But it doesn't seem fair, because small farmers couldn't afford to match those offers. Growers smile at each other around town. But they are trying to nab your piece of the pie."

As a result of the sharp decline in the tobacco economy, U.S. tobacco growers have received various forms of monetary assistance. They received special consideration in 1998's Master Settlement Agreement, which settled the various lawsuits brought against the tobacco industry by states seeking compensation for social costs related to smoking disease, with more than $200 billion going to the states. Perhaps as a political strategy to appease growers, the major tobacco companies involved in this legal settlement also agreed to provide growers with $5 billion. As with the other relief programs, this money went to active growers, and those who had already exited tobacco agriculture were left shortchanged. Growers also received assistance from the federal government, namely, $700 million in emergency and disaster relief appropriations in the late 1990s. These financial infusions definitely minimized the rate of farm exodus during the tumultuous market shift (Womach 2004b). Even still, the impact of the cash transfers was sometimes paradoxical. Since each active grower received an annual payment proportionate to the amount of the tobacco he produced that year, there was a clear incentive for growers to grow the size of their operations, even though tobacco profits decreased. In fact, the cash infusions were the new tobacco profits. Bigger farms got bigger checks, so bigger farms got bigger. In North Carolina, 28 percent of farm relief from the federal government in the late 1990s went to the top 1 percent of producers, who received an average payment of roughly $70,000 per year. The bottom 80 percent of producers received 15 percent of the funds, an average payment of about $500 per year.[4] Relief created the incentive and means for large operations to pursue land and quota acquisition as aggressively as possible.

Farm relief was a source of political controversy. The mostly black manufacturing workforce in tobacco towns, just as dependent on tobacco revenues as growers, did not receive compensation, even though there were also major declines in leaf-processing plant and cigarette-manufacturing jobs. Nor did farm labor receive public or private assistance, even though, likewise, farm wages only continued to stagnate and farm consolidation led to more rural unemployment and more seasonal and flexible kinds of work. So ignored were the hardships endured by farm labor that in all of my archival research in the *Wilson Daily Times*, I found only one article (2002) noting the impact of the farm crisis on the landless workforce and no critical commentary from the editors about the obviously partial system of reckoning who is suffering hardship and who is deserving of relief. To labor advocates with whom I spoke, the exclusion of these groups from government and industry responses indicates a degree of racial bias in these determinations. "The whole thing is about the grower," a labor organizer in North Carolina, a Mexican American woman in her twenties, told me in an interview. "Even though hardships for growers translate into all kinds of hardships for workers, there is the idea that workers do not deserve to be compensated. To understand this, you need to think about race. Who is the grower and who are the workers?"

---

[4] These data are taken from the Environmental Working Group Farm Subsidy Database and the statistical archive at the Center for Agricultural and Rural Development in Iowa.

Coalitional Politics

Although claiming to be friends of tobacco farmers, the major tobacco companies, including R. J. Reynolds and Philip Morris, used their political power to successfully oppose a farm relief package proposed by Senator John McCain in 1998. His bill would have directed more than $28 billion in economic development funds to historically tobacco-dependent constituencies, including both rural farming communities and tobacco-manufacturing towns. The funds would have come from either a cigarette excise tax or a direct assessment on tobacco companies. The legislation was an attempt to bring about comprehensive reforms in tobacco agriculture, assisting decimated communities while also addressing the basic structural problem of international competition. McCain's bill proposed to do away with the imploding New Deal program where tobacco leaf production rights were tied to the land and restricted by the quota system. A new system would involve production licenses like quotas, except they were to be owned only by active producers, so as to remove the leasing of production rights linked to the land from the cost of production. This would have reduced the price of domestic leaf and made it more competitive, while continuing to control production and protect the viability of small-scale operations through licenses that dictated the maximum that an individual could grow. This last aspect was also intended to prevent further growth of tobacco agriculture in the United States, which is something for which public health groups were lobbying. The bill also included a mandate granting the FDA regulative authority over tobacco products (National Institute for Tobacco-Free Kids 1999).

Despite the defeat of this comprehensive proposal, it indicated a rare but important political collaboration. Building on the momentum of the McCain bill, public health groups, most notably the Campaign for Tobacco-Free Kids, now endorsed policy approaches to support tobacco farm businesses and help farmers diversify away from tobacco. As tobacco companies were making political inroads in rural regions, public health groups began to see growers as potential allies, too. More than this, limiting competition and the scale of tobacco agriculture, and keeping domestic leaf prices high through a tax on cigarettes, made good public health sense. While high leaf prices elevated the cost of tobacco products and thereby helped to limit demand, public health groups also sought to have "fewer people depend on tobacco production, either directly or indirectly, for their livelihoods," given the overarching goal of vastly reducing tobacco use. This quote comes from a landmark report that was the result of a collaboration among antitobacco advocates, tobacco growers with different-sized operations—some large, some very small—and agricultural economists. The group was assembled at the behest of President Clinton, and its report, entitled *Tobacco at a Crossroads*, insisted that the two sides of tobacco, production and consumption, were "unavoidably linked." The report put forth a set of policy recommendations to control smoking, sustain rural communities, and facilitate diversification options all at once (U.S. Department of Agriculture 2001).

The report formed the basis of years of policy debate. Like the Mc-Cain bill, it called for the elimination of the existing quota system, cash infusions to growers funded by an excise tax, an incentive program to encourage crop diversification (growers who transitioned would receive additional compensation), and the ongoing support of domestic leaf prices subsidized by financial assessments on growers. It also recommended the licensing system that was part of McCain's bill to disallow tobacco cultivation from moving outside of traditional areas. There was also the call for the FDA component, as well as a recommendation to create economic development centers in tobacco regions and towns to promote job diversification and undercut the power of tobacco companies as employers (U.S. Department of Agriculture 2001).

Along with all the major public health groups, leading agricultural economists, and the elected leadership of the tobacco farmer population, President Clinton endorsed the report. But the major tobacco farm policy reform that was eventually passed—the Tobacco Buyout of 2004—did not include any of these recommendations. It was a classic case of a government committee making evidence-based proposals and politicians, beholden to powerful corporations and working with constituencies swayed by defining ideologies, instead legislating watered-down, almost meaningless, or rather dangerous policy.

Politics of Plight

Despite its innovative framing, which bridged the gap between the seemingly strange bedfellows of tobacco growers and antitobacco groups, the report was flawed. It spoke of the "crisis situation that has engulfed U.S. tobacco farmers and their communities." The recommendations were described as "sound public policy that can make a real difference in the economic plight facing tobacco farmers and their communities over the long term and that is in the best interests of public health" (U.S. Department of Agriculture 2001). All of this sounds good, except it also makes plight and hardship seem like universal conditions, replicating the story spun by the tobacco companies.

The report was a golden opportunity to address the uneven pattern of farm loss in the South. The "plight of tobacco farmers," the report plainly states, "has been caused by declining demand and rising costs" (U.S. Department of Agriculture 2001: ES1, ES4, 23). While this historical assessment rings true from one perspective, it fails to account for the fact that in many cases other factors besides market forces—factors intrinsic to southern agriculture, such as racial bias and uneven access to education and public resources, as well as the acute problem of intensified competition and land consolidation—also contributed to "plight." The idea of sociological differentiation in the farmer ranks was perhaps not conducive to the report's goal of government attention to and special financial compensation for the cultivators of a harmful crop. Rather than developing an alternative language to highlight the race and class structures that mediated how farm crisis was felt in tobacco states, public health advocates and other leaders involved in the report did not challenge the social construction of the tobacco farmer as part of a generic and homogenous group.

The myopia about race and rural class composition evident in the report is perhaps more troubling when one considers that it came together in the late 1990s at the exact moment that southern black farmers were litigating against the USDA for losses due to institutional discrimination in the distribution of public resources through the Extension Service (as discussed in chapter 2). A class action lawsuit, settled in 1999, involved nearly 100,000 black farmers, most residents of Mississippi and Alabama, about 3,500 from North Carolina. This was the country's largest ever civil rights litigation. The plaintiffs received $2.3 billion from the federal government as compensation for injuries and losses (Environmental Working Group 2004; A. Martin 2004; *New York Times* 2004). Remarkably, there is not one passing mention of this lawsuit, the disproportionate exodus of black farmers, or the historical weight of racial projects in whitening agricultural livelihoods in the president's report, which was published after the settlement.

I interviewed dozens of black farmers who participated in the lawsuit and others that had farmed in the past but chose not to participate. Many described how their grievances and hardships were compounded by a complex legal process. For one thing, the pool of eligible plaintiffs was underestimated by the USDA because of poor record keeping, and eligible parties were not always or quickly informed of their right to participate. Although the court mandated that the USDA undertake a comprehensive outreach initiative to inform the public about the settlement, there was considerable foot-dragging on the part of the agency. Consequently, thousands of black farmers came forward with claims of discrimination after the official deadline for filing grievances because the USDA had not reached them in a timely or effective manner. But late claims were only accepted if farmers could demonstrate that extenuating circumstances had prevented them from meeting the deadline. The very basis of the lawsuit, the inadequate and uneven service that the USDA provided to rural black people for decades, now redoubled as further discrimination and structural violence. On top of this, some tobacco-state newspapers ran articles and editorials that raised doubts about the legitimacy of the settlement and the reality of discrimination. Newspapers quoted black farmers who denied, at least to the white reporters, that bias occurred in their cases (e.g., E. Fitzgerald 1997b). Here is what one black farmer, now retired, told me in an interview:

> Of course white people say it never happened. If it did happen, then they had an unfair advantage. Every newspaper in North Carolina ran a story where one black farmer says, "No, nothing happened to me." But something did happen to them. The problem is that it's embarrassing to say it publicly, to tell a reporter, a white person, that you were disadvantaged.

The legal settlement was in fact based on an internal investigation, conducted and sponsored by the USDA, which found evidence of pervasive racial bias within the agency (Ginapp 2003; U.S. Department of Agriculture 1997). "I was heckled at the country store for filing a complaint with the federal government about bias that was happening right there in my county extension office," a black farmer, a small producer who stopped growing tobacco in the late 1990s but has managed to keep going with grains and livestock, told me. "The county agent told some of the white farmers. Then they ridiculed me for asking for a handout." His farm truck was keyed in the Piggly Wiggly parking lot, retaliation, he suspects, for involvement in the plaintiff class. The discourse that doubts the veracity of institutional discrimination, linked to acts of hostility, has a relationship to the silence about black farmers in the president's report. These are two distinctive ways in which the particularities of hardship that impact one segment of the population are abstracted into an image of uniform agrarian plight as something that impacts even the best farmers, as the newspaper had reported. This logic is crucial not only for delegitimizing the claims of black farmers, but also for legitimizing the idea that mostly middle-class, white farmers are themselves not seeking special treatment when they make claims on the state.

Many black farmers who sought to participate in the suit were turned down for one reason or another. Access was severely limited because the burden of proving injury fell on the injured black farmers. They had to provide written and official documentation demonstrating that the USDA responded to a request for farm loans or relief in a manner that was discriminatory and that a formal complaint was filed. When these pieces of evidence were not satisfactorily provided, entry to the settlement was denied, locking thousands out. Farmers seeking to participate also had to locate "specifically identified, similarly situated white farmers," as the USDA stated, so that individual cases could be compared to isolate race as the unadulterated factor of differential treatment. Complicating matters, the USDA refused to provide black farmers with requisite information about white farmers, citing privacy issues. According to a farm policy watch group, black farmers had to obtain this information on their own, tracking down a specific farmer in their county who applied for the same benefit program at the same time, with the same acreage, the same type of crop, the same credit history, and who had received a higher payment or better treatment. This is "a feat," the group states, that "the most sophisticated lawyer would not be able to achieve based on public information alone" (Environmental Working Group 2004). That black farmers have been disproportionately illiterate and had limited access to public education further compounded matters. And discussing issues with a white farmer might not be the most inviting opportunity given the skepticism and violence black farmers claim to have faced. By 2004 less than half of the compensatory funds had been delivered. Meanwhile, the USDA spent an estimated $330 million in public funds to challenge individual claims about discrimination and withhold compensation (Environmental Working Group 2004).

The ideal of a "similarly situated" white farmer reflects a cultural view of agriculture as a system of individual production units defined by quantifiable microeconomic variables. It also reflects a cultural view of race as a simple demographic characteristic that applies to individuals, not a context of collective experience (Lipsitz 1995: 381). The mandate to legitimize injury via individual comparison made racial discrimination a contingent rather than institutional feature of farm policy, happening to this individual or that individual, but not a social group. How is it possible to hold all other things except race constant when social segregation was an official state policy? Empirically speaking, all of the microeconomic variables that are part of the financial profile of any farm business reflect the impact of institutionalized practices.

More than one white grower privately admitted to me that they were aware of various forms of racial bias taking place in county offices. I learned of a large-scale producer who worked in conjunction with the county agent to access the financial records of struggling black farmers so he could conveniently offer to purchase their land (and the tobacco quota attached to it) at a discounted price. "That kind of shit happened all the time," a grower told me. "But the same thing happened to white farmers. I've had big farmers try to rent land out from under me. It's not just a race thing, it's a farm thing." Against this recuperation of an image of uniform plight, which falsely equates losses due to economic competition with hardships caused by institutionalized discrimination, black growers commonly reject the notion that the racial bias perpetuated at the county offices was limited to agriculture and frame their rural struggles as part of the broader freedom and civil rights struggles. "This is about something bigger," one black grower told me, "not just farming. People know about other stuff: the bus rides and the boycotts, all the 1960s civil rights stuff. That's all taught in schools. No one learns about what has happened to black farmers. But that's just as important."

Buyout

By 2001 tobacco growers widely supported the elimination of the New Deal program in order to end the quota system, stop the rental wars, and increase the competitive advantage of their leaf. The *Wilson Daily Times* (2001b) opposed this idea, fearing that more rapid farm consolidation would ensue. They were correct. Many small-scale and less capitalized producers also opposed the measure for this reason. Tobacco companies opposed the idea because the latest legislative proposal, the McCain bill, had entailed taxes and company payments, so they pushed for a drawn-out legislative debate in order to water down what the ultimate reform package would be (E. Fitzgerald 2003a).

This part of the story begins in 2002 with a heated senate race in North Carolina. Republican Elizabeth Dole was nominated to fill Helms's seat when he retired. Thirteen years prior, her husband, Robert Dole, authorized the bill Helms introduced, facilitating the process of offshoring, which brought about the complex economic pains in rural North Carolina that she was now claiming to hope to resolve via further deregulation. The Democrat challenger was Erskine Bowles, former chief of staff for President Clinton, who also supported a liberalization of the New Deal program, a project now referred to as a "buyout." Generic endorsement of this project became a prerequisite for all political hopefuls in North Carolina, indexing their support for growers as a community or kinship group (even though some producers didn't like the idea). There was no discussion about exactly what a buyout proposal would mean. In expressing a vague level of support, the candidates never specified a preference for the strong, comprehensive McCain bill or the weaker bills that were being proposed.

Nearly a dozen versions of buyout legislation emerged in Congress that fall. The common cornerstone was the direct cash transfer of billions of dollars to tobacco growers and landowners to "buy out" their historical franchise. All of these bills also endorsed a new production license model to replace the quota system. A few bills, including one proposed by the lame duck Helms, included the quite illiberal proposition of funding economic development centers and alternative livelihoods in rural communities in tobacco states. The high cost of the bills, ranging from $15 to $19 billion, limited their appeal in a Congress already criticized for excessive largesse in farm bills and influenced by resistant tobacco corporations (Capehart 2002; *Wilson Daily Times* 2004a).

In 2003, more bills emerged. In the House, a bill sponsored by North Carolina Democrat Bob Etheridge most resembled the president's report recommendations. It cost $19 billion. There were rural economic development centers, production licenses, and an assessment on tobacco corporations to fund the whole thing. Rivaling this version was a much more neoliberal bill sponsored by Mike McIntyre, also a North Carolina Democrat. It lacked the production licenses, therefore calling for complete deregulation of tobacco agriculture. It had no rural economic development centers. Nor was there a clear funding mechanism to pay for the cash transfers to growers and landowners. But it did include the FDA mandate, perhaps reflecting McIntyre's close financial ties to Philip Morris. By this time the company had begun to support buyout legislation, the only one to do so, but only legislation that included the FDA component. "By opposing a stand-alone buyout," the firm stated, referring to the need to incorporate this public health element, which, as discussed in chapter 1, was strategic for the company, "we believe we are standing up for the growers' interests. A stand-alone buyout can't pass; the votes aren't there. The only way to preserve the political viability is to keep the FDA linkage" (Keown 2003a; *Wilson Daily Times* 2004b). With minor modifications, and lacking an FDA linkage, this is the proposal that was eventually legislated, a far cry from John McCain's $28 billion proposal.

For its part, R. J. Reynolds had to justify its opposition to a buyout, which conflicted with its presumed friendship with growers. Why didn't Reynolds want to pass legislation that would benefit active producers when Philip Morris was on board? Reynolds claimed that the bill would actually harm growers because the buyout would be funded via an assessment on tobacco companies, thereby, the firm said, leading them to purchase less domestic leaf, a market strategy they were pursuing anyway. The company framed it as an unfair "tax" on tobacco companies, the proposal "totally unpalatable," Reynolds said, alluding to "an absolutely devastating consequence for tobacco manufacturers and their employees in North Carolina." The company's opposition to the reform deceptively implied that it favored trade frameworks to protect traditional industries. "R. J. Reynolds made a big deal about the . . . bill, saying they would lose jobs," a leading agricultural economist in North Carolina told the *Wilson Daily Times*. "But before [the bill] was introduced they laid off 40 percent of their workers in Winston-Salem" (*Wilson Daily Times* 2003; E. Fitzgerald 2003a).

With the clear competitive advantages that the FDA component would entail for Philip Morris (as discussed in chapter 1), Reynolds needed to decouple agrarian reform from this public health aspect while also seeking to reduce the overall cost of the buyout to tobacco companies. The key player would be Congressman Richard Burr, a Republican from Winston-Salem who was being groomed to eventually replace Helms. From 1998 to 2002, Helms received roughly $60,000 from Reynolds and Philip Morris each in addition to the untold thousands he received in the decades before. Burr was also funded by Reynolds. Public records show that he accepted roughly $350,000 in campaign contributions from Reynolds since his first run at Congress in 1998. But Burr's real concern has always been the growers. Articles from the *Wilson Daily Times* from 2003 find the congressman speaking about the plight of "my farmers" and the "smallest" farmers who have gone "bankrupt." As a member of the House agricultural committee, Burr advanced the corporate interests by opposing the Etheridge bill, the most supportive of agricultural interests, and echoed Reynolds's talking points in referring to the proposal as a "tax" (Keown 2003a, 2003b).

By the end of the 2003 legislative session, further lobbying from tobacco companies led to the removal of the FDA component. Public health groups were now vocal about their opposition to a tobacco reform bill that lacked this crucial feature. Philip Morris also withdrew its support, and it seemed evident that no reform would be passed. Reynolds and other tobacco companies had sponsored town hall meetings and rallies across tobacco states in which they politicized the FDA component as capitulation to antitobacco groups and a threat to farm livelihoods. I attended dozens of town hall meetings on the issue across North Carolina in 2004, some of which were organized and funded by the major farm groups and tobacco companies. "Keep the FDA off the farm!" This was the mantra in stump speeches and on bumper stickers distributed at the meetings. Thousands of farmers in attendance were told by corporate reps, politicians, and farm group leadership that FDA agents would be on farms doing inspections. Rumors circulated about food and drug regulators inspecting chemical application records and workplace and worker housing conditions. "There is enough regulation as it is," a farmer who I met at a meeting told me. "With the environmental regulations, all the records on chemical applications that we need to keep, and now they want the FDA on farms doing inspections. That worries me." Growers commonly told me at the meetings that the FDA agents would "make trouble." There was also a keen sense among growers that Philip Morris was uniquely supporting the FDA component as a means of limiting corporate liability. Some perhaps feared that liability, in extending further to consumers, would also backtrack onto farms. "The FDA is about health," a grower told me at a town hall meeting in Wilson. "That's something to take up with the companies. There is a lot of talk that the FDA thing will mean a new tracking system. So if a smoker gets sick they track that tobacco back to my farm. What I grow is a plant. It is a legal crop, not a drug." The *Wilson Daily Times* editors opined that FDA regulation would "disrupt" the tobacco farm business, which would be "shattered by tobacco's demise," but they didn't share any details as to exactly how and why this would happen (E. Fitzgerald 1996; *Wilson Daily Times* 1997a, 1997b, 2001a; Zuckerbrod 2004a).

Only a couple of the farmers I interviewed were vocal in their support for FDA oversight. They saw new quality control standards on their farms as the flip side of federal oversight over leaf imports and imported tobacco products. FDA regulation seemed to them like a way of leveling the playing field to some extent and hindering the flexible sourcing capacities of tobacco companies taking advantage of lax environmental and quality control standards in developing countries. Some growers also supported the FDA for its positive public health benefits. "It is a good thing for public health," a large grower contracted with Philip Morris tells me. "It is a good thing for smokers. Tobacco is a legal product and we depend on it. As long as it is legal, it ought to be regulated like other products to make sure that consumers are informed," an attitude that sounds an awful lot like what is found on the Philip Morris website. "I also see FDA as a way of taking some heat off of the farmers," he continues. "No one can say that we're part of an unregulated industry anymore."

The 2004 Election

In 2004, the buyout legislation was finally passed. It eliminated all price supports and restrictions on leaf production, depressing the price of domestic leaf by about 25 percent (Dohlman et al. 2009; Tiller et al. 2007). Whereas producers of other crops have long fought to safeguard subsidies, tobacco farmers widely supported the bill, their short-term interest in reacquiring market position meshing with the long-term aim of tobacco companies to liberalize and further globalize the industry. Built on neoliberal ideals, the buyout was intended to end government protectionism and improve the free-market competitive advantage of domestic leaf. Regional newspapers called the buyout a "miracle." A reporter for the *Wilson Daily Times* wrote that it was the result of an "invisible hand lining everything up." Tobacco state politicians scrambled to take credit for what one dubbed "the most important change in agricultural policy in this new century" (Beard 2004; E. Fitzgerald 2004).

The passage of the buyout was neither mysterious nor miraculous. It happened for a few concrete reasons. President Bush was up for reelection and North Carolina was an important swing state. The junior senate seat was vacated and, after losing to Dole in 2002, Bowles was after it, now running against Burr, whose earlier opposition to Etheridge's buyout proposal while a congressman conveniently set the stage for him to now make this his pet project, as Helms had done a decade earlier. Newspapers said whichever candidate could "get the buyout [would therefore get] the farmers' vote" (*Wilson Daily Times* 2004e).

The core recommendations of the president's report were no longer viable in a context of overriding corporate power and staunch divisions among tobacco companies and public health groups over the FDA component (Womach 2004c: 9). The buyout was now watered down enough so that Reynolds no longer held out. There was no licensing program to limit economies of scale and no excise tax on cigarettes to subsidize domestic leaf prices. The legislation that came out of the Republican-led House was more than $5 billion less than previous versions. The plan to fund the buyout via an assessment on tobacco companies was also shelved. The direct cash payments to growers and landowners, billions of dollars worth, would now be funded by the Treasury. The Campaign for Tobacco-Free Kids called the bill "irresponsible," "an enormous, undeserved gift to the cigarette companies [that] shortchanges small family farmers and provides an unwarranted windfall to the tobacco companies." The *Washington Post* called it a "handout" and chastised the Republican leadership in Congress for managing "to transform this worthy public policy into an expensive corporate handout, paid for out of the public till and without any public health benefit. [The bill] would not even protect the struggling small tobacco farmers in whose name it is being pushed" (cited in *Wilson Daily Times* 2004c, 2004d).

Public health groups urged Democrats in the Senate to refuse to authorize this proposal. They pleaded for a bill that upheld the recommendations of the president's report. The Senate passed such a bill, sponsored by Ted Kennedy. It funded a buyout of $11.6 billion, including more than $200 million in economic development funds for rural communities, all paid for directly by the tobacco companies. That version also retained a system of production licenses to limit the expansion of tobacco production, contain economies of scale, and ensure some kind of price floor.

Most important, it was the first time that either chamber granted FDA regulative authority. In Kennedy's bill, the two sets of issues that defined the debate for half a decade—public health and farm business—finally came together.

Two drastically different versions—one in the House, the other in the Senate—split down partisan lines, influenced by competing tobacco companies: Reynolds had its hands in the pockets of Republicans in the House, especially Burr, while Philip Morris held sway over much of the Senate. A joint committee sat down to hash out a compromise version for a vote in the full Congress. A media campaign of radio and print ads, sponsored by a dozen religious and public health organizations, as well as tobacco grower groups, blitzed rural North Carolina with a positive appraisal of the senate version. If "those who represent tobacco-growing states work with those who support FDA regulation," the campaign announced, "we cannot be stopped" (*Wilson Daily Times* 2004g, 2004h, 2004i).

Republican Dennis Hastert, the Speaker of the House, appointed Burr to serve on the joint committee. This was clearly a motivated appointment, given Burr's hopes of claiming credit for a buyout in his senate run. Leading up to the committee meetings, Burr traversed North Carolina, stumping to tobacco growers. He told them that tough compromises and work would need to be done to satisfy politicians, much like Helms had used cynicism and the threat of reprisal to convince rural residents that in fact what was in their best interests should not be pursued. To a crowd of several hundred who were gathered at the regionally famous Bill's Barbecue in Wilson (a meeting sponsored by Universal Leaf Tobacco Company, which, like Reynolds, was a vocal opponent of Ted Kennedy's version), Burr said, "I don't buy the fact that you have to have FDA regulation, but I will accept it at the end of the day." But Burr surely knew that the FDA would drop, given the lopsided composition of the joint committee (only six of the eighteen appointees were Democrats) and his leadership role on it. He came across as compromising at all costs, all for the benefit of the grower, even though what was happening backstage was benefiting his corporate backers (Stair 2004; Keown 2004a; Lillard 2004; Mooneyham 2004).

Twice in the joint committee Burr, with three other tobacco-state Republicans, voted against a package funded at $2 billion more than the House version because it included an FDA mandate. Those votes kept that money from flowing from tobacco companies into the hands of growers in the tobacco states. North Carolina's tobacco growers lost nearly $800 million as a result. "There is no excuse for Richard Burr to refuse to stand up to the special interests," Bowles said. When the final bill emerged out of the special committee, Kennedy threatened a filibuster because it was so appallingly geared to appease Reynolds. But there was no stopping this bill. Republican leadership channeled the spirit of Helms. Just as Helms had done in 1985, the 2004 buyout legislation was tucked into the massive "omnibus bill," which contained multiple pieces of legislation, tax breaks, and programs appealing to myriad interests, avoiding the possibility of a filibuster and assuring support throughout the Congress (Crustinger 2004; Zuckerbrod 2004c; Holmes 2004). The final bill authorized the transfer of roughly $10 billion from tobacco companies to tobacco growers and landowners. Having the tobacco companies, as compared to the Treasury, fund the complete deregulation of tobacco agriculture was the only remotely compromising dimension of the bill.

Helms and Burr: the first time it was a tragedy. Now, with no criticism from the tobacco-state newspapers, no critical analysis of how Burr helped to dilute the bill and shortchange North Carolina communities, it was a farce. Two Republican senators, both from North Carolina, both backed by Reynolds—it is as if decades of political wrangling, the two buyouts, 1985's fire sale for tobacco companies and 2004's liberalization of a globalized industry, and this pair of politicians, having played a defining role in shaping each moment's outcome, had been wonderfully orchestrated just so one might cite Karl Marx: "all great, world-historical facts and personages occur, as it were, twice" (1972: 594).

On the eve of Election Day, a full-page ad appeared in the *Wilson Daily Times*, urging "Fellow Friends of Tobacco" to cast a vote for Burr (*Wilson Daily Times* 2004j). Paid for by various individual and corporate supporters of the Burr campaign, the lengthy appeal was cosigned by a litany of tobacco growers. These were the recognizable proper names of mostly large producers around Wilson County. Most of them were Reynolds contract growers. The next day Burr won the senate seat vacated by the retirement of Helms. "Each of us who make our living from tobacco owe a debt of gratitude to Richard Burr for his leadership in getting a tobacco buyout passed," the newspaper ad stated.

> The buyout saved countless tobacco farmers from losing their farms. For years, tobacco farmers have been promised relief from Congress, but Richard Burr was the first to deliver for North Carolina's farmers. ... The tobacco buyout has been called a legislative miracle by farmers and Congressmen alike. Tobacco's greatest friend, Jesse Helms, said that it would have been the toughest bill he ever could have passed. Jesse Helms also said that it would not have happened without Richard Burr's leadership. (*Wilson Daily Times* 2004j)

Figure 3.2. Cartoon published days after the buyout legislation was passed. *Wilson Daily Times*, October 14, 2004. Reprinted by permission of the *Wilson Daily Times*.

A Certain Key Figure

This chapter has examined the political influence of the tobacco industry in the lives of North Carolina growers since the 1970s. This particular constituency, which supported economic protectionism and the preservation of the New Deal program in the Reagan era, desperately sought its elimination two decades later. Understanding this change requires an analysis of the social context in which popular support for market liberalization was established. The American Studies scholar George Lipsitz insists that such allegiance to neoliberal policies does "not exist in a vacuum." It is fomented in "a culture and set of social relations that make them seem natural, necessary, and inevitable" (2006: 455).

Part of my analysis points to economic desperation as a reason why tobacco farmers largely supported liberalization. The role of corporate strategy and an inaccurate media also contributed. Tobacco-state politicians never pushed back against the tobacco companies and were the very mechanism for delivering a neoliberal fantasy to the world's most harmful industry. Tobacco companies were savvy so as not to seem to ad-

vocate for a bill that pulled a safety net out from under growers. They indirectly encouraged support for a neoliberal bill by promoting suspicions
about government, blaming public health for farm household hardships
and even construing public health groups, which endorsed the comprehensive president's report, as the reason behind the need to dilute the bill.
Far-reaching reforms like Charlie Rose's proposals in the early 1980s or
the collaborative efforts of the late 1990s were made to seem like dangerous partnerships with enemies. The experience of complex realities of
farm loss among growers were structured by the social construction of "a
certain key figure" or "nodal point" (Jacques Lacan's *point de caption*),
which became a unified threat (Žižek 1989: 72, 87). Fictive kinship was a
key cultural resource whereby tobacco corporations fomented allegiance
among growers and pushed this group to feel distinguished from stereotyped others and threatened by the public health.

The philosopher Theodor Adorno's concept of "exact fantasy" is
helpful for understanding the popular support for neoliberalism in the
grower ranks. It refers to an ideology that has a dynamic relationship
to empirical realities, one that does not just obscure how realities are
perceived and discussed but also compounds material conditions in a
feedback loop (cited in Buck-Morss 1977: 86). Keywords like *pride, heritage, plight,* and *family* accrued powerful ideological meaning, steering
growers away from a view of the contradictions that existed between
the tobacco companies and them and toward a familylike loyalty that
provided some sense of security in the face of acute economic calamity.
Why these keywords became so meaningful among growers has to do
with the real effects of international leaf-sourcing practices. Plight was
an ideology that was also "actively lived and felt," as the literary scholar
Raymond Williams might say (1977: 132). For example, the "Pride in
Tobacco" campaign took advantage of the fact that growers did and still
do have pride in tobacco, and this has been at stake in the threat of farm
loss. Reynolds tapped into something real and definitive in the moral life
of tobacco farmers and family members, literally playing with people's
emotions. Tobacco companies took hold of this sense of pride and the
abiding politics of race and regionalism that came out of the Civil War
and encouraged a protectionist attitude in which allegiance to the tobacco industry was like an act of familial membership and a key response
to hostility against southern white families and undeserved government
assistance for a stigmatized underclass.

The main component of the buyout was direct cash transfers to eligible recipients. These payments did nothing to challenge the distribution
of agricultural livelihoods in rural regions or redress the problem of farm
loss that had been so devastating in the preceding decades. Only active
farmers received payments. Those who had gone out of business were

not eligible. Most of the money went to landowners anyhow, many of whom were absentees who had no direct involvement in tobacco production except in renting their land (and its quota) to growers. Of the nearly half a million recipients of cash transfers, about five hundred individuals received more than $1 million each. The bottom 80 percent of recipients received about $5,000 each. Proponents justified this payment schedule in terms of private property rights. "If you acquired more tobacco quota through the sweat of your brow," the North Carolina Farm Bureau, one of the bill's most vocal advocates, said to the *Wilson Daily Times*, "then you are entitled to more of this buyout money" (Shreiner 2004). This equation of hard work and private property neglects the historical reality of how tobacco land was acquired and consolidated over time.

Of course, many growers and landowners acquired land through entrepreneurial efforts. But a common mode of acquisition was inheritance. "We worked hard in tobacco," a middle-aged lawyer from Raleigh told me in an interview. Like many other absentee landowners, he acquired tobacco land through an estate and rented it to producers in Wilson County. "The payment I receive will help pay for my kids to go to college. I see it as a heritage, something we worked hard for, and now it's being passed on to keep supporting our family." This common justification overlooks the fact that his family did not farm in any active way. The tenant families that did most of the manual labor were excluded from the buyout payments because they owned no land. The language of heritage also makes quota ownership seem natural. In fact, tobacco allotments were created out of thin air in the New Deal. The buyout thus effaced the history of land distribution in the post–Civil War era leading up to the New Deal, with questions of how land wound up in whose hands and who owned the legal rights to produce tobacco dissolving into a story about birthright, heritage, and family.

North Carolina received about half of all buyout payments, $3.9 billion transferred to 76,000 residents. Media accounts heralded this as a windfall for the state economy. Yet the idea that cash transfers simply turn over into local economic growth is misleading. Economists predicted the modest creation of 3,000 new jobs for the state, which pales in comparison to the 16,000 new jobs that would have been created had a stronger bill, such as the McCain bill, been legislated. There is no evidence that the money that went to landowners has been spent locally rather than invested as capital outside of North Carolina. My interviews with growers suggest that cash is being used to repay farm loans and invest in new farm equipment, often through local lenders and agricultural suppliers. Many growers also indicate they invested the money in stock markets, with the recipients of very large sums establishing trust funds for their children, hardly the ideal of compensating struggling businesses for hardships or helping to diversify the regional economy. No growers told me that they used the money to improve labor camps. Nor did recipients see the transfers as a means of exiting tobacco production in favor of another cash crop. The transfers were basically used to support the retirement plans of landowners and aging growers or to enable active growers to further mechanize their operations to increase global and local competitiveness. With no restrictions on the use of the money, and no incentives to diversify crops, the buyout undermined the central goal of the president's report to phase out tobacco production and create more sustainable livelihoods. The legislation even diminished public revenues and undercut local funding for the social infrastructure. Wilson County lost about $200,000 in annual tax revenues because the eradication of quota lowered the value of farmland. The total value of real estate in the county was immediately reduced by about $25 million upon the passage of the legislation. "That's a pretty significant impact," the county manager told the *Wilson Daily Times*. "It would be hard to absorb a loss like that without cutting somewhere else. It would probably mean a reduction in some other expenditure area to make up for it" (Zuckerbrod 2004b; E. Fitzgerald 2003b; Keown 2004b; *Wilson Daily Times* 2004f, 2005). These losses might have been remedied had the legislation taken into account such impacts, included funds for local economic development centers, or entailed a more equitable means of compensating people—not just growers, but also workers, warehouse people, farm lenders, and retailers—who have been involved in and dependent on the tobacco industry.

In fact, the legislation created a new set of uncertainties and challenges for growers. Tobacco had been geographically frozen since the 1930s. Now tobacco can be lawfully planted anywhere—on those same plots of land, on nearby lands, in the front yard or garden, or in a faraway state, like Texas, California, or Kansas. Geographical liberalization led to even more farm loss and more rapid farm consolidation than in the immediate buildup to the buyout and the complete reorganization of the tobacco agriculture landscape. Farm loss has been disproportionately higher in regions with less-ideal soils and less-mechanized production, such as Appalachia. In 2005, the first crop year under the new legislation, more than 50 percent of all growers in those areas exited. Aging growers who retired with the buyout accounted for the bulk of those who got out of farming, and they now rent their land to active producers or are selling it off for development. Others were forced out earlier than planned because of new challenges in a free-market system (Capehart 2004b; Dohlman et al. 2009; Snell 2004; Snell et al. 2008). In contrast, eastern North Carolina has seen increased levels of production, a new wave of capitalization, and the consolidation of many farms. This new world of tobacco leaf factory farming—the advantages and challenges for active farmers and the impact on the farm labor workforce—is a key theme of the second half of this book.

More than anyone else, the key political figures celebrated as the heroic saviors of the tobacco family, Helms and Burr, enabled the current configuration of tobacco agriculture in North Carolina, which is characterized by industrialized farms, intense corporate power, a preference for defensive responses when it comes to the legitimacy of tobacco farm livelihoods rather than potentially more fruitful and profitable alliances with the public health, and widespread unemployment in decimated tobacco regions. They received the praise, but it was their actions that led to the steady decline of North Carolina's tobacco industry. Growers and those who have supported these politicians might not like these facts, but they are the facts. Helms and Burr lied to their constituencies, advanced the interests of a criminal industry, enacted policies that have kept public resources out of the state, and limited the possibilities for economic diversification and growth in rural regions and tobacco towns. Where are the editorials in tobacco-state newspapers that complicate the image of the enemies of tobacco by pointing to the work of these figures? Why have tobacco-state newspapers been so silent when it comes to the role of these political monsters in helping to hurt the state's economy, disadvantaging working-class populations and marginal farm families, to be sure, but also creating conditions for unprecedented corporate power over active producers?

PART II

INNOCENCE AND BLAME IN AMERICAN SOCIETY

Chapter 4

Good, Clean Tobacco

ECONOMIC RESTRUCTURING IN THE TOBACCO INDUSTRY induced changes related to how growers manage their businesses, interact with and talk about the farm labor workforce, and derive symbolic and material worth from tobacco farming. With the Tobacco Buyout of 2004, discussed in chapter 3, the government distanced itself from leaf production. Growers are at the mercy of cutthroat companies with flexible international sourcing mechanisms. The traditional marketing system for tobacco (public auctions at locally owned warehouses) has been dismantled. The new system operates on one-year private contracts between growers and tobacco companies. Temporary contracts are now the only way to market tobacco, and they give companies unprecedented control over production. The ongoing critique of the industry by the antitobacco movement and the expansion of the government's regulation of smoking also influence how growers talk about the tobacco business and their own moral worth, both as members of the national community and as parents. This chapter and the next are about how structural changes in the tobacco industry, the intensification of corporate power on farms, and the societal problematization of smoking and health play out in the lives of North Carolina tobacco growers and workers.

To coincide with the FDA bill passed in 2009, which, as discussed in chapter 1, includes the potential for the development of potentially reduced-risk tobacco products, Philip Morris's grower contracts include stringent quality control standards aimed at producing a "good, clean" product. For example, bales of tobacco leaf must be free of "trash" (nontobacco materials) and register only moderate levels of certain carcinogenic agricultural chemicals. Philip Morris can cancel the contracts of noncompliant farmers, effectively putting them out of business, and says stringency makes tobacco safer for consumers. This is part of the company's effort to induce the profitable illusion of a "safer" cigarette while at the same time reconfiguring itself as a kind of public health advocacy group.

When analyzed at the farm level, these presumably health-driven industry changes involve a morass of paradoxes. Contracting fosters fragmented workplace conditions where various problems cluster and thrive. Prices are tightly ratcheted to fully mechanized production methods, which has pushed many farmers out of business, enabled further farm consolidation, and deepened dependency on low-wage seasonal and migrant labor. Contracting makes farm businesses less stable and disciplines and partly deskills farmers while also promoting company loyalty. Local cultural values of independence and pride are challenged as growers are reclassified as service providers who are part of corporate teams. Many active growers increasingly share a sense of economic insecurity and subordination with the seasonal workers they employ; however, these differently situated actors often respond to insecurity through antagonized interactions and assertions of authority in the context of a continuously racialized workplace hierarchy. Drawing on broad cultural stereotypes, growers commonly associate migrants with "trash," which reflects a local biopolitics of community and national belonging that aligns with Philip Morris's push for "good, clean" tobacco and hampers efforts to rectify health and housing problems that affect migrants.

In my analysis, *safe, clean, risk,* and *trash* are keywords. *Clean* and its opposite, in this case, *trash,* denote qualities associated with the product on tobacco farms but readily become associated with workers. Mexican and Latino migrants, along with other immigrant and minority groups, face stigmatization in many forms, including institutionalized discrimination, state surveillance, government neglect, racial segregation, and the promulgation of negative stereotypes in the media. Given the ethnographic focus of this book, my emphasis is on how stigma is manifest on a local level among growers and other "native" North Carolinians influenced by these widespread trends. Stereotyping and blaming in this rural region, I argue, reflect a local practice of stigmatization that is galvanized under the weight of rapid industrial restructuring. Tracing stigma's social course highlights how biocapitalist activities can compound social dilemmas for certain groups despite—or because of—emergent ethical and biological interests claimed by corporations. Workplace antagonism also reflects the trickle-down effects of the negativity that surrounds smoking on a national stage. Feelings of blame felt by growers as a result of their participation in the tobacco business intersect with their experiences of financial pressure and instability to yield defensiveness and the displacement of blame as common social strategies.

Tobacco Talk

There is remarkable commonality in how individual growers talk and think about smoking. A stock script involving several patterned lines of defense exists. Only a handful of the growers I met vehemently deny that smoking is harmful. This is far more common among older growers and retirees. For many in this aging cohort, tobacco is only one area where the government has overreached and where science is manipulated by a liberal agenda, alongside climate change, evolution, and multiculturalism. This view represents a mix of libertarian values, the hyperbole fueled by conservative talk radio and the idea, which goes back at least as far as the Reconstruction, that the South is under attack. "I tell you," a grower told his local newspaper in 1990, "I've got about as much use for the Surgeon General as I've got for flying a kite. People pay no attention to that man in North Carolina" (Bivens 1990: 1). This linkage of tobacco with individualism and agrarianism was promoted by the tobacco industry for decades, as seen in the Marlboro Man campaign (Brandt 2007: 261–64).

Most growers now affirm the science about smoking and health, while also emphasizing the importance of education. "The older generation was different," says a grower in his early sixties, reflecting the common sentiment of baby-boomer growers.

> Being honest about smoking, that's the best policy. I admit smoking is bad for you. Some farmers say it's all a bunch of lies. But those of us out here farming right now, we don't adopt that old way of seeing things. I talk with my children about smoking. But we are producing a legal product, just like any other business. Do I want my children to smoke? The answer is no. Do I think other people have a right to smoke? Yes. When my children are of age it will be their right to make that decision. What I can do as a parent is to educate them and that is what my wife and I do.

The shift in the tenor of grower attitudes about smoking reflects the influence of public discourse. Honesty about smoking risks became politically expedient in the 1980s amid criticism that the federal government should stop subsidizing tobacco agriculture. Senator Charlie Rose, seeking to preserve economic protections for tobacco agriculture (as discussed in chapter 3), routinely said, "I don't smoke; I don't want anyone in my family to smoke; it'll kill you" (White 1988: 58). Tobacco-state politicians used a seemingly apolitical language about good parenting and wholesome families to argue that the tobacco business is as legitimate as any other business. By the 1990s, even though some tobacco-area legislators such as Jesse Helms remained tobacco industry allies, agricultural-based interest groups and state agronomy officials reacted to national-level changes in tobacco attitudes and policies by shifting away from efforts to refute public health science and contain public health measures toward a neutral position on tobacco control (Sullivan et al. 2009a).

   Likewise, acknowledgment of the health risks of smoking became common in the tobacco grower population (Wilson et al. 2004). Cynthia Kettle, the wife of a tobacco grower and an art teacher, affirms the smoke-free campus policy at the public high school where she works. But she felt chided by a school assembly focused on informing students about drug use, which lumped tobacco with illicit drugs.

> I know smoking is bad for you and I don't smoke. But our livelihood depends on people smoking. That's a fact. But it's not something that I lose sleep over. This is a legal product. It is for adults. I do have a problem with how the companies advertise to children. But I felt like the school attacked my family. Our kids learn that tobacco is in the same category as cocaine. They come home and wonder what is wrong with our family. We explain the history. We tell them about how we grew up on tobacco farms, that tobacco is part of our heritage, and that people have lost respect for it. We also talk about health and making smart decisions. I hope they will not smoke when they are adults. I really discourage it. But I've got to say that it's ultimately their choice. There are a lot of things that are dangerous, and what I can do as a parent is provide my children with information and skills so they can make good decisions.

Like many active tobacco growers, Cynthia emphasizes tobacco's important role in the region's and the nation's economy and talks about cultural property or heritage. "Tobacco is not all negative. It has done a tremendous amount for this country," a grower who does not smoke tells me. "There is no house in North Carolina that does not have some tobacco money in it." He talks about the hypocrisy of a government that derives much tax revenue from tobacco products and the thousands of jobs still linked to tobacco production in the United States. While the idea of heritage helps to frame tobacco in a favorable light, individuals in these farm families are also realistic about tobacco. "Yes, there is a heritage component, but at this point," a grower tells me, "this is a business just like any other. It is about profit, and if there is not profit in it, then we're not going to do it." Yet Cynthia does not defend tobacco in terms of economic contribution alone, or by retracting into the seemingly antiquated regional agrarianism, or simply in reference to heritage; rather, her justification for the tobacco business is a mixture of factors, and prominent among them is the notion that tobacco—both production and consumption—are family matters.
   Members of tobacco farm families feel attached to aspects of the vocational identity and class standing that were consolidated through the state-sponsored rural modernization project of the postwar decades.

They perhaps also feel "underdescribed" (Berlant 1997: 2) by the label of "tobacco producer," as if all that they are as members of the nation is explicable in terms of their contribution to a vilified industry. This ambivalence about livelihood helps explain tobacco farm families' claims that their business is legal and normal and unproblematic and that they are just like other mainstream farm families who are trying to make a living off the land. Their involvement in tobacco farming, a potentially delegitimized kind of work, is reconciled in talk about meanings of citizenship that are more broadly construed. Cynthia claims a social identity in terms of what one does in the family more than in relationships throughout the wider society and economy. The dominant theme of parenthood helps frame an industrial tobacco business as something that simply puts food on the table, pays the bills, and maintains a family, rather than as a means of making profit or procuring class standing in society. Tobacco farming is "our heritage," but also "our business," suggesting its primacy in the household economy, in spite of the fact that her salary as a schoolteacher has in various years comprised a majority of their income. Nor does she claim that education or mentoring is her heritage, even though her two sisters are also schoolteachers, as were their parents.

Cynthia basically says that tobacco is not a crop that they started to grow for monetary gain alone, but that there is a backstory here, and tobacco consumption is lawful. In some sense, she is arguing for an understanding of tobacco as an "embedded" commodity culture (Polanyi 1957). This is also a claim about not having chosen to do anything wrong and about living life as an unmarked citizen, "normal" in other words, thus lacking the negative distinction that would pigeonhole tobacco farmers. "My husband and I like to go out to eat on the weekends," Cynthia says later in the interview. "Sometimes we drive into Raleigh, only an hour. We might catch a show or a movie. We don't like to be around smoking. So we're just like everyone else in that regard. We sit in the nonsmoking section."

Defending tobacco as a means of seeming normal and identifying with the exit culture of suburban sprawl and an imagined baby-boomer generation characterized by middle-class consumption patterns and signs of distinction (Ortner 2003) is sometimes the flip side of subtly distancing oneself from scenes of the abnormal and the classless. In the social text of local moral defenses for tobacco, talk of good parenting and mainstream lifestyles traces a faint racial divide, the self-making and the distance taking, which plays out through intertextual references to geography, blameworthiness, and legality, and becomes vivid when tobacco is contrasted with illicit drugs.

What Would Jesus Do?

Given the uncertainties about the long-term sustainability of tobacco agriculture, diversification away from tobacco was widely promoted by agronomic experts in North Carolina and other tobacco states in the 1980s. The *Wilson Daily Times* ran dozens of articles on alternative crops. By the 1990s public health groups were advocating for federal investment in economic development in tobacco-dependent regions, most notably in the president's report discussed in chapter 3.

Although recent economic pressures in the tobacco business are changing attitudes about diversification (Beach et al. 2008), social surveys conducted in the late 1990s found that the vast majority of tobacco farmers never expected to discontinue tobacco farming for reasons other than retirement. There was never a widespread transition to other crops for several reasons, including tobacco's profitability compared to other crops, the need to acquire new specialized knowledge or equipment, difficulties of market access and maintenance, the heritage value of tobacco farming, and the age of the majority of growers (Altman et al. 1998; Swanson 2001). Besides, most of the funds from government lawsuits against the industry that were earmarked to spur diversification went to fund state projects unrelated to tobacco (Rosen 2002; A. Jones et al. 2007). Not surprisingly, there has also been a problem of trust between growers and public health groups, just as there is often distrust and animosity between growers and farm labor advocates (Benson 2010a). Many growers opposed the collaborative president's report. Growers have rightly, I believe, sensed that the public health goal of containing and phasing out domestic tobacco agriculture was linked to the idea that growers should get on board because tobacco is harmful, rather than a primary concern for the economic well-being of tobacco-producing families and communities. "Public health groups are condescending and accusatory," a grower tells me in an interview. "They tell you that they sympathize with your plight, but then they want to put you out of business. So it was more about them than us."

As a result of many factors, the growers who have considered diversification have almost always done so for economic rather than health or moral reasons (Altman et al. 1998, 2000; Beach et al. 2008). Yet, some do admit to feeling moral ambivalence about their crop. "Growing tobacco is a subconscious problem for me," a nonsmoking grower tells me in an interview.

> Tobacco pays my bills but it kills people. It is bad for smokers, but it is good for me and mine. I don't know. Being a Christian, I want to be a righteous person in whatever way. But I grow tobacco. Does that make me un-Christian? Would Jesus grow tobacco? Would he vilify me

> for growing tobacco? I know, I know, it's a legal product and an individual choice. That's basically my position. That's what all of us farmers say. If you smoke, sip liquor, it's up to you. But it still nags at me. I can't quit tobacco because I've got a family, and at my age.

Such moral reflection is most evident in the story of Ricky Flint, the one grower I met who diversified away from tobacco primarily for health and moral considerations. Until 1992, tobacco was the main cash crop for Ricky and his father. When his father retired, Ricky decided to transition. "All of a sudden I was not just a farmer," he said. "When I was farming with my dad, I was a farmer. Now I was in charge, and that meant I was a tobacco farmer. I was never comfortable with that label. I always grew other crops and worked more with the corn and beans. I always loved farming, just not tobacco. There was always something about the label that bothered me. I think I always had this deep nagging that it is sinful."

Ricky switched to peanuts and fruits and vegetables. Other growers in the region who made a similar switch as the tobacco economy went into decline have not always been successful. Many growers who know Ricky or know of him question the idea that his decision was made on moral grounds. His choice seems to make perfect economic sense. Because his father was frugal, never expanding tobacco production capacities through debt financing, Ricky would have needed to invest in specialized tobacco equipment to remain profitable. But Ricky apparently began to consider exiting tobacco production in the mid-1980s, as evidence of a link between secondhand smoke and disease piled up (Brandt 2007: 279–318). This bothered Ricky because it contradicted the industry's talk of consensual adult consumption. "Back in the 1970s it wasn't a big deal for me," he says. "Some people smoked, some people didn't. But now there was proof that tobacco hurts people who don't have a choice or choose not to smoke. As a farmer, I could no longer just say, 'It's up to the smoker.' I felt it was up to me now."

All tobacco farmers are exposed to antismoking messaging. In Ricky's case it brought about a different moral understanding, leading to a concrete personal and business decision. But he carefully negotiates what can seem threatening about this decision for neighbors and colleagues. His moral stance toward tobacco is dynamic, seems to arise in the narration itself, and involves multiple registers of engagement with questions about what is right and wrong. Sitting in his kitchen sipping coffee, he continues:

> It was unheard of to not have tobacco on a farm. This is North Carolina! Everyone knows our crop kills people. But people don't talk about it around here. When I stopped growing, people were shocked. Other farmers seemed irritated. They asked, "What the hell are you

going to grow?" Some rolled their eyes. They knew my father and I were good tobacco farmers, and they knew I could have stayed in the business. I tell everyone that it was a personal decision, not for everybody. I do think questions about morality are fair game for tobacco farmers. But I don't think there is one single answer.

Legislatures are beginning to improve tobacco-control efforts in states where tobacco is grown, largely the result of waning opposition from agricultural groups and advocacy work by public health groups in these states (Sullivan and Glantz 2010). However, there has historically been much less support for tobacco control and less negative attitudes about tobacco there, including lower cigarette taxes, fewer clean air ordinances, and considerable support for the idea that it is not morally wrong to profit from tobacco business (Altman et al. 1997, 2000; Fishman 1999; Sullivan et al. 2009; Dixon et al. 1991). Consequently, tobacco states have comparatively higher adult and adolescent smoking rates. Industry advertising exceeds $2 billion annually in the major tobacco states, 20 percent of its nationwide advertising spending (National Institute for Tobacco-Free Kids 2005a).

In my fieldwork I heard stories about rural pastors of small churches who advocated against tobacco decades ago, instructing parishioners to plant other crops or find other work and landowners to sell tobacco land. This religious critique goes as far back as the first commercial tobacco plantings in North America. Today some Protestant denominations continue to discourage relationships to tobacco. These are not the churches growers attend. The Protestant congregations to which growers belong sometimes discourage smoking but rarely challenge the morality of tobacco business. Churches in tobacco states have tended to avoid stigmatizing leaf cultivation, instead emphasizing the importance of the work ethic, which is reflected in successful farm management and the idea that parenthood is the proper arena for inculcating certain kinds of ethical or healthful behaviors in adolescents. Churches have been less likely than agricultural-based interest groups, the Extension Service, or other community organizations to conduct activities aimed at helping growers cope with economic decline or think about diversification (Altman et al. 1998, 2000).

"I don't get a good response from other farmers," Ricky says. "They are not going to agree with my decision. They have their whole life invested in something. They don't want to hear that it's bad. They are more or less obligated to finish this course. I'll admit, for me it was easier. We had old tobacco equipment. It was in bad need of replacing. Other growers expanded to keep up with the tobacco business, but I didn't want to."

At a foundational level Ricky does not challenge the legitimacy of tobacco business. "I want to make it clear," Ricky continues, "I am not judging or condemning any other farmers. I am not saying it [his decision to diversify] is the only one or the best one. It was the decision that made sense for me. I tell other farmers that. But they know that part of my decision was about me not feeling good about the health aspect. So there is always going to be awkwardness; they assume I'm also judging them. At farm meetings we'll say hello to each other. But they'll always ask, 'How's the peanut business?'"

This story is told to me in a tone that seeks to convince as much as narrate and to personalize a decision that might imply a broader principle. He places himself within the first-person plural to index that his consternation has in fact been common. "We always knew that what we were growing wasn't good for you," he tells me. "But we didn't think it was bad to grow it. A lot of us don't smoke because it's not good for your health. We never thought that if you grow it then you are a bad person. But then there was so much criticism. You know you are a good person, but everyone is saying you're not, and so you start to question yourself." In this interview excerpt, the shift to the second person comes when Ricky speaks specifically about his personal experience, and it frames his personal feelings as colloquial and situational.

To stay true to the religious dimension of his decision without implying its universality, Ricky discusses religious faith in largely Pauline terms, although with a curious twist of legalism. What was "sinful" was not the act of tobacco farming itself but a felt lack of alignment between the inside and the outside, or, in Paul's language, faith and works. "There's plenty of moral, Christian people growing tobacco," Ricky tells me. "Sin is a complicated thing. It's got to be how you define it in each case. That's what Paul talks about. If you're a tobacco farmer and you say, 'I don't see a problem with this. People have a choice whether they smoke or not. I'm not holding a gun on them to buy these cigarettes,' and that's the way you really believe, then I think you're fine. What is important is that you don't believe one thing and do another. I felt I needed to do something else." What seems evident in theory is much more complicated in practice. I suggest to Ricky that this idea might imply that anything goes. He sees the national law as a firm threshold, not allowing leeway in the case of an illicit substance, for example. "Illegal drugs, well, that's always going to be wrong," he says, "There you are breaking the law."

Commodity Fetishism

Ricky reconciles his own misgivings about tobacco with the idea that it's okay for neighbors. His reluctance to link his personal decision to a broader public health or ethical approach reflects the social pressure on even a man with important reservations about tobacco, responsibility, and harm. He ultimately shares a dominant cultural view that legality is one of the most basic determinants of the legitimacy and morality of work.

Tobacco growers commonly insist that they produce a legal crop and distinguish themselves from criminal elements. "I'm not a drug dealer," a grower told me in an interview after I asked him to comment on perceptions of tobacco growers in the society. "Tobacco is legal. It's a real livelihood. I'm not out here peddling drugs. Go into town, that's where the problem is, not out here." Here the defense of livelihood legitimacy also differentiates classes and cultures. Spatial metaphors reflect a tacit divide between urban and nonurban, while reference to the formality of the tobacco economy helps map moral meanings of worthiness and illegitimacy down geographical and legal lines.

In general, willed commodity fetishism, flattening what is unique about tobacco in comparison with other products, is common in rural North Carolina. Here is an excerpt from one of my interviews with an active grower in 2006:

> There are a lot of things that are bad for you. If you eat a hamburger and fries every day you are going to get fat. Drinking and driving is irresponsible. It is the same with guns. Lots of people don't know how to use guns and accidents happen, or guns fall into the hands of criminals. It's the same with smoking. I grow tobacco. Consumers need to know the risks and make responsible decisions. But ultimately it is their choice to consume a legal product. If they are okay with the risk, then that is their choice.

There are countless quotes like this in the tobacco industry archives. While under oath in a trial in 1994, one industry executive stated:

> To me it's like any other form of pleasure, whether it's jogging, drinking beer, or smoking cigarettes. If it provides a benefit to the person . . . in the eyes of the beholder, if it makes that person feel better about himself or herself, [then there] is a benefit, otherwise you would not sell the number of cigarettes that we sell every year. (cited in Balbach et al. 2006)

Here is another example: In a lawsuit in 2001, tobacco industry defense attorneys argued to the jury that in "our society there are lots of risky products that are not defective. Guns can shoot you, knives can cut you, and we all unfortunately know what eating too much fatty food can do to you" (Cummings et al. 2006: 85). The tobacco industry's goal in using this language is to portray whatever injuries or harms might derive from consumption as the result of human user error, not industrial design or product defectiveness (Lochlann Jain 2004). Reference to other commodities is a means of misleadingly casting tobacco as an ordinary consumer product, neglecting that it, unlike other legal products, is intrinsically harmful, and suggesting that risks related to tobacco use are equivalent to other kinds of risk. These comparisons understate tobacco's specific public health toll.

But growers, industry reps, and the media do not pair cigarettes with just anything. There is no comparison to baseballs or automobiles, even though these products entail risks. The comparisons pit tobacco alongside firearms and alcohol (legal products that are also regulated by minimum-age requirements) and foods (also regulated by the FDA). Thus, the comparisons refer to a subset of products where risk and harm are the subjects of public debate, perhaps also special regulatory frameworks, and where optimal consumer behavior is framed in terms of moderation and appropriate kinds and levels of use. A model consumer is rhetorically and socially constructed against a latent image of abusive, excessive, and irresponsible consumption. As in a Pauline model of sin, normal consumption seems to be a matter of alignment between what is external to the subject (in this case, warning labels and health discourse) and the internal power of being a free agent who is responsible for individual decisions. In this logic, the harmful outcomes of consumption, whether smoking disease, injuries or fatalities related to gun use, or obesity, are pinned on the users, and the abuse of products is narrowly understood in terms of an individual lack of control or willpower, inherent blameworthiness, or malice rather than issues of access, social determinants of health behavior, industrial predation, or product design. In the 1980s, the tobacco industry was adamant that it is not "proper to say that smoking a cigarette is the same thing as using heroin or crack." The industry's public relations organization, the Tobacco Institute, claimed that a focus on tobacco as a significant health problem "trivializes, and almost mocks, the serious narcotic and other hard drug problems faced by our society" (1988). In fact, the mortality associated with tobacco use has always far outweighed what illicit drug use causes.

Together with the emphasis on the role of the family in health behavior, this conception of health and risk management as decentralized individual prerogatives obviates the population health perspective. In a class action suit in the 1990s, a lawyer for the tobacco company Brown and Williamson asked the company's executive in charge of youth smoking prevention initiatives, "Why do you care why kids smoke?" "I'm a mother," the executive replied while under oath. "I have two small children, two girls, eight and six. I don't want my children to smoke. I don't want anybody's kids to smoke. So it's very important to me" (Wakefield et al. 2006).

A vilified industry is humanized in terms of responsible parenting. These are normal people who do what seems natural in the family domain. "Tobacco supports my family and pays the bills," growers commonly say. "That makes me a good person, not a bad person. I provide for my family. I don't smoke and I don't let my children smoke." This issue of parenting is only one slice of the history of how the tobacco industry has crafted a "set of powerful rationalizations" (Brandt 2007: 398) for internal elements such as growers and their wider communities. Defensive strategies that trickled down from corporate headquarters through various media became the common language among growers who were also being coached to feel threatened. These attitudes and rationales became common in tobacco states, as evidenced in this excerpt from an editorial in the *Wilson Daily Times*:

> Tobacco opponents harp on tobacco health hazards, and reasonable people can have little doubt that smoking is not a healthful habit. However, the government does little to restrict other habits that are harmful to health. Alcohol, a far more dangerous drug than tobacco because of its contributions to traffic accidents and assaults, is advertised freely. . . . A multitude of other freely advertised and distributed products also pose a health risk. Rich, cholesterol-laden foods constitute a proven health risk. (1989a: 4)

Tobacco causes more mortality and morbidity than alcohol. What really matters in this discourse more than the facts is the project of normalizing risk so as to both diminish tobacco's immense public health toll and to imagine a society loaded with risky decisions. This discourse shifts responsibility and accountability for smoking disease onto consumers, in the same way that gun advocates insist, "Guns don't kill people; people kill people." Keeping in mind the industry's role in crafting key rationalizations and tropes for its dependent constituencies, the importance of tobacco growers distancing themselves from smokers may be about defending a livelihood amid other limited options. It also has to do with the contrast with the stereotype of illegitimate activity and the advancement of a more general claim about the geography and culture of normalized social belonging and family life.

Total Recall

Growers are often quick to insist that they make an agricultural product. "I grow tobacco," they say, "not cigarettes. They are different products. The tobacco companies make cigarettes; I grow an agricultural crop." Yet, as tobacco companies are becoming more involved in farm decisions, an important buffer between tobacco and cigarettes is disappearing. In 1995, Philip Morris instituted the first ever recall of cigarettes after the

Centers for Disease Control received complaints from smokers and determined a pattern of acute respiratory illness linked to Philip Morris brands. Some smokers had asthma, pneumonia, bronchitis, and laryngitis, and a number were hospitalized. Philip Morris attributed what it called "temporary discomfort" to high traces of a pesticide that is used as a soil fumigant on tobacco farms. Philip Morris pulled 8 million units of cigarettes off the shelves "out of an abundance of caution." The firm framed this as an isolated incident. But an analysis of cigarette samples by the CDC did not reveal a unique chemical profile in the recalled items. Pesticides identified by Philip Morris as harmful were found in cigarettes manufactured in pre-recall and post-recall periods. The CDC concluded that prolonged smoking rather than acute exposure caused the health problems. The agency emphasized that while pesticides have been linked to adverse health effects, there is no evidence that inhaled pesticides endanger smokers in an unusual way compared to presumably nondefective cigarettes (U.S. Centers for Disease Control 1996). Nonetheless, the recall had symbolic power for Philip Morris, which took the opportunity to pin the cause on agronomic practices rather than inherent product design.

Whereas tobacco leaf sold at auction was not traceable back to the farmer, contract systems now feature computerized tracking systems that affix barcodes to bales, which can be linked to individual farm operations. Because in the contracting structure tobacco companies also demand that growers keep detailed records about plantings, chemical applications, and harvesting, it is not out of the question that specific bales of tobacco and the batches of cigarettes they fill will be traceable back to a particular field. Growers and agricultural officials I interviewed remain unsure about how this new system will potentially reconfigure liability issues. Aware of cases such as salmonella-infested spinach recalls that led public health investigators to a parcel of land somewhere in California, some growers are wary that contracting will devolve some new degree of legal liability for smoking disease to them.

While contracting has been widespread in U.S. agriculture for decades, it arose in tobacco in the late 1990s. As production levels dwindled, tobacco companies provided desperate farmers with incentives to sign private contracts and bypass auctions. Companies offered to share costs for an expensive and mandatory farm-level upgrade (aimed at reducing carcinogen levels in tobacco) with farmers who signed.[1] This limited the

---

[1] Tobacco companies mandated the installation of heat exchangers in bulk barns used to cure tobacco, which had previously been done using open flames that increased nitrosamine levels in cured leaf. The companies refused to purchase, at auction, tobacco cured in barns that lacked heat exchangers (Brown and Vukina 2001; Rice 1999).

possibility of developing an alternative marketing system, such as a joint endeavor or cooperative in which farmers could sell a combined product, distribute risk, and bolster prices. Companies invoked product safety to reorganize market access and used economic incentives to force farmer compliance. Whereas only 9 percent of flue-cured tobacco was contracted in 2000 (the first year Philip Morris offered contracts and the third year for R. J. Reynolds), fully 81 percent was contracted a year later (Brown and Vukina 2001: 1; Dimitri 2003: 2). There was a "mad rush to sign" built on the fear of being locked out, farmers told me. By 2005, all U.S. tobacco was produced under contract (Dohlman et al. 2009; Tiller et al. 2007).

For tobacco companies, there are clear advantages in the contract system: enhanced quality control, improved supply management, and lower marketing costs. Leaf moves from farms to cigarette factories more quickly, and firms can purchase tobacco with specific qualities desired for cigarette blends (Dimitri 2003). Signed in the winter before planting, contracts provide a price schedule based on internal company grades and stipulate the leaf poundage the company intends to purchase. Companies reserve the right to reject tobacco that does not match noted stipulations. The farmer assumes all risk of loss, which is exaggerated by the temporary duration of all contracts. Companies make annual decisions on an individual basis, reviewing the quantity and quality of each farmer's leaf, as well as subjective factors not specified in the contract (described below). Each year the contract might be augmented or reduced, increasing or decreasing the farmer's income and ability to repay farm debt. The company might decide to "cut" a contract altogether, forcing the farmer to contract with another company, which is difficult, or the farmer may exit tobacco farming, as word of reputation or quality problems travels quickly. The official framing of contracting is as a "pay for performance" system. If one meets demands, then one is rewarded with high grades, good prices, and a bigger contract (Dimitri 2003: 5). Indeed, many contracting farmers report concrete benefits. "You might wait two hours to get unloaded at the auctions," one small grower tells me. "Then you would return a few days later, wait for graders to arrive, and then the buyers. It might take up the entire workday. A lot of the bigger farmers could afford to wait around because they had an employee back on the farm looking after everything. But small guys like me don't have that luxury. That's what I like about contracting. You have your check in an hour."

But the shift to a free-market system has been experienced as quite closed by some groups. Durable patterns of race and class differentiation are at work, despite official claims that contracting has ended the auctions' biases. Contracting favors those who have access to large and productive tracts of land, but adversely affects small farmers whose ability to "remain low-cost producers is questionable under the structure of a freer market environment" (Brown et al. 1999: 22; Algeo 2002). Though some small-scale producers have realized benefits in contracting, others complain that the efficiency demands of tight pricing lock them out. "The companies say they want quality tobacco and if it's on a small farm, it doesn't matter," says a small farmer, who had difficulty accessing a contract and recently sold his business. "But that's not true. Bigger farmers come to the warehouse with a truckload, not just with a few bales on the back of a pickup. That's more efficient and the prices are tight. Plus, the company would rather deal with a transfer truck, so I'm pressured out." Because diversification is limited by several factors, not accessing a contract usually means not being able to farm. Many growers have sold their equipment and moved into off-farm work. Access to contracts has been especially limited for black farmers, who tend to operate smaller, less mechanized farms on poorer-quality land, the accumulated result of discrimination in federal farm programs (chapter 2). Black farmers roundly complained to me that emphasis on scale has pressured them out of business, although the free-market rhetoric silences any consideration of racial bias. "They offered me a contract," says one fifty-six-year-old black former farmer who now works as a wage laborer on a neighboring farm. "But it was only for two acres. They say, 'See, we did not exclude black farmers.' But that's what it amounts to. They cut you out with a measly contract and it doesn't seem like a race thing. I've got equipment for ten acres and planned on a few more years. But, see, those acres can go to a bigger white farmer."

Owing to ideal soil types, more mechanized farms, and an existing infrastructure of tobacco warehouses (many of which have now been reconverted into tobacco company-owned contract stations) and leaf-processing facilities, eastern North Carolina has seen a new wave of capitalization and the consolidation of a class of entrepreneurial managers who benefit from increased short-term profits through contracting. Beginning in 2005, farmers I interviewed ambitiously leveraged capital to expand, investing hundreds of thousands of dollars in specialized machinery to optimize efficiency, increase output, and maximize profit. "Contracting is much better," one of the region's farmers told me a couple of years after the buyout of 2004. "It's more efficient and I can grow as much tobacco as I want now. No more government restrictions. It's wide open." He portrays himself as "open to change," an entrepreneur willing to "upgrade equipment, get faster, and show the company that I am invested in tobacco." Farms like his are not romantic family farms.

They are capital-intensive businesses that tend at least fifty (sometimes upward of one thousand) acres of tobacco (as compared with just a few acres tended by each tenant family decades ago). Tobacco is now typically harvested by machine. But it is commonly still loaded into barns and packed into bales manually. Farmers are deeply dependent on a flexible supply of seasonal labor during the summer harvest months. This structure of dependence, coupled with the heightened moral demands of demonstrating entrepreneurial self-reliance and ambition, fosters a context of accountability in which racialized social relations at the farm workplace become the medium through which growers take out the frustrations, uncertainties, and feelings of lack of control that, despite the optimism of many growers, are part of the contract system.

Keep Tobacco Clean

Approximately 60 percent of farmers contract with Philip Morris, which buys more U.S. tobacco than other companies and offers the highest prices. Philip Morris (2008e) has used the phrase "Tobacco Farmer Partnering Program" to describe its contract system. Many contracted growers proudly wear hats with TFPP embroidered on the front. But, farmers routinely mention, its contracts also contain more "bullshit," namely, stringent professional and quality standards related to the company's overarching goal of padding tobacco with the value of being clean and safe.

In the 1990s, the firm began its push for "cleanliness" by furnishing auction warehouses with red garbage barrels and immense red banners strewn taut between exposed wooden rafters. These items said "Keep Tobacco Clean," with white lettering against a red background that mimicked Marlboro packaging and announced, without a trademark or corporate signature, that these items were put there by Philip Morris. At a time when the auctions were still operating and growers were not yet directly contracted with firms, the signs expressed corporate power and subtly implied that more stringent demands were coming down the pike. Traditional practices such as "nesting," where growers bury heavy objects (e.g., pieces of metal) deep in a bale to boost its weight, were increasingly labeled as threatening to a declining industry. Corporate-sponsored messaging about quality was an emergent form of labor control, relocating the cost of quality control from firms to farms and auctions. Philip Morris plastered posters all over auction warehouses that said, "Your quality tobacco is always in demand." This gesture of apparent respect also suggested that the decisions of firms to pursue cheaper foreign leaf could perhaps be justified in terms of quality problems and the faults of growers, and that growers wishing to remain in the business ought to exhibit a renewed commitment to cleanliness and compliance.

Beginning in 2005, Philip Morris encouraged its contracted farmers to minimize use of the chemical MH30 (a plant growth inhibitor sprayed on tobacco to kill the reproductive system and divert more energy to leaf). Although this chemical minimizes the grueling manual work of removing the plant's flowers, it is carcinogenic and an environmental hazard with serious risks for smokers. Industry officials have long expressed concern about the toxicity of agricultural chemicals. In the 1960s, the toxicology of chemicals such as MH30 was examined by a special committee composed of representatives from the tobacco industry and the USDA. Mice exposed to high doses of MH30 showed high levels of toxicity. Tests on cigarette smoke also produced "disquieting" results. It was clear that "an agricultural chemical could detectably increase the already high toxicity of tobacco" (Glantz et al. 1996: 205, 208). Ultimately, the chemical composition of MH30 was slightly modified through partnered research by tobacco companies and federal officials that largely sought to cover up this potential "powder keg," as insiders called it (205). The chemical has remained in use to the present, and traces have been found in cigarettes (202–12).

Philip Morris's contracts also stipulate that tobacco must be free of any "non-tobacco-related material (NTRM)," such as paper, string, metal fragments, plastics, fiberglass insulation materials, foam materials, excessive sand or dirt, rocks, debris, and other contaminants (see Cooperation Centre for Scientific Research Relative to Tobacco 2005: 8–9), what farmers call "trash" or "foreign matter," that is, anything that can get mixed in with tobacco on the farm. If a bale contains NTRMs or high levels of MH30, Philip Morris can cancel the producer's contract. Philip Morris says that stringent contracts keep tobacco clean, making it safer for consumers and the environment. In this way, Philip Morris is aligned with a dominant public health approach that aims to reduce harm to consumers and promote safer tobacco products (Fairchild and Colgrove 2004; Hatsukami et al. 2004; McDaniel et al. 2006).

Stringent contract stipulations are core, farm-level components of Philip Morris's corporate social responsibility image overhaul and push for FDA regulation of tobacco products. Philip Morris's website features a link to information about "High-quality tobacco" under the heading "Reduced Harm," directly associating agricultural practices with cigarette safety. The website states, "For those adults who continue smoking . . . we are searching for ways to reduce the health risks of smoking. . . . The primary component in each of our cigarette brands is tobacco. Therefore, quality control of the types and grades we use is critical" (Philip Morris USA 2008d). The website goes on to emphasize that direct contracting allows the company "to work directly with U.S. farmers to ensure that sufficient amounts and the right qualities and grades of tobacco are available for our products." In contrast to "certain inherent limitations" of the old auction system "that created concern about our ability to procure the qualities and grades we needed," the website frames the benefits of contract marketing in terms of "enhanced supply security," "improved [leaf] quality and consistency," "improved product traceability," and a "mechanism to monitor agricultural practices" (Philip Morris USA 2007b, 2008e). Ultimately, the website implies that because contracting enables the procurement of "good-quality tobacco," it also contributes to the engineering of potentially reduced-risk tobacco products (Philip Morris USA 2008c).

Because the majority of farmers I interviewed have been opposed to FDA regulation, and because Philip Morris linked its stringent quality control standards to its public support for such legislation, the firm has attempted to induce grower support. In 2001, the company launched a newsletter, entitled *Tobacco Connections*, devoted to disseminating tobacco policy information relevant for farmers. The first issue, mailed to 130,000 tobacco farmers and landowners, outlined Philip Morris's support of FDA regulation and emphasized the importance of implementing quality control procedures on farms to ensure the future economic viability of the tobacco industry (McDaniel and Malone 2005: 196; Philip Morris 2001). Although the exact language of the 2009 FDA bill did not provide any farm-level authority, "the impacts would likely spill over," one agricultural economist predicted, and "requirements of manufacturers would be passed along to leaf producers."[2] This is exactly what is happening. Part of what is meant by "good-quality tobacco" includes delivering a bale with minimal amounts of sand or soil. This has led to a new wave of mechanization among growers, who are purchasing systems that move leaf through a tumbler to remove fine grains and particles. The upshot for tobacco companies is that they no longer pay for dust. With the new tumbling machine, a medium-size grower with about one hundred acres of tobacco will extricate several thousand pounds of dust from his tobacco crop each year, amounting to a potential loss of tens of thousands of dollars in revenues. Growers who have adopted the new tumbler

---

[2] This quote is from "2006 U.S. Tobacco Outlook," by Tiller, Brown, and Snell (2006), Tobacco Economics, Department of Agricultural and Resource Economics, North Carolina State University. The report was accessed in April 2007 from an online source that is no longer available.

technology have done so to curry favor with the tobacco companies, a display of an entrepreneurial spirit and a willingness to go into debt and put private resources on the line for a cleaner product and industry image enhancement.

The Grower Profile

Tobacco farms have become the front line for quality control and product safety. For farmers, contracts mean market access but also new pressures related to keeping tobacco clean. The trip to Philip Morris's contract station, a trip farmers make every week in the fall to sell tobacco, is fraught with uncertainty. Their bales are weighed and graded and may be broken open to spot-check for NTRMs or chemically tested for MH30 levels. I have frequently ridden with farmers to the marketing stations of various companies, accompanying men like Fred Warren, who operates a farm an hour east of Raleigh with two hundred acres of tobacco plus rotational fields planted in corn and soybeans. Fifty years old, Fred took over the farm from his father in the 1970s. He says that tobacco is a meaningful heritage but also a business "just like any other." He has worked hard to make the farm business successful and takes pride in having expanded and mechanized in a careful manner that allowed him to weather difficult years and avoid crushing debt loads. At his age, diversifying away from tobacco is not a realistic option. He depends on tobacco to put food on the table, make mortgage payments, and pay tuition for his child at a major state university. Nor does he want to quit growing tobacco. He will tell you that it is all he knows; "tobacco is in my blood," he says, using a phrase that is ubiquitous in grower speech. Farming is something he mostly enjoys, and this cash crop and inherited livelihood allow access to material possessions and social status that set him and his family apart in the locale.

Fred signed on with Philip Morris in 2001, part of the mad rush to contract: "I figured if my neighbors were doing it, then I needed to also. I was afraid of losing out. None of us really knew what we were getting into." Fred has seen neighboring farmers go out of business and now says that contracting has finally gotten rid of "bad farmers." But he knows that his own standing within the firm's contract structure is perpetually uncertain. Fred delivers tobacco to the company in an eighteen-wheeler that he owns: thirty bales (more than $5,000 in profit) each week during the harvest. Philip Morris's station is like a corporate campus. A U.S. flag flies in front of the facility, with its tree-lined driveway and new metal-sided warehouse surrounded by a well-kept lawn, flowerbeds, and stone walkways. Clean and new, it is definitely not like an old auction warehouse where hundreds of farmers once congregated to socialize during sales.

Today, marketing is a private affair. Farmers are supposed to arrive at a scheduled time to avoid gridlock. They pull into lines that move through large bay doors. Fred and I always arrive a bit early, his punctuality a strategic rehearsal of a subjectivity that he needs to adopt inside the station. After pulling the truck to the side of the driveway, he does a once-over—perhaps tucks leaves loosened on the highway back into the bales, ducks underneath the flatbed to ensure there are no fluid leaks, tucks his work shirt into his khaki pants, and, in the truck's side-view mirror, makes sure none of the ham biscuit he ate on the way is caught between his cigarette-stained teeth. "Everything has to be perfect," Fred says. "If you go into Philip Morris and everything is not just right, you're a fool. They can tear you up. You need good, clean tobacco, no leaks, nothing falling off your truck or out of your pockets, not messy and dirty." Double-checking is a common strategy for farmers. "It all depends on you. You need to be a professional," another farmer says. "If Philip Morris doesn't like the mud under your truck or the kind of tires you've got, then you'll have to change. There are guys who don't do the extra stuff. He could drive in here with an oil leak. Then a Philip Morris guy will yell at him, 'Don't bring that truck here again or you'll lose your contract.'"

Eventually, Fred pulls his truck into the building's bay openings and parks beside the grading station. The entire operation is "clean." Automatic sweepers motor about in circles and figure eights, maintaining a spotless floor, free of tobacco dust, errant leaves, dirt, grime, and grease. The tobacco, never touching the floor, is always in motion and connected to a machine. On automated forklifts, it moves from Fred's flatbed to the conveyor belt, passes by the grading station, where printed receipts are affixed to each bale, and is finally put on a freight truck, which will haul it to cigarette factories. "You'd eat off of that floor," Fred says. "Professional and efficient, that's contracting." With a company pride that is actively promoted by Philip Morris, perhaps Fred is covering over the jitters that he will later admit to feeling as we climb three metal steps onto the platform where the grader stands.

Philip Morris hires graders from various regions to ensure against biased relationships with farmers. Fred's tobacco bales begin to pass in front of us on the conveyor belt, then in front of the grader. The grader does not say the grade aloud, a major difference from the auction, at which grade and price were hollered loudly. Here the grader punches each grade into a computer interface. It then registers on another computer situated low in front of Fred. The computerized circuit distances the grader from the grade, as if the grade appeared magically on the screen, as if it were not his decision. The system seems set up to squelch confrontation, digitized graphic representation being more polite, less potentially insulting than direct verbal exchange. But this rationalized scenario incites conversation. Fred says it is important to "kiss the grader's ass a little." In learning that the grader is from the western part of North Carolina, Fred drops names of respected farmers he knows in that region. Brushing Fred back, the grader brags that their "crop out there" is "the best in the state, a bit stronger than here in the east." This makes Fred nervous; the person judging his tobacco has said he has seen better, displacing Fred's common sense about the high quality of tobacco in eastern North Carolina. So Fred accelerates his chatter, turning to sports, college payments, and the weather.

Once the grading is complete, Fred gets a printout of grades and prices received. This printout, which Fred awkwardly reads over the steering wheel as we head back to the farm, is like a report card. Overall, his tobacco brings high grades, but not as high as he would like. A form of discipline, the printout indicates to Fred that he can improve and compels him to internalize disappointment for the sake of maintaining a business relationship with Philip Morris. I ask Fred why he does not complain about lower-than-expected grades. "You cannot complain about the grades. Rule number one is you keep your head down and your mouth shut. What Philip Morris gives you is what you take home." Fred expresses a view that is common among contracted farmers. "If they say, 'This is worth $1.25' but you think it's worth $1.50, tough. You have no choice. You nod in approval. Did you see the paper in front of the grader? Well, that's the 'comments section,' where he can write you up." Each contracting farmer has a so-called grower profile, a statistical record of the individual's production history, including his crops' average grades, chemical levels, and instances of trash. The profile also includes the "comments section," in which the grader can make notations on attitude and appearance (e.g., if a truck is leaking or a farmer disheveled or ornery). The grower profile is part of the basis on which firms make decisions about renewals, increases, or cuts.

On its website, Philip Morris describes contracting as an "opportunity" for farmer and company agents, such as graders or station managers, to "talk and share ideas about how to maximize the quality and value of the tobacco" the farmer delivers. "If the grower agrees with the assessment of the crop, he receives immediate payment . . . based on a price schedule." The contract marketing scenario is described as "an opportunity [for farmers] to engage in face-to-face conversations" with company officials and "raise any issues in person" (Philip Morris USA 2007c). This is not how farmers describe their experiences to me. They generally see little opportunity for conversation; what counts as dialogue is confined to chitchat, and unmet expectations about grades are suppressed. The traditional auctions were raucous places where farmers were encouraged to speak their minds, express distaste for company buyers, and brag about their tobacco. Each bale was seen by multiple buyers, and farmers had a safety net. If a bale received no bids, a government-sanctioned cooperative bought it, giving the farmer a minimum price for that particular grade of leaf. A farmer could also reject the sale of any bale, opting to sell another day, potentially for a better price. I do not mean to romanticize sometimes corrupt auctions, but the system did allow farmers more control over the value of their product.[3] Today, complaint, culturally valued stubbornness, and expressions of independence limit market access. Reputation matters greatly. Aspects of personality such as "bad attitude" or "being difficult to work with," farmers tell me, get noted on the grower profile, which functions as a technology of government individualizing responsibility for streamlined production and marketing. This technology is like forms of record keeping and government in the history of penology and criminology, in which individual files were built up out of observed behaviors, a moral science of how to read people's character in their attitudes and transgressions, and a desire to incite docility and limit confrontation between officials and prisoners (Lingis 1994: 61; Foucault 1979).

Grading is now an exemplary form of "coercive harmony," a controlling process that eschews acrimonious troublemaking in favor of efficiency and harmony (Nader 1997: 712–15). The invitation to dialogue at the grading station is not unlike Philip Morris's emphasis on information sharing and individual risk assumption in its multimedia campaign, a framing that elides a broader consideration of social forces that influence behaviors and loyalties. The requisite display of company loyalty at the station moves criticism to the farmer's psychological interior. Fred often second-guesses his performance while driving back to the farm shop, rethinking conversations with the grader and wondering if some aspect reflected positively or negatively on his profile. Adding to the uncertainty, most NTRMs are identified at leaf-processing plants and only then are noted on a grower's profile. The actual material (e.g., a piece of metal) may be shipped to the farmer's mailing address. Farmers see this practice, which to my knowledge is unique to Philip Morris, as a threat. "If you get your shoe sent to you in the mail," a farmer tells me, "if the return

---

[3] It must be noted that there were real limits to competitive bidding at tobacco auctions. In May 2003, a class action lawsuit filed by U.S. tobacco farmers against tobacco companies was settled. It alleged that companies colluded to fix auction prices.

address says Philip Morris, you're in trouble." When I ask what the repercussions might be, he shakes his head, "Luckily, it's never happened to me. The first time would be a warning, and then you'd be cut."

Philip Morris Washing Its Hands Green

The centerpiece of Philip Morris's contract system is its "Good Agricultural Practices" (GAP) program outlined in a company-produced handbook distributed to contracted growers annually. The program aims to "ensure that quality tobacco is produced under conditions that protect the environment, create a safe working environment . . . [and] ensure economic viability for the farm." The bulk of the handbook is a blank calendar that growers are urged to utilize in planning the year's production process, with reminders about when to plant and cultivate, apply chemicals, and so on printed in the margins. The handbook "encourages" growers to establish individual business goals and self-monitor their management activities and outcomes over time. Philip Morris lists a set of examples (e.g., "To use varieties that offer disease resistance," "To use less nitrogen fertilizer," "To monitor production costs more closely throughout the growing season," "To improve my record keeping," among other goals). From a sustainability standpoint, the GAP program is a vague set of objectives that may serve more of a symbolic function than anything else, a case of "green washing," where Philip Morris appropriates environmentalism without an attendant set of sustainable practices or environmental objectives.

Enumerated examples of possible management goals are "a long list of good intentions phrased in apolitical language" (Pottier 1999: 16), making the grower seem like the sole arbiter of good or bad agriculture, deflecting attention away from the corporation's role in reorganizing production in such a way that perhaps makes farms less, not more self-sustaining, given the financial and managerial resources growers must invest without the benefit of even medium-range contractual security. The handbook's examples of "good agricultural practices" are in all likelihood practices that growers already undertake to some extent, thus serving more of a disciplinary function than an educational one. They reassert basic agricultural practices and goals so that they are now clearly linked, in the handbook's opening pages, to the industrial and ethical problem of making new and different tobacco products and a new and different industry. The GAP handbook explicitly states that among the principle advantages of adhering to Philip Morris's production regime is "enhanced public image" and "better public relations." The irony is that growers are being sold a program that is very plainly about image maintenance at the same time as contracting poses serious obstacles to their ability to stay in business. The GAP program is one resource among many others by which Philip Morris is seeking to become innocent in the eyes of the public and the government. Part of this ambition involves putting the responsibility for health and environmentalism on individual growers, who are encouraged to anxiously monitor their contribution to this project, while the financial and moral pressures of contract production are conveniently left out of the handbook.

A Clean Cut

At agricultural meetings farmers routinely ask each other, "Who are you [contracted] with?" Farmers discern consequential differences across companies: R. J. Reynolds is known for stingy prices and, deeply dependent on foreign leaf, seemingly less permanent contracts; Philip Morris offers the highest prices but makes stringent demands; and other firms are somewhere in between. Farmers "with" Reynolds often bury the implied instability by responding, "It's been good so far; I'm confident they like my tobacco." In contrast, to be "with" Philip Morris is to have secured a competitive contract that imparts economic status and pushes competitor farmers to tactically offset this apparent security against the firm's stringency by saying, "Well, I hope you don't mind all the extra bullshit." In response, Philip Morris farmers complain about "the 'no MH30' rules, a real headache" yet are always sure to emphasize, "We get a premium for that clean tobacco." Such conversations would not have occurred a decade ago, before contracts replaced auctions. The shared class and race affiliation (given the auction's segregation and cronyism) of selling publicly and standing against company buyers has given way to divergent relationships to tobacco capital, a process of class differentiation driven by variable pricing and company demands. Premiums associated with health-driven stipulations impart status to those at the industry's cutting edge, whereas for others they subtly negotiate downward class mobility. "My tobacco is the same as my neighbor's, same exact quality," one farmer told me. "But he's with Philip Morris, so he gets ten cents more per pound, twenty thousand more per year. That extra money hitting his pocket hurts. He's got a new truck this year and my tobacco's just as good. But, look, my company's not breathing over my shoulder. And that's important. He's got more pressure."

Neoliberalism in the United States has often been accompanied by a public discourse of "winners" and "losers" that discounts an uneven geography of economic and symbolic capital and privileges an ideology of individual accountability (K. Stewart 2000). Agricultural industrialization usually fosters such a division between surviving and failed farmers (Dudley 2000). Despite fragmented loyalties to corporations, active tobacco farmers still see themselves as part of a surviving class that is distanced from the auction's corruption and inefficiency. "The only thing I miss is the socializing, but I'll gladly forget the crookedness and slowness," farmers routinely say. Liberalization becomes a decisive turning point between old and new, a clean break and a technology of cleansing, whereas the auction is recollected as an antiquated heritage. The neoliberal depiction of farming as a business optimally managed by market principles creates a context of moral accountability in which marginal farmers are allied with corruption and seem to deserve their dislocation. Disparities of rapid restructuring are justified in terms of industry health and the public good (Dudley 1996: 51). In other words, the shift to contracting has been a "critical event" (Das 1995: 5–6) that has altered patterns of discourse, action, and identification in a local world. Traditional categories have been redefined and social types invested with residual and emergent moral valences. Surviving producers commonly speak in a language of economic eugenics: "The whole point of contracting is to cut them, get the bad farmers out, and then the efficient ones, we'll make a living." They talk about "messy farmers with heaps of trash everywhere, old tractors sitting on blocks" who do not care "about quality, always cut corners, [and are] wasteful and inefficient." Although this appraisal might be true in some cases, the blanket effect is to obfuscate historical forces that have placed chances for success beyond the control of many producers.

Private company decisions become public signs of personal moral deprivation, and a biopolitical discourse about industry health frames "cutting" as a justified surgical procedure that excises waste from organizational efficiency (Coronil 2000: 365). Insofar as they threaten the cleanliness of tobacco and, writ large, the industry, marginal farmers are like "trash" or "foreign matter," logistically separated out as not tobacco related. The portrait of their inefficiency and uncleanness implies, in turn, the efficiency and professionalism of survivors. "Aesthetic order in the agricultural . . . landscape," James C. Scott writes, gets "replicated in the human geography as well" (1998: 227). Philip Morris's public tobacco-cleansing campaign gets matched by a local mode of aesthetic class judgment that depicts structural outcomes in terms of individual skills and responsibility, reflecting the discourse of stereotypically backward "dirt farmers" used in the last century (see chapter 2). Fred's metaphors are telling: "Contracting is about culling, like when you pick rotten apples from a bushel, get rid of bad apples."

The optimistic, rather austere outlook of surviving producers contrasts sharply with bitter and vehement criticism from others. Dislocated warehouse managers, their auctions suddenly undermined, tell me that the system is a dangerous way for companies to supervise all aspects of leaf production and intimately control farmers. Some go so far as to use the term *brainwash*. If true believers like Fred describe contracting as a new independence, an invitation to entrepreneurship and market-based mobility, many producers, large and small, were reluctant to sign a contract because they saw more independence and control in the auction. They saw contracting for what it is: being at the mercy of a single company. "The auction was a good deal," says one farmer who signed a contract only after the buyout. "Right now, we're doing better, we're competitive again. But I'm worried about long-term security. The companies care about price. That is why they got rid of the government program. I'm in my forties. I've got years in tobacco still, but if the price is right the company moves my pounds to Brazil. That's the problem. There is no security anymore."

Tobacco farmers like this one are also aware of the vertical integration of North Carolina's poultry industry over the past few decades (see Durrenberger and Thu 1996, 1997). They have seen neighboring poultry producers lose contracts on a whim, leaving the producers with huge debt loads. Buying firms micromanage production and own inputs, including animals, rendering the farmer a service provider who owns expensive buildings and farm equipment. Tobacco's susceptibility to weather makes total integration unfeasible for companies, which prefer to leave meteorological risk to the farmer, who retains ownership of the leaf until sold. But tobacco companies are beginning to establish wholesale contracts with seed and chemical manufacturers in order to facilitate bulk distribution throughout the contract network. The aim is to reduce input costs to growers, although this also undermines their autonomy about input decisions and dislocates established relationships between growers and input suppliers: "profits are extracted and accumulate in distant places rather than locally" (Durrenberger and Thu 1996: 19). Philip Morris's stringent contract requirements signal a tendency that some see as dangerous. "Right now," says one tobacco producer, "it's not that bad. But if the company is out here telling me when to plow, when to put fertilizer, then I would think hard about stopping. That's not farming; that's just doing a job."

Despite decades of reliance on a federal subsidy program, independence has historically been a key part of class affiliation for tobacco farmers and distinguished them from farm labor (Kingsolver 2007). Now farmers who are cut sometimes strategically emphasize independence as something they retain over increasingly deskilled contract producers. Consider Derek Parker, who took the termination of his contract as a "personal attack, a matter of pride." Derek's neighbors told me that he

was always "inefficient" and "hard to get along with." But Derek claims
to be "just as good as any other farmer." He says simply, "The company
did not like my style of tobacco. It just wasn't right for their cigarette
blends," excusing the cut in terms of consumer preference, not personal
shortcoming. "But it's just as well," Derek goes on. "I wouldn't want to
farm now anyhow. I'd rather not grow tobacco than kiss their ass. I won't
ask Philip Morris, 'What can I do to do a better job?' They know how
to sell cigarettes. I know how to grow tobacco." Derek is understandably
bitter about being cut. Whether he was cut for stubbornness is debat-
able. To Derek, though, "favoritism, who you know at the company,"
is very much at work in contracting. "Some of the worst farmers are
contracted with Philip Morris," he says, then adds sarcastically, "unless
Philip Morris magically taught them how to farm tobacco. Somehow I
doubt that." For Derek and others locked out, resistance is found in individual expressions of pride and stubbornness. As the "contrast between
the multi-skilled independent farmer and the factory laborer, whose skill
is to follow the production algorithms of the contract" (Durrenberger
and Thu 1996: 20), begins to blur, ousted farmers like Derek continue
to assert local knowledge and independence in refusing to accede to the
firm's disciplinary power and dislocation of expertise.

Good, Clean Tobacco

Rural class dynamics also involve shifting relationships of farm management and labor that are shaped by agricultural industrialization (Wells
1996). Although liberalization alters farmers' class position vis-à-vis
multinational capital, the everyday hierarchy at the farm workplace has
largely remained the same. Farmers still make decisions about production, plan the workday, and supervise workers (although the exact organization of work differs across farms). Small farmers often do some
manual labor alongside seasonal workers. Huge operators with several
hundred tobacco acres are more like factory supervisors, with a handful
of labor camps, dozens of migrants, and permanent foremen and machin-
ists, usually local black men. Fred's farm is a typical medium-size setup.
He hires a crew of ten migrants, whom he houses in his camp in the harvest months, and three aging black men who have worked on farms all
their lives. One of these men, Donald, drives the tobacco harvester, and
the other two transport tobacco from field to farm shop in pickups. The
migrant crew performs the manual labor, including putting tobacco into
bales. Fred spends most of the day in his pickup truck, which he calls "my
office." He scouts land, makes regular trips to sell tobacco, and routinely
cycles back to the shop to check on the workers.

Like all farmers, Fred tells me that he monitors workers more intensely under contracting than he did under the auction system. His contract hinges on keeping trash out of his tobacco, but trash can be common in bales because workers may smoke, eat, or drink around the baler. Doing all the manual labor, workers are usually the only ones to handle the tobacco. Farmers lack an important measure of control over a bale's contents. Workers frequently joke about the practical power in their hands; they know how contracts work and realize that farmers have a direct relationship to tobacco firms. One young man, Pablo, sometimes held a soda can over the baler and motioned as if he were tossing it in with the tobacco. Fred knew it was a joke. But he would also scowl and become noticeably nervous. Laughing, Pablo turned to the crew and joked, "The company will cut his contract and fire him [*lo corren*]." In interviews with me, workers frequently used the phrase *correr* (literally "to run off") to describe their own experiences of being suddenly released from employment and forced to leave the labor camp in the event of a weather disruption or a labor surplus. The joke conveyed an element of sympathy for Fred yet also played on the increased scrutiny workers experience with contracting. "Like the other men, I know how to work: what goes in the baler, what you throw out," says one Mexican man. "The boss watches all the time now. It's like he doesn't trust us." Manual laborers are peeved when the farmer stands over their shoulder, points, and instructs in simple English: "Yes, that's good tobacco—that, no, trash." They sometimes respond by cussing the boss in Spanish under their breath, saying, "You think I haven't done this before?" or "You are not working, I am." Such are the minor tactics of class positioning deployed by seasonal workers to note the lopsided distribution of manual labor and rub against the official framing of their jobs as unskilled. Farmers are not the only ones who experience contracting's stringency as a threat to independence.

Pablo never sabotaged the baler. His own employment was on the line. Workers, too, must adhere to codes of professionalism in producing a "good, clean" product. Farmers can easily replace them with other temporary hires. Besides, if the farmer loses his contract, the crew also loses future work; many workers return to work annually for the same farmer and have something at stake in the tobacco's quality and the operation's success. It is not out of goodwill but a need to strategically negotiate their own impermanent contract that workers become invested in "getting good prices for the farmer," as they routinely say. "If the company likes the employer's tobacco, there's more work for us." Farmers sometimes utilize an incentives model (a bonus at year's end) to exert control. Feigned sabotage plays on, while ultimately upholding, the uneven distribution of authority and manual tasks at the farm workplace. It also tugs at farmer anxiety, spotlighting the sizable amount of money that farmers have invested in tobacco equipment and that rides on keeping a contract.

In contracting, the flip side of the market-based emphasis on individual accountability is partial lack of control over the content of bales and, more broadly, long-term economic security. "I'm really out of control with contracting," Fred tells me. "The Mexicans are the last ones to touch the tobacco. You can't get someone who trashes the camp to keep tobacco clean." Trash can end up in tobacco in many incidental and accidental ways. But farmers commonly blame migrants as the only source of trash, just as they deem them culpable for squalid labor camp conditions. "Philip Morris is big business," Fred continues. "Do you think they care if that trash in my tobacco is not my fault? Right here, that's where the buck stops. I can't pass this shit on. If Philip Morris finds trash in my tobacco, I can't say, 'Well, go talk to Pablo.' They cut me out, not the workers." Blaming others and publicly marking one's own professionalism and cleanliness are strategic ways to mitigate risk and affirm a dominant ideology of individualism.

Whereas some have stubbornly refused the transition to contracts, farmers like Fred go out of their way to appear professional and compliant. Given the possibility of delivering trash along with one's bales, a constant display of professionalism becomes an essential defense against implications of moral culpability and bad management. Here entrepreneurship amounts to the docility of being attractive to the company (i.e., as a clean and efficient producer). Farmers invest in professionalized loyalty as much as in technology, often going deep into debt, which leaves them with little choice but to comply with whatever company demands might come down. In the end, the very class dynamics that set survivors apart from dislocated farmers also challenge the independence that defines a crucial part of their class affiliation and differentiates them from farm labor (hence, the moral importance of establishing such distinctions rhetorically and through demarcated cultural and spatial boundaries and stereotypes). Because U.S. farmers generally believe that "we are each responsible for our own fate," the anthropologist Kathryn Dudley theorizes, they are also led to affirm, often at the expense of others and themselves, the very processes that give "rise to the economic disorder we experience" (1996: 56).

Morass of Paradoxes

Some assume that neoliberalism in the context of the tobacco industry has "not, often, been about consumer health issues" and has "emphasized a diminishing role of the state in regulating the market and de-emphasized corporate accountability to producers or consumers" (Kingsolver

2007: 88). Yet contracting is itself a technology of government, a form of political organization that is premised on neoliberal ideals and organized by multinational corporations. It might usefully be thought of as a broad-scale mode of industrial discipline, an innovative combination of disciplinary and regulatory regimes built on a transnational production network, including ethnicized labor migration (Ong 2006: 20). Wielding control over leaf inspection and marketing, and dependent on lax enforcement of hiring and housing laws in the United States (and lax environmental and labor laws in other countries), private firms have displaced and utilized, not eroded, state functions (Trouillot 2001: 132). Philip Morris uses new private regulatory mechanisms that are built into contracts to capitalize on public values associated with "safer" cigarettes and harm reduction. In turn, the firm emphasizes smoking risks to influence federal policies and control crop production. In these ways, rapid changes in tobacco agribusiness are directly linked to the politicization of health issues. Just as firms like Tyson and Perdue ensure minimal variation in their products by disciplining poultry farmers via strict, all-encompassing contracts (Boyd and Watts 1997; Heffernan and Constance 1994; Scott 1998: 338–39), so, too, Philip Morris aims to ensure quality control, optimize profitability, and secure FDA approval partly via the contract. In many ways, the seemingly "new" face of tobacco agriculture looks a lot like the historically durable institution of merchant capitalism, which, when seen from above, as the anthropologist Gerald Sider points out, incorporates producers into a larger and larger interregional economy and, when seen from below, yields heightened differentiation within locales and often galvanizes cultural difference "as a moral or political rallying point" among the populations affected (1986: 191).

Philip Morris claims that its stringent contracts improve public health. In fact, liberalized health-driven production in the tobacco industry fosters contextual factors that promote social and health problems. Year after year in the contract system, more and more tobacco farmers have lost their contracts, leaving fewer and fewer in business. In some years, there have been unprecedented numbers of cuts, including in 2010, when upward of 40 percent of farmers in some regions were pushed out of business by tobacco companies that decided not to renew those contracts. "Philip Morris is doing what they should do as a business," a farmer who lost his contract recently told a reporter, "They're taking care of their stockholders" (Schreiner 2010). At the same time that the contracting system contributes to local patterns of job loss and dislocation, it also puts downward financial pressure on farms, individualizes production risks, and deepens dependency on an illegal labor system characterized by squalid housing conditions, government neglect, and clustered health problems. Although Philip Morris demands that growers comply with all laws related to agricultural production and hiring, contracts do not provide incentives for farmers to improve labor camps, and pricing makes farmers' ability to comply questionable. So this ostensible health campaign may actually compound migrant health and housing issues. Consider Philip Morris's new emphasis on limiting MH30 levels, which is intended to reduce health risks for smokers. Workers are no longer exposed to this dangerous chemical in the field, but MH30 is a laborsaving chemical, so the ban translates into extended workdays for migrant crews who manually do the work in the dewy mornings and evenings that MH30 used to do. Because working in wet conditions is a principal risk factor for green tobacco sickness (Arcury et al. 2001), the MH30 ban might actually increase its incidence. "Concrete biological phenomena," the anthropologist João Biehl writes, "are thus intertwined with environmental conditions that are part of a larger context" (2004: 476). Farmers often get blamed for these outcomes, but like farm employees, they are also partly disadvantaged within the contract system. Understanding what it is like to be a tobacco grower in this antismoking era requires apprehending what it is like to sell tobacco to Philip Morris, a company guided by one motivation, that now facializes its cutthroat, stomach-churning power as the friendly face of humanitarianism and web-designs its calculating, neoliberal machinations as the honest voice of consumer freedom.

These complex ethnographic dimensions were lost in the debates leading up to the recent passage of FDA legislation. In the United States, there will be some positive results from enhanced regulation over cigarettes (as discussed in chapter 1), but FDA regulation does nothing to address economic instability and conditions of exploitation in tobacco farming regions, worldwide smoking prevalence, and the ongoing redistribution of leaf production to the developing world. Insofar as contracting aims to simply optimize production and minimize labor costs, in North Carolina this historic tobacco-control measure and cornerstone of Philip Morris's corporate makeover risks shifting the financial, moral, and political burdens of health-driven production onto the shoulders of insecure farmers and subordinated farmworkers. Research at the farm level reveals important contradictions on which enhanced consumer health and safety measures are established. It demands assessment of FDA legislation in its complexity and on multiple levels, because the legislation stands to benefit tobacco corporate interests and builds on uneven spheres of risk and vulnerability.

Chapter 5 _____

El Campo

Payday

FRIDAY IS PAYDAY ON THE FARM. At noon, before heading back to the labor camp for lunch, the crew gets paid. Bartolo, the crew's foreman, handles a manila envelope that Craig Tester, the owner-operator, gave him that morning. It contains a dozen paychecks, each in a sealed envelope. He gives one of the envelopes to Diego, an older, frail man who moved to the United States from Central Mexico during the late 1970s' wave of Mexican immigration. Diego has worked in various regions and sectors of the U.S. economy, recently settling in North Carolina. His checkered shirt is unbuttoned and his hairless chest is grimy and sweaty after a morning of heaving thousands of pounds of cured tobacco leaf into hydraulic baling machines on Craig's industrial farm. Diego tears into the envelope with his index finger, which is caked with gooey bits of tobacco. He scans the check's surface, his finger circling, as if avoiding the bottom line. Once located, he says, scowling, "The pay is *muy campo*."

"*Muy campo*?" I ask, not exactly sure what he means.

"It's nothing, this paycheck," he bitterly comments. Diego walks with the crew to a run-down white van, which Craig owns and calls the "Mexican van." Bartolo will drive a half-mile stretch of country road to *el campo*, the squalid labor camp where the crew will eat lunch—today beans, eggs, tortillas, pickled carrots, onions, and chili peppers—and relax before returning to the afternoon's tobacco grind.[1]

The term *campo* is used commonly among migrant farmworkers in North Carolina to characterize various aspects of their life and work. Campo means rural, having essentially to do with the countryside and farmwork. Campo also refers to a field where crops are cultivated and the housing facility, the labor camp, where workers reside. In North Carolina's coastal plain, it is as if campo were not just this or that thing, but the social condition of farm labor itself, characterized by interlocking

---

[1] Bartolo is not a crew leader (i.e., a labor recruiter), a term described later. He lives with the crew in the labor camp, and having worked for Craig for successive years and being able to speak more English than other migrants is considered the foreman and charged with operating the van and dispensing paychecks. Craig does not employ a crew leader. Instead, he recruits workers by word of mouth and solicitations posted at local Laundromats and grocery stores.

Figure 5.1. Seasonal tobacco worker in a tobacco warehouse in Wilson, North Carolina, 2005. Photograph by author.

forms of subordination and marginalization. When migrants find a job in construction, a restaurant, or an office, anything that is not farm labor, they say it is "outside of the campo" and regard it as a socioeconomic advance, not just because of higher wages but because it extricates them from a situation that is largely experienced as embarrassing and dispossessing. The difficulty of manual tobacco work, the neglected condition of labor camps, and the meagerness of agricultural wages—each is stingingly indicted as campo. Something like a paycheck becomes a synecdoche, an illuminative fragment of the mean face of depravity and structural violence.

Facing Structural Violence

Through useful concepts such as "social suffering" (Bourdieu et al. 2000; Kleinman et al. 1997), "structural violence" (Bourgois 1996; Farmer 2004; Farmer et al. 2006; Singer 2006), "everyday violence" (Scheper-Hughes 1992), and the "social course" of suffering (Benson 2008b; Kleinman et al. 1995), medical anthropologists have emphasized the systemic constitution of inequality and suffering. Whereas violence is typically conceived in terms of physical harm, and although responses often seek to pin praise or blame on individual actors, a tendency Paul Farmer calls "the erosion of social awareness" or "desocialization" (2004: 308), this literature emphasizes societal, institutional, and structural dimensions of suffering, including the role of corporations, markets, and governments in fostering various kinds of harm in populations (Benson and Kirsch 2010). Farmer defines structural violence as social arrangements that systematically bring subordinated and disadvantaged groups into harm's way and put them at risk for various forms of suffering (2004: 307–8). Anthropologists have sought to "resocialize" suffering by tracing its origins to political-economic processes, social structures, and cultural ideologies (Benson et al. 2008).

Apart from important exposés, such as John Steinbeck's *Grapes of Wrath* (1939), James Agee and Walker Evans's *Let Us Now Praise Famous Men* (1941), and Edward R. Murrow and Fred W. Friendly's *Harvest of Shame* (1960), farm labor conditions have remained hidden from the public eye (Bletzer 2004: 532). Romantic cultural representations of plighted family farmers have covered over the menacing living and working conditions endured by laborers (Thompson 2002b). Farmworkers in the United States endure conditions of structural violence, including deplorable wages and endemic poverty, forms of stigma and racism, occupational health and safety hazards, poor health and limited access to services, and the constant threat of deportation (Arcury and Quandt 2007a; Griffith and Kissam 1994; Oxfam America 2004; Smith-Nonini 1999; Thompson and Wiggins 2002; Villarejo 2003). In the peak tobacco harvest season (late June to early October) employees work between thirty-five and sixty hours per week without overtime pay, earning the federal minimum hourly wage, which amounts to a few hundred dollars weekly. About half of the 2.5 million individuals employed in agriculture in the United States earn less than $8,000 per year, making farm labor one of the country's poorest social classes. Relative agricultural wages have fallen by 10 percent since the late 1980s (Oxfam America 2004: 12). In this chapter, I analyze the interlocking political, economic, and cultural processes that are involved in the continuous reproduction of the particular system of structural violence (what Farmer calls "the social machinery of oppression" [2004: 308]) that affects farm labor. I analyze how inequities of political and social power, differences in living conditions, and the unequal distribution of citizenship and belonging become embedded in long-standing social structures, normalized in institutions, and naturalized in everyday experience in rural North Carolina.

Farmer suggests that structural violence is often perpetuated on the basis of visibility. Certain factors are seen as "causes" of suffering (and/or disease), while others are overlooked, as when government policies and programs focus on individual behaviors and ignore underlying systemic conditions. He encourages anthropologists to scrutinize dominant frames of perception that remove historical and societal forces from an account of how structural violence, attendant inequalities, and responses are constituted. For example, Farmer (1992) emphasizes the enduring impact of the slave trade and an uneven geography of capitalist accumulation in shaping the HIV epidemic in Haiti, as well as pernicious stereotypes that inaccurately blame Haiti as the source of the epidemic. His aim is to open a "field of vision" that includes historical, material, and symbolic conditions or phenomena that might fall outside of what is "ethnographically visible" to researchers and observers, and what is culturally visible to participants in a given system (Farmer 2004: 305–8).

Given this emphasis on visibility, a field such as the phenomenology of perception would seem indispensable to the anthropology of structural violence.[2] However, the strategies Farmer outlines for opening new fields of vision are premised on a positivism that involves the integration of more bodies of scientific or objective knowledge. He writes, "[the] anthropology of violence necessarily draws on history and biology, just as it necessarily draws on political economy. To tally body counts correctly requires epidemiology, forensic and clinical medicine, and demography. The erasure of these broad bodies of knowledge may be seen as the central problematic of a robust anthropology of structural violence" (308). But an adequate understanding of how visibility sustains or challenges structural violence must involve ethnographic and phenomenological accounts of the frames of perception through which people interpret relations of inequality, experience familiarity and alterity, and respond to suffering. It is not only scientific knowledge that influences the visibility or invisibility of suffering and harm but also the subjective acts of meaning making, patterns of moral reasoning, and cultural logics of accountability that can encourage people to look at suffering (and each other) in particular ways. Oftentimes, the problem is not that suffering is invisible or its causes unknown, but rather that individuals and whole groups can have something at stake in actively overlooking and taking distance from other people's suffering. "Oppression is a result of many conditions," Farmer writes, "not the least of which reside in consciousness" (307).

---

[2] The phenomenology of perception is a subfield of phenomenology that comes out of Edmund Husserl's concern with acts of intentionality that constitute human perception. Maurice Merleau-Ponty (2002) expanded beyond the Cartesian underpinnings of Husserl's work to develop a more dynamic and worldly sense of perception as constituted at the nexus of consciousness, body, and world. The descriptions undertaken in this chapter are influenced by this social approach to how people see themselves and others (see Lingis 1998; Schutz 1967).

Among the interlocking factors that cause and maintain the structural violence that impacts farm labor are downward economic pressure on agricultural production, the power of agribusiness corporations, systemic government neglect, and mass-media stereotypes. On a local level, in North Carolina tobacco country, structural violence is also underpinned by a mode of perception built on specific understandings of alterity and community, an optical regime evidenced when tobacco growers and other "native" North Carolinians envision farmworkers as people who belong to a fundamentally different and devalued "culture," an essentializing way of seeing that links up to national efforts to criminalize "illegal" immigration. The view of undocumented immigrants as a threat to U.S. nationalism leads to harsh policy approaches that do not acknowledge the realities of societal integration and the dependence of U.S. economic growth on low wages paid to Mexicans and other immigrants (Gledhill 1998).

Negative stereotypes about immigrants and collective racist attitudes limit ethical responsiveness in the face of the hardships immigrants typically endure (Chávez 1992: 16–20; Cowan et al. 1997). When some people look at a migrant farmworker, they do not see a sentient face that bears witness to the vulnerability of existence and commands the self to infinite responsibility and hospitality, as in the ethics idealized by Emmanuel Levinas (1969, 1981, 1998). Instead, they see someone who, despite living down the country road in a labor camp and doing the backbreaking work of harvesting the area's tobacco crop, does not belong to the fabric of "who is here with us," and are thus excluded from what counts as community (Joseph 2002: 174). As tobacco industry declines and recent neoliberal reforms intensify farm-level economic pressures, this way of seeing allows growers to strategically distance themselves from illegal yet financially beneficial hiring practices and noncompliance with labor camp housing standards, routing blame onto people differentiated as Other, blameworthy, and threatening.

Farm Labor and Labor Camps

In the pre-1950s U.S. South, a predominantly insular regional labor market confined African Americans to manual agricultural labor, tenancy, and low wages, conditions rooted in plantation slavery (Daniel 1972). There was also a less visible system of seasonal and geographically mobile labor. As early as the 1890s, black and European immigrant workers followed the harvest from truck farms in the Northeast to produce operations in Florida (Hahamovitch 1997). As with the sharecropping system discussed in chapter 2, this mobile workforce was built on well-organized strategies of social control, including vagrancy laws, forced labor, and physical brutality. Migrant crews were often segregated into dilapidated labor camps, company towns, and ghettoized enclaves that were placed outside city limits (Rothenberg 1998: 33–34). Agricultural company towns in Florida, where vagrancy laws required all "Negroes [to] be off the streets" at a certain hour, were colloquially called "black towns" or "slave camps" by growers. One was called "Harlem." Workers were generally not permitted to write home, while those who complained about wages or attempted to flee were sometimes killed. Supervisors wore guns, carried batons, and routinely threatened workers with death and beatings (Hollander 2006: 281–82).

A tradition of legal exceptionalism has historically regarded farm labor as distinct from other kinds of work (Schell 2002). The New Deal excluded farmworkers and domestics from rights and protections that were guaranteed to workers in other industries, including the right to organize, minimum wage standards, overtime provisions, child labor laws, pension plans, unemployment insurance, and workers' compensation (Rothenberg 1998: 36). These exceptions disproportionately denied minority groups—the bulk of farm laborers—aspects of citizenship that were afforded to white workers in other sectors (Lipsitz 1995: 372). Indeed, the federal government has generally backed the social power and economic interests of growers. In the wartime labor shortage of the 1940s, Florida growers maintained depressed wages and a controllable workforce by importing foreign-born workers from the Caribbean through a formal government "guest worker" program (Hollander 2006). The trend to rescale the labor pool to an international level to maintain a supply of unskilled laborers drove dramatic changes in the regional workforce for the rest of the century.

Farm mechanization and market globalization intensified the postwar need for flexible and inexpensive labor arrangements (Winters 1998). The crew leader system, rooted in the 1950s when Mexican American farmworkers migrated to Florida and established themselves as labor contractors, filled this niche. The regional workforce has since undergone a "steady process of Latinization" (Rothenberg 1998: 44). Rural dislocation and poverty in Mexico, exacerbated by international economic liberalization (e.g., the North American Free Trade Agreement), have driven northward migration (Delgado-Wise and Covarrubias 2006; Kingsolver 2001; Massey et al. 1987). North Carolina's Hispanic population has increased tenfold since 1970, which is triple the national rate (Kasarda and Johnson 2006: 1).[3]

---

[3] While the term "Hispanic" is used in the census and demographic studies, it is not preferred in the academic literature on Latino and Mexican anthropology, geography, and cultural studies. The term, as De Genova documents, was formulated by the U.S. government as a census category and flattened and erased particular histories of several ethnic groups (2005: 256).

Farmers I interviewed commonly explained their switch to using migrant labor in terms of the "laziness" and "unreliability" of black people. This rationale echoes the familiar "displacement" thesis, which presupposes an immutable, antagonistic social division between poor black people and immigrants, and neglects the role of industrial forces and relationships between classes in recomposing the labor market as a whole (De Genova 2005: 74). This scenario implies that the government and agribusiness are not complicit in an illegal hiring system that has fundamentally shifted the farm workforce, depressed wages, and dislocated many residents, especially in low-paying, labor-intensive sectors, and has substantially reduced costs and made North Carolina agriculture more competitive (Kasarda and Johnson 2006). The existing federal "guest worker" program is rarely utilized. Farmers save money by hiring undocumented persons who are often willing to work for minimum wage and live in substandard housing, and the government takes a punitive approach characterized by raids and deportations, and only laxly regulates hiring practices writ large.

There is no precise count of migrant farmworkers in the United States, but roughly half of all agricultural workers are migrants according to the U.S. Department of Labor. Although 95 percent of migrant farmworkers are of Mexican descent, others come from Central America and the Caribbean. More than half of all agricultural workers are undocumented (Oxfam America 2004: 7–8). Nonpermanent guest workers are legally hired through the federal H-2A program, which issues temporary, nonimmigrant work visas. In North Carolina, H-2A hiring expanded from 168 to 10,500 employees during the 1990s, making the state the country's largest user of guest workers (Oxfam America 2004: 19). Since then, H-2A hiring has slipped to a few thousand workers, a sliver of the state's roughly 100,000 total farmworkers, owing to escalating wages, transportation costs, and labor-organizing activities associated with the program (Smith-Nonini 1999, 2005). While most Latinos in North Carolina have settled in metropolitan areas, more than 40 percent of the rural economic impact of the state's Hispanic labor force is concentrated in a handful of counties with specialized farm industries like poultry or tobacco (Kasarda and Johnson 2006: 4–8; Larson 2000; North Carolina Farmworker Institute 2007).

Important farm labor reforms came out of the cultural and political struggles of the civil rights era. New legislation required labor contractors to register with the government, maintain wage records, disclose working conditions, and ensure workplace protections. But not until 1983 were federal standards for labor camps established (Griffith and Kissam 1995: 17–21). Even then, implementation was slow. Only in 1990 did North

Carolina establish uniform inspection standards, ending a long-standing rule that excluded growers from housing fewer than twelve workers from regulation (*Wilson Daily Times* 1989c). State law stipulates specific standards for the housing site and the structure itself, which must be kept clean and free from debris, garbage, rodents, and insects (North Carolina Department of Labor 2008), but because labor camps house people who belong to a marginalized social class, government neglect and noncompliance in the private sector are the norm. Farmers are rarely penalized for housing code violations. Workers often lack command of English and knowledge of their rights, and they fear deportation and unemployment, such that compliance issues are underreported (Smith-Nonini 1999).

North Carolina law defines "migrant housing" as "any facility . . . that is established, operated, or used as living quarters for migrants" (North Carolina Department of Labor 2008: 7). Mobile homes, single-family homes, duplexes, apartments, tenant houses, converted barns, and large barrack-style structures that house hundreds of people can all legally be registered as migrant housing. Camps thus belong to that category of power-saturated spaces created not by architecture but by the status of the inhabitants (Low 2003: 144–46).[4] Camps come in all shapes and sizes, but they are almost always overcrowded and run-down. "Farmworkers are among the worst-housed groups in the United States," writes one observer (Holden 2002: 169; Early et al. 2006; Gentry et al. 2007). One study of farm labor camps conducted in the eastern United States found that 10 percent of units lack toilet facilities, have broken toilets or dysfunctional stoves, and have structural problems, such as damaged windows and sagging roofs, as well as interior problems, such as water leakage, broken plaster, and peeling paint. Thirty-eight percent of units are classified as "severely inadequate," with serious plumbing problems, damaged heating elements and electrical systems, and extensive structural damage. This compares to the 2 percent of all housing (including nonfarm labor housing) that is severely inadequate on a national level (Holden 2002: 169–93). There are active efforts to improve these conditions in North Carolina, most notably by the Farm Labor Organizing Committee (FLOC), a national labor union affiliated with the AFL-CIO. Farmworker advocacy groups, public health outreach workers, church groups, and some growers have also joined these improvement efforts (Agricultural Missions Incorporated 2000; Oxfam America 2004; Smith-Nonini 1999). But national farm groups are powerful and capable of opposing improved standards in legislative processes (Schell 2002: 139–40).

---

[4] While this is the case in North Carolina, where growers usually own a labor camp, it is important to note that in other parts of the country farmworkers do not always live in housing owned by employers (Holden 2002: 172).

About two-thirds of North Carolina's thousands of labor camps are unregistered, one-quarter get inspected, and a measly 1 percent comply with standards (Holden 2002: 180; *Wilson Daily Times* 1989c).

Faciality

> Violence can aim only at a face.
> —Emmanuel Levinas, *Totality and Infinity* (1969: 225)

In this epigraph, Levinas means that harm is meaningless if it is understood as being directed at an inanimate object (1969: 225). One cannot harm a stone, for example (Kosky 2001: 39). Violence can only target an animate and sensate existence, which for Levinas is signaled in the human face. The face is different than objects in that it bears the trace of the infinite alterity of the other person (i.e., the other's singularity) and thereby confounds cognition and eludes masterful powers of perception. The face cannot be "synthesized" like any old object (Levinas 1969: 33). Individuals, in their singular existence, are irreducible to totalized representations, such as "culture" or "ethnicity" (Benson and O'Neill 2007; Kleinman and Benson 2006). For Levinas, the face's singularity also means that the face is always the face of vulnerability because it can be materially or symbolically annihilated (1969: 251). According to Levinas, it is the sentient face—the singular existence of the other person—that totalizing representations, physical acts of brutality, and systemized forms of violence target, and this is why he says, "Violence can aim only at a face."

Building on this phenomenology, Levinas idealizes the "face-to-face" encounter, the immediate interpersonal frame, as the basic scene of ethics. He imagines a self held hostage and propelled to infinite goodness in the face of the suffering of another person (Levinas 1998: 93–94). For Levinas, the very possibility of annihilating the other's singularity, which shines through in the face, makes hospitality an imperative for the self. One is always already bound to the other by an ethical relationship because of the possibility of turning away or doing harm (Benson and O'Neill 2007: 32–33). However, the modes of perception that guide ordinary interactions in empirical life tend to squash this esoteric principle into hard realities of *faciality*, or people seeing each other as typified objects and, on that basis, circumscribing suffering as an event that belongs to, or is even caused by, the sufferer. The other's suffering dangerously and easily becomes an event in which the self is not complicit (Levinas 1988). Levinas speaks of the "transmutation of the other into the same," the reduction of alterity into a model of what is expected or already known, and the triumph of formal legal codes, moral models, and social

contracts over face-to-face ethics, the isolation and partitioning of responsibility over the impulse to unconditional goodness (1969: 113). As
used in this book, the concept of faciality refers to how power and perception overlap, as well as to how ethical orientations are formed and/or
inhibited on the basis of what people see when they look at other people's
faces. Faciality is crucial to the constitution and perpetuation of structural violence because how people see others can help legitimize patterns
of social subordination, economic exploitation, and spatial segregation.

The term *faciality* (*visagéité*) comes from Gilles Deleuze and Félix
Guattari (1987), whose analytic of power emphasizes the social production of faces, that is, how faces are perceived in light of media images,
social typologies, and power relations: "the face, the power of the face,
engenders and explains social power" (Deleuze and Guattari 1987: 175).
To say that faces are socially produced means they are perceived in a
fundamentally different way than Levinas wishes. Deleuze and Guattari
write sarcastically of "glum face-to-face encounters" between pre-given
social types (171). They argue that faces are seen as generic types that do
not confound cognitive synthesis in their infinite alterity. Rather, the human face becomes a medium through which finite differences are established, as when the aesthetics of the face play an important role in racial
schemes, class structures, and other classificatory logics (185–93).[5]

Human faces never simply signify in terms of phenotypical features,
and their composition does not mechanically reflect the structural or societal position of the individual. Amid a transpersonal set of strategies
operating throughout society (i.e., an abstract machine [Massumi 1992:
26]), faces are actively coded as allegorical signs and invested with cultural meaning in practices of everyday life. Faces have a figurative quality.
They can be perceived in terms of a stereotype, a capitalized "Face," as
Deleuze and Guattari (1987: 129) put it (what Levinas [1969] might call
a "totality"). Deleuze and Guattari cite the face of "a rich child in which
a military calling is already discernable, that West Point chin. You don't
so much have a face as slide into one" (1987: 177). In this conceptualiza-
tion, faces are perceived in terms of a metonymic relationship between
a particular feature and the discursive coding of who a person is, what
that type of person is like, where they live, and what capabilities, propensities, and other traits they have (168). It "is not the individuality of
the face that counts but the efficacy of the ciphering it makes possible"

---

[5] On the role of the face in marking race and class differences, see Roland Barthes's
(1972: 56–57) analysis of Greta Garbo, Sander L. Gilman's (2001) cultural histories of
plastic surgery and the aesthetics of anti-Semitism, and Kathleen Stewart's (2002) analysis
of facial gesture and cultural style in photographs of Appalachian people.

(175). Faciality is thus constituted in a "zone of frequency or probability" involving the coproduction of empirical features and their significance.

> A child, woman, mother, man, father, boss, teacher, police officer, does not speak a general language but one whose signifying traits are indexed to specific faciality traits. Faces are basically not individual; they define zones of frequency or probability, delimit a field that neutralizes in advance any expressions or connections unamenable to the appropriate significations. . . . Concrete faces cannot be assumed to come ready-made. They are engendered by an abstract machine of faciality. (Deleuze and Guattari 1987: 168)

Generic facial representations are detachable images that can circulate as symbols of place, icons of a group of people, and tools of power and resistance. Think of the confident face of a political leader on a campaign poster, the stenciled face of Che on an expatriate's shirt, or the destitute face of a migrant worker on the cover of a news magazine. Deleuze and Guattari note that many sociopolitical structures or movements "need face" as a fundamental component of their constitution and reproduction (1987: 180), as when flags and other symbols seem to represent the face of a nation or when the faces of rulers are spatialized in monumental architecture and public spectacles. Not only human visages but also spaces and landscapes are facialized. Particular social and spatial features resonate as a "face-landscape" (175), as when a neighborhood or gated community is said to have character or personality. Cities stand out as skylines that are recognizable faces, and the great heights of skyscrapers personalize wealth and power as character traits of the city itself. Furthermore, human faces can be structured or staged by landscapes; spatial arrangements and the literal lay of the land dramatically shape how faces are configured and interact, as we will see in the case of farm labor camps.

It is precisely the detachable and allegorical quality that makes faces, especially the face of power, readily available for parody and defacement (Taussig 1999). The face of the Boss, for example, is constituted in the watchful eye, furrowed brow, and persistent scowl that resonate as the stern face of management, a cluster of features that might be parodied in a cartoon, by a mime, or by a worker who resents the constant glare over his shoulder. Migrant workers in North Carolina are not silent in the face of structural violence. In the gripes and grimaces of people like Diego, we find parodic acts of resistance that take command of the stigmatizing quality of vision in rural farm regions and in national media to expose the mean face of depraved labor camps and the hostile face of a nationalist and nativist public that ironically thrives on their labor.

This is what is meant by campo—a metaphoric expression used to disparage structural violence and facialize its inhospitable and menacing character. Wages are campo not simply because they are meager, but because they are part of an unremitting slap in the face that plasters symbolic denigration into the materiality of such things as a paycheck or a labor camp. Diego calls the paycheck campo because he knows Craig condescendingly sees him as naturally belonging in a field or labor camp, in el campo. His use of the term conveys an experiential aspect of farm labor, the feeling of being "other" and on the "outside," that is produced and naturalized in relations of economic exploitation. In this chapter, I examine how the visages of farmers and farmworkers, as well as labor camps and other "Mexican" spaces, are facialized. Drawing on the anthropologist Michael Taussig's (1999) concept of defacement, I also investigate how subversive practices of defacement take hold of faciality to levy a political and moral indictment against structural violence. This study enhances our understanding of the dialectics of domination and subordination in U.S. agriculture and provides fruitful ground for theorizing the dangerous constitution of structural violence and racial stereotypes in the context of transnational labor migration and international agricultural restructuring.

Culture of Blame

Many growers take pride in being reasonable and responsible employers. Farmers commonly say that seasonal workers are "part of the family," having employed the same crew for several consecutive years. Good feelings and working relationships are not easily disentangled from the paternalism that has historically been a core part of white identity on southern farms and helped justify racial domination and socioeconomic inequities (Hollander 2006: 269). For people who share a hegemonic common sense about who belongs where and understand a racialized division of labor as more or less natural, treating workers with respect and dignity, abiding by labor regulations, and even getting to know workers can seem like consequential moral acts.

But farm labor advocates critique the sometimes romantic overtones of how farmers talk about workers. "They tell stories about coming of age on their farms. But this is a complete dehumanization of the workers who they now hire. They try to make the farm seem like a regular life, a normal part of the countryside," a labor advocate tells me. "But the reality is that it's not a regular life. We can all appreciate the fact that farmwork is important work. But if your standards of living are degraded, then that's a huge discrepancy and not regular or normal."

Craig, a medium-scale grower (with 150 acres of tobacco), registers his camp and has it inspected by state officials every year. He ensures it is up to code (e.g., the smoke detectors and light fixtures are working, the kitchen and bathroom facilities are clean and functional) before migrants move in for the harvest season. "It is a right or wrong thing," Craig says in an interview.

> My neighbors don't comply and they don't get in trouble with the government. I think that is wrong. They furnish a run-down tenant house that is not up to code. So they have an advantage. I spend money and time to abide by the law and they don't. The workers work damn hard, hot weather, doing work that I don't do, and I understand that. I manage the farm, and my work is more and more about putting a pencil to paper. So the least I can do is make sure the camp is decent, livable. The workers deserve that. But most farmers could care less. The workers are here for a few months, so why should they give a damn—that's the mentality.

In Craig's mind, part of being a responsible employer involves regularly visiting the camp to have what he describes as quality "face time" with workers:

> Most growers don't know what's going on in the camps. They let the place get wrecked and then they complain when the place is wrecked. What do they expect? If you are not there, there is no contact. If there is no face time, then you don't know the workers. You are just *el patrón* [the boss], and that's what happens. The camp is trashed. You've got to be there. You've got to show respect to workers, and then they will respect the camp, keep it clean.

Each night, Craig visits his camp for about ten minutes. He walks around and greets workers, who nod and try their best to look innocent. He does not speak Spanish, although some growers—people Craig would regard as both "good" and "bad" actors, farmers who abide by housing laws and those who do not—have acquired language skills to facilitate work-place communication, which workers see as a mixed blessing, a potential mechanism of social control. The crew admits that Craig is "not like other bosses. He is more relaxed and kinder," as one migrant puts it. But the crew is also aware that Craig's intentions with face time are partly economical. "The boss is here, but he is not really here," one worker, Marcos, a frail young man from Veracruz, said to me. "He comes and looks at everything. But he just comes to make sure there are no problems. He wouldn't come and eat dinner in the kitchen here. He wouldn't use this bathroom." Another worker believes Craig "does not trust us." He discerns that Craig seems concerned with garbage and the order of things, staring at a pile of dirty laundry, rolling his eyes at beer bottles on the ground, smearing the grease caked on the rusty stove with his finger as if to point out a glaring problem, like a sergeant with bleached gloves fingering a cadet's sole. Although Craig sees himself as going above and beyond, distrust arises as the crew senses some other motive besides a genuine desire to interact. They sense the pastoral power that wants to sanitize their living space through the incitement of self-regulating behaviors and a boss's desire to maintain order and livability so as to maximize labor's productivity and minimize his own financial and legal liability.

These power dynamics and managerial strategies may not be what Craig sees in his own actions, but they are part of the crew's interpretation. The rigid division of labor and its reflection of stark differences of citizenship and wealth—and, therefore, the larger system of commodity production in which farm management and labor are situated—create subjective barriers that make workers suspicious of face time, and their faces and bodies targets of a kind of monitoring that is not altogether innocent, even though it might dutifully fulfill official government regulations. From the standpoint of Levinasian ethics, what Craig idealizes as face time falls short of being an ethical relationship. This is not because Craig directly causes some kind of harm to workers, but rather because his engagement with them is already couched within a particular set of relations that are embedded in economic transactions and dependencies. In contrast, Levinas imagines ethics as a "relation without relation" (1969: 79), a situation in which the other person calls the ego into question and holds the self hostage precisely because an economy of expectations or debts has yet to be established. Only in such a hypothetical setting—the unmediated face-to-face—does the face of the other defy totalizing representations and command a kind of respect that is not linked to self-interest (Derrida 1995).

Although he complies with standards, what Craig shares with other North Carolinians is a tendency to blame migrants themselves for depraved living conditions. Indeed, for Craig, compliance with standards is a strategic way to ensure his own innocence, such that when a problem does arise in the camp—perhaps the grounds are rife with garbage or the kitchen has broken fixtures—he can claim, "It was fine and good before the crew moved in. Now it's trashed. That's not my fault." As labor organizers visit camps with greater frequency to check on compliance issues and report problems to the North Carolina Department of Labor, farmers increasingly face costly fines, and many resort to a similar strategy of blame deferral. Growers say workers trash what are, in fact, adequate housing facilities. "The labor camps are nasty, yes. But it is the nastiness of the workers. The media and the labor union say it's our fault," a farmer who hires a dozen migrants each year says. "But migrants are over here illegally to start with. We furnish good, clean housing, nicer than what they had in Mexico. Then they trash it—beer bottles and garbage everywhere, a damn pigsty. It's not my fault; the workers are to blame."

This reasoning may be true in some cases. "I refurbished a mobile home and wanted to make it look nice," another grower tells me. "I put in brand-new appliances, windows, carpet, everything. But the crew moved in, and by the end of the season, it was ruined." One room was filled with emptied and crushed beer cans, and insects infested an unkempt kitchen. "Look, I am a fair person," he continues. "I realize that you can't expect a bunch of guys to keep the place spotless. But they trashed it." However, such reasoning about responsibility neglects important aspects of the context in which camps become trashed. Workers are tired after the workday and rarely feel compelled to keep the camp clean. Garbage tossed on the ground only contributes to an already squalid environment. "It's impossible," one Mexican worker tells me, "to keep a refrigerator clean when it is shared by twenty people. It's impossible to keep a stove clean when it is shared by fifty people."

The fact that workers inhabit dispossessed space, a space that they do not own or even call home, surely limits their desire to keep the place up. Without regular inspections and strict regulation, it is difficult to simply attribute the obvious depravity of most labor camps to workers. Migrants and farmworker advocates make stinging moral claims about the deprivation of camps and the difficulties of living in substandard housing (see below). That workers are blanketed with blame depends on forms of social stigma and cultural conceptions of alterity that are marshaled by nonmigrants to reassert status hierarchies, distance themselves from the trash associated with migrants, and justify squalor. On farms, spatial relationships are often clearly marked. Some farmers do not permit migrant workers (or black employees, for that matter) to enter the farm office or nearby family home. Migrants typically eat apart from the other workers. Jobs are coded as white jobs, black jobs, and Mexican jobs. Aging black workers often insist that only blacks and whites should ride in the front of a pickup truck, that "the bed was made for Mexicans," as one man says. Although the black worker has a class relationship to migrants, sitting in the cab implies his affinity with the farmer who owns the farm trucks, and it establishes a shared sense of locality based on belonging to the workplace in a permanent, substantial way.

In addition, many nonmigrants exhibit anxieties about getting close to camps, which are usually set off the road and tucked away in a field, because this implies a class and cultural association with devalued figures (e.g., migrants and prostitutes who frequent camps in the evenings and on weekends). "I don't go into the camp," a black worker tells me in an interview. "After work, I drive the crew to the camp and drop them off at the road. I'm no Mexican and I'm not going to fool with the camp." Avoidance marks the camp, like the back of the pickup truck, as "Mexican" space. Despite the multiethnic composition of the workforce on most farms, often including Latinos of various backgrounds, local white and black folks commonly call labor camps "Little Mexico." The term *Mexican* is used to refer to all migrants and is defined as someone who does a devalued, stigmatized kind of work and lives in stigmatized spaces (Rothenberg 1998: 181–84; Striffler 2005: 164). These acts of separation and differentiation reflect the influence of mass-media images, popular stereotypes, and political discourses that consolidate the generalized category of the "Mexican" as a temporary, "illegal," deportable subject who is said to be linked to a natal country and is therefore not properly a part of the local or national society (Chávez 2001; De Genova 2002, 2005).

As an analytical tool, stigma has been applied to various circumstances that afflict individuals and groups, especially discrimination and disparity issues owing to disease, race, ethnicity, and language. Researchers regard Erving Goffman's (1963) pioneering work, which portrays stigma as a "spoiled identity" or deeply discredited attribute that devalues a person, as a still influential if also somewhat mechanistic model, and they have sought to more complexly document experiential, moral, and sociopolitical dimensions of how stigma is constituted in local cultural contexts (Kleinman et al. 1995; Kusow 2004; Yang et al. 2007). Stigma is currently seen as a dynamic social process linking interrelated components such as labeling, stereotyping, emotional reaction, and discrimination (Yang et al. 2007). Much stigma theory has focused on the psychology of stigma (Major and O'Brien 2005). Anthropologists have emphasized an "experience-near" approach that is focused on the contextual processes, historical conjunctures, and social fields in which stigma takes shape and affects persons (Good and DelVecchio Good 1994; Kleinman et al. 1995). This approach combines knowledge of the macrosociological forces, such as discrimination, that underwrite stigma with the ethnographic understanding of how stigma is configured within a local world amid contextual interpretations of what stigma means, historical patterns of social affiliation, and evolving experiences of danger and uncertainty (Yang et al. 2007; Castro and Farmer 2005). Anthropologists are not interested solely in the lived experiences of the stigmatized but also in the experiences and motivations of stigmatizers (Eichelberger 2007; Lee et al. 2006; Nations et al. 2009; Reddy 2005).

For example, some white farmers are an important source of forms of stigma that affect migrants (Kingsolver 2007). Blaming migrants for poor conditions and "illegality," farmers strategically distance themselves from compliance issues and criminality. Such blame is also stigmatization because it links labels and stereotypes to an "us versus them" logic, which leads to shunning, avoidance, and discrimination (Link and Phelan 2001: 367). Institutionalized and informal discrimination against immigrants is widespread in the United States and is manifested in xenophobia, harassment, segregation, and criminalization. Social stigma is built on uneven structures of economic, political, and symbolic power, as in the case of farm employment. The public nature of stigma influences interactions across local settings, as when signs of inferiority are marked out, commented on, and sanctioned at farm workplaces. Farmers draw on a public universe of stereotypes to homogenize Mexicans as part of an essentialized "national culture" that is "fixed, simple, and unambiguous" (Herzfeld 1992: 73), and to devalue that culture as morally inferior. Here, the social production of the face is a mechanism of power that does not render people faceless or invisible as much as it facializes individuals as having the Face of a culture that is alternately seen as friendly and familial, docile and hardworking, threatening and nonlocal, or morally inferior and filthy.

Stigma is a social phenomenon that can have various ramifications. One interesting intersection is with the ecology of disease on farms. In North Carolina, tobacco workers are commonly afflicted with an illness that results from dermal exposure to dissolved nicotine from wet tobacco leaves, called "green tobacco sickness" (Arcury et al. 2003; Quandt et al. 2000). Prevalence among the state's tobacco workers is about 25 percent. Symptoms include nausea, vomiting, headache, dizziness, weakness, abdominal cramps, breathing problems, and diarrhea (Arcury et al. 2001). Tobacco sickness is common among foreign-born workers partly because they do the bulk of the manual work; limited work experience is also a risk factor (Arcury, Quandt, and Preisser 2001). Among farmers, tobacco sickness is culturally framed as an ethnic disease, a "Mexican disease," as farmers sometimes put it (see also Quandt et al. 1998). The disease is interpreted according to "biosocial" groupings (Rabinow 1996: 91–111), which naturalizes the epidemiological distribution of disease in terms of nationality, with culture itself becoming a risk factor (Kleinman and Benson 2006). Farmers sometimes attribute symptoms to drunkenness (e.g., the migrant worker is hungover from a night of partying in the camp, which might be true) or say that workers who vomit in the field are malingering. Stigma becomes a dangerous lens through which illness is interpreted and valued (Kleinman et al. 1995). This may be one reason why efforts to reduce risks (e.g., beginning work later, after dew has dissipated, or utilizing protective clothing) are uncommon. When the disease is demedicalized, its reality is discredited, and cultural beliefs and lack of knowledge become obstacles to efforts that seek to medicalize, treat, and prevent sickness (Arcury, Quandt, and Russell 2002; Arcury, Quandt, and Simmons 2002; Rao et al. 2004).

Face Time

"I have thought about why someone would trash the house they live in," a farmer tells me. "I think it's because he was raised that way. I can't raise him again. It's part of his culture." Implying that poverty and trash are inherently part of Mexican culture, farmers naturalize the nastiness of camps in terms of stereotyped ethnic pathology, masking the role of government neglect and agribusiness in helping make those conditions. "That is the way they are," this grower continues. "The Mexicans pile up toilet paper with shit on it high as their heads. What the hell can I do about that?"

This grower refers to an incident that occurred at his rural church, where an early-morning Spanish service is offered on Sundays in partnership with a separate Hispanic "sister church." One Sunday, white parishioners arriving for their regularly scheduled service found toilet paper on the bathroom floor. They blamed "Mexicans" for defiling sacred space. In their eyes, the gesture of allowing people who are seen as outsiders to use the facility was abused and disrespected. One church leader, Sean, who had been a missionary for decades in Mexico, tried to explain the situation to irate Southern Baptists. "In Mexico, poor plumbing demands that toilet paper not be discarded in the toilet, but rather in a wastebasket or even on the floor," he tells me during an interview. "This is what happened—a simple misunderstanding. We have to educate both groups about cultural norms and hygienic practices. We put signs in the stalls for those who can read, and many cannot, and we've added trashcans." This well-intentioned intervention did little to alter white parishioners' attitudes. They saw floored toilet paper as unclean and unsafe, evidence of cultural backwardness and a lack of what Sean calls "hygienic practices," even though, as he rightly insists, for Hispanic churchgoers, this disposal method is perfectly normal, hygienic, and safe, a responsible way to avoid sewage backup. If Sean wanted to "educate" parishioners, he started from the premise of a cultural clash between two "groups" that possess unwavering "norms." In an evolutionary hierarchy—note his reference to lower literacy rates for Hispanic parishioners and inadequate sewage infrastructure in Mexico—the particular relationship to feces he frames as normal in Mexico is equated with less educational achievement and underdevelopment, and seems premodern by comparison.

In the European colonial imagination, according to Dipesh Chakrabarty, phenomena such as dust, dirt, disease, and crowds were equated with the colonized population, who were seen as backward and as threats to the colonizing population's modernity, cleanliness, order, and well-being. The colonial subject was thought to be "blind to the unwholesome aspects of their public spaces" (Chakrabarty 2002: 65). The bazaar was luridly narrated in Orientalist literature in terms of "filthy drains," "disgusting" vendors, and overcrowding, an "Indian chaos" that "was opposed [to] the immaculate order of the European quarters" (67). For Chakrabarty, these views did not simply comprise a set of stereotypes that were passively embodied as a cognitive model, but were "evidence of a particular way of seeing" (66), a regime of visibility and a lens that pleasurably examined things from afar with a keen interest in discerning and reasserting hierarchies of cultural difference and moral value. The particular spatial sensitivity to aesthetic aspects of human habitation and exchange that defined this colonial gaze was evidence of a more generalized mode of perception and technology of power that, Chakrabarty stresses, underwrites the very grammar of modernity, including visceral sensibilities about public health, a tendency to equate filth with otherness, and knee-jerk responses to disorder (65–79).

This optical regime frames how many North Carolinians look at migrants. One parishioner, Trisha, left the church because of the toilet incident. "The church was trashed," she said, "and this scares me because I am interested in my community and the neighborhood. Will it be okay, you know?" She was also dismayed by her church's plans to relocate to a larger, presumably less "Mexican" and more "modern" building located near the current facility, which would now be used exclusively by the Hispanic church. "Churches want to partner with Hispanic groups," she tells me. "I understand those outreach goals. That church was my home, my community, my ties. Now they are giving it to the Mexicans, even after what they did to it." An evangelical Christian who discerns a basis for universal hospitality in the Bible, Trisha is not seen by friends and family as a mean person who wishes to exclude others simply on the grounds of racial otherness and discomfort or lack of understanding about differences. Like her fellow parishioners, she values religious and social outreach to marginal and minority groups. But it is in wanting "my community" to be clean and safe that she excludes forms of life and embodiment that are different from her own, stops short of being able to understand difference or discomfort in the context of broadscale conditions and diverging norms, and grounds a narrow image of belonging in stereotypes and misunderstanding.

Levinas wants people like Trisha to see singular traces of a vulnerable existence in the faces of the migrants, and then to be held hostage at that sight, infinitely responsible for their well-being, and unconditionally hospitable, an experience Levinas calls "epiphany" (1969: 213). The face-to-face he idealizes assumes that self and other are cohabitants of shared time and space: an immediate, proximate encounter with vulnerability galvanizes ethical responsiveness (Levinas 1981: 139). In practice, this interpersonal dynamic is rare. The temporal and spatial coordinates of alterity are culturally shaped and politically consequential. People who reside within a geographically defined community can sometimes seem the most out of place owing to practices of exclusion, segregation, and racialized mappings of belonging (Benson 2005).

Among the many paradoxes of "community" is the fact that "it can provide a medium for the fullest expression of belonging or the ultimate suppression and exclusion from one's closest surroundings" (Greenhouse et al. 1994: 175). Migrants are seen as traveling repositories of an essential culture, excluded from what counts as the here and now, or "my community," as Trisha puts it. They also seem to belong to a different time, a primitive past that makes them available targets of outreach at the same time as they are said to deserve depravity. The interpersonal event of sharing time and space is denied in cultural stereotypes and colonial optics that see others as underdeveloped and backward (Fabian 1983). Growers commonly justify labor camp squalor by saying, "The camp is nicer than what they had back home in Mexico" or "In Mexico they live in mud huts and shacks, so the camp is better than what they are used to." The language of modernity and an evolutionary view of cultural progress—the flush toilets and vinyl siding of middle-class U.S. citizens at the zenith—underpin the "ethical variability" (Petryna 2005) of seeing different people as deserving different standards of living. Despite their integral connection to the ongoing flow of tobacco leaf off industrialized farm operations, labor camps seem to somehow exist in an earlier time, while migrants are facialized as people whose proper space and time is always elsewhere, neither proximate nor immediate.

The trace that migrant faces exhibit is that of cultural difference, but also economic value. The actual face time of growers interacting with workers on the job would seem to unravel a blanketed denial of coevalness. Farmers sometimes get out of their pickup trucks or tractors, leave the farm office, and work in fields alongside migrants. To be sure, there is constant interaction, a mix of the camaraderie and antagonism that is common at any workplace, despite language barriers. Folks like Craig are conscientious about the implications of being proximate to others and sincerely see their relationship to workers as a moral struggle against prevailing tendencies of employer aloofness. But face time is also about managing property: the labor camp and the labor that it houses. When Craig visits the camp and meets with workers, he is literally facing time, a commodity, labor hours that he has purchased and that are assumed to be continuously at his disposal and available for monitoring and managing, even though the workday has ended (Taussig 1983: 26). Because workers inhabit space owned by the boss they are, in effect, perpetually on the clock, although they are not paid for the face time Craig "spends" with them, which he conceives as labor, as well as a tactical investment, on his part. Workers recognize the economic basis of this relationship and rightly attribute to Craig the distrust of someone keeping watch over private interests.

Craig once told me, "I don't know what these guys do after the season, and I don't even want to know. But as long as they're in my camp and working for me, I want to make sure there are no problems." When this contract is up, workers leave the camp and move on, to other states or economic sectors. But Craig knows that those workers or others like them, people with the same Face, will return, because he believes that "Mexico," the imagined space and time of migrants, is inferior. Faciality becomes a mask that conceals the forces that drive labor migration in Mexico and allows growers (and workers, as we will soon see) to maintain distance between one another despite realities of having conjoined lives. The basic fact that industrialized agriculture depends on flexible arrangements with mobile workers—that face time with workers has been made possible by the international economic restructuring that puts migrant populations at the disposal of U.S. employers—is converted into a set of beliefs about cultural superiority and imagined personalities that are the stereotyped face of imagined communities.

Insomnia

When North Carolinians give directions, labor camps are not counted in a string of houses. One can say "fourth house on the left," for example, a count that might exclude a camp, marking it as something other than a house. Nor do migrant farmworkers call the camp a "casa," preferring campo.[6] As discussed earlier in this chapter, this term also refers to a field and farm labor itself, as when workers answer the question "What kind of work do you do?" by simply saying *campo* or *trabajo de campo*. Flexible word usage reflects a phenomenological sense of campo as manifold rural space, an overlapping sphere of life and labor that is owned by the boss and defined as that which is "outside" (of the social order). "Everything is el campo," one migrant, Pancho, tells me. "I go to work and am in the field [*campo*]. Come back for lunch, in the camp [*campo*]. The grower [*ranchero*] has a house. But we are peasants [*campesinos*], always in the campo." Note that Pancho foregrounds class affiliation as part of a peasantry in which he would include his family in Oaxaca who work

[6] Hispanic migrant farmworkers distinguish North Carolina's camps from rental housing (*casas de renta*) found in Florida, where workers pay rent to contractors or growers. The term *casa* is almost never used to describe housing facilities in North Carolina.

Figure 5.2. Farmworker from Nayarit, Mexico, on a Wilson County farm, 2005.
Photograph by author.

in agriculture and to whom he sends monthly remittances. Although he considers his family's home a casa, his life and labor are now experienced as contained within el campo. The farmer is distinguished in terms of the place he lives, which Pancho and other workers call the *mansión*, and also his class affiliation as someone who is, Pancho tells me, neither a *campesino* nor an *agricultor* (farmer or agriculturalist), but a manager who does very little manual labor. He mostly monitors the production process from inside his pickup's cab, as compared to the work Pancho does, which is always outside in the hot sun.

In the reluctance of farmworkers to call the labor camp a casa, we are reminded of the spatial indistinction that James Agee spotlighted in his portrait of sharecroppers and tenants in Depression-era Alabama.

> [The] fields are workrooms or fragrant but mainly sterile workfloors without walls and with a roof of uncontrollable chance, fear, rumination, and propriative prayer. . . . The fields are organic of the whole, and of their own nature, and of the work that is poured into them: the spring, the garden, the outbuildings, are organic to the house itself. . . . The fields [are] the spread and broken petals of a flower whose bisexual center is the house. (Agee and Evans 1941: 129)

By emphasizing the spatial and experiential indistinction that defined tenant life, Agee undertook a kind of cultural critique. He sought to challenge the ostensible universality of the modern opposition between home and workplace, a split that arose as part of an emergent bourgeois imagination in the eighteenth and nineteenth centuries (Coontz 1988). Changes in domestic architecture separated living and work spaces. New practices in leisure and mass culture, and moral values of gentility, inflected spatial sensitivity with a politics of class differentiation (Smail 1994). The home became a metaphor of modern habitation, while practices of boundary maintenance and hygiene, such as housekeeping, were seen as microcosmic of a community-level imperative of delineating insiders from outsiders. The "deeply ambiguous character" of the colonial bazaar, for example, challenged a modern bourgeois sensibility that was centered on the home and a strict division between what is "outside" and the "ritually enclosed inside" of both private life and community (Chakrabarty 2002: 73). In this theory, spaces linked to trash and garbage (e.g., bazaars and labor camps) become dangerous realms of "matter out of place" (Douglas 2002) that need to be policed in order to protect the public sphere of sociopolitical membership, but never relinquished as cozy, private spheres of domesticity.

The spatial and architectural composition of camps informs a phenomenology of habitation in which social ostracism and stigma seem spackled onto the facility itself. The barracks-style camp Diego and

Pancho live in, for example, seems inside-out, a surface without interiority, thin metal walls apparently assembled with the minimalist aim
of making enclosures that resemble bedrooms to the extent that people
(try to) sleep there. The building's outside wall is wrapped with doors
that each open into one of a dozen bedrooms. Metal walls absorb heat
and make the interior more humid and sultry than the outside. "There is
no air, no movement," Pancho says, "no relaxation here. It is not comfortable. You cannot sit in your room. You cannot sleep." Small vents
cut into the top of the outside wall do not circulate fresh air. Pancho
has a fan "but it does not help because the air is hot. It moves hot air."
He sometimes props the metal door open, but this leaves the bedroom
exposed at night and makes him feel as though he is sleeping outside.
"Anyone can come into my room," Pancho says. "I don't use a bank. I
keep [*guardar*] my money in the camp. It is difficult to fall asleep, out
of fear, with the door open. But that is the only way to remain cool. It
is so fucking hot. You feel like walking around because you can't sleep.
But you need sleep because of the morning [or tomorrow, *la mañana*].
You think about tobacco and how difficult [or mean, *pesado*] the work
is when you are tired."

Here, insomnia is not experienced as a negation of the natural phenomenon of sleep, but as a sleeplessness caused by the experience of not
being able to go home and leave work behind (Levinas 2000: 207–12).
"It's too hot, Pete," Diego tells me. "I don't know what to do, every night
with the air and the heat. There is nowhere to go. I don't have a car. What
can I do? How long can I sit outside? El campo is burdensome [*pesado*]." (Note that the Spanish term for nightmare is *pesadilla,* something
that is especially mean or heavy.) Insomnia and a felt lack of privacy
are also linked to the problem of constant illumination. Powerful flood-
lights perched high in a tree make the camp a bright-eyed island amid
unlit, winding country roads that disappear into the night. This allows
the grower to survey the camp from a distance—perhaps on an evening
drive home from the string of chain restaurants out near Walmart—but
workers are unable to catch sight of anything other than the beaming
lights of a motoring vehicle. Panoptical effects push workers inside. "I
stay in my room and close the door," Roberto, a stout man in his thirties,
tells me, "because screw the boss if he wants to drive and check." Invisibility becomes a tactic of positioning within a rural optical circuitry. Still,
light seeps through vents like an unavoidable spotlight the boss projects
onto the camp: "The electrification of human habitats maintains the twi-
light and stops the oncoming of the night" (Lingis 1998: 9). The bath of
light and heat at labor camps is like a tepid pool in which insomnia is
cultured. "How can I sleep with that light?" Roberto goes on. "It is so
difficult [*pesado*]."

Levinas describes the home as more than an overhead shelter; it is commencement. It is the place from which one starts out and to which one returns each day, a private repose walled from the outside and a maze of hallways that warmly burrows any proper home (Levinas 1969: 152; Lingis 1998: 74–79). The labor camp lacks this interiority and achieves no separation from the workplace. In architectural terms, the camp is a conglomeration of cells, each bedroom an "elementary structure" with a single opening (Hillier and Hanson 1984). Variations on this kind of facility are found cross-culturally. In its simplest form, the single cell is the architectural model for the traditional shop: goods are displayed in front of the opening during the day and stored inside at night. This structure is ideal for shopkeepers because it allows a continuous flow between interior and exterior; shoppers can freely enter without feeling they have penetrated a private space, whereas thresholds established within the shop separate the vendor's backstage from the accessible space of wares on display (Hillier and Hanson 1984: 176–77). In the context of a labor camp, it is difficult for workers to establish thresholds of privacy, either internally (bedrooms are cramped and often shelter more than one worker, who are perhaps strangers) or externally (closed doors often mean unbearable heat). More like a warehouse or a shed, it is not surprising that the camp is commonly referred to by the workers as a *bodega* or *galera*, a generic storage facility. What workers are left with is an experience of being on display, available for surveillance.

Shopkeepers can board up their doors, freely exercising control over a space that is their own, but the camp's bedrooms open directly into the rural surrounds. Because most labor camps are adjacent to work fields (Holden 2002: 175), workers rise from bed and step right into their workplace. Agee described this experience as a "concentration of living and taking." In the context of southern sharecropping, the perpetual debt that bound families to landlords was the material side of an existential predicament of dispossession. The fields were "the wrung breast of one human family's need," a need to survive and make a living, "and of an owner's taking," survival always tied to a process of extraction (Agee and Evans 1941: 113). Similarly, many migrant farmworkers in North Carolina inhabit a space that is not their own: the labor camp, the farm shop, the fields, and the Mexican van. Even when they go to Walmart to get basic necessities on Sundays (their day off), they are transported in the grower-owned van. Dispossession is a constant experience for people whose bodies and energies are warehoused at night and carefully managed during the workday; they are never permitted the privacy of a home place except to the extent that growers do not often care about—and prefer to strategically distance themselves from—the camps. Ultimately, the very survival of workers, their ability to make a living and send a remittance back home, depends on inhabiting a space that could never be a home.

Face-Object

Diego walks me through the camp, a tour of impotent things that do not live up to the adequacy and fulfillment to which they gesture. "Look at this bathroom," he begins, pointing at the splintered toilet and nonfunctional light fixture. "This is not a bathroom. There is no door. The toilet is broken. The light is not steady. A real bathroom would have these things. It's ugly, nothing but a shed." Diego swivels, marches out of the bathroom and moves into a bedroom. "Look at this window. No air passes. What sort of bedroom is this? The beds are uncomfortable. It's not a bedroom," he says, embarrassment in his voice. Then he takes me to the kitchen, where a bilingual list of labor and housing codes is posted. "These laws don't mean anything. The camp complies with the rules, but the rules are not good. One doesn't want to live here. Would the boss live in this camp? This is not a house. It is an edifice. It is *muy campo*."

To Diego, the camp is belittling and degrading, as if his life were worth less than the owner's. The pretense of the whole thing is utterly demeaning: laws posted on the kitchen wall seem like a seal of approval, but they are also a slap in the face. The legitimizing force of the law is experienced as a double negative: the poster announces that the camp is not not regulated, compounding the sense that depravity is sanctioned, even deserved. It legitimizes conditions that Diego knows do not fit the image of human habitation that the grower would accept for himself and his family. In fact, the camp is not better than what Diego and other workers had in Mexico, as many North Carolinians assume. Workers tell me that the camp makes them long for the homes from which they migrated, houses that may resemble the camp's minimal accommodations but resonate in an entirely different way, houses that slide into the faciality and felt interiority of home.

Diego calls out aspects of the camp as incomplete, as if the camp were masquerading as a home to conceal its shallow character. Moving back and forth between naming and negating, the camp is made into a "dialectical image" (Taussig 1987: 369), containing an inherent contradiction that is simultaneously disclosed and covered, a house that is not a house, like Magritte's pipe (Deleuze 1988: 66). Diego's narration opens a gap between object and subject, the thing pointed to and the caption he provides, which "reveals, as with film montage, not only another view via an-

Figure 5.3. A farmworker from Central Mexico, who goes by the name of Don José, on a Wilson County farm, 2005. Photograph by author.

other frame, but released flows of energy" (Taussig 1999: 3, 43; Benson 2004). The tour illuminates the camp's double negativity: growers, with the law on their side, insist that the camp is not a bad house, whereas Diego insists the camp is not a house at all, a negation of a negation. When the camp emerges, in the flow of Diego's tour, as something other than what it portends, an occasion opens in which he might rename what the camp actually is. The camp begins to take on a kind of personality. What Diego sees is failed seriousness and pretense, the campiness of the camp. Diego reveals his embarrassment at having to live in such conditions, but also refacializes the camp as itself an embarrassment and disgrace, thereby socializing his own negative feelings and identifying the locus of affect in conditions of existence themselves. The bathroom, the kitchen, and the bedroom are farcical and condescending gestures of ethically variable livability that resonate for Diego as a "face-object" (Barthes 1972: 56), mean and heavy, somewhat nightmarish even. The face of structural violence is what Diego recognizes in his meager paycheck and the menacing labor camp, both of which are indicted as *muy campo*.

Divisions of Labor

The conditions in which farmworkers live are influenced by broadscale forces of international agricultural restructuring. The "culture of blame" that exists in tobacco country is shaped by the public nature of anti-immigrant sentiment as well as interlocking economic, political, societal, and ethical forces that shape the subjective lives of tobacco growers, threaten their farm businesses, and challenge the sense of self-worth that has historically been wrapped up in successful farm management. Workers viscerally sense that farmers are more curious and intense managers in the new contract system because trash can be common in tobacco, and because growers have so much at stake financially in keeping trash out of bales. Diego frequently allows himself—his face—to take on the characteristics of the boss. He mimics a diagram of nervous energy and frustration that he notices in Craig's face. The boss makes a mean face and so does Diego, grimacing just so, sarcastically, and subtly peering up at the boss from beneath his sweaty ball cap. Diego tells me, "The boss is very facial [*muy cara*], very much like this . . . " and he scowls as a scowling Craig walks by, anxiously monitoring the baling operation, "like he is going to snap," Diego says.

On one level, Diego's parody of the boss is a classic example of a "weapon of the weak" (Scott 1985) that is meaningful in the context of a workplace division of labor. Protected beneath his brim, Diego is reversing the optics of management and its one-way street of visibility, doing what bosses and others driving by the camp can do to him, mimicking the panoptical act of "seeing without being seen" (de Certeau 1984: 197). Done behind the boss's back, Diego's face work provokes other workers to smirk and mumble about how the boss is constantly bothering or nagging them. On another level, Diego is calling attention to forces that impinge on the boss himself. Diego is like a clownish street performer who pantomimes the money-driven earnestness of a businessman without time for diversion. By parodying the stiff's gait, walking behind with exaggerated gestures, straightened back and robotic striding arms, the mime achieves an allegorical effect by objectifying the Face of the on-the-go culture of capitalism as the driving force behind (or inside) the seemingly autonomous and self-motivated suit. This release of symbolic energy—unmasking a secret, defacing a Face—is what rouses laughter among the crowd, not just the impersonation.

For Taussig, defacement is an act of "criticism" that harnesses the power of faciality to undermine the authority and integrity that adhere in a Face. Defacement is a "cut into wholeness and holiness" that "engages internally with the object defaced, enters into its being" (Taussig 1999: 3). Defacement places the Face in a new context, shedding light on webs of power and meaning that underlie its social production. Defacement alters the way a Face looks and looks at observers, linking the semblance of gestures to agencies that might not be immediately visible in the visage. Diego is not necessarily attentive "to the tenderness of face and of faces facing each other," as in Levinasian ethics (3). Much like the work of the mime, his sarcasm is instead evidence of attentiveness to the networked forces in which the boss's face is caught up. The face here does not signal the radical neediness of the other person, but the worldliness of the face, the fact that the face bears traces of social processes and pressures, not the asocial singularity of an individual.

Taussig writes, the "face is the bubble of the public secret" (1999: 229), which refers to knowledge that is generally known but not often articulated (5). This is what bubbles up in the boss's nervous energy like a face "ready to snap," as Diego says. What is this secret? As has happened in other agricultural industries, the shift to private contract production has reclassified independent growers as service providers who carry out the mandates of a contract and are at the mercy of distant corporate decisions (Durrenberger and Thu 1996). Diego's parody reveals that the boss is not fully what he claims to be, that his autonomy and authority are unreal, a farcical pretense, just as Diego had negated the labor camp's adequacy. The boss's stern face is read as an index of local authority that seems exaggerated and ambivalent in light of Craig's dependency on both corporate goodwill and the manual labor of migrant workers. "I have worked on other farms and everywhere I see the same thing,"

Diego tells me. "The boss is nervous in the face. It's because the company can cut his contract and put him out of business." Here, the parody does not seem to simply poke ad hominem fun at the boss, but also builds an affective bridge that recognizes in the boss's earnestness and nervousness the heaviness of a system that bears down on both men and makes the boss look mean. "Why should the boss improve the camp," Diego asks me, sitting in the camp's kitchen, eating hardened tortillas from yesterday, "when he can use that money to improve his farm?"

Much like an ethnographer, Diego sympathetically realizes that the hardships he endures as a farmworker are partially the result of systemic pressures exerted on growers and the power of tobacco companies that can cut growers on a whim. If the illicit underpinnings of industrialized agricultural production—illegal hiring practices and noncompliant labor camps—are a public secret "never appearing on food labels" (Thompson 2002a: 8; see also Bletzer 2004: 531), then what bubbles up in the boss's face, what Diego's parody illuminates, is the fact that growers are not a simple cause of structural violence. They become a vector of harm when networked in globalized systems of production and consumption. Growers do not furnish labor camps that they themselves would inhabit because pressures of international competition and intensified company demands are a trickle-down economics sanctioned by government neglect that keeps wages low and motivates against improvements in the farm labor infrastructure, and, regrettably, because growers often see migrants as deserving less.

Growers are perceived as labor from the standpoint of the buying firm and increasingly share a sense of economic insecurity and subordination with the seasonal workers they employ. Rather than envisioning themselves as inhabiting shared time and space with workers, and rather than acknowledging that when Philip Morris USA looks at a grower like Craig the company sees time and economic value, growers turn to culture to reassert power and authority in the context of a continuously racialized workplace hierarchy. They negotiate the nervous system of contract production by translating structural problems of intensified quality demands, a felt lack of control, and international competition into cultural problems having to do with Mexican backwardness. "The companies have us right where they want us with this contracting thing," one grower tells me. "I could lose my business at any time. It's really about making sure you produce good, clean tobacco, and that means I've got to look after this crew. But look at how they keep up the labor camp. I've got people who trash the house they live in baling my tobacco." In fact, trash can end up in tobacco in many incidental and accidental ways (see chapter 4). Farmers commonly blame migrants as the only source of trash, just as they deem them culpable for camp conditions. Managerial demands and

threats of farm loss galvanize a way of seeing, a way of looking at other
people and talking about how they and the spaces in which they reside
"look." This regime of faciality is a strategic and dangerous coping strategy among growers, a way to save the face—the face of someone in control—that is associated with managerial authority. This strategy deflects
attention from the role of governments and corporations in making farm
businesses less stable and adversely impacting farm labor conditions.
When considered within the context of the kinds of pressures farmers
face, the critical force of Diego's parody seems multisided: it challenges
the integrity of the boss's authority while simultaneously opening an alternative field of vision in which growers and workers are seen as part of
the same subordinated scene.

The Social Course of Stigma

In this chapter and in chapter 4, I documented a multisided context of
accountability that defines how growers contend with the various forces
that have challenged their businesses and morality, as well as the cultural ideologies and stereotypes that have been marshaled to reaffirm national belonging. This context helps explain stigma's social constitution
on farms and how active growers become a conduit for stigma against
a multiethnic workforce. Farmers blame other people because all that is
at stake in their tobacco bales (e.g., livelihood, capital investments, and
the pride and public status of being a successful farmer) hinges on keeping a contract that is perpetually insecure. If stigma is shaped at a broad
societal level, on farms stigmatization arises a coping strategy under
conditions of economic fragility, class politics, and moral risk. In fact,
Donald, the harvester driver on Fred's farm who was introduced in chapter 4, tells me he would not want the pressures of being a farm operator.
"I used to want to farm, tried to get something started back in the sixties.
It never did work out," he says in an interview. "Now I see all the shit
that Fred puts up with. I wouldn't want it. He's got farm trucks, barns,
balers. Why would I want to own a tractor that costs $150,000 and still
be paying it off? Plus, he's got this Mexican crew to look after. What
do I want to own a damn labor camp for?" If Fred is anxious about his
contract, Donald also feels economic insecurity. Donald dropped out of
a segregated high school in the 1960s to become an independent farmer.
He says humbly that it "never did work out," and institutional discrimination in federal farm programs would have been a major obstacle to his
success. Today, lacking a diploma and other job training, hampered by
arthritis, and without health care, Donald has few options. He can easily
be replaced for a lower wage by younger migrants. One day Fred tried

to train Alfredo, a young man from Central Mexico, to operate the harvester, a job Donald has done for decades. Here is how Donald reacted: "What does Alfredo know about driving the harvester? Mexicans didn't even know where North Carolina was until twenty years ago. Where were they before that? Never saw cotton or tobacco either."

"Don't worry, Donald," one of the pickup drivers half joked, "Alfredo will be in Raleigh next week working in construction." That young migrants like Alfredo can more flexibly access low-wage labor markets because their undocumented status economically benefits employers is referenced here as an ambiguous kind of job security for black tobacco workers. For this group, a crucial part of class affiliation involves locality, a sense of being permanently attached to farms, and operating machines, not doing manual labor. Donald insists to me that driving is "a black job, my job," whereas manual tobacco work is "for the Mexicans." Donald claims a certain right to his job on the basis of local loyalties and accumulated work experience, a kind of flexible labor that is experientially and sociopolitically different from that provided by migrants. "Mexicans don't stay in one place," Donald tells me in an interview. "I know all the farmers, all the white farmers. I've always been working in tobacco." As for other black workers, Donald's defensive claim to employment turns on a localized relationship to tobacco capital that is mediated by farm owner-operators.

Donald sees Alfredo as a threat to this relationship, potentially cutting him out. In addition, Donald faces ongoing discrimination and is called "lazy" and "unreliable" by white farmers, and is blamed for his possible dislocation. This experience of threat is an important part of the context in which Donald, like other black workers, exhibits antagonism toward migrants. "Show me your papers, motherfucker," Donald regularly yells, "if you're not illegal then let me see them," arousing chuckles among the other black men and intimidated downward glances from the migrants, who are not passive about being berated. They muster resistance back at the camp in conversations that stereotype black people as lazy—the reason, they commonly claim, that farmers hire migrants (echoing farmers' own explanation). The anthropologist Nicholas De Genova offers a richly detailed account of racial stereotyping among Mexican migrants in Chicago. He finds a "rampant, explicit denigration of African Americans as 'lazy' in the racial discourses of many Mexican migrants" (2005: 192) and understands this process as some kind of response to the migrants' "extraordinarily laborious and exploited condition" (194). The discourse draws on dominant stereotypes while affording subordinated people a tactic of resistance amid threatening economic and sociopolitical circumstances. Alfredo speaks as someone empowered to displace local workers but also as someone whose physical experiences have him feeling exploited, as if aspiring "for some measure of relief from [his] own laborious plight," as De Genova writes (189). De Genova concludes that "Such a climate of insecurity could thus quite readily inspire migrant workers to disparage . . . proximate competitors in the labor market" (207). Griping and self-defense within the ranks of low-wage workers who actively delegitimize one another so that they stand out as hardworking constitute a subtle mechanism of labor control. Such tactics localize animosity, deflecting attention from the role of white employers in shaping the parameters of the labor market, the power of a corporation like Philip Morris to dictate prices and production, and, ultimately, the government's role in ineffectively enforcing labor laws to the benefit of both farm employers and the corporations with which they contract.

Shared experiences of economic insecurity brought on by agricultural restructuring in both Mexico and the United States are fragmented as variously racialized and classed persons—farmers and farmworkers—engage one another and gripe, stereotype, and backbite in the context of a historically shaped social order and workplace hierarchy. Antagonism arises in active strategies to advance self-worth and dignity and negotiate earnest threats. Under certain conditions, embedded values such as status, health, or livelihood can seem threatened, and people respond in ways that can negatively affect others (Kleinman 1999, 2006). "This is what makes stigma so dangerous, durable, and difficult to curb," Lawrence Hsin Yang and colleagues theorize (2007: 1528). "For the stigmatizer, stigma seems to be an effective and natural response, emergent not only as an act of self-preservation or psychological defense, but also in the existential and moral experience that one is being threatened" (1528). What specifically characterizes stigma among other kinds of conflict and discrimination is its public nature, institutionalization, and a distinct power differential between social groups (Link and Phelan 2001). Whereas workers of varying ethnicities participate in antagonizing and stereotyping one another, farmers who are set apart because of race, class, and access to capital stigmatize these Others as a "highly pragmatic, even tactical response to perceived threats, real dangers, and fear of the unknown" (Yang et al. 2007: 1528).

Tobacco money puts food on the table. More than that, it establishes moral standing within the social order and important class and race distinctions vis-à-vis farm labor. Philip Morris's website claims that direct contracting benefits growers by offering the "predictability" of knowing the buyer before planting season and the "fairness" of "competitive pricing" (Philip Morris USA 2008e). But prices have been tightened in line with global competition, input and production costs continue to rise (Foreman 2006), farms have gone out of business, and temporary contracts can be torn up at any moment. "We do the best we can and hope they grade it well," Fred tells me. "But we don't know. I could lose my farm right now because Philip Morris cuts up my contract. Indeed, tobacco agricultural economists highlight the unprecedented control that buying firms enjoy under contracting, and the serious risks and uncertainties growers face in the absence of a government safety net. Growers now "have limited market power to influence contract offers or terms, with contractors determining which growers will be offered contracts and where they will be located, and under what conditions and prices they will purchase contracted tobacco, all absent federal grading requirements" (Tiller et al. 2007: 3).

On top of this uncertainty, the negativity of smoking trickles down to the farm. Farmers tell me that they feel vilified and demonized for growing tobacco. On family vacations, when people ask them what they do for a living, they lie to avoid confrontation and embarrassment. The experience of blame that farmers themselves report (i.e., public blame about growing a deadly crop and hiring "illegal" workers) meshes with deepening financial and moral risks in a free-market situation and creates a volatile context of accountability that results in defensive responses. Blame is dynamically routed downward, which positions surviving white farmers, however fragile their contracts, above ousted "bad farmers" and low-wage employees who are dubbed "lazy," "filthy," and "criminal." Maintaining boundaries of essentialized differences of worth and power is a way to eschew culpability amid economic instability and one's own experiences of being blamed, diminished, and even stigmatized.

Ann Kingsolver (2007) has documented antagonistic social relationships between white farmers and a multiethnic farm workforce in Kentucky's tobacco region. Drawing on rich oral histories, she argues that white farmers have rhetorically stigmatized farm labor as Other to mask a legacy of deep economic dependency on African slaves, Irish immigrants, and, now, Mexican and Central American migrant workers and to sustain an ideology of independent yeomanry. She dubs this practice "strategic alterity," defined as a "shifting between strategic assertions of inclusion and exclusion . . . to both devalue a set of people and to mask the very process of strategic devalorization" (Kingsolver 2007: 89). This model usefully orients attention to a fundamental nexus of class, race, and culture on tobacco farms. But it tends to isolate farmers as the source of stigma, only briefly touching on the public nature of stigma in the wider culture, changes within the tobacco industry, and the ways subordinated workers themselves actively participate in practices of discrimination and stereotyping. In Kingsolver's account, strategic alterity seems to be a static process that is duplicated among farmers across generations, with migrants now filling a particular "slot," a subordinate structural position. Although my use of the term *stigma* also implies a certain slot of absolute Otherness (Trouillot 1991), with migrants portrayed on multiple levels as exterior to locality, community, and nation, I am pushed to emphasize how this "geography of imagination" is fundamentally linked to a shifting "geography of management," that is, political-economic changes and the shifting relationship of working- and middle-class citizens to transnational commodity and labor markets (Trouillot 2003: 2).

To analytically frame stigma as running a social course is to analyze interwoven political, economic, and cultural processes that contribute to the stereotyping and discrimination of subordinated actors in light of historical forces and broadscale cultural representations. Emphasizing the changing relationship of farms to tobacco capital and the state provides a more dynamic and complicated picture of stigma's societal and organizational production. Among growers, agricultural industrialization creates psychosocial stressors that link debt, economic insecurity, rural class dynamics, and moral meanings of farm failure that deeply inform emotional states and self-processes, and often jeopardize social relationships and access to support networks in the wider community (Dudley 2000; Ramírez-Ferrero 2005). Farmers become vectors of stigma against ethnic and racial minorities not simply to uphold an unwavering yeoman ideal but to cope with threatening conditions.

Likewise, when workers antagonize each other or parody bosses, they do so in contexts of impending threats to what is at stake materially and symbolically in their jobs. The constitution of stigmatized and antagonized relationships is linked not to static structural positions but to shared experiences of economic insecurity and various moral and social risks of class differentiation galvanized by market liberalization and labor force restructuring. In large measure, interpersonal antagonisms, forms of stigma, and the institutions and processes that foster them keep people like Fred, Donald, and Alfredo from realizing "they had more in common than they had differences" (Kingsolver 2007: 91). Stigma's social course at the farm workplace reveals dynamic relations of power and resistance and the continually racialized composition of the working class (De Genova 2005: 74). Racial segregation and inequity still prevail in North Carolina and elsewhere in the rural South, even if race relations have been recoded within a neoconservative language in the post–civil rights era (Omi and Winant 1994). Moreover, race relations remain structured by a state that is complicit in illegal hiring practices despite neoliberal reforms and the waning role of governments in regulating markets (Sider 2006).

Strategic Essentialism and Visibility in Farm Labor Struggles

The capacity for making growers and workers part of the same economic and ethical picture has been a driving force in FLOC's successful boycotts of several major food producers. The union targeted Campbell's Soup early in its history. A boycott campaign that began in the late 1970s and lasted eight years resulted in a labor contract that, according to the FLOC website, changed "the structure of the agricultural system, putting all parties [corporations, growers, farmworkers] on equal footing in negotiating relationships and benefits, under the mediation of a labor relations board representing all parties in the contract" (cited in Griffith 2009b). Similar contracts were eventually signed with other large food companies such as Heinz. Rather than simply taking on individual farm operations, FLOC set a precedent in farm labor organizing with its innovative efforts to triangulate disparate interests and to hold accountable the corporations purchasing commodities from growers and wholesalers, thereby largely dictating farm labor wages and conditions (Griffith 2009b: 55).

The union's boycott of the Mt. Olive Pickle Company, the country's largest independent pickle producer (which is headquartered in North Carolina), began in 1999 and was endorsed by more than two hundred organizations, including the National Council of Churches (Broadway 2003). The union was initially unsuccessful in negotiating with management for improved wages and working conditions. In an editorial in the Raleigh *News and Observer*, the company framed the issue as a localized problem between cucumber growers and workers, claiming negotiations ought to occur on that level. "Since we do not employ farmworkers," a company spokesperson editorialized, "it is inappropriate and unfair for us to interfere." The company sought to deflect attention from its role in competitively sourcing cucumbers and thereby influencing agricultural wages and labor camp conditions (Bryan 1999). FLOC emphasized that a large company like Mt. Olive is "an integral part of the system that contributes to and benefits from the exploitation of these workers" and "Mt. Olive is in a position to influence and improve the conditions of farm workers" (Agricultural Missions Incorporated 2000).

By 2004, the company conceded and the boycott successfully ended. The contract, which was signed by FLOC, the Mt. Olive Pickle Company, and the private North Carolina firm that recruits guest workers for growers, resulted in a set of reforms that entail significant benefits for each of these groups, as well as for growers and farmworkers. It resulted in higher wages for farmworkers who work on farms that supply cucumbers to the company. The boycott also led to a company mandate to expand the code of conduct for its suppliers, who must permit ready access to labor camps and workplaces for inspection. Growers benefit from modest annual financial supplements to help them pay for the fees associated with importing legal guest workers and maintaining labor camps. At long last, the contract led to the establishment of a formal grievance procedure to elide many of the problems that have plagued the H-2A program and that have made guest workers vulnerable in spite of the program's formality. There can be no retaliations on the part of growers against workers who file grievances, no terminations without just cause, no prohibitions against the right to receive visitors (including labor organizers) in labor camps, and the right to compensation for lost time due to injury, medical leaves, and religious leaves (Collins 2004; Farm Labor Organizing Committee 2010).

Although all of this seems very threatening to growers, who now face a new level of exposure and oversight, and whose employees are now empowered through the institutional support of the labor union, organizers with whom I spoke regard the grievance procedure as a benefit to growers, too. "This kind of contract system benefits growers in several ways," a FLOC organizer told me in an interview. "Even though growers complain about the union, this boycott won them higher commodity prices and creates a new framework of collective bargaining. Rather than having to face individual lawsuits and the uncertainties that were in place before this contract, where workers felt vulnerable and growers felt protective, there is now a formal process where grievances against particular growers can be negotiated through a fair process that benefits everyone and makes the workplace safer and more productive." FLOC touts this contract as "a model transnational labor agreement" that is intended "to benefit all sides in the production of agricultural products" (Farm Labor Organizing Committee 2010). In fact, the Mt. Olive boycott was limited in its capacity to alter material conditions because the union is legally permitted to organize documented workers only, which is a small fraction of the workforce. Government neglect in permitting employers to hire a more vulnerable, undocumented workforce continues to allow buying firms to depress commodity prices and reap the financial benefits of squalid living conditions. FLOC's partnership with the H-2A program also means that the union is currently dependent on guest workers as the core of their membership, which creates a structural problem when it comes to their capacity to critique the forms of servitude and company-friendly policies that will inevitably be a part of proposals for new guest worker programs (i.e., "immigration reform") in the future (Griffith 2009b: 63).

My concern is that the tobacco-producing region of North Carolina is a social setting where criticism of labor conditions can bring about backlash among growers who have been coached by the tobacco industry to regard outsiders and critics as enemies and who face real financial hardships in their abilities to maintain farm operations. The strategic problems that labor organizers face in this context involve not only the problem of reaching a diverse and dispersed workforce, but also the challenge of making growers the allies of labor unions. FLOC organizers comprehend this possibility and have built the union's entire organizing strategy upon recognition of the important fact that growers and workers have a great deal in common. But the union's boycotts have involved protests at the roadside in front of big farms in order to attract public attention and publicly shame individual growers, whose names appear in the newspapers. FLOC organizers told me in interviews that while they understand that potential backlash can occur, shaming can be tactical in a context in which growers can easily evade legal oversight and union organizing by employing undocumented workers. Farmers and farm labor advocates, not surprisingly, usually do not get along in North Carolina. Tobacco growers feel that FLOC portrays them as the sole culprit of farmworker suffering in media accounts. In other words, growers feel that FLOC facializes them as bad people, and this leads growers to facialize labor organizers as mischievous and threatening. At this local level, the project of remaking farm labor conditions is not simply about making farm labor more visible to consumers but also about remaking facialized strategies and responses that divide growers and labor organizers and that give rise to a parochial blame game that corporations conveniently transcend.

Enrique Ortiz is a Puerto Rican man in his midthirties and a public health worker who makes regular visits to camps during the harvest season to do basic medical checkups. Enrique is good at establishing trust with workers. He sees them as dignified and worthy of attention and care. He talks about pop music with the younger men and always asks permission before entering any room in a camp. Enrique usually has open access to labor camps, if only because growers benefit from the free medical care he provides to employees as a migrant healthcare outreach worker and an employee of a publicly funded clinic. And, admittedly, he does not search out signs of noncompliance and otherwise make trouble (which is how growers see FLOC's activities). Even though he intentionally depoliticizes his interaction with workers to ensure access and facilitate the provision of health care, Enrique has a political perspective on farm labor that comes out of his work as a broker between the social service sector and the labor class. Although he realizes that growers profit from noncompliance, Enrique also regrets FLOC's tendency to blame them in ad hominem fashion and place social conflict and suffering in a vacuum. He sees the blame game as a process that ultimately detracts from an understanding of the role of macroforces and the government in creating the conditions of structural violence that FLOC seeks to rectify.

I frequently accompanied Enrique on his visits to camps. This allowed me to get to know workers in many different camps and crews. However, the following event occurred on a day when I was not with him. Enrique tells me that he was talking confidentially with a worker about chronic back pain and headaches that were keeping the worker from working at his usual pace, and the verbal abuse and threats of dismissal his sluggishness had garnered from the crew leader. Enrique was organizing a discreet way for this worker to obtain medical attention without further infuriating the crew leader, who is skeptical about workers frequenting migrant health clinics and strategically seeks to maintain a barrier between workers and social services, perhaps to protect his own power and limit exposure of the abuses for which crew leaders are known. Enrique sees crew leaders (who recruit, transport, pay, and supervise farmworkers) as the most dangerous part of the labor system. They frequently take advantage of worker vulnerability and the lack of opportunities that recent immigrants and undocumented persons have in the wider economy. They also sometimes use physical and verbal abuse to control workers and illegally deduct fees from paychecks for services like food and transit (Bletzer 2004). For example, in 1989, at one camp near Wilson County, a federal inspector uncovered the ledger of a crew leader that tabulated fees for food, drinks, cigarettes, and other expenses that had been deducted from the employees' checks, as well as debts for border crossing and smuggling fees, payments that were fronted by the crew leader (*Wilson Daily Times* 1989d).

Clinics like the one Enrique works for usually provide a shuttle service that transports workers to and from the labor camp at a date and time that fits with the worker's schedule. In the midst of trying to secretly hatch out a plan to smuggle the worker from the camp at night or on a weekend, such that the crew leader would be unaware, FLOC organizers arrived at the camp. They were visiting various camps, talking with workers, and asking about abuses. One organizer overheard part of Enrique's conversation with the worker and blew up, yelling at the crew leader for inhibiting access to services. The trust Enrique had worked to establish with the worker over a period of several weeks suddenly collapsed. The crew leader barked at Enrique, threatened him with physical abuse, and told him never to return to the camp again, while the chances of that worker getting to the health clinic evaporated. Enrique also sensed that the worker probably lost trust in the ability to interact with social service providers. Furthermore, news of his back pain, which the worker had tried to keep quiet, reached the crew leader, jeopardizing the worker's status as a viable part of the crew. Enrique told me that FLOC planned to approach the grower who owned this particular camp and demand that he contract with another crew leader. "But that's not easy," Enrique says. "The grower needs those workers. He needs them tomorrow to bale tobacco. He can't just get rid of the crew."

Enrique remains despondent about this event, even though he has had positive experiences at other camps and regards FLOC as an indispensable part of farm labor struggles in North Carolina. He sees crew leaders and growers as part of a systematic problem that is underwritten by government neglect and potentially compounded by interventions, even well-intentioned activities by labor organizers, who sometimes blame individuals rather than structures. Enrique tells me, "Farmers say, 'The workers destroy the facilities.' The labor advocates say, 'The farmers are to blame, because they have bad facilities.' But there is no enforcement. There is no incentive to be good. Why should a worker keep his room clean when it's not a decent place to live? Why should a farmer improve the facilities when there is no enforcement? The conditions destroy the facilities."

In advocating for a broad critique of the conditions themselves, Enrique sounds a lot like a critical medical anthropologist, not surprising for a social medicine practitioner concerned with delivering healthcare services to a marginalized population. "Structural violence," Farmer writes, "is violence exerted systematically—that is, indirectly—by everyone who belongs to a certain social order," which runs against "a moral economy still geared to pinning praise or blame on individual actors" (2004: 307).

Another Toilet Problem

The project of making farm labor and labor camp conditions more visible through public educational initiatives, social advocacy, and product boycotts is one practical implication of an account of faciality. These activities can put a human face on farm labor and alter what amounts to a stereotyped Face. Faciality matters on the most basic levels of public policy. Public policy debates and measures can challenge or reproduce how bodies, faces, and spaces are facialized and spatialized as alterity.

By federal law, farm employers must comply with requirements for workplace sanitation, such as providing toilet facilities in the field. Until very recently, farmers were noncompliant. In the 1990s, only about 4 percent of North Carolina's farmworkers had access to adequate drinking water, toilets, and hand-washing facilities in fields (Agricultural Missions Incorporated 2000). Workers defecated in the woods, using toilet paper brought from the camp or the leaves of trees and bushes. But the federal government has cracked down on this issue and farmers now uniformly comply. The portable toilet, a Porta Potti, is towed on a flat, steel trailer and driven to the field with the labor crew. But at the farms where I studied, workers did not use the toilet. They called it a *discriminación*.

"We used to shit in the wilderness [*el monte*]," Bartolo tells me. "In the woods you can be with the animals, be alone, and be quiet. You can think. You can jack off. The woods are cool and refreshing. You are away from work and outside of the field [*campo*]. The woods remind me of my hometown." Importantly, migrants commonly use the term *monte* to refer to the vast expanse of desert, the wilderness that must be traversed on the cross-border trip. In Bartolo's spatial imagination, this expanse is private and concealed space divorced from work and linked to activities of excess and expenditure that do not yield salable commodities: masturbation, defecation, and reminiscence. The wilderness is imagined as punctuated by el campo, a patchwork of clearings (i.e., fields and camps) linked to agricultural production, spaces exposed to the light of capitalist discipline and the labor camp's ceaseless glow.

This spatial imaginary helps us understand why the toilet is seen as discriminatory. Workers describe the law as a racialized form of isolation that makes defecation into a public spectacle and moves them and their bodies into the light of day. The toilet's discriminatory feel comes out of a combination of there being a "Mexican law" and a "law about shit," as Bartolo complains. "They oblige you to use it. If you are a Mexican, you must use that toilet, you must shit in there. It is a Mexican toilet. It's like the law sees Mexicans as people who shit." Workers also commonly describe the toilet as uncomfortable and dangerous. Although federal law specifies that the toilet must be "adequately ventilated [and] . . . constructed to ensure privacy" (North Carolina Department of Labor 2008: 16), the toilet ends up sitting in the sun and becomes unbearably hot and smelly. It is not the least bit private. Typically parked in the front of the field, at the roadside, it is in plain view of motorists.

The toilet law comes out of good intentions that aim to protect and enable migrant life and work. Its reasoning is founded on the sound logic of rights and protections that is applied across other professions. In practice, the toilet interferes with a fleeting experience of freedom and spatializes human biological processes as properly belonging to the campo; shitting is dispossessed, brought from the woods into the john owned by the boss. This biopolitics of defecation reproduces a regime of visibility in which individual bodies—those running for the toilet, for example—are visualized as part of a population associated with trash, filth, and transience. A tobacco field's faciality is profoundly altered when a portable toilet is placed in it. The field looks different, and it looks at one differently. Bartolo calls attention to the power of vision when he says that the law sees Mexicans in a particular way. He knows passing motorists perceive the toilet as part of a moving cultural zone of Mexican space, like labor camps, a landscape facialized as a "recurring, detachable face," which is the "face of the permanently Other" (Taussig 1999: 88). Rather than remake migrants' relationship to society, the toilet law, in seeking to dignify work, contributes to the framework of faciality in which Mexicans are associated with manual labor, trashed labor camps, toilet paper on the floor, and now, roadside defecation.

Faciality and Policy

The explosive growth of agricultural output and consumer surpluses over the last half century has been built on the structural violence that puts workers in harm's way, while international agricultural restructuring, persistent government neglect, and cultural barriers such as stereotyping collude to create a context of ethical variability in which farm labor seems undignified and deserving of squalid conditions and inadequate social response. Farm labor advocates realize the power of vision and the face in constituting this system. They utilize faciality in struggles over farmworker rights and social justice—the reproduced images of destitute faces in an Oxfam America report are meant to morally and politically challenge a food system that mystifies labor as faceless beneath the cellophane of product packaging and depersonalizes workers as "machines in the field" (2004; Thompson and Wiggins 2002). The trope of faceless labor is repeated in scholarly literature on farmworkers, evidenced in Daniel Rothenberg's (1998) "hidden world" and Leo R. Chávez's (1992) "shadowed lives." Although the invisibility of labor is surely a problem on a national level, my analysis suggests that on a local level, in places like rural North Carolina, farm labor is not shadowed. In addition to macropolitical-economic forces, the perpetuation and justification of structural violence on tobacco farms is the result of a mode of active perception. Faciality is coproduced alongside structural violence and is part of the social constitution of the specific landscapes on which symbolic and material forms of violence are played out. Migrant farmworkers are often viewed through a prism of faciality that frames them and spaces linked to their life and work as "other" and belonging on the "outside." They are people who do manual field labor under the beating sun, run headlong for the portable toilet, and live in an archipelago of labor camps that are literally not counted in the string of houses that anchor people inside the moving borderlines of community.

Recent efforts to criminalize undocumented individuals and militarize the border reflect a narrow understanding of immigration that seeks to punish individuals—employers and employees—and overlooks the role of macroforces of economic liberalization in driving transnational labor migration and applying downward pressure on farms (De Genova 2005; Massey et al. 2003). Noncompliance for growers is a beneficial and strategic way to compete in international commodity markets, while consumers, who may know very little about how agricultural products are harvested, reap the benefits of cheaply priced products. To locate growers and workers as part of a shared predicament is not to neglect the division of labor that very clearly exists on farms or to let growers off the hook for noncompliance and prejudice. But, with my informants Enrique and Diego, I find it more helpful to depersonalize blame and spotlight broader conditions that make noncompliance and low wages viable strategies in the first place. As Walter Benjamin writes, "Sudden shifts of power such as are now overdue in our society can make the ability to read facial types a matter of vital importance" (1999: 520). Indeed, this was exactly Diego's tactic: to discern in the facial type of the boss traces of structural forces that put both men in a similar situation.

To explore how faces are socially produced and perceived is to gauge the workings of power and resistance in the most intimate of ways. Several practical implications come out of an analysis of faciality as part of structural violence. My analysis suggests that collective responses and farm labor advocacy ought to focus on transforming political-economic conditions and corporate power over agricultural operations, rather than on growers, who seem like a commonsensical target of advocacy because they are often noncompliant. A medical anthropological perspective pushes us to see the structural violence that affects farm labor as originating in economic policies and (a lack of) government regulation over farm labor conditions. Farm management is a node through which harm passes and at which it is localized. Efforts that seek to improve farm labor conditions will be most effective when they do not also facialize growers as blameworthy, because the antagonism tobacco growers exhibit toward workers and labor organizers is partly a face-saving response to the multiple kinds of blame they themselves face—blame for growing a lethal crop, potentially failing as a farmer, illegally hiring undocumented workers, and maintaining substandard labor camps (Benson 2008a). Possibilities for collaborative political action between farm labor and management would be enhanced if farm labor advocacy sought to improve economic security among growers along with the conditions of workers. Targeting agribusiness corporations as complicit in localized antagonisms and noncompliance is crucial to such an orientation, as FLOC's successful boycott initiatives show. My analysis of faciality is also useful toward an assessment of protective policies, suggesting the importance of ethnographic research on experiential aspects of the farm workplace to determine how a seemingly beneficial measure such as the portable toilet law might actually contribute to stigmatization and social stereotypes.

The seemingly hypocritical face of growers often masks the difficulties they face and their stakes in clinging to tobacco. The face of public health seems to threaten growers, even though tobacco states bear a disproportionate share of smoking disease, and whether growers like it or not, tobacco is addictive and kills people. The face of the smoker is wrinkled and seems to deserve blame for a choice. The industry's humanitarian face masks its globalizing ambitions and its aggressive advertising, and the pursuit of civic virtues masks strategic efforts to contour and contain regulation. The neoliberal institutions facialize developing countries as needing tobacco in order to develop. The face of the farmworker who may have a home in a developing country where smoking rates are on the rise seems to not belong to North Carolina communities where farms would go under without immigrant labor. Growers and farm labor advocates facialize one another in ways that overlook overlapping structural and experiential conditions and localize the industry's contribution to workplace stress, depraved working and living conditions, and economic insecurities as seemingly unmovable problems of race and culture. Faciality is an analytical tool that emphasizes questions of ethics. In directing our attention to how and why people, governments, or corporations may or may not respond to structural violence, faciality is helpful for organizing political responses that eschew stereotypes and go beyond narrow framings of blame to bring social systems into account. Faces contribute to the reproduction and legitimization of harm industries and the perpetuation of harm in populations. Faces can also be a basis for partnerships that seek to remake the conditions in which people look and look at each other.

Chapter 6 _____

Sorriness

A COMMON JOKE IS TOLD among white North Carolinian tobacco growers at the country store, farm meetings, the gas pump, and, in the past, the tobacco warehouses where their cash crop was sold. It goes like this:

> A tobacco farmer is at the warehouse, waiting to sell his tobacco. He walks the rows of tobacco to see how his bales were graded. One bale got the grade N1GR. He turns to a group of farmers chatting, waiting for the auction's start, and says, "My tobacco is so damn sorry that they wrote nigger on it."

During my fieldwork, I heard this joke dozens of times. Amid variations and elaborations, two words remain the same: *sorry* and *nigger*. This twinning is the joke's gist, its laughter-crowded, easy hostility. The auction system involved more than a hundred standardized government grades. Tobacco leaf was distinguished by a government grader according to such characteristics as color and texture. N1GR was nearly the lowest grade a bale could receive.

The grader would write N1GR on any bale that was of such poor quality that it was barely recognizable as tobacco: disheveled, discolored, dirty, perhaps moldy or rotten. The joke's punch line is that this grade graphically resembles the racial epithet. The joke plays on this resemblance to associate sorriness, meaning low human value, with African American farmers and workers.

One possible reading of the joke is that it converts a potential moral hazard (the grower's sorry tobacco might say something about him) into the essential property of the tobacco itself, which embodies the labor of the racialized farm labor workforce. In claiming rightful ownership of the tobacco, thereby alienating this labor, the joking grower also takes distance from it, insinuating that even he is the victim of the niggardly ways of workers that put him in this precarious position. Not blaming the grader for the low grade, the joke actually implies an affinity—the grader got it right, yes, the tobacco is *so damn sorry*—a kind of collusion among white men who seem burdened by having to deal with sorriness and empowered with the visual powers of objectification and evaluation.

This explanation is appealing, although it misses much of the nuance of what sorriness means and why it matters, and how multiple layers of

Figure 6.1. Summary of standard grades

23 Grades of Leaf						10 Grades of Smoking Leaf		
B1L	B1F	B1FR				H3F		
B2L	B2F	B2FR				H4F	H4FR	H4K
B3L	B3F	B3FR		B3K		H5F	H5FR	H5K
B4L	B4F	B4FR		B4K		H6F	H6FR	H6K
B5L	B5F	B5FR	B5R	B5K				
B6L	B6F	B6FR		B6K				

10 Grades of Cutters		10 Grades of Lugs		8 Grades of Primings		6 Grades of Greenish			7 Grades of Variegated Mixed		
C1L	C1F	X1L	X1F								
C2L	C2F	X2L	X2F	P2L	P2F						
C3L	C3F	X3L	X3F	P3L	P3F	B3V		X3V	B3KM		X3KM
C4L	C4F	X4L	X4F	P4L	P4F	B4V	C4V	X4V	B4KM	C4KM	X4KM
C5L	C5F	X5L	X5F	P5L	P5F	B5V			B5KM		
									B6KM		

20 Grades of Variegated								7 Mixed Grades			
B3KL	B3KF	B3KD									
B4KL	B4KF	B4KD	B4KV	C4KL	C4KF	X4KL	X4KF	X4KV	M4F	M4KR	M4KM M4GK
B5KL	B5KF	B5KD	B5KV						M5F		M5KM M5GK
B6KL	B6KF	B6KD	B6KV								

15 Grades of Green						6 Grades of Variegated Red or Scorched			5 Grades of Excessively Scorched		
							B3KR			X3KR	B3KK
B4G		B4GK	C4G	C4GK	X4G	X4GK	P4G	B4KR	C4KR	X4KR	B4KK C4KK
B5G	B5GR	B5GK	B5GG		X5G		P5G	B5KR			B5KK
B6G		B6GK									B6KK

6 Grades of Slick			4 Grades Whitish-Lemon		2 Grades of Cutters (Primings Side)		13 Grades of Nondescript			1 Grade of Scrap
B3S		X3S		X3LL	C5LP	C5FP	N1L	N1KV	N1GG	S
B4S	C4S	X4S	C4LL	X4LL				N1XL	N1GL	N1PO
B5S			C5LL				N1K		N1GF	N1XO
							N1R		(N1GR)	N1BO
										N2

Figure 6.1. Summary of standard grades.

Source: "Official Standard Grades for Flue-Cured Tobacco U.S. Types 11, 12, 13, 14, & Foreign Type 92," Tobacco Division of the Agricultural Marketing Service of the United States Department of Agriculture, 1989.

meaning and force reverberate in the joke. In North Carolina, the word *sorry* is used in various ways. Anything disheveled is described as sorry: a beat-up truck, a leaky faucet, or a long line at Walmart. Also, sorry is anything meager, such as a skimpy buffet at a local restaurant, a small portion of pie at the holidays, or a wimpy handshake. The more potent use of the word is a cultural resource for interpreting dynamic processes of rural class recomposition. The unusually high unemployment levels, aversion to work among many residents, and increased dependence on social services in counties like Wilson were brought on by waves of agricultural industrialization and a mix of capital flight and concentration. Those who remain relatively secure amid the change and dislocation often interpret disparities in terms of a logic of winners and losers, with the outcomes naturalized as stemming not from historical and structural advantage but from sorriness, the characteristic flaws and deficiencies of categories of people. This process reflects "dominant ideologies that rank individuals on the basis of culture, race, and ethnicity, thereby facilitating the cultural . . . inscription of individual achievements and failures" (Ong 2003: 6). In a hegemonic white vernacular usage, the language of sorriness amounts to an explanatory model for relaying a common theory of misfortune and the duties of men and women in society. It helps to configure scenes of decrepitude, squalor, and chronic subordination as public signs of a semipsychological, semimoral problem of the resident populations. Facializing the social landscape in this way lets historical processes and mobile global industries off the hook. It also circumscribes zones of accountability in intensively narrow ways so that neighbors are only responsible for each other to the extent that the backwardness and indolence of the one is said to sometimes unfairly encumber or jeopardize the other.

Sorriness reflects a local way of dramatizing the story of the white man's burden. Sometimes race and class are tethered in such a way that poor white people who are labeled sorry are equated with trash. Anyone who does not own property (perhaps not even a vehicle), does not pay child support, and does not have a family that was planned, or that is moving on an arc of social mobility, does itinerant wage labor, speaks in a way that is the butt of jokes, is foreign and a burden to comprehend, lives in trailer parks and labor camps, or in old, neglected, and falling-down tenant houses—all of these public signs of Face that exaggerate, overlook, or misconstrue realities of dispossession and concretely determined differences—is similarly classified. The one who idles in a pickup truck and manages migrants doing manual labor in fields is somehow different than the one who idles on the porch because he does not want to do grueling labor for nothing and for someone who will watch him in this way because the discourse and optical regime of sorriness is a lens. It involves assumptions about the economic and moral worth of different categories of subjects—cultural assumptions having to do with such issues as the meanings of property ownership, the division between knowledge work and manual work, the composition and composure of families, capacities to accumulate and consume, different kinds of houses and living arrangements, and different relationships to capitalism and the state. The extent to which, and the specific ways in which, different groups are seen as positive or negative national icons has a lot to do with the power of perception—what I have called faciality—in understanding all of these phenomena as rather arbitrarily indicating something innate about idealized or stereotyped imagined communities. In the process, a face-landscape is made where local space is carved up so that certain spaces and families are perceived and treated as somehow out of place, hard facts of local economic integration annulled, and the affinities and solidarities that are necessary to any social setting—but often denied and crosscut within them—are circumscribed in terms of a class that is innately sorry and a class that is entitled to name others that.

Sorriness is the local vocabulary through which a class of industrial tobacco growers, and other middle-class white people in the region, invoke their status as burdened professionals as a means of staking out affinity within the local context of what professional work and two-story households mean, and within the broader context of an imagined national mainstream. This chapter explores how this pervasive ideological process and strategy of social stratification, spatial segregation, and moral indifference works by showing that a politics of innocence, and also a will to be innocent, is really at the core of these cleavages. While the work of social distinction and differentiation in the United States is, of course, infinitely complex, my aim is to demonstrate that the fantastical image of a normal mainstream distinguished from various illegitimate, criminal, or generally morally inferior constituencies has a lot to do with the idea that the nation is tacitly white, inherently innocent, and burdened by having to support, deal with, or accept those facialized and typecast as substandard or abnormal. Even still, this conception of the political valences and projects that the language of sorriness helps to advance remains limited, only part of the story.

Sorriness can involve a serious denigration of others or a positive measure of selves whose aestheticized agronomic practices and products, and way of life more generally, reflect pride in a job well done. To establish self-worth in terms of work ethic, to claim to not be sorry in speech or practice, is not necessarily to participate in a racialized discourse about laziness, although these trajectories cannot be finely separated. There are surely a thousand plateaus in any genealogy of morals (Deleuze and Guattari 1987). My exploration of some of the contexts that are useful for understanding sorriness diagrams transverse rather than linear connections between the times and places that lend sorriness its accumulated historical meanings and in this way emphasizes the polysemous and heterotopic character of sorriness as a political and cultural resource for drawing images of selves and others.

Rooted deeply in the Germanic tradition, sorriness hurdled across the Atlantic system, and positive and negative meanings have been cultivated over the span of a millennium. On tobacco farms, sorriness also reflects the influence of an old aesthetic regime rooted in the mercantile system of the Chesapeake colonies, where leaf quality was closely linked to planter reputation and status, the "quality of a man's tobacco often serv[ing] as the measure of the man . . . as an index of worth and standing in a community" (Breen 1985: 22–23). These historical meanings were further layered in the twentieth-century context of sharecropping, and later when the local language of sorriness became associated with intensely politicized meanings of race and geography amid the decline and restructuring of traditional industries like tobacco and textiles, and the national war on welfare. Yet this discourse, which can be mean, does not go uncontested. Some of the black farmers I have met turn the language against itself and talk about what is sorry in terms of social justice. Whereas a dominant white vernacular use focuses on the innate sorriness of certain classes of people, this resistant use indicts those social structures and institutions that have yielded uneven life chances in rural North Carolina as a sorry state.

Help

During my fieldwork, I drove around with dozens of farmers, talking with them for hours. No one explained sorriness more clearly than Andrew Blevins, a farmer in his late forties, and a deeply devoted, born-again Christian who believes in and practices the prosperity gospel, the notion that success in business is external evidence of God's blessing, that hard work and faith are the means to economic prosperity, and that those who are impoverished need religion rather than government to help them. Like most growers, he is a staunch Republican. He need not reference Jesse Helms to speak in terms of big government as a bogeyman. Since the 1980s farmers like Andrew consumed the rhetoric of blame about public health advocacy and aggrieved minorities just as voraciously as the billions of dollars of government relief payments sent to their mailboxes.

On most days, Andrew arrives at the shop early with his thermos of hot coffee. Even in the muggy summer, he drinks it hot, loaded with sugar. He sports Oakley sunglasses, a blue work shirt, khaki pants, and a custom farm hat with his surname embroidered alongside golden tobacco leaves. The shop is a large metal barn where equipment is warehoused and maintained. Like most farm offices, here bilingual posters are tacked on walls and detail federal and state occupational safety and health laws. The shop is cluttered, not what some would consider a neat and tidy farm business. This reflects poorly on cool Andrew. "It used to be worse," a neighbor grower says. "He's trying to be a good manager like everybody else now. But it's still a little sorry there in his shop." But Andrew produces good, clean tobacco and has favorably kept a contract with a major tobacco company for a decade, so the shop's messiness is not really a sociomoral deal breaker. "He's a good farmer," his neighbor says, "works hard, just needs to clean up his act."

Heading out from Andrew's shop one day in his pickup, we pass a row of tobacco fields that he tends, then the labor camp he owns. He tells me about the difficulties of "the labor problem," lamenting that an older generation of black men who worked for his father and later for him no longer comprises the bulk of the workforce.

> I work all week because that's all I know. But it's tough to find help that's willing to do the same. You can't find people who want to work in the heat. I understand why young people don't want to work on farms. But I can't afford all of the benefits. In farmwork there are no good benefits, no health care, and no good salary. How can I afford those extras when, look at the tobacco prices. I've got heaps of debt to keep this business competitive. There would be no jobs if I didn't invest in the new equipment I've got and if I wasn't frugal in managing this business. I can't afford to pay the help all the extras.

The inflation-adjusted cost of tobacco leaf production has increased 200 percent since the 1980s (Foreman 2006). Growers like Andrew contend with escalating input costs, tightened leaf prices, and new debt loads. They can't compete with higher wages paid in other industries. This is one reason why growers employ undocumented migrants, even though they often gripe about having to do so, but it is also part of why there is lots of aversion to farmwork among local people. Indeed, Andrew acknowledges that many people do not want to do agricultural labor because of these evident reasons. But when a handful of the migrants that he employed that year up and left in the middle of the season, having found construction work in Raleigh, this common affair, periodic and unpredictable labor shortages faced by growers, Andrew did not take out his frustrations on the tobacco companies that leave him unable to increase wages to attract workers in a more reliable way or the government's role in permitting all kinds of employers to take advantage of undocumented labor. His explanation comfortably points blame at another vulnerable population.

> People have to work. That is what people are meant to do. Working on a farm is better than nothing. It is better than sitting on your porch collecting welfare. That's the basic problem. Farmers all run Mexicans now. The blacks don't want to work. They have gotten used to government programs, where a man doesn't have to work anymore. Go hang around a black crew and tell me what you see. They sit around and drink, won't work early, won't work late. Then look at the young Mexicans who haven't been here for a while, haven't been "Americanized," gotten like the blacks. They realize that a man needs to work hard. Americans could care less about hard work. Why should they? With food stamps, welfare, there will be something. The blacks are damn sorry.

This is volatile language that is probably more common nationally than people want to acknowledge or believe. Sometimes Andrew casts a wide net in talking about what he calls the labor problem, rightly pointing to the fact that people of many backgrounds and social locations refuse to do menial labor. Sometimes he narrowly talks about one group only. He rationalizes the illegal employment of migrants in terms of generalizations about another group, employing slogans about government assistance, immigration, and racial minorities that come from the conservative pundits he listens to on the radio and watches on television.

"The only ones who want to work are the Mexicans," Andrew says. "But that is a hassle. There is a language barrier and culture barrier. They trash the labor camps. I would just as soon not deal with migrants. I think they ought to put a sign in the airports that says, 'If you don't speak the language, get the hell out of the country.'"

"But you employ those workers," I mention.

"There's no choice. I'd rather hire blacks or whites. But they're damn lazy."

I ask, "The Mexicans that you employ; they are undocumented?"

"No way," he responds, "I don't hire illegals. They are legal to me. I hire men who have social security cards. If they're fake cards, then that's not my problem. It's their problem."

Existing labor laws do not mandate that Andrew (or any other employer) validate employee identification materials. He need only ensure that employees present identification, which may be fraudulent. This framework of accountability, where workers, not employers, are responsible, lets him off the hook. Here Andrew sounds like the operator of a

big farm near Wilson County that was raided by Immigration and Natu-
ralization Service officials in 1992, resulting in the detention and deportation of nearly two hundred farmworkers. "We have workers with valid
documents," the grower said. "As far as I know everything is completely
legal here" (*Wilson Daily Times* 1992: 1).

The negative publicity and fines that employers face amount to a very
different kind of punishment than what happens to migrants and their
families. With relatively small businesses and some level of social power in
the region, and with undocumented labor so prevalent, tobacco growers
like Andrew have never really faced a serious threat of law enforcement.
But public criticism of employers of undocumented labor has increased
in recent years, and residents of the area gripe in private. For example,
the banker or realtor will tell you that she doesn't like the demographic
changes that industrial agriculture is helping to drive, but she would never
directly confront an employer. Lots of people in counties like Wilson
have financial relationships to growers, or they share a pew with them
on Sundays, so these employment practices remain a public secret that
is rarely discussed in the open. There is certainly a register of backstage
complaint among working people who feel that their own standing in the
labor market has been diminished as a result of the hiring practices that
benefit growers. Just as there are patterned ways that tobacco growers
rationalize their involvement in the cigarette business (see chapter 4),
there are common strategies to reframe their advantageous relation to
"illegal immigration" in terms of victimhood and a lack of alternatives.
Andrew also speaks as someone supporting the common good by not
hiring lazy people and instead hiring productive workers (Dudley 1996:
51). That Andrew benefits from a government that permits a stagnant
minimum wage and illegal hiring practices that disadvantage many residents and add to the chronic unemployment in his region is removed
from the ethics of what counts as wrongdoing in this scenario or what
defines the ethics of citizenship.

Teutonic Plates

The English word *sorry* comes from the Germanic tradition.[1] It derives
from the Old English *sār* (sore, painful, sad, sorrowful), which connoted
sickness, disease, suffering, and pain, an early usage derived from the Old
Frisian, Old Saxon, and Old High German *sār*, the Old Icelandic *særa*,
and the Gothic *sair*. Hence, the modern English term is etymologically

---

[1] This etymology is taken from *The Oxford English Dictionary* (3rd ed.) and *Alten-
glisches Etymologisches Wörterbuch* (2nd ed.), by Friedrich Holthausen (1963).

linked to the Finnish *sairas* (sick or ill). It is also related to the Old Irish *sáith* or *sōeth* (to injure, harm, pain, or disease), the Latvian *siev-s* or *sīv-s* (harsh, vexing, cruel), the Latin *saevus* (raging, fuming, thrashing, convulsed with rage), and to a Greek word possibly meaning scurvy.

The modern English usage developed along two etymological vectors within the Germanic tradition. One vector began in the 800s with the Old English *sārig* (sad, sorrowful), a combination of two words: *sār* and the Old Saxon and Old High German *sērag* (grieved, distressed, injured, wounded). So the word had to do with loss and sorrow, as well as the feeling of being pained or afflicted. This first vector culminates in today's expression, "I'm sorry." Whereas *sārig* originally signified potent expressions of distress (as when people today say that they feel sorry "for" someone), the modern term has largely been diluted into a weak expression of sympathy, a mundane apology.

The second vector arose in the 1200s with the English *sori* or *sorie* (vile, wretched, of little account or value, worthless, mean, poor). In contrast to the diminution of meaning and force in the first vector, the second vector's attribution of a negative judgment has been maintained in some contexts. In 1386, Chaucer wrote that "the more strong that the fleisch is, the sorier may the soule be." This second vector links the pathologies of the spirit and the body, as in a lay mass delivered in 1405 to "al that er sek and sary." In North Carolina's tobacco region these deep meanings also continue to resound.

"Sorry is what you say when you apologize," I say to Andrew, our conversation in the pickup truck continuing.

"Yeah, that's one meaning. But how we use it down here [in North Carolina, the South] is different.[2] Sorry essentially means 'not good,' like a 'sorry worker.' But it is more than that. It means 'not good' because of lack of ambition and effort. That is the key. It means 'not good' plus 'it's your fault.'"

"Can you give me an example?"

"Take basketball. If I lack talent and am not tall, then you'd say, 'I'm not good.' But you wouldn't say, 'I'm sorry.' But if I woke up late every morning and did not practice, then you'd say, 'I'm sorry.' Take farming. It's the same way. If I have a bad crop on account of the weather and it wasn't my fault, then I'm not sorry. But if I have a bad crop because I'm in bed, watching television all spring, hanging around the country store instead of checking fields, then I'm a sorry farmer."

---

[2] In her book on schooling in North Carolina, Shirley Brice Heath (1983) briefly touches on the local meanings of the word sorry, and her discussion reflects the meanings of industry, moral character, and race that I describe in this chapter.

The discourse of sorriness involves a moral judgment about the cause of misfortune: some people get slack, others get pinned. Go back to the Elizabethan poor laws of the 1600s, when this kind of division was crucial for the governance of poverty and the distribution of relief. The laws required communities to assist permanent members and emboldened them to refuse others who fell outside of culturally and geographically constituted borders, a distinction, therefore, between strangers and members. The New Poor Law of the early 1800s reframed this division in terms of separating "the genuinely needy from rogues, vagabonds, and sturdy beggars," the historian Michael Katz (1986: 4) writes. This more modern division reflects a moralization of those excluded from assistance as being blameworthy, with beggary seen as the result of characteristic indolence, an aversion to doing right, or some other abnormality. Social membership was now constructed not simply in contrast to the foreign but also to the abnormal and the delinquent, and a legitimate if not definitive part of normalized modern belonging—citizenship in the capitalist nation-state—involved judging others as a routine part of class identification and differentiation and social affiliation. Those deemed "able-bodied" were excluded from social assistance by the New Poor Law, reflecting the interest of the growing capitalist class in England in limiting the scope of sympathy and relief and incentivizing work. Institutionalizing a theory of human behavior as promoted in the classical liberal economics of the time, where social assistance was said to dangerously encourage "idleness" and "improvidence," the New Poor Law, which involved the threat of being imprisoned in notorious workhouses, forced millions of rural people to sell their labor to large estates or migrate and work in growing cities (17), thus creating a labor surplus for the factories and scenes of overcrowded misery for Dickens.

In many ways, this modern conception of social welfare as a disciplinary tool to induce wage labor while maintaining significant social disparities is the contemporary policy in the United States and in many other countries. The war on welfare of the 1980s had a distinctly "nineteenth-century ring," Katz writes, because, much like the New Poor Law, it was a punitive approach that was geared toward contracting social assistance and labeling certain categories of people as the "undeserving poor" (1986: ix). There remains a broad distinction between poverty as a condition that carries little or no stigma, and that can be understood as the result of concrete historical or social processes, and "pauperism," which is described in the public discourse concerning the New Poor Law as the "fault" of disadvantaged persons and groups and/or the consequence of "willful error," "shameful indolence," and "vicious habits." Pauperism was said to be "the lamentable consequence of bad principles and morals," and, Katz continues, this "transmutation of pauperism a moral category tarnished all the poor. Despite the effort to maintain fine distinctions, increasingly poverty itself became not the natural result of misfortune, but the willful result of indolence and vice." This moral politics "served," Katz continues, "to justify the mean-spirited treatment of the poor, which in turn checked expenses for poor relief and provided a powerful incentive to work" (Katz 1986: 17–19; 1989: 11–14).

Deeper in history, the moralization of industry and poverty as outward signs of an innate character reflects the cultural meaning and function of the Protestant work ethic as described by the German sociologist Max Weber. From the sixteenth century onward, being industrious was regarded by the Calvinists he studied as more than the source of productive power; perhaps more important, industry was a protection against sin and vice. Working hard was, Weber writes, "the specific defense against all those temptations which Puritanism united under the name of the unclean life." The prescription to "work hard in your calling" was meant to discipline the behavior of community members and encourage strict sexual control, spiritual reflection, and familial obligation. This moral economy was also a basis for judgment and discrimination. Weber describes how Calvinists regarded "unwillingness to work" as "symptomatic of the lack of grace." Those who did not work steadily for whatever reason were understood as not being one of the elect nor predestined to go to heaven, hence Weber's well-known argument that the sociological function of industriousness was to publicly display election, because this meant a great deal in context. Material poverty was seen as evidence of a lack of divine blessing. "Wealth," Weber wrote, "as a performance of duty in a calling . . . is not only morally permissible, but actually enjoined" (1958: 108–09). The limits of sympathy and membership were thus also drawn. "Waste of time," Weber wrote of the Calvinists, "is thus the first and in principle the deadliest of sins. The span of human life is infinitely short and precious to make sure of one's own election. Loss of time through sociability, idle talk, luxury, even more sleep than is necessary for health . . . is worth absolute moral condemnation" (104–5). Anyone who was able-bodied and was not working was theoretically deemed unworthy of sympathy or assistance because it was assumed that they were inherently sinful and possessed a desire to be unhealthy and unproductive, as in Saint Paul's claim that "He who will not work shall not eat" (2 Thessalonians 3:10), which Weber cites as the central thread of the moral politics of worthiness and membership for Calvinists (105).

"Look, it is all in the Bible," Andrew keeps going. "'He who will not work will not eat.' That's what sorriness is. A person needs to work to support a family, put food on the table. If a person does not work, that person is sorry. They drag on the government and people like me out here hard at work. The government does not understand sorriness. The government feeds you even if you're sorry. And that is the basic problem in society today."

"So, I take it, you are not sorry?"

"No, it's more complicated. Sometimes I can be sorry. We can't do anything on our own. That's in the Bible. Paul talks about how we can't do anything unless it is Christ living in us. You might be doing a great job on the farm, but if your heart is not with the Lord, then it's bound to crumble. Sometimes you get a gut feeling that you ought to do something, and that is how you are not sorry. Where does that come from? I think it comes from God. There was a piece of metal that fell out of the back of my truck near the farm shop. I saw it. I had that gut feeling. I said, 'I need to pick that up because it's going to tear up my equipment.' But I didn't do it, Pete. Sometimes I'm not the best about keeping up the shop. Two weeks later, my tobacco harvester is coming into the shop and the front tire throws the damn rod up. It cost me a few thousand dollars. That's sorriness, and we all have it. It costs us."

"Does that make you a sorry person?" I am playing a bit dumb here, nudging Andrew to help me understand how he is using the term.

"Do I provide for my family and work hard? Am I out there asking for a handout? Everyone is sorry sometimes. But are you a sorry person in terms of working hard and supporting your family? That's a bigger issue. Working hard is the most important thing."

Ironically, tobacco growers have been "out there," in the public sphere, asking for government assistance for decades, and they have gotten lots of it. But to be fair to how Andrew sees things, this relationship to the state is legitimate because it has helped hardworking families. The cultural work that went into depicting the tobacco grower as a meritorious plighted citizen in the last half century is implicit in how Andrew defines sorriness and what he believes about entitlement. In other words, sorriness is a flexible idiom that can be adapted to empirical circumstances in ways that reconcile contradictions and reconfirm expectations about achievement, accountability, and assurance. Growers like Andrew speak mercifully about the impact of weather or the tragedy of neighbors who are in over their heads. "Take my neighbor," he says. "You've seen his tobacco this year. They haven't had much rain. It's sorry tobacco. He's a good farmer, but got a rough crop this year. It's not his fault," he goes on. "If you have rough weather, really and truly it's not your fault. The man is working hard, doing his best, but just unlucky. There might be no rain over here where I'm farming next year and my crop will suffer. It doesn't mean that I'm sorry." Whereas there is some leeway in what a bad crop of tobacco says about its producer and how the meanings of sorriness are

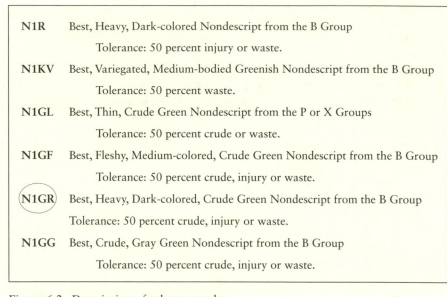

N1R   Best, Heavy, Dark-colored Nondescript from the B Group
                 Tolerance: 50 percent injury or waste.

N1KV   Best, Variegated, Medium-bodied Greenish Nondescript from the B Group
                 Tolerance: 50 percent waste.

N1GL   Best, Thin, Crude Green Nondescript from the P or X Groups
                 Tolerance: 50 percent crude or waste.

N1GF   Best, Fleshy, Medium-colored, Crude Green Nondescript from the B Group
                 Tolerance: 50 percent crude, injury or waste.

N1GR   Best, Heavy, Dark-colored, Crude Green Nondescript from the B Group
                 Tolerance: 50 percent crude, injury or waste.

N1GG   Best, Crude, Gray Green Nondescript from the B Group
                 Tolerance: 50 percent crude, injury or waste.

Figure 6.2. Description of tobacco grades.
Source: "Official Standard Grades for Flue-Cured Tobacco U.S. Types 11, 12, 13, 14, & Foreign Type 92," Tobacco Division of the Agricultural Marketing Service of the United States Department of Agriculture, 1989.

applied, the attribution of an essential moral character is crucial in the dominant white discourse, as in the N1GR joke.

As part of the government's tobacco program, the USDA published a list of standard grades each year, detailing the dozens of grades and assigned price values for tobacco leaf. In this old system, the official technical definition of N1GR was "heavy, dark-colored, crude green nondescript from the B Group" with a "tolerance" of "50 percent crude, injury or waste." In lay terms, this is a bale comprised of matter that is not well cured, looks damaged and bruised, and is dark and green, rather than the ideal bright yellow. A significant portion of the bale is made up of very poor quality leaf and also nontobacco material.

I asked growers to explain exactly what N1GR means. They told me that it is "nondescript, green and red," or "sorry, ugly tobacco, not worth anything," or "dead tobacco." The most common explanation was that it stands for "no grade." This is an important misconception because the "N" in N1GR officially refers to "nondescript," which is a generic kind of tobacco matter not recognizable as originating from a particular stalk position but nonetheless recognizable as tobacco leaf. Nondescript tobacco is recognizable as belonging to the tobacco plant species. It is not just the "bare life" of generic organic matter (Agamben 2000), which is what "no grade" would mean—a bale that, upon inspection by the grader, was deemed unrecognizable as tobacco. According to the government handbook, such bales often had a "foreign odor," were "off type," and were "of distinctly different characteristics" and "cannot be classified" as tobacco. Technicalities mattered when the distinction between "nondescript" and "no grade" carried economic value. Bales with "no grade" fetched no price support; their price was not buoyed or subsidized by the federal government program. Even though tobacco companies sometimes purchased these bales, perhaps to use as cheap cigarette filler, from the standpoint of the government they were worthless. A bale graded N1GR, although of low value, was "supported," in local parlance, and fetched a minimum price for the grower's benefit. Growers were intimately familiar with the old grading system and could describe the attributes of the most common grades, like B3K, with incredible precision. To them the differences between B3K and another similar grade were a matter of several cents per pound. That these men mistake N1GR as "no grade" reveals the extent to which the grade functions as a general concept, not an acronym indicating specific leaf characteristics. This confusion is part of the joke, which speaks to the ambivalent relationship of the white growers who tell and laugh at it to black workers who are simultaneously regarded as abstract labor value ("nondescript") and, in a fantasy about an older social order, a different species ("no grade"). Either way the joke construes blackness as a commodity that is owned by and at the disposal of white people, defines the "utterly degraded bottom" of the social hierarchy (De Genova 2006: 2), and in this way helps to distance growers from the racialized labor and manual labor that is embedded in their bales, in spite of their dependence on it.

Americanized

In the Depression era, white sugar growers in Florida attributed labor shortages and high wages to a problem of "idle negroes." Growers commonly said that local black people were not "interested" in working steady, but rather making a "quick" sum of money. One Florida grower said at a federal hearing in 1937, "If you were to give the 'nigger' more money than he gets now he would leave two months sooner because he has too much money to spend." These stereotypes masked the interest of those growers in maintaining low farm wages, suggesting that increased wages would undercut the productivity of laborers, while the predictable act of faulting local black workers naturalized the idea that they ought

to make themselves disposable for white people. Based on these stereotypes, the growers successfully petitioned the USDA to rescale the farm
labor workforce to include a broader regional pool through the forced
resettlement of underemployed, mostly black rural and urban residents
from across the South (Hollander 2006: 277–79). A few years later, in
the wartime labor shortage, Florida sugar growers again spoke with great
urgency about the "idle negro farm hands" who threatened their ability
to harvest cane. Now their lobbying efforts portrayed Caribbean ethnic
groups as the ideal farmworker. These groups, "mostly belonging to the
negro race," growers publically said, have a "different set of mores and
social patterns," being "generally honest, law-abiding, church-attending
citizens." An enduring regional white paternalism depicted immigrant
workers as "happy" and "contented." These images led the federal government to establish a formal "guest worker" program so that Florida
growers could import Caribbean labor, much like the Bracero Program
was established to help California growers maintain low farm wages and
a controllable workforce by importing Mexican seasonal labor. Recalci-
trance among diverse classes of local workers in the United States was
never understood as resistance to austere farm management conditions
and low wages or to the division of labor in southern agriculture in general (266, 283–85).

How growers like Andrew use the term *Americanized* reflects a dominant view of assimilation as having gone awry, suggesting that some positive dimension of foreignness has irrevocably been lost. Claiming that
Mexican migrants become Americanized over time, Andrew means that
they learn that they do not have to work to survive, by which he specifically means migrants have "gotten like the blacks." This rationale is
premised on the assumption that immigrants are docile and happy field
hands and that their natural station in life is stoop labor and labor camp
living. It converts the fact that migrants become less intimidated by employers and more capable of securing employment in other sectors into a
scourge of blackness and a backhanded and condescending compliment
about why vulnerable immigrants work hard. "Oh man," another farmer
says, "the Mexicans work hard, buddy, they just go as hard as they can
go, and now they've got a little on the sorry side. They have gotten to be
like the blacks."

The discourse of Americanization thus encodes a set of Faces. Migrant
farmworkers are said to become Americanized because they were apparently not American to start with, and they devolve into that category
through a pathological kind of assimilation. The "America" implied in
the term Americanized is a victimized nation where white middle-class
people do not have to apologize for anything because they are said to be

threatened—in their business interests and patriotism—by people who are called sorry, just as Calvinists centuries before felt threatened by the unhealthful desires of neighbors and strangers. Migrant farmworkers are said to "have gotten to be like the blacks" because the attainment of full citizenship for black citizens and civil rights guarantees enacted since the 1960s are often culturally perceived as a ticket that African Americans did not pay for. The civil rights struggles also pointed out that white people have been the historical beneficiaries of forms of comparative advantage, and that private property and capital accumulation were not obtained in vacuums or the result of individual achievement in a simple way. These struggles implied that many white people are, in a word, sorry, in the sense of being complicit in a system stacked against others, but also in the sense of being dependent on largesse and entitlement. Andrew does not see himself as having been involved in the practices of racial discrimination that have disadvantaged black farmers in his vicinity and maintained the racialized division of farm labor. Yet civil rights policies like affirmative action, a frequent topic on Andrew's favorite radio talk shows, imply a degree of inherent complicity and culpability. Use of the term *sorry* to denigrate black workers and justify the illegal employment of migrants is not just an economic strategy to depress wages by using cultural explanations to incite and maintain competition in the working classes, but it is also a moral project having to do with the idea that to be American is to be white, and to be a white American is to be an innocent person burdened by the pathologies of selfish racial minorities. It makes it seem as though white Americans manage their businesses not in the pursuit of profit or out of self-interest but rather as an altruistic act of taking on the burden of employing the underclass. National icons feel themselves at odds with a state that is said to not understand sorriness even though its contraction and reorganization in large measure engendered the sorry social conditions of poverty and chronic underemployment that are now misrecognized as the stereotyped Face of people "naturally disposed to be lazy and indolent" (Katz 1986: 23). The discourse about people being Americanized reflects the idea that America is in trouble precisely because of policies like affirmative action, which came out of the civil rights movement. Andrew and other people who use this language feel empowered to frame these as unfortunate turns in American policy, and to believe that the imagined Christian, white roots of America are threatened and need to be recuperated. The ways that North Carolina growers talk about labor relations and social inequalities thus reflects a conservative approach and set of strategies, keywords, and talking points that are broadly evident in the United States.

The Sorriness of Structural Adjustment

Idleness in rural North Carolina is undeniable. Poor black and white people sit jobless on the porches of old shotgun houses and loiter around the service stations and country stores of tobacco towns. In the lobby at the Department of Social Services, unemployed young men and women with crying babies slouch in vinyl seats and read tabloid magazines and talk on cell phones. Rural unemployment and an aversion to the harshest forms of manual labor do not so much index their laziness as show a clear awareness of how certain forms of employment deeply exploit them, are impermanent and lead nowhere, and perpetuate a kind of caste system in which different categories of people are supposed to know and stay where they belong.

From the 1950s to the 1970s, the value of manufacturing in North Carolina increased from $2 billion to $18 billion. The manufacturing labor force increased by 96 percent. Only seven states had a larger manufacturing workforce. The release of tenants and the gradual consolidation of farm operations in the countryside were offset by increased urbanization and industrialization. However, the structural adjustment policies that began in the 1970s led to major changes, including the decline of communities built up around industry, new kinds of residential segregation, and the worsening of social epidemiology there.

From the 1970s to the 1990s, tobacco manufacturing in North Carolina declined from 16 percent to 12 percent of total manufacturing, and from 8 percent to 3 percent of the total workforce (Wood 1986: 16–19). Nearly 82,000 jobs were eliminated in the state's textile industry. The passage of the North American Free Trade Agreement in 1994 quickened capital flight. Since the 1990s the textile workforce declined another 60 percent, plummeting from 250,000 to less than 100,000 jobs. On the tobacco side, there were major layoffs in important tobacco towns like Wilson and Durham, with multinational tobacco companies (both leaf wholesalers and cigarette manufacturers) dissolving and consolidating local factories and moving a good deal of the production apparatus to the developing world. Since 1995, the state's tobacco manufacturing workforce has declined by roughly 40 percent, and further layoffs are perpetually on the horizon. Meanwhile, wages in existing tobacco facilities in urban North Carolina have stagnated and benefits have been retracted in order to justify keeping those jobs there. In the late 2000s, North Carolina boasted fifteen counties with unemployment rates more than a few percentage points over the national average. They were all rural, and most were in the heavily tobacco-dependent eastern section. Social surveys conducted at the time found that 59 percent of the unemployed in rural North Carolina were able to find work in one year, and just 62 percent in two years. With only 22 percent of rural residents in North Carolina having a college degree and 27 percent lacking a high school degree, the movement of industry offshore, combined with the influx of immigrant workers onto farms and into the technical vocations, leaves many rural residents, who are often unable to access the knowledge jobs in the new economy, with limited job options. Record payouts in unemployment benefits since 2001 led local politicians to divert money from public education and job-training programs. Those who have found jobs earn about 10 percent less than in their previous work, owing to the shift to less-skilled employment in the growing service sector and the impact of transnational migration on local wages.[3]

The power of international trade agreements in driving northward migration from Latin America and lax government enforcement of existing labor laws has allowed the North Carolina economy to expand by leaps and bounds in spite of the collapse of traditional industries and high unemployment levels. Employers in the state save about $2 billion per year as a result of wage stagnation attributable to labor surpluses made available because of transnational migration (1.4 percent of total wages). Nearly all Hispanics in North Carolina work in labor-intensive jobs where wage stagnation has been the most evident. Remarkably, while manufacturers in North Carolina shed 325,000 workers between 1995 and 2005, the number of Hispanic immigrant workers employed in manufacturing industries increased by 15,000. The per capita income of the state's Hispanic residents is about $9,000, and 26 percent live in poverty compared to 14 percent of all state residents (Kasarda and Johnson 2006; East Carolina University Regional Development Institute 1999).

The combination of structural adjustment economic policies, the war on welfare, failures to raise the minimum wage, the contraction of low-income housing, the recomposition of residential and industrial zones around cities like Raleigh, and the depredation of rural and urban tax bases for public schools—all of these are concrete historical factors that have worsened living standards and made life precarious in many communities since the 1980s and increased dependence on social assistance. They comprise the complex cause of why black people came to make up a substantial proportion of welfare rolls (Katz 1986: 267, 274–91). Yet the "demonization of black families," George Lipsitz argues, through

---

[3] These data come from the Center on Globalization, Governance & Competitiveness at Duke University (http://www.cggc.duke.edu), the North Carolina Rural Economic Development Center (http://www.ncruralcenter.org), and Wagner (1999).

cultural stereotypes about indolence has justified harsh social welfare policies and been one reason to continuously legitimize the neglectful governance of employment and labor laws (1995: 378–80). For example, in 2005, Vicente Fox, then president of Mexico, made the controversial comment that "Mexicans, filled with dignity, willingness and ability to work, are doing jobs that not even blacks want to do there in the United States" (Orlandi 2005). Fox was perhaps politicking, playing to nationalist sentiments in the Mexican diaspora. The migrant workers with whom I worked agreed with him. But they broadened the scope of the critique. Here is what a young man in his twenties from Central Mexico told me: "What Vicente Fox said is true. They won't do it, much less the whites. The farmer comes to the field and says, 'Slow down, be careful, it's hot out here.' But he does not have to tell us it's hot. The blacks don't like to work. The whites [*americanos*] don't either. Look at the farmer. He drives. He checks everything. But he is not in the sun. He is not sweating. I would prefer that, too."

Like the white farm employers, many black workers are in their fifties or sixties. Their ability to do difficult manual labor is usually waning. Anxiety about the direct threat that younger migrant workers pose to their livelihood arises in the kinds of workplace antagonisms analyzed in the last chapter. "I'm not going do that shitty work," an old black employee tells me in an interview. "Mexicans do all the shit work. That's what the Mexican is for. But when I was young I did it, too." Aversion to manual work among black workers, their strong preference for operating farm machines and serving as supervisors, is not just the result of age. Whereas migrants travel in crews and are commonly provided free accommodations in the labor camps (part of how their vulnerability and usually undocumented status is exploited), the real value of farm wages is worth less to black workers who live in neighborhoods, pay rent, and usually supply their own transportation. Hence, when a black worker needs to temporarily borrow a truck from his employer or to catch a ride with other workers or with the grower, who now needs to leave the house that much earlier, the worker will face derision and be seen as a mooch who is unable to support himself and who is inherently dependent on others, a worker who is not frugal, is wasteful, spends his paycheck on alcohol rather than saving up for a car, and is spoiled in becoming accustomed to dependence. However, this interpretation personalizes what is at least partly an effect of the higher cost of living that nonimmigrant workers face and the capacity for growers to reduce labor costs through the warehousing of migrants. Besides, the preference for operating machines and expecting higher than minimum wages among black workers is also due to pride, a critical perspective on employer power, and the simple fact that the manual work is difficult.

Willie, an aging black man who I got to know well during my fieldwork, lives in a mobile home in Wilson County. He related the following story to me as we smoked cigarettes together during a break in the workday and read the newspaper article reporting what Vicente Fox said.

> Years ago, this white dude came uptown. I'm just sitting outside on the porch. He asks me if I want to harvest some tobacco. I was in good shape then. Damn if I harvested all day long. The man gave me a dollar an hour. Fuck that shit. He just sat there watching. He gave a few bucks to a few black guys and sat in his pickup truck listening to the radio. I don't have a problem working. But I've got a problem with that.

Willie encouraged me to see work ethic as more than a simple matter of doing work. For him, it is wrapped up with the cultural meaning of work and supervision, and the air of entitlement that emanates from pickup trucks and weighs down on tobacco patches.

> Say a white man goes into town right now and asks a bunch of black guys sitting on a porch if they want to harvest tobacco. A couple of guys might jump in the back of the pickup truck and go to the field. When they find out that the farmer means harvest by hand, they are going to say, "For what, five or six bucks an hour? You better take my ass back to town, and you can forget that shit." But if the farmer wants them to ride a harvester, or drive a pickup truck hauling leaf, then that's fine. That's more skilled work and you've got to pay more. And another thing: is the white farmer going to get out of the truck and harvest tobacco by hand, too? If he won't do that then why should a bunch of black guys do it? Why didn't Fox say that Mexicans are doing work that Americans won't do? You don't see any white dudes out there doing that kind of work.

Willie sees himself as a skilled worker and takes offense at the suggestion that manual labor is his natural disposition. Yet this inclination pushes him to affirm that trait in the migrants he works alongside. Manual work is tied to racialized forms of power that have for centuries positioned experience and knowledge on the side of white landowners and farmers, and made it seem as though black people were at the disposal of white people and ought to happily serve their interests, which helps to explain the politics of why someone who is treated like an object, and whose wages and position at the farm do not permit the level of social mobility that white farmers expect for themselves, might not want to do this kind of work. It also helps to explain how and why the use of the term *help* to refer to workers is pejorative and paternalistic.

Thirteen-Month Crop

On most summer days, retired farmers and aging landowners visit the farm shops of their neighbors to watch the action: ripe tobacco hauled from fields in trailers towed behind pickup trucks, heaved into bulk curing barns, and packed into bales that emit the same dank and musky smell that tobacco had in the past. They do not tire of shaking their heads at the sight of a mechanized assembly line. They repeatedly comment, as if surprised again with each new day, about the "shame" of leaf being handled so "carelessly," dumped from trailers onto concrete floors, trafficked through a mechanical tumbler, and tossed in mass quantities into a baling machine. "We would never consider doing such a thing," a former tenant farmer tells me one afternoon, pants jacked to his belly button. "We took care of tobacco. It hurts me to see it treated like this." He understands the mandates of the new production regime, but he indicates that an important element of human contact and care has been lost to industrialization.

The new model of production, based on company contracts, is geared to having as little human contact with the tobacco leaf as possible, ensuring "cleanliness" and reducing contamination possibilities, while also using machines—the mechanical planters and harvesters, the leaf-tumbling machines, and hydraulic balers—to generate economic efficiencies. In the past tactile contact with leaf was definitive of the work of tobacco cultivators and was linked to a different approach to quality control. The anthropologist Fernando Ortiz evocatively describes the craftwork involved in an earlier stage of tobacco production in his historical study of Cuba's tobacco industry.

> [T]obacco-raising is such a meticulous affair. . . . The tobacco-grower has to tend his tobacco not by fields, not even by plants, but leaf by leaf. . . . In tobacco quality is the goal . . . The ideal of the tobacco man, grower or manufacturer, is distinction, for his product to be in a class by itself, *the best*. . . . The cultivation of tobacco demands the most delicate attention at every stage . . . It is as though tobacco demanded the solicitous, pampering care of its cultivator. (1995: 24, 27)

The relation of leaf quality and farmer reputation was strongly developed in colonial Chesapeake, as discussed in chapter 2. In the Deep South, planters of other crops often fled the humid weather, partly to avoid malaria, hiring supervisors to manage the plantations. But tobacco planters were always present because of the intensive supervisorial and managerial requirements: "Each step in the annual process required skill, judgment, and luck" (Breen 1985: 45).

Figure 6.3. Tobacco harvest near Wilson, July 1938. Photograph by Bill Baker. Courtesy of the North Carolina Office of Archives and History, Raleigh, North Carolina (image #ConDev1243C).

Of all facets of production, curing has historically been most definitive of producer skill and reputation. It involves innumerable microdecisions related to temperature and time, where a working knowledge of how to evaluate the curing process depends on an ability to feel the texture of the tobacco, the way it is sticky and gummy, to smell its musty aroma and perceive ripeness or rotting, and to decipher the colorful progression from Jurassic green to bright yellow or yellowish brown (50). Although the curing process is now highly mechanical, with digital controls for barn temperature, airflow, curing schedules, and moisture control, active growers insist that no amount of technology can replace the artisanal aspects. They can touch the tobacco and tell you the water content to a percentage point. Even though the dials are all preset, they check them every two hours because this is how it has always been done and something can happen, such as a malfunction in the barn's power supply or an inaccurate digital gauge. The machines are not fully trusted. Growers complain that once curing begins (in mid-August when the lower stalk positions are harvested), there are no vacation getaways and, as if caring for a newborn baby, they sleep in spurts and awake a few times without an alarm clock to drive a golf cart down the road from their house to the farm shop where the gas-burning barns murmur. They stand in front of the industrial barns where air exhaust blows wickedly out of vents, and they talk about how human sensations of heat and odor indicate what is happening to the leaf. Here is what one grower told me.

> I cannot teach this. You'd have to learn it by doing. What am I looking for when I smell the tobacco? What I'm looking for is the color of the leaf. You can see that the leaf is yellowing and drying, but there are shades of color and texture in there. You need to know about them because that's where the quality and the aroma are. You only know what these things mean—where to move the temperature, if you need to add heat or pull back on the heat, if you need more exhaust—these things come from experience. Pete, I've been doing this for thirty years. I went to college and I learned a lot about agriculture. But curing I learned from my father and from doing it.

Now here is what Ortiz said about Cuban tobacco producers more than a half century earlier.

> The grower visits his treasure every day, first to touch the leaves and gauge their degree of dryness, then to smell them and judge the progress of curing by their scent. . . . It is here that the painstaking skill of the grower comes into play to keep the leaves at the right degree of flexibility. (1995: 31)

There is a complex anthropology of the senses in the relationship of the grower to curing tobacco, where an ability to smell is also a way of "looking for" and "seeing that." Digital technology is supposed to make these skills unnecessary and allow the grower to take weekend trips or perhaps a longer break before the kids or grandkids go back to school. But a practical relationship is crucial at this stage for maximizing leaf quality. "The computers, the digital monitors, all of that," a grower says, "that's a mediocre approach. You rely on those machines and you'll get a crop that's just okay. You really need to be there, because if something goes wrong, and because a damn machine doesn't know how to cure tobacco. That's all there is to it. It cannot make the adjustments that need to be made. That's why you see the grower reach [through the air vent, into the barn] and grab a handful of leaf." This grower distinguishes between the theoretical knowledge that guides mechanical production and the practical knowledge that comes from experience and is not part of the functioning of the computerized barns. Being there makes the grower the sovereign power and allows a level of emotional satisfaction having to do with self-assurance. "Yes, I could probably go to the beach for a weekend, and let the barns run, and they'd turn out fine," this grower continues. "But I'd be worried the whole time. I'd get to the coast and be miserable. It's just what you do; come August you stay awake all night and monitor your barns. It's just how we do it and how it's always been done." While being present at the farm throughout the harvest season is an economical matter having to do with quality control, it is also a means of everyday coping in a business where farmer skill is increasingly mechanized, made obsolete, and even depicted as threatening by corporations preferring to streamline and standardize things and minimize human involvement. It is also pleasurably excessive. The grower likes the smell and the touch, and rummages in the air vent to an extent that is perhaps more than what is necessary for quality control, because this contact with the leaf is also a kind of contractual obligation that comes with being a grower and actively maintaining a human element, which has been so important in the history of tobacco production and seems passed down through generations.

Many other artisanal aspects of tobacco agriculture have gone by the wayside. For the entire history of tobacco up until the 1990s, tobacco was marketed in "bundles" of six leaves, the seventh and highest-quality leaf wrapped around the stems to hold them together. The requirement that cultivators bundle their leaf and stack it in orderly piles on the auction floor was completely gratuitous. The leaves were neatly wrapped only to be shredded and adulterated at the processing facilities and cigarette manufacturing plants. The function of bundling had to do with the exhibition of skill and pride among producers. It was about publicly presenting what farmers continue to call "pretty tobacco," meaning leaf that is well cured. As compared to tightly stuffing leaf into bales, which replaced bundles to allow for more efficient transportation from ware-

Figure 6.4. North Carolina tenants swapping help, 1938. Photograph by Bill Baker. Courtesy of the North Carolina Office of Archives and History, Raleigh, North Carolina (image #ConDev1244B).

houses to processing facilities, bundling was a way of staging the intricacies of color and the substantial texture of each individual leaf. Decades ago tenants worked hard to weed their fields and maintain straight rows to curry the favor of landowners (perhaps as an eviction-avoidance strategy) and establish a reputation within the local tobacco world in which tobacco farming was construed as having an obligatorily excessive and obsessive aspect. Tightly wrapped bundles of bright leaf staged the tenant family as being dedicated and devoted to an arcane kind of care, which perhaps also reflected a level of docility or industry that would appeal to the landowners who supervised them and shared in their takings. Reputation and hard work, linked to involvement in artisanal techniques and an institutional system of public display, were important strategies of economic survival and social power for tenant families. "Those who accepted the gospel of hard work received community support even if they failed, but the community scorned the idle," Pete Daniel, a historian of southern agriculture, writes, whereas for "those who did not work . . . the community had pillorying terms—lazy, good for nothing, no account, trash" (1986: 66).

The vernacular meaning of sorriness is sensed in these adjectives. Just to nail it down—the idea that the intensive and obsessive managerial care in the history of tobacco farming has been a context in which being deemed sorry, being seen as a certain kind of person, and having access to important material and social resources is at stake—let me cite another historian who reiterates that rural North Carolinians "always associated crooked rows with sorry people" (Crews 1978: 119). Not being sorry or deemed lazy, good for nothing, no account, or trash mattered for tenant families because the morality of hard work was linked to the security net of being deemed worthy of social assistance and having access to the collective labor of neighboring tenant families cooperating during the harvest. "Neighboring farmers shared labor," an old tenant farmer told me in an interview at his house. He is in his early nineties, a white man who never owned land and reminisced about pretty tobacco as if the shift to baling was the day pride in tobacco died. "We rotated, working here one day and then there the next day. But you had to work. We wouldn't work with the families that didn't want to do it right or wanted to take advantage." For sharecroppers and tenants facing the constant threat of eviction and the vagaries of weather, the "only feasible response to the uncertainty of the times was to insure the best crop possible" (McKinney 2003: 11). Not just an economic strategy, an investment in working was also a thing of pride. "Pride was all we had," another former tenant says, a white man whose family swapped labor for years with black tenant families. "It was hard work. Now I look back on it and think it was silly. We spent so much time tying tobacco into bundles, dressing it up. But it mattered. That was how you got the grades. That was what other farmers looked at. That was what you thought about when you finished the season. You thought about whether your tobacco looked good, and you wanted other people to know it."

Farm Truck

Jeff Hart drives a brand-new red Ford F-150. The color nods to his alma mater, the major state university where he earned a joint degree in agriculture and business. Just weeks old, the truck already has a defensive bumper sticker: "Tobacco Money Pays My Bills!" It is more luxurious than his older trucks, half a dozen beat-up Fords parked at the farm shop that are used during the harvest season to transport workers and supplies to fields. In his new truck, Jeff enjoys air conditioning, automatic windows, and leather bucket seats, plus a brilliant satellite radio toggled for country music, conservative talk, and weather reports. Whereas imagined community was once broadcast as a regional identity in local call signs like WGTM, the radio now rallies a broader sense of affiliation for people like Jeff, who see themselves as part of a victimized and intensely patriotic mainstream of decent, hardworking families, an identity promoted as much by talk radio hacks as nationalistic pickup truck advertisements. In his daily trips from field to field, Jeff gets an earful about the demise of family values, the dangers of a liberal political agenda that promotes resource redistribution and entitlements for people who do not work hard, and the problem of illegal immigration.

Jeff has a nervous tic. Having recently quit smoking, he anxiously taps the wheel or the dashboard. He is off beat, not keeping time with the music, his loud and forceful taps annoying me. I wish he would roll down the automatic window and smoke a cigarette, frankly. He is frustrated about something, everything maybe, anxiety that is expressed in fidgets, excited by Rush Limbaugh, and certainly not allayed by flatlined leaf prices and dry weather. Jeff says he quit smoking to get his wife, Christine, off his back: "She likes to scrimp and save, and we were paying double on health premiums when I was smoking, so I quit." I believe part of his decision also involved a desire to hang around long enough to see his grandchildren grow up, so he can spoil them as he likes to do with stuff bought with each year's tobacco profits and the payments he receives as part of 2004's buyout.

Christine is not stingy when it comes to the new truck. She says Jeff, in his midfifties with graying hair and a big belly, looks damn good driving it and deserves it after decades spent in the throes of tobacco's demise. But she wonders why he insists on using the new truck as an everyday vehicle, sometimes towing equipment or driving into muddy fields, with so many old trucks available. "Some farmers have an 'everyday' truck and a new 'weekend' truck," she tells me in an interview.

Other growers avoid the muddy fields and other wear and tear because of scale. They manage their operations from offices, paved roads, or clean paths, distributing tasks to workers driving older trucks. With 110 acres of tobacco, Jeff is able to afford a new truck on credit but does not have the scale that would allow him to hire more supervisors, stay in the farm office, and avoid muddying the tires. In this context, Christine knows that his preference for regularly using the new truck is also a matter of visibility and status. It indicates that he is like these other growers, adhering to an ideal of ambitious and expansive farm ownership. But it is also about the pleasure that Jeff derives from technology and the assured feeling that he gets from driving it. Large growers stockpile soda and snacks that employees are given at break times—once in the morning and once in the afternoon—in a refrigerator at the farm shop. Even though this makes more sense economically, Jeff is a middling producer who prefers to drive

Figure 6.5. Liberty Warehouse on opening day of the Wilson Tobacco Market in August 2004. Photograph by Keith Barnes. Reproduced by permission of the photographer.

during break times to country stores that sit at crossroads. He pulls up, eight cylinders loud, blasting classic rock on his satellite radio, and is in a particular class—he and the truck—compared to farmers who cannot afford new trucks and who might see a new red Ford as ostentatious. "He's just showing off," a retired farmer, a man in his late seventies who drives his old truck down to the corner store and sits all morning with his coffee and a handful of other old timers, says to me in an interview. "But I understand. That's part of the game. If you're farming right now, you've got to get a new truck every couple of years. Otherwise, what are you doing? Are you not making out? But you look beneath the surface. All of a sudden that new truck doesn't seem so affordable. Does he need a new truck? Does it improve the quality of the crop? Absolutely not, but, you know the truck is more than a truck."

The switch from bundling to baling, and then the rise of private company contracts, dramatically changed the aesthetics and politics of public displays of success in tobacco farming. The public nature of the auction, where growers saw and heard each other's tobacco grades being hollered out, has been replaced by a system in which all growers privately sell as individuals. Having a contract has become the most definitive marker of distinction, indirectly indexing the quality of a grower's leaf, since it is presumed that those who possess and maintain company contracts are doing well. But what it means to be successful in tobacco farming is being redefined by contracting in other ways, with the historical and practical knowledge that growers have about leaf color and texture being replaced by a set of company standards that involve technocratic language, as seen in this excerpt from the Philip Morris website, which describes aspects of how the company evaluates its contracted farmers each year:

> Achieve SAP Vendor Evaluation scores in Quality of 99% for four consecutive quarters in a calendar year with no reportable R4, R45, R55 or R6 usage decision scored as Super High in the Impact Elements of the Vendor Evaluation. . . . Receive a Satisfactory rating on PM USA Supplier Audit . . . No identification of areas of concern requiring immediate attention in order to do business with PM USA. . . . Receive no material rejections for sensory issues, non-tobacco-related material (NTRM), mixed material or misidentified material (applies to flavors and ingredients) . . . Have no reportable nonconformance to PM USA requirements.[4]

Not to worry, the growers I interviewed also have only a vague sense of what this verbiage means. "It means produce good, clean tobacco, no trash in it, deliver it on time, look sharp, and don't complain," is a common response. This is "a bunch of bullshit that just means deliver them a good product and don't start any trouble," another farmer says. They tacitly know what is expected because having been in the tobacco business for a long time they know the kind of color, aroma, and texture that tobacco companies desire. The effect of this verbiage is not informative as much as disciplinary and organizational, linking the status of growers within the corporate system and issues of income and promotion to a system of quantifiable measures, while also identifying Philip Morris as the true sovereign power in a context where growers have long valued their accumulated expertise and power as managers and even artisans.

Public displays of success still happen, but this is now done through consumerism rather than in the bundling of pretty tobacco, and consumerism, of course, hinges on the extent to which the grower is willing to go into debt and acquiesce to company standards to avoid, as Philip Morris puts it, "reportable nonconformance." The grower can have a personality, as long as it doesn't interfere with the company's goals of strategically deskilling and standardizing tobacco farm management. Given this sce-

---

[4] This information, which I originally found on the Philip Morris website in 2007, is no longer available. I include it here to demonstrate the kind of technical agronomical language that is found in the internal literature that Philip Morris distributes to its contracted farm suppliers.

nario, growers have tactics of their own to achieve some economic lever-age and manage their reputation, for example, handpicking the "prettiest leaves" and "placing them around the outside of the bale, so that's what Philip Morris graders see." There is also the strategy of focusing more attention and resources on tobacco fields that are bordered by country roads, because these fields are publicly visible and will be judged by other growers, who all know which fields belong to which growers. "The front of the field is what everyone sees. You make sure to plant the crop next to the road with special care," a small farmer nearing retirement age tells me. "You want it to be the prettiest crop you've got. It's in the front of the road that people judge you. Farmers are always riding around, talking about who has sorry tobacco this year."

Mechanization limits this tactical posturing by homogenizing the aesthetics of the tobacco farm landscape. Seed varieties have been bred and modified to produce high yields and limit disease incidence, there is now less tobacco biodiversity than in the past because a select handful of seed varieties are marketed and utilized, tractors ease the practice of transplanting tobacco seedlings and maintaining straight rows, and chemical applications that kill weeds and control suckers are technologies that destroy signs of sorriness while rendering the close supervision and careful labor that mitigated sorriness in the past partly obsolete. A grower who got out of the tobacco industry in the 1980s farm crisis puts it this way:

> Success in farming used to be about making a pretty crop. That's what tenants did. It was family work, and they worked hard to make tobacco pretty. Now everybody is producing a decent crop and facing the same challenges: weather and prices mainly. A bad crop is a string of bad weather. That's what happened to me. Making it in farming is not really about the little attention to quality. Everyone is using machines and chemicals. Technology has taken out a lot of the art that was part of tobacco in the past. You're probably not going to come across a bad farmer. Most of the people who farm, they know what they are doing. They know how to grow crops, probably were raised on a farm, know their way around equipment. It's second nature to them. Even someone like me—I didn't grow up on a farm, but I worked on farms all along, and I knew how to put crops in the ground. Making it in farming today is more about managing cash flow and management. You've got to know how to manage a crew. You have to handle your loans and your investments. You can ride around the country roads and tell the difference. You look at the equipment, the farm shop, and the trucks. Who has junk spread out all around the farm shop and the equipment is not parked under shelters? The good manager is the one who keeps a neat and clean farm operation. I think this says something about the way

they manage their finances, too. I had cash flow problems and you could tell by looking at my farm. The equipment was old and neglected. I had soda cans piled high in the back of my pickup truck and tractor parts piled up in the grass around the shop. The good farm managers do not.

With increased uniformity in leaf quality, consumer practices and the aesthetics of the farm shop and farm equipment have become only more crucial to the presentation of a lack of sorriness. The color of pickup trucks and brand preferences in farm equipment are not miniscule manipulations of a regime of taste and class but reflections of personalities and inborn proclivities. Growers monitor the farms and fields of other farmers to look at quality issues, but they also look at the cleanliness of the tractors and harvesters, the orderliness of equipment, and whether weeds are kept down around farm shops. But the idea that there is a simple equation between the newness of farm equipment and the capabilities, skills, and merits of the manager neglects the important structural differences that have different growers facing different constraints and chances. There are many growers who go deep into debt in order to purchase new equipment so as to maintain the appearance of success, even though in reality their business is shaky. "Some of the farmers out there are in trouble, but you could not tell by looking at the business," an active farmer who takes pride in keeping frugal books and minimizing debt loads tells me. "They use debt and that can work for a while. But come a bad year, the cash flow is not there to pay off the bills, and that is why lots of farms fail. It's not that they're bad farmers. They're not good managers, but really it's because there is pressure to keep up appearances. There isn't always lots of equity behind the new trucks and tractors."

Consumption practices locate growers as part of a successful cohort at a regional level, while indicating middle-class preferences and tastes in relation to the wider society. These practices also mark distance from the workforce, where vehicle ownership and home ownership are essentially nonexistent, and reflect traces of the gentility and paternalism that was part of the colonial planter society. "I can afford to have our uniforms dry-cleaned by the service in town," Jeff tells me, referring to custom uniforms for all employees. "That's something nice for the workers. And it's nice when other farmers come over to the shop. They don't see a sorry mess. We're all wearing clean uniforms." Everyone at Jeff's operation wears gray work shirts, although Jeff, like most other growers, wears khakis, a contrast to the dark blue work pants that workers wear.

Farm Crisis

Morris Hyde did not inherit land or equipment. In the mid-1970s, he rented 450 acres of cropland by borrowing from the Farmers Home Administration (FmHA), a government lending program geared to supporting marginal producers. Dry weather and a bad crop in the first year put him in debt. Then it was a string of wet weather. Encouraged by the local FmHA officer, who at the time was urged by federal officials to expand farm operations to cheapen agricultural prices for consumers, Morris expanded rapidly to boost revenues and, ideally, repay the debt. While Morris was encouraged to expand, black farmers in the region faced denial and discouragement. These divergent policy trends worked together. Morris admits that part of the additional five hundred acres he rented to expand output was tended for decades by a deeply indebted black family who had been encouraged to exit production by the same loan officer, who, in his capacity as a resource broker, killed two birds with one stone.

Rising assessments under the "no-net-cost" compromise of the early 1980s drove Morris further into the hole. Meanwhile, in 1985 the Reagan administration decided to cut FmHA funding as a way to eliminate inefficient and indebted producers and to "maximize activities that are profitable and marginalize those that are not" (Ong 2003: 9). The administration also slashed—by 60 percent—existing agricultural training programs that provided mostly marginal growers with resources to help them generate cash flow, manage debt loads, and negotiate the farm crisis. In 1986, after a two-year moratorium on farm foreclosures, the government called in its loans. Some 2,400 delinquent farmers in North Carolina alone had one month to begin repaying (Minehart 1985b; E. Fitzgerald 1986; *Wilson Daily Times* 1986a, 1986b). Morris was one of those people. He owed $1.5 million, and with limited access to the government program that had initially encouraged him to expand, he now tried to cut costs however possible: he moved into a mobile home, drove an old pickup truck, learned to rebuild motors and fix equipment himself, and never dined at restaurants. He gained a reputation in the community as lacking managerial skill and making bad decisions.

Morris went through a difficult divorce, the spillover impact of workplace stress and financial strain. He says all of this, plus his smoking habit, contributed to two heart attacks.

> I was not fair to my wife. She tried to provide emotional support for me, but I always brushed her away. I was embarrassed. Taking her support, or a loan against her car or her family's home, would have been

> admitting I was incapable of clawing my way out of the hole. Eventually she had enough of me being quiet all night, pretending everything was fine when it clearly was not, and staying up nervous all night. I was not talking to anyone about it. I stopped going to church because there were the other farmers who knew I was in the hole, and they weren't fairing as bad. And I thought a lot about suicide. I'd drive the tractor to the back of the field and, it was weird, I was happiest back there, because I could look out over the crop, and I knew I was trying my hardest, but it wasn't working, and so I thought why not end it all back there.

Morris purchased a gun but never used it. In 1990, he exited farming. He endured the ritual embarrassment of a farm auction. All the equipment he could not afford was on display for farmers who came from far and wide to buy it at a deep discount. He took a job in the public school system and has worked there ever since, with a decent salary and summer hours that let him tend a vegetable garden that he calls a "farm." He is still paying off loans and still struggles to get to the local eating places where folks like Jeff park their new trucks. The felt disgrace of sensing that others see him as a failure keeps him in the garden on the weekends and in front of the television at night. His children come to visit on Sundays.

Morris sees himself as a good parent and a role model despite what others might consider to be serious failures. What matters to Morris and what he emphasizes to his children is that he is working to pay off the bills. Perhaps Morris is in this way attempting to maintain a sense of dignity and position himself on the hither side of sorriness.

> Lots of farmers went bankrupt, but not me. It got to the point where I couldn't drive through town. I didn't want to face them: the equipment dealer, the fertilizer dealer. These were people who I saw at church, the barbecue place, the post office. I wanted to pay them so I could hold my head up and not have to move up to Raleigh for work. These were people I knew and I wanted to look them in the face again. I never declared bankruptcy, even though it made sense financially. And I'm still paying off my bills. I guess you could say it was a pride thing.

Like other forms of economic dislocation, farm failure is interpreted and experienced through a cultural lens. It can indicate a personal failing, a capricious event, political oppression, or a blessing in disguise (Dudley 2000: 47). Talk about farm failure and folk theories about why it happens also reflect the sociology of rural communities in the United States, where there is often a particular context of accountability in which praise or blame is attributed to individuals. "For while surviving farmers were quick to attribute *someone else's* loss of a farm to 'bad management' and the 'go-go' mentality of [factory farming]," Kathryn Dudley writes in her study of the farm crisis in the Midwest, "farmers who lost their farms saw *themselves* as victims of circumstances beyond their control" (1996: 48; original italics). There is a local politics of victimhood and misfortune in agrarian settings where farmers constantly "monitor each other's behavior," but in their own cases, "make excuses for personal shortcomings" (49–50). This politics reflects the fact that all agricultural producers are to some extent impacted by forces that are beyond their control, but it also reflects the preponderance and legitimacy of a cultural ideology of personal accountability.

Even though admitting that he was an ineffective grower in many ways, Morris spoke frankly with me about the role of limited resources. As his debt load increased, he could no longer afford to employ a full-time worker to assist with planting and cultivating. Consequently, his fields were often sewn late in the season, weeds grew out of control and limited yield, and the work just piled up. Morris acknowledges some responsibility, telling me, for example, that he should have better utilized the educational resources provided by the Extension Service. And yet he also asks, "How was I supposed to go to a farm meeting to learn about, I don't know, weed control, when my weeds were out of control? Besides," he says, "asking for help is hard." Morris understands his farm failure as the result of several factors, including problems of skill and management, an eager government that prodded him to go into debt, and a culture of personal accountability that limits help seeking.

"My son once said I was a sorry farmer," Morris tells me.

"He called you that?"

"Yes, he told me one day. This was right after the divorce. We had an argument and he blurted out, 'Sorry farmer.' He was a young teenager. I'm not sure he knew exactly what he was saying, or what it means, or that it hurt me—and that it hurt to know that this was probably how lots of people saw me. He never apologized, but he doesn't need to. We have a good relationship now. Sometimes I still think he looks down on me, you know, because I didn't make it as a farmer. And he's got plenty of friends where their families are doing well in tobacco farming. I can understand why he was upset. We'd be living in a brick house if I was still farming, not just me in this trailer. His mother's got a new husband who works in town and they've got a brick house. So I'm kind of on the outside."

"Do you think you were a sorry farmer? Is that how you'd describe yourself? It's so easy to say, 'Look, farm loss, okay, he's a sorry farmer,' but how do you see things?"

"Parts of me were a bit sorry. But that is true with everyone. I was a farmer. That was my job and I did the best I could. I like to say that I was a bad manager. I had mediocre yields. But there was the weather. When I was in debt I didn't know how to get out. I wasn't using chemicals right. I couldn't afford labor but had to expand production. I didn't want to use my wife's income to pay off debts because I didn't want to talk to her about the situation. That is a big pride thing around here. The man is the farmer and you don't talk about the farm when it's having problems, because you always hope, in the back of your mind, that things will turn around. I was working damn hard out there. The ones who are sorry are the ones who don't put out the effort. That was not me. But I understand why my son said that. He was in high school when the farm was failing miserably. Other fathers were doing better than I was. It was just as embarrassing for him as it was for me."

"Do you know anyone who would admit to being a sorry farmer?"

"Well, not really, nobody would ever admit that. Maybe the guy who piddles around in his back yard with an acre of this or that, he might say he's sorry. But it doesn't really matter for him. For a farmer with debt, the guys who put food on the table, it's never your fault that you didn't make any money this year. It's the weather's fault. It's the market's fault. In my case, there was a combination. I was behind from day one. If I had to do it again, I wouldn't have taken those big loans."

"Why did you?"

"That's easy. I took out the loans because you want to be successful, with a nice farm, nice equipment, you want new things. You go into debt to get more acreage, ultimately to succeed. But when you're not succeeding you use debt to make it seem like you are, and you hope that a really good year will get you out of debt. No one wants to admit that they've made a mistake or that they cannot make it as a farmer, especially when their father did, and when your neighbors are doing well. I wouldn't admit it to my wife."

Morris was open and honest with me about the emotional tone of farm failure and the ways social context can compound stress and fragment relationships.

Let me again quote Kathryn Dudley:

> Economic failure is a stigma in virtually all walks of life, but is especially discrediting in rural townships, where viable farms remain in the family for generations . . . Particularly in rural settings, where the forces of nature and capitalist society exert direct control over farmers' productivity and material fortunes, the question of what the individual may claim credit or responsibility for is ever present. (2000: 5, 7)

Morris's story helped to clarify for me what it means to be sorry. He had a great deal at stake in succeeding. He did not want to fail. He wanted to uphold a certain image of masculinity as the head of the household. To not be sorry in this context is about all that is wrapped up in the success or failure of tobacco farms and the tendency of community members and family members to interpret these outcomes in terms of individual merit and achievement rather than shared conditions and incomplete control. Morris continues:

> When you go deeper into debt you try to put it out of your mind. You try to cope anyway you can. Sometimes it is alcohol. Sometimes it is suicide. Sometimes you take it out at home, like I did. You get depressed and you neglect your family. You try to convince yourself that it is alright. Winter is spent begging for more loans. You want to make it one more year. Springtime was sitting down at the table, working the numbers, convincing yourself that you can be successful at this, trying to hide the budgets from your wife so she won't look down on you or think you're not an adequate husband or man.

Morris had a lot at stake in responding to risk and failure in a certain way. Social support can be an effective means of reducing the harmful effects of stress, providing not only resources but also important coping mechanisms and an outlet for coming to grips with doubt and uncertainty. The masculine model of confidence and control promulgated in Marlboro Man advertisements and contoured in the postwar Extension Service framed the modern tobacco grower as an expansive business owner and head of the household, and wound up leading Morris to interiorize economic trouble and avoid seeking help, which limited possibilities for more effective personal and social responses to the common condition of financial insecurity.

Sorry State

Willis and Eve Stanton raised a family as yeoman farmers from the 1960s to the 1990s. They owned some land so were not sharecroppers. Willis's father bought the seventy-acre farm upon returning from military deployment in the late 1940s. During our interview at their modest house, Willis speaks of the white landowner who sold his father the property as a "good neighbor" who did not want "a white person to have the land because he cared about wrong and unjust things happening to black people." But over time the five acres of tobacco quota attached to that land was not enough to make ends meet and support their three children. Like many other smallholders, the Stantons supplemented farm income with wages from "public jobs." Willis worked in textile factories and pork-processing plants, Eve as a domestic worker. They talk about long days and little sleep, decades when complaint did not provide subsistence in the way hard work did. These narratives of work ethic in-

form a larger sense of themselves as people who are not sorry but have
been adversely impacted by institutional processes that are themselves no
good. Work schedules had a detrimental impact on household dynamics.
Willis admits detachment from the duties of child rearing, which largely
fell on Eve, who was no less busy. This created a constant interpersonal
rift in their marriage and at times threatened to end it. The difficulties
of farm life were impressed on their children, who moved to Raleigh
after graduating from high school to avoid having to do weeknight and
weekend tobacco work. "Watching us struggle for years with four jobs
and raggedy-ass equipment," Eve says, "tractors that won't start, running
out of money, buying Christmas presents with tobacco money that was
supposed to pay bills—we can see why our kids wanted to get away from
the farm and find public work."

In the early 1990s, the textile factory where Willis worked moved to
Mexico. In his fifties, he could not find another job that would let him
flexibly work around the farm schedule. The farm struggled to stay afloat
when quotas were slashed. "Besides," Willis tells me, sounding a lot like
other growers we have heard from, "it was impossible to get good help.
No one wants to work anymore, ..." The Stantons harvested and sold
their last tobacco crop just before the turn of the millennium. Eve says
they should have exited farming earlier; they'd be in better financial
shape today. Debts incurred to stay afloat cut into social security checks
and put added pressure on their children to help them subsist. In terms
of the buyout, they only receive payments for the value of the quota that
was attached to their land, since their eligibility as active growers was
annulled when they exited production. The roughly ten thousand dollars they receive annually as part of the buyout is barely enough to pay
property taxes.

They do not regret that the children overheard kitchen conversations
about how their operation received differential funding and assistance
compared to white farmers. That difference, Eve says, was the primary
reason they had to operate with raggedy-ass equipment.

> Why can't the white farmer imagine being in that situation? That is
> what I want to know. We are all farmers. We all face the weather. So
> why can't he understand my situation? When your farm is threatened,
> you risk losing everything that is attached to you. All the white farmers
> know what happened to black farmers, but they deny it. They'd come
> by our house at night and say, "Look, if you end up getting out of farm-
> ing, I would like to rent your land." They saw the old equipment and
> knew we were not able to get the funding we needed.

Willis and Eve have a somewhat different take on the word *sorry* than
white farmers I interviewed. "That word came about because some

farmers just don't care about their crops and aren't as clean and orderly as they could be," Willis says. "In the older generation, lots of tenants were sorry farmers, just making whatever kind of crop they could and taking the government support price."

"Sorry means bad," Eve says.

"Sorry is when you don't keep the weeds out and the grass doesn't get cut, the ends of the rows aren't straight, and the edges aren't trimmed. You're going to have sorry tobacco."

"Some people just carry tobacco to the market any kind of way. That's sorry."

"Yes, that's a sorry farmer. I wouldn't use the term, though," Willis cautions.

"Me neither; you say someone is a no-good worker or no-good farmer."

"I've seen some crops where I might say, 'There's a sorry farmer.' I'm driving around and I see a field that hasn't been cultivated; yeah, then I might say it."

"But you say it to yourself," Eve qualifies.

"What is it about the term?" I ask. "What's the difference between calling someone a sorry farmer and a no-good farmer?"

"When I say that someone is a no-good farmer, I'm talking about his crops. But if I say he's a sorry farmer, I'm saying something about the person, the man."

Eve adds, "You know, we never allowed our children to say 'I'm sorry.' That is not how you apologize. We always told them to say 'I apologize,' because they did something wrong. They are not sorry people, so why should they go around calling themselves sorry?"

Perhaps the Stantons are positioning as polite for me. Here I am doing an interview about a word frequently used to denigrate people like the Stantons, who were forced into difficult circumstances in their efforts to grow tobacco. Maybe they are not entirely comfortable in this interview setting. The ineluctably marked space between us is crosscut by differences of educational attainment and different implications of sorriness. They are perhaps implicitly sorry because they are the subjects of research about farm loss—or I am obviously sorry because I do research rather than the more manual labor that supported their family. Sorriness looms in this conversation where the attainment of an academic degree on my part is subtly referenced in their descriptions of struggle. Or maybe the Stantons are trying to delegitimize what they see as a dangerous word and confine its meaning to the aesthetics of fields.

Willis continues, "It was always important to me to keep a clean crop. In anything I did, I wanted to do my best. Some people do just enough work to get by. But it's just as easy to do it right. I would rather do the work than duck around to do less work or, you know, do a sorry job. It is important to do a good job."

"That is what we did," Eve says. "We didn't know any different. That is in our blood. That is how we were raised—to do a good job, keep the crop clean, pack it nice, and don't let the tobacco fall on the floor. People try to take a lot away from you in this life. You want to be proud of your work because people cannot take that."

Willis starts to talk about the factory. "The plant manager would come through the line and everyone would get uptight. But it never bothered me because I was doing my job the way I was supposed to." Willis tells me about the biases of factory managers and varieties of verbal abuse that disrespected his efforts and his pride. Less-experienced white employees were shown favoritism in promotions. He was repeatedly overlooked for the supervisor's post. Not only deserved, it was a job he wanted: better hours, better pay, and timely bonuses at Christmas. In the mid-1980s, during the farm crisis, Willis and Eve wanted to stop producing tobacco because of the high assessment costs that put Morris Hyde out of business. A supervisor position opened at the factory. Willis knew he was the most qualified person: no demerits, no troublemaking, an impeccable attendance record, no signs or traces of sorriness anywhere on the uniform that Eve washed at home to save money. He applied. One week later he had a new supervisor lurking over his shoulder. Willis, the most qualified and experienced employee on the floor, had to train him.

> It was a white dude who didn't know which way to enter the factory, let alone how to manage it. I trained a man half my age for a job I could do without needing any training. I would use the term sorry to describe that situation. If you are my boss and you know that I am more qualified than you, but I train you and you still take the job, I would call you a sorry person. It is a sorry state of a person is what it is.

Maybe Willis took the word in this direction to make a point. Sorriness here is about social justice and accrues the sense of being a state of affairs. Maybe Willis is partly talking to me, or about me, or with me—someone half his age interviewing him as part of a research project that will allow me to supervise and instruct other people about such things as farm livelihoods without the kind of experience in that field that Eve and he have. There is a hint of sarcasm as Willis tells me about how he was excluded from a supervisor position filled by someone my age, with my skin color, and my relatively limited experience. The performative act of defining a term while literalizing exactly what one means locates me as part of a system defined as a sorry state and makes me partly complicit, without having known Eve and Willis in the past, for the kind of inequity that, he suggests, defines this system in a fundamental way. Calling the system sorry is like calling the kettle black. It only needs elaboration in this interview, because in my questioning and prodding I am, sorry to say, not as intimately aware of this fact as he is.

> It was because I am black, plain and simple. That man did not have my experience. He had a degree, an education. But I had experience, real experience, and that's why I was asked to train him. I didn't get paid to train him though, and he was already making more money than me. His degree didn't make the difference; his skin did.

For Willis, to call something a sorry state is to call it unjust, but also duplicitous, willfully and woefully negligent about its defining unfairness and violence, returning, in fact, to the older meaning of the term *sorry* as wounding and injuring, and a context of grief and loss.

The Stantons participated in the recent black farmer lawsuit against the USDA to acquire financial restitution for the discrimination that kept them in a lower technological stratum than neighboring white producers. "If you gave black farmers another chance and did it fairly, give everyone the same chance with loans, equal everything for farming," Willis tells me, "that would be fair. But how can that happen? You can't just go back in time. If you gave me that promotion at the factory, that would be fair. But you can't go back in time. That is the only fair way, but it cannot happen." Financial compensation now helps support the Stantons in retirement. But they are bittersweet about the lawsuit. What they really wanted was to maintain a sustainable farm business, which is not something that the lawsuit can deliver. They are keenly aware that institutional discrimination creates divergent life trajectories that the lawsuit, in focusing on individual injuries, does not redress. Eve puts it this way:

> It's tough to walk around town. You run into the children or grandchildren of people I worked for, people whose parents paid me, but not much, working weekends washing their dishes as my second job so they could do their first job and make more money than my two jobs combined. And what those people made, they could save and pass on. I'm not sorry about working hard all those years. But then you see people uptown who don't know who I am, don't know how I worked so hard for their parents or grandparents. They don't know that all that they have—their houses and their education—I helped, that they could have that. Not all of it—their folks worked hard too—but part of it.

Eve and Willis do not see themselves as people whose life conditions and chances correlate with hard work and effort. Societal and historical forces have not valued their desire to not be sorry as one worth supporting at all costs. For some people who have put in loads of hard work and faced serious resistance to their efforts and institutional discrimination, not being sorry may be all that matters and all that is left. The public face of their farm or fate might imply sorriness, but the critique borne out of these conditions locates sorriness on a much grander scale.

Headache

Jeff Hart used the first installment of his $250,000 sum from the 2004 buyout, payments distributed over ten years, to purchase his new pickup truck. One year later, it is muddied and scuffed, as his wife had worried it would be, but the bumper sticker still proclaims desperate pride and defensiveness. The money has also helped to revive his farm operation. It seems intuitive why the buyout was an attractive policy for nearly all growers. The cash transfers and short-term boom in competitive advantage permitted access to the mix of material and symbolic capital found in new farm technology. Jeff repaid some farm debts and the home equity loan he took out to keep the farm afloat. He also purchased new equipment, such as a tobacco tumbling machine, to reduce labor costs and make his operation more attractive to tobacco companies desiring a cleaner product. But the wide support for this neoliberal policy among growers was not just financial. There was an important moral dimension. Here is what Jeff told me during one of our drives around the country roads:

> The buyout is exactly what we wanted: no more headline crop, no more "tobacco this" or "tobacco that," no more wake up in the morning and read that what you are doing is bad, what you do for a living kills people. Now we can make our crop and that's it. We are just like everyone else now.

This is a common sentiment among active growers. The idea is that now that the government is out of tobacco farming, it seems, or it is claimed, that there is no longer anything controversial or suspect about the livelihood. However, tobacco growers continue to depend on the state in a couple of key ways. Even though the cash comes to growers straight from tobacco companies, it was the work of Congress to authorize this transfer. There was public funding for the late 1990s president's report, which was the backdrop for the eventual passage of the buyout. As mentioned previously, growers also continue to depend on lax government regulation of employment practices and migrant labor housing laws. The idea that growers are the truly victimized constituency, as seen in Jeff's

feeling about being unfairly under attack or singled out from the mainstream, helps erase these beneficial relationships to the state.

Even still, as discussed in the preceding chapters, the free-market environment has also forced growers to contend with new challenges related
to corporate power and health-driven production demands. There is a local idiom for talking about the stress that growers now experience. They
call it *headache*. They complain that there is "a lot of headache," "too
much headache," and "a mess of headache" because of the contracting
system. Here is what Jeff tells me when I ask him what he means when he
says that his livelihood entails headache.

> I still enjoy farming. But I get aggravated now, more than ever. There
> are times you wouldn't want to be around me. I get crazy, angry at the
> world. It is not just one thing that frustrates me. There is the weather.
> I can't control that. Then there is the contract that I've got to fill and
> I'm always thinking about whether I'm doing a good job for the com-
> pany. And then there are labor problems: workers do not show up one
> day and I've got to manage these guys who would rather not be work-
> ing. That's a world of damn headache.

Here is what another farmer who contracts with Philip Morris says:

> Sometimes I think about how nice it would be to have a nine-to-five
> job at a factory. You clock in, do your job, and clock out. You leave
> work at work. You don't take it home. But, see, I'm always thinking
> about what's happening on the farm and what needs to be done. That's
> headache. It's that pressure that doesn't want to leave you alone. That
> is what I mean when I say that farming is a mess of headache. It is
> because it never ends. There is always the pressure to do better in the
> eyes of the company. And there is always something that happens on
> the farm that causes aggravation: the weather, the workers, these are
> things that farmers cannot control, but we have to deal with them.

This cultural model of frustration and stress encodes several specific
meanings. Headache is an indefinite substance. Growers never say "*a*
headache." This phenomenology of stress refers not to some definite bio-
mechanics that is located inside the person but rather to a set of external
material conditions, a "world," the grower states, "of damn headache."
Headache also seems to be autonomous. It does things to people, makes
them feel a certain way, and in a way that involves a felt lack of control
and an inability to resolve it, an affront to expectations about privacy
and comfort in modern life. Headache is not only overwhelming and
unrelenting, but it follows you. It does not respect the division between
home and work. It doesn't want to leave you alone, and it never ends.
Talk about headache places the microaggravations of daily farm man-

agement into the larger context of a "world" where there seems to be no clear end and no control. Talk about headache indexes larger predicaments about aging and retirement in the United States, the sense that life really ought to be easier, but for some reason things are getting harder and more frustrating, such as the need for people like Jeff, who are in their late fifties, to work long hours, and the paradox that making a living often means being beholden and threatened. Talk of headache encodes an expectation of entitlement at the same time that it reveals the deep anxieties that are part of tobacco management and the extent to which this work is experienced as precarious and unstable.

What most Americans see and have seen of the farm crisis is "farmers who chose to make public their private distress" (Dudley 2000: 4–5). Dwight Watson went public. Jeff Hart stayed local. On one trip to the contract station to sell his tobacco, his nervous tic came out from behind the steering wheel. The company grades were too stiff. The prices were too low. Lowering his sunglasses, Jeff hollered in the face of the grader. The station agent pulled him aside and tried to calm him down. Jeff then yelled at him, too. The prices were not fair, he said. *Growers deserve more for their tobacco. There is a lot of hard work that goes into making that tobacco. Do you think it is easy managing a farm with a dozen employees? This is the same tobacco that I've always grown—I know it is good, clean tobacco—so how dare you give me these low grades? Are you, the company, playing some kind of game with me, using low grades as a way to get me to work harder, when I'm already working damn hard and there's a world of damn headache?*

These complaints went nowhere. The grades did not change. Nothing is negotiable at the contract station. Yes, the 2004 buyout renewed the competitive advantage of domestic leaf, but grades and prices will continue to stay tight, and in this context headache has no perceptible end. Here is what another active farmer tells me when expressing frustrations about autonomy, value, and change, which were likely a part of what Jeff was venting.

> The companies are not stupid. The prices are set so that we can have a lower-middle-class living. But that is it. The companies know exactly what the cost of production is. The prices are set right at that point where you can make a decent living, nothing over the top, if you are willing to go into debt to mechanize your operation. The farmer has no choice in this. We might want a little more for our work. Things feel tight. But really we are employees now. The company pays us a salary based on a standard of living that they determine for us.

Jeff was lucky. That instance was the first time he got in the company's face. Because he has a reputation for being likable, his outburst was taken by the grader, the station manager, and other growers who heard about the incident as evidence of a misstep. Jeff has been close friends with the station agent for years. That Jeff was a loyal patron of the auction warehouse that this agent used to administer paid off in this new context where both men are part of a corporate team but where the agent is now something of a supervisor. Afterward, I talked with Jeff about the incident.

> It was not just about low grades. My company pays less than Philip Morris. The same damn hard work. But the farmers with PM earn more. So I felt that I'm not getting paid what's due. It's the same tobacco. It comes right off fields that are next to mine. Just because it goes to a different company—they have a different contract—means that I get lower prices. That means they can afford to do things that me and my family can't afford to do. Where is the fairness in that?

Jeff evidently does not feel just like everyone else as he had hoped. The impact of free-market competition is experienced in intimate ways and leads to an experience of headache, where the work and its purpose seem to make less sense than before. Talk about fairness seems out of place for someone who adamantly supported the neoliberal buyout, which opened the door to new levels of competition. While Jeff can attempt to switch to a Philip Morris contract to accrue the higher income, mobility is contained by the fact that Philip Morris already has an existing roster of growers who work hard to maintain those more lucrative relationships, and his relationship of patronage with his current company allows for missteps, where Philip Morris would not.

But it seems that what Jeff and other growers like him want is something rather common and understandable: dignity in work, some degree of autonomy and stability when it comes to paying the bills, and a meaningful station in life. The possibility of a collective conversation about the stress and pressure of competition has often been limited in the United States by the cultural context of accountability and the structure of corporate discipline. Coping is made into an individual psychological ordeal or a problem that affects families. "Most folks are going to manage something like this in private," an official at the North Carolina Tobacco Growers Association, the leading tobacco agriculture trade group, said of the tractor man Dwight Watson. "But . . . it was more than he was mentally able to cope with" (Collins 2003: B1). However sound at a structural level, the class standing tobacco farmers enjoy as employers, business owners, and white citizens is precarious within the contract system and is a source of workaday stress and social strife. What the neuroscientist Robert Sapolsky says about the social determinants of stress reads like a powerful critique of the waves of neoliberal economic restructuring that have made headache a common experience for growers and many others in the United States: "As a culture, America has neglected its social safety nets while making it easier for the most successful to sit atop the pyramids of inequality. Moreover, we have chosen to forgo the social capital that comes from small, stable communities in exchange for unprecedented opportunities for mobility and anonymity. As a result, all measures of social epidemiology are worsening" (2005).

Failing to rectify historical ills in southern agriculture, the 2004 buyout also missed a chance to stabilize tobacco farm businesses and provide resources for diversification, goals that were at the center of early policy debates. It forced the surviving growers to be more closely tied to tobacco corporate power and less able or likely to diversify, because continued reliance on this cash crop in the new free-market environment requires financial and technological intensification. These changes come at the expense of what Sapolsky has in mind in referencing social epidemiology, including social capital in communities, feelings of satisfaction and well-being, and economic security.

The American middle class, a wide swath of the population that is perhaps more imagined than empirical, constitutes what Lipsitz blisteringly calls the "most disgruntled, embittered, and angry agglomeration of 'haves' in the history of the world" (2006: 465). Some people roll their eyes when tobacco growers complain that they are frustrated and contend with headache. They do not find merit in the victimized experience of people who grow an inherently harmful crop, employ vulnerable workers, and receive special treatment. They roll their eyes at congressional authorization of cash transfers to them when the tobacco workers do not have healthcare premiums to worry about or new trucks to show off. But if growers' claims to victimhood and talk of headache are part of a broad political project that seeks to assure a long-standing structure of entitlement rather than fundamentally remaking the social epidemiology at large, they also index a mounting experience of insecurity for people at higher rungs of the social order. Those who have retained employment and have not seen the worst of economic crisis nonetheless confront decreased levels of job security, increased financial indebtedness, and the realistic possibility of downward mobility (Storper 2000).

The restructuring of North Carolina tobacco agriculture in the wake of the 2004 buyout has been characterized by new levels of job loss and farm loss, uneven access to capital accumulation, and a new regime of corporate power and patronage. These effects have led not to collaborative behavior among put-out and surviving growers, but rather routine backbiting, diminished levels of trust, a motivation against supporting each other (since growers now compete as individuals for company contracts), and a tendency to invest in private production capacities rather than public goods. The optimism of new pickup trucks and paint jobs guards against public awareness of precarious financial realities. For a decade leading up to the buyout, Jeff's tobacco operation was on-again, off-again dependent on Christine's salary to pay farm debts. In fact, his relatively small-scale business has never been independent. The pressed work shirts and custom farm caps, and the slow time he takes in ordering coffee and breakfast—this tempo of not being hurried—are consumption acts that mask as much as they reveal. Public secrets bubble up when headache breaches the levy at the contract station. What spills over is "the vulnerability of personal existence" that results from "the instability of capitalism and the concretely unequal forms and norms of national life" (Berlant 1997: 4). I admonish that it is important to not roll eyes and to recognize the experience of vulnerability that can affect even relatively advantaged groups, because the instability of capitalism can lead to moral and emotional investments in preserving something that seems to be slipping away, as well as collective efforts to maintain unequal forms and norms of national life.

"The company treats me like a nigger" is how Jeff explained his outburst to me. He interprets capitalism not as a powerful, disorganizing force in which supportive and trusting social relationships are often fragmented and levels of control in workplaces and families are diminished but rather in terms of assumptions about race and deservedness. Jeff means that the feeling of being treated unfairly has to do with being exploited and being at the disposal of a powerful employer, being treated in a way that is different than what he feels he deserves given a racial order that he wills and takes for granted.

During my field study, Philip Morris employed a black man to oversee operations at its receiving stations across North Carolina. I met this supervisor briefly during a visit with one farmer to deliver tobacco at a Philip Morris contract station. The farmer told me that the supervisor had a graduate degree in business administration "from a university in the North." And he grumbled to me after we left that a black man was in charge of the local market. "He doesn't know the first thing about tobacco. He didn't grow up around here. Where's he from? New York. What does he know about tobacco?" To be chided by the supervisor's skin color is to link place and power in a way that implies that white people own tobacco expertise and the tobacco business. But this farmer knew that having a black supervisor was a symbolic statement for Philip Morris: engaging with the historical subordination of black labor in North Carolina comes across as threatening to white contract growers and is part of the company's disciplinary apparatus, which regards growers as labor, time, or an input cost in the price of a cigarette and no longer local experts.

Keep the two sides of sorriness together. Rambling around the roads one day, Jeff and I talk about why he does not drive a tractor most days (which would save him labor expenses), instead preferring to remain in his pickup truck and monitor operations from the roadside.

> What do you think I'm worth? Am I worth minimum wage? That's how much I'm worth if I fire one of those guys and do what he's doing. What if something goes wrong? That is the difference. Labor does a job. I make decisions for the whole operation. That's why I need to be available. I can't be bogged down in field work. I'm worth more than minimum wage because I manage this business, and none of the workers could make it in what I'm doing. They would last a month, maybe. They just don't have what it takes. They don't have the smarts or the ambition to manage a farm, with all that is involved. The reason I have what I have, my business and my house, is because of financial discipline. The workers do not put aside a little money each week. They do not plan to buy that used car. They know they can take advantage of me because I need them at the farm shop every morning. So I let them use my old trucks for free. The workers waste their paycheck on who knows what. They drink or gamble. Some of them have child support, and they try to avoid paying that, so it gets deducted from their paycheck.

Jeff sees himself as worth more than the workers he employs and feels unfairly treated, like they are by his tobacco company, which implies that unfair treatment for workers is acceptable or normal but not for him.

Sorriness is a moral discourse that is used to assert innate character: that of the self as much as the other. As Jeff says:

> There is satisfaction in seeing your crops grow, a different value than you put on money. It's not what it used to be. There's more pressure now. But you can still take pride in a good crop. That's what got me at the contract station. It's not like I'm delivering sorry tobacco. I'm delivering good tobacco, and I know it because that's what I produce. I am meticulous in what I deliver. I take great pride in having clean tobacco. You can take any piece of a bale of my tobacco and it will be the same all the way through. It is good and clean. I don't do that for the company. I do it for myself. When I get up in the morning and make my bed, is the company watching me then?

In his outburst Jeff was hollering as an expert with decades of experience. In worlds built up around pride, expectations of modernity, and a social order premised on assumptions about supremacy and inferiority, economic instability and change often induce anxieties about status and power. Many kinds of people would and do make similar claims and respond to change in similar ways. They might not use the word sorry, but they too would cast aspersion or blame on other classes or categories of people and in the process claim to be experts in something and to be good people, as well as being iconic of what is valuable and endangered in the nation.

Conclusion _____

Reflections on the Tobacco Industry
(and American Exceptionalism)

DESPITE THE IMMENSE BURDEN of disease caused by tobacco and wide-spread critical awareness about the tobacco industry, ten times more people will die from smoking in the current century than died in the last century. This may be surprising to readers. In the United States, adult smoking prevalence has significantly declined since the peak in the 1960s. This decline contributes to the common misperception that the smoking problem lies in the past.

"At no moment in human history has tobacco presented such a dire and imminent risk to human health as it does today," writes Allan M. Brandt (2007: 450). As smoking declined in Western countries, the multi-national tobacco industry worked aggressively to expand and open ciga-rette markets around the world. The Philip Morris website proclaims a newfound responsibility concerning smoking issues. Visitors to the site do not learn about the billions of dollars tobacco companies spend each year on cigarette ads and political contributions in every world region, and their lurid pursuit of new smokers in developing countries where there are often relatively limited public health resources or regulations (Nichter and Cartwright 1991). On the website there is, conveniently, no mention of the 2006 U.S. Department of Justice lawsuit *United States v. Philip Morris,* which deemed tobacco companies "racketeers." The website does not cite the presiding judge in that case, who found that the "defendants have marketed and sold their lethal product with zeal, with deception, with a single-minded focus on their financial success, and without regard for the human tragedy or social costs that success exacted."

Philip Morris's claims about responsibility are abetted by the com-pany's vocal support of FDA regulation of tobacco products. Compared to the other tobacco companies, are Philip Morris's actions, including support of FDA regulation, better or worse for public health? Would U.S. consumers be better off if Philip Morris, like the rest of the tobacco indus-try, had continued to fight FDA regulation, not decided to fully acknowl-edge smoking risks and provide consumers with information about quit-ting, and not required their contract farmers to discontinue use of certain hazardous agricultural chemicals? The idea that Philip Morris (or any corporation) would pursue regulatory mandates that would undermine the long-term position of shareholders seems unlikely. Unfortunately, in the case of the tobacco industry, this means that Philip Morris is counting on growing its business in spite of (or because of) FDA regulation. This legislation will perhaps limit the serious threat of litigation for tobacco companies and strengthen the industry's financial solvency and its ability to exploit market conditions around the planet. The politics and ethics of tobacco regulation in the United States thus have truly global consequences. National policies that regulate smoking without posing a serious challenge to the functioning of tobacco companies and the international free-market environments in which they operate do nothing to address the increasing levels of risk and mortality to which many other populations are now being exposed. There is therefore a need to holistically assess national tobacco-control policies and coalitions between the tobacco industry and the public health in terms of their global impact and the extent to which an approach like FDA regulation might have positive outcomes in a narrow view but more negative ramifications over the long term and across a wider demography and geography. One of my two goals in this conclusion is to draw reflections out of my study of southern tobacco farms that are relevant for global public health. My other goal is to address an important theme in contemporary politics in the United States, namely, the politics of victimhood and reprisal.

Capitalism and Global Public Health

In 1995, the World Health Organization (WHO) began to forge an international treaty on tobacco control, a multilateral agreement enunciating core principles and policies to be implemented by member states. Multinational tobacco companies, including Philip Morris, expressed opposition by claiming that tobacco products do not meet the international criterion for collective action, meaning, the companies argued, they do not threaten populations and governments in a manner that transgresses sovereign borders, like amorphous billows of pollution, for example. The industry argued that tobacco products ought to be regulated and managed on a national basis. The chairman of British American Tobacco also referred to cultural diversity and economic underdevelopment as reasons to not "foist" a "developed world obsession" with tobacco control on most countries (Brandt 2007: 483). Antitobacco advocates have maintained that tobacco use is an inherently transnational phenomenon because of the pervasiveness of advertising and the likely failure of unilateral approaches given the tobacco industry's multinational organization, its tremendous political influence, and the appeal of tobacco tax revenues and direct foreign investment from tobacco companies for governments in poor countries.

The Framework Convention on Tobacco Control (FCTC) was drafted between 2000 and 2003. Tobacco companies lobbied hard to obstruct and influence it in many ways. They invoked the World Trade Organization's controversial determination that tobacco is a "conventional product," a ruling that disallows the implementation of special trade restrictions in the name of national health, safety, and security (Brandt 2007: 474). Philip Morris held powerful sway over trade negotiators who were working on behalf of the Bush administration and who emphasized the legal weight of trade agreements and the conventional nature of tobacco, which limit the ability of countries that are signatories of free trade agreements to treat tobacco as a special case and to implement regulations such as tariffs or marketing restrictions. The Bush administration also urged negotiators to push for a clause in the FCTC that allowed individual nations to ratify the treaty while electing to opt out of particular protocols on cigarette taxation, advertising bans, and smoke-free environments legislation (these policies were ironically already widely and favorably implemented in the United States). Congressman Henry Waxman, a Democrat from Ohio, said the Bush administration was spearheading "a breathtaking reversal in U.S. policy—going from a global leader on tobacco control to pulling back and advocating the industry's position." In a letter to the president, he stated, "the U.S. is seeking to undermine world efforts to negotiate an international agreement to reduce tobacco use" (476).

The Philip Morris website does not discuss how the company contracted with expert public relations firms to develop a strategic response to the FCTC. The consultants told management that "currently proposed and drafted, the framework convention will provide the means to eradicate the tobacco business worldwide." They told the company that "the WHO is in the fight with substantial resources, unshakeable determination and powerful allies. It also has all the emotional issues on its side—health, children, women, the poor and a host of others." The consultants advised Philip Morris that "delaying the adoption of a convention" was optimal but not completely realistic given the momentum behind the WHO's efforts. Thus, the firm instructed Philip Morris that "the company is best served by participating in the development of the agreement." They further admonished that it "would be in the company's best interest to have the treaty focus entirely on protecting children and leaving adult choice protected" (cited in Brandt 2007: 475–77).

In 2003, the WHO unanimously adopted the framework convention, the organization's first multilateral treaty. Even though the federal government was reluctant to sign until the last minute and Congress has still not ratified the treaty, the U.S. Department of Health and Human Services praised the occasion as a major advance in tobacco control. Even Philip Morris came around to affirming the framework, part of its eagerness, Brandt writes, "to show that it had turned over a new tobacco leaf and become a 'responsible corporate citizen'" (2007: 482). One of the firm's lawyers said, "What we hope and expect is that this treaty can be a catalyst in every country that signs on for meaningful and effective treatment of tobacco" (482). However, as Brandt notes, "such posturing had little immediate cost," since the FCTC remains somewhat limited in its capacity to bring about substantial tobacco-control reforms. The treaty recommends that countries impose a set of universal standards to provide a baseline of minimal tobacco regulation worldwide (478–79). But the WHO is fundamentally constrained in what it can do in terms of policy development and law enforcement, and the implementation of its recommendations falls on legislative bodies where tobacco companies exert powerful influence.

At present, global tobacco-control programs are dominated by a decidedly demand-side logic, one that ends up favoring tobacco companies and their supporters within government finance ministries. This is strongly visible in the FCTC, which requires that participating governments take programmatic steps to alter the behavior of citizens, steps aimed at helping people avoid smoking, quit, and more generally better self-manage risks posed by tobacco exposure. Largely left out of the equation is supply. The FCTC requires states to do very little to disrupt cigarette production, distribution, and sales. Meanwhile, institutions such as the World Bank and the International Monetary Fund continue to encourage developing countries to open their borders to foreign direct investment from tobacco companies. The World Bank's official position is that tobacco-related public health interventions ought to target demand through negative incentives such as taxation and product labeling rather than through trade restrictions. The World Bank continues to affirm that tobacco agriculture may make good economic sense in developing countries and that cigarette demand helps drive economic development and the growth of governments through taxation policies.[1] These institutions are important protagonists of economic and consumer dependencies on tobacco in the contemporary world. The philosophy and ethics of trade should be central to policy development in contemporary tobacco control. Anthropological research has a role to play in disclosing the inner workings and costly effects of this regime, and such research can be leveraged for improved tobacco-prevention policies.

---

[1] The World Bank home page las links to various policy reports and fact sheets concerning tobacco economics and regulation, as well as a link to a formal report on these issues (World Bank 1999).

At a time when Philip Morris disseminates information about smoking and health risks on its website and throughout its public relations, the dominant emphasis in tobacco control on demand issues and the informed decisions of citizens is at best incomplete. The convergence of seemingly opposed interests—Big Tobacco and the public health advocacy community—around the creation of regulatory frameworks to help citizens self-manage risks and health behaviors (as in the FDA bill) suggests the need to revitalize a more sweeping and more critical perspective in the antitobacco movement. Not only is there a need for more research on the tobacco industry's appropriation of the language and values of public health, adoption of corporate social responsibility agendas, and nefarious engagement in public health policy development, but there is a need for trade issues and protection to be part of a broader assessment of tobacco-control strategies (Bettcher et al. 2000; Yach and Bettcher 2000). In other words, there is a need to further scrutinize the tobacco industry and international trade regimes as vectors of disease and to use trade policy as a means of containing rather than abetting the spread of sickness and mortality.

Although it seems as though the U.S. government has taken a bold new step in regulating tobacco, this really only pertains to consumer behavior. In fact, the passage of FDA regulation is the flip side of the deregulation of tobacco production, namely the Tobacco Buyout passed in 2004. Philip Morris would not have supported the FDA bill if the legislation had included measures to promote economic development and alternative livelihoods in tobacco-producing states like North Carolina and to maintain guaranteed minimum leaf prices as a means of limiting economies of scale. That the company indeed refused to support legislation coupling FDA regulation to these other measures (see chapter 3) is indicative of what corporate social responsibility means at the company. It means being responsible when it comes to policies that shuffle responsibility onto consumers and induce profitable illusions that tobacco products are now less harmful than in the past. It does not mean being responsible when it comes to attending to problems of farm loss, job loss, and social suffering in the rural regions where the industry sources its primary raw materials. The reason that Congress passed two separate bills—the buyout in 2004 and FDA regulation in 2009—even though President Clinton recommended an overarching approach is because Philip Morris, R. J. Reynolds, and other tobacco companies used their political influence to fragment the coalitional politics that arose between the public health advocacy community and leadership in the grower population. Their interest was in gutting the buyout so that there was no funding for measures that would have kept tobacco prices higher, created new and different job options for groups historically dependent on tobacco money, and loosened their loyalties on the tobacco industry. The improvement of social conditions and economic diversification in rural regions where tobacco is produced is a direct threat to the tobacco industry. Production and supply issues and farm labor conditions thus need to be at the center of international tobacco-control efforts.

Research in rural regions exposes a widening range of health and social problems for which the tobacco industry can be held directly accountable. This helps incite critical awareness about industry predation and has the potential to build public health alliances in rural regions where the industry relies on and works hard to cultivate dependencies and loyalties of farmers (Otañez et al. 2009). In the process of strategically negotiating the political and legal problems of accountability, malfeasance, and responsibility that are related to smoking disease, tobacco companies also exact a powerful impact on rural communities in a way that often disadvantages growers and workers at the same time. Public health policies that narrowly focus on educating consumers about health risks are preferred and even endorsed by tobacco companies because they frame smoking as a matter of informed adult decisions and neglect a broader approach to controlling the international leaf trade, free trade agreements, and supply-side harms and health problems. The international tobacco-control movement clearly needs to continue to develop critical perspectives on international trade and the ways that globalized leaf production detrimentally impacts rural communities at the same time that free trade policies allow populations to be exposed to harmful products. The health problems associated with tobacco, as with other chronic diseases, are ineffectively controlled when the focus is on informing and optimizing consumer choices and establishing individual consumption as the locus of health and risk management rather than providing effective health education or public health regulation. The preponderance of harmful behaviors depends only partly on informed adult decisions. It also depends on a loose affiliation between millionaires and billionaires, a lax government stance with regard to capital and its rights, shameful government and civil society collusions with industry that put producers and consumers at risk, and a general public resignation about capitalism and its products.

New Faces

"Now is the time to revisit and improve the governance of global tobacco control," Derek Yach, a leading public health advocate and researcher, writes in an editorial that assesses how to move beyond the general platform of the FCTC to implement tangible changes. "New players must be brought in to deal with new realities" (2005: 148). The tobacco industry is built on the labor of millions of people in many countries who work on farms and in processing and manufacturing facilities. It is crucial that public health groups work with these constituencies to counterbalance the influence of the tobacco industry (Yach and Bettcher 2000). The FCTC itself, namely, Article 17, addresses policies of crop diversification and alternative livelihoods for tobacco growers and workers and calls for governments to provide "support for economically viable alternative activities for farmworkers and growers," while Article 18 calls for environmental health and safety protection with respect to tobacco cultivation (World Health Organization 2009). The WHO acknowledges that a holistic framework is required to address all aspects of tobacco and health, including the economic dependence of farming and manufacturing communities and social and health problems related to tobacco work (World Health Organization 2008). The WHO's position builds on several years of engagement of global tobacco-control advocates with grower and farmworker issues. The most promising collaborations so far have been seen in emerging alliances in developing countries, such as collaborations between public health groups and trade unionists in Malawi that demand tobacco worker rights (Otañez et al. 2007). Public health groups have also been involved in addressing the problems of child labor, deforestation, agrochemical exposure, and debt servitude, which are common in tobacco-growing regions, by building on research by anthropologists and other social scientists in South America, South Asia, and southern Africa, where tobacco farming is an important contributor to poverty (Amigo 2010; Efroymson et al. 2001; Faria et al. 2006; Geist 1999; Geist et al. 2009; Otañez et al. 2009; World Health Organization 2004; V. Brown 2003). The creation of the Human Rights and Tobacco Control Network in 2008 is another example of the integration of global health groups and tobacco grower and worker issues (Simpson 2008). The network pulls together disparate advocates and groups that have been working to improve the rights of farmworkers and growers while simultaneously promoting tobacco control.

Anthropology rightly belongs on the list of essential resources in international tobacco control. Public health groups interested in working with tobacco constituencies to promote policy agendas must not discount the local moral perspectives of growers and must engage growers in the context of other powerful influences. In North Carolina, the dependence of tobacco growers on a harmful plant and an uncertain economy has been maintained through a combination of industry strategies and the various influences that render tobacco livelihoods legitimate and moral on multiple levels. The defensiveness about tobacco that is common in North Carolina may be common in other tobacco-producing regions around the world but for different reasons and with different histories of industry in-fluence and political representation. Intense loyalties to industry may be present. Critical anthropological reporting on the impact of tobacco capi-tal in rural communities may help to inform advocacy work that seeks to educate rural populations about industry impact and remake these relations. The avoidance of tobacco ethics in many southern churches and communities may be subsiding as knowledge about smoking risks increases and the size of the tobacco grower population and the number of people financially dependent on tobacco dwindles. Meanwhile, as the industry evolves, new sources of economic strain are emerging in North Carolina and other tobacco states. It is unclear whether U.S. tobacco growers would now be open to partnerships with public health groups, a prospect that did not really work out in the 1990s. The company loyalty and docility demanded in contracting may make this impossible. Howev-er, lessons from my case study may be helpful for thinking about tobacco control and livelihood diversification issues in the U.S. South and other geographical areas.

I have documented various sources of resistance to alternative agri-culture in North Carolina. The complex of material and cultural reasons that make tobacco seem essential needs to be better understood across diverse national contexts. There is also a need to understand how the tobacco industry works to limit what options are available for tobacco farmers and workers, as in the case of the tobacco industry using its paid politicians to prevent billions of dollars' worth of funding for economic diversification in the United States since the 1990s. A more diverse rural economy and expanded options for agricultural producers increases the supply of jobs relative to tobacco, thereby increasing the price of tobacco leaf and the cost of tobacco products. Funding for economic development could also be a means of addressing disparities and inequalities in the tobacco sector, so that what tobacco control can focus on in attempt-ing to foment critical awareness in tobacco-dependent communities is not limited to the industry impact on farm families but also on laboring populations and the unemployed. The antitobacco movement can also become further involved in prioritizing international labor standards for agricultural workplaces and throughout farm and food chains. Helping to organize grower cooperatives, supporting farm labor advocacy and worker unions, promoting the enforcement and expansion of labor and environmental laws, and improving occupational safety and health stan-dards are ways to counterbalance industry power and its extraction of surplus value from rural regions.

For new partnerships to be successful, it is important that public health groups work with rural communities in sincere ways rather than stereo-typing them as prosmoking adherents. The cultural and moral value of tobacco for growers must be understood and acknowledged not simply as a means to tailor public health programs and strategies but as a basic human act and the starting point of a potentially transformative relationship. What may seem unethical to many outsiders is completely normal, if not obligatory, on a local level. Ricky's story from chapter 4 suggests that people who exit tobacco may feel like traitors because of real and imagined social pressures. Exiting tobacco production implies wrongdoing or failure. Defensiveness about tobacco may not reflect a lack of ethical reflection or moral conscience. If the ability to live unmarked, the sense of having done nothing wrong, is important to growers because it is part of the wider cultural politics of regional and national belonging, then potential collaborative efforts will be most effective when they do not impart a feeling of blame or wrongdoing. The public health intervention literature suggests that the first step in prevention should be to address feelings of stigma and shame that are linked to specific behaviors or conditions, and I am thinking of the need for a similar kind of contextual sensitivity and social approach in tobacco control. Financial dependence on tobacco revenues may often be related to status and a sense of group membership that must be acknowledged as an important reality for grower households. Growers themselves might feel diminished or stigmatized because of the public nature of antitobacco messaging or politics or because of the changing tobacco economy. Therefore, policies that seek to promote alternative livelihoods must take into account cultural dynamics and involve effective means of connecting with tobacco farmers in terms of their lives and subjective experiences. These approaches appreciate the potential for backlash in workplaces and communities that are defined by historical racial divisions and the cultivated spirit of defensiveness that industries like the tobacco industry strategically promulgate to contain critique.

Agricultural anthropology's traditional strength in studying political and social ecologies of agriculture in specific locales (Chibnik 1987), a "human-centered perspective" (Rhoades 1984: 40), is relevant for tobacco control. In working in tobacco-producing regions, tobacco-control groups will need to present themselves as having respect for growers in a way that is not interpreted as a hidden pursuit of the demise of growers' livelihoods or as a way of using growers to attack the industry. The partnerships will need to be built on sincere desires to improve grower livelihoods and to make friends with people who are ambiguously, sometimes staunchly, and sometimes uncomfortably part of the tobacco industry. New senses of self-worth might arise as growers begin to cooperate and collaborate in light of sincere expressions of shared understanding in how the industry has profitably taken advantage of rural regions through the promotion of ideologies of kinship and pride.

Coda

In 2010, at the same time that I was completing this book, the conservative politician Mitt Romney, who was my governor in Massachusetts when I was in graduate school, published a book entitled *No Apology: The Case for American Greatness*. The book's blurb begins with a reference to President Obama's diplomatic European tour and his supposed apology to European countries for America's international power. The book claims that President Obama repeated this message when visiting Latin America and when speaking in an interview broadcast to the Muslim world.

The book's central thesis reflects the conservative punditry of the period and the conservative backlash against the Obama presidency. Much of this rests on the idea that there is a large proportion of the American constituency—Democrats, people living on the coasts and in cities, liberals, whatever—that is un-American, because in advocating for progressive public policies they imply not only that there are core problems in the American present, but also that these problems derive from problems and structures that are rooted in the American past.

Romney's phrase "no apology" means that he believes that America does not have to apologize for anything, and that all the wretched history of slavery, imperialism, discrimination, and inequality is the indiscretion of an inherently and naturally innocent nation. Politics that stem from a desire to not whitewash history and to redress these historical burdens, policies of redistribution and attempts to reduce inequality, and efforts to come to terms with what Cornel West (1999) dubs the "ignoble paradox of modernity"—the sordid facts and realities that are an irredeemable part of economic growth and political power in the contemporary world—are condemned as threats to the nation. It is really a quintessential American attitude that one does not have to apologize for anything since one has done nothing wrong.

What historical realities are disavowed and what economic and social systems are tacitly authorized when people are said to have a non-relation to slavery? In chapter 5 I argued that the ethics idealized by Emmanuel Levinas—absolute responsibility for the other person—does not reflect the actual ways that people interact with one another, because histories and realities of suffering are often overlooked through the circumscription of zones of non-responsibility. Who are those people in the United States who, in sending their children to college, in saving for retirement, in purchasing a home, in making a career, have a non-relation to the structures of accumulation that undeniably come out of plantation slavery?

Figure C.1. "I smoke," tobacco advertisement, circa 1973. Courtesy of TobaccoDocuments.org. http://tobaccodocuments.org/pollay_ads/Vant05.07b.html ?ocr_position=hide_ocr.

The tentacular nature of tobacco leads me to think about innocence and complicity in this sweeping historical way. What is most interesting about tobacco is perhaps not the irony that people make a legally sanctioned living from this most harmful drug but rather the opposite: that the majority of people in the United States probably feel that they have no relationship to tobacco or its harms. How is it possible to have a non-relation to tobacco when it shaped the society in determinate ways? This ethical dilemma is exactly what growers are hinting at when they talk about the importance of tobacco in North Carolina history, saying, for example, that there is not one house in the state that does not have tobacco money in it. The flip side of this discourse is the one focused on the social life of tobacco sin, as in the question of whether landowners who lease their land for tobacco cultivators are sinful. Is it sinful to own a shop and sell products to tobacco farmers who purchase goods with the fruits of the harvest? Is it sinful to send one's children to a public school funded partly by taxes from tobacco farm households or consumers? Where does complicity for tobacco disease end? While this question challenges the industry's ideology of individual choice, I intend it as a rather facetious rhetorical device to make the point that understandings of responsibility are built on assumptions about the relationship of the past to the present and of different segments of the society and the economy to one another. Hence, the conservative "no apology" attitude espouses an ideology of individual responsibility and a politicization of family values (the very resources the tobacco industry has used to make smoking into a problem of parenthood) to reconcile the paradoxical idea that historical burdens are a thing of the past at the same time as historically disadvantaged and discriminated groups and families are responsible for their own present conditions. The carving up of the social body into frequencies and probabilities of responsibility and wrongdoing is a project that seeks to preserve the Face of the nation as innocent and exclude segments of the population from full social membership, delegitimize the reality of hardship faced by much of the population in terms of personal and family flaws rather than problems of government and political economy, and exonerate inequality and its beneficiaries through idioms of equal opportunity and the merits of individual achievement (Lipsitz 1995).

Is it sinful to attend a major research university funded at its founding by tobacco money? With its concerted focus on medicine and biotechnologies, what relationships to tobacco continue to permeate these academic halls and its sports fields? In the media spectacle surrounding the criminal investigation of a rape accusation made against three members of the men's lacrosse team Duke University in 2005, considerations of innocence went beyond the category of legal guilt to involve racial stereotypes and assessments of moral character based on the vastly different social backgrounds and locations of the parties involved. Moral innocence, as compared to legal non-guilt, is a condition that is not permitted all citizens, and is culturally defined. The Duke students accused of sexual assault were exonerated and proclaimed not only "not guilty," but also "innocent." They were said to be the victims of media frenzy, wrongful accusations, and the problem of troublemakers in Durham. Indeed, the district attorney for Durham County was eventually found guilty of professional misconduct for advancing false allegations, even withholding evidence. But, early on in much of the media reporting, doubts were cast about the accuser's story and credibility, presumably because of what was molded as her identity, a black sex worker with a sorry history of drug abuse. Whiteness served as a powerful signifier of innocence when juxtaposed with racialized, hypersexual, criminalized blackness, and the moralized and gendered distinction of worth between formal and informal economic participation (Leonard 2007: 26–27). Whiteness was presumed innocent when juxtaposed against social norms that "define which category of subjects is more or less valued as citizens of the nation" and influence "degrees of undeserving or deserving citizenship" (Ong 2003: 9, 11).

A most iconic figure of moral innocence and national identity in the United States is the "future American," who, according to Berlant, "can feel firmly placed in a zone of protected value while on the move in an arc of social mobility" (1997: 6, 8). This is the college graduate who, despite some indiscretion, has a whole life ahead of him. Various cultural factors, such as youthfulness, whiteness, class status, and educational attainment conspire to portray certain university students as naturally predisposed to having some fun, but not to crime, much as Dwight Watson's fate and the citizenship of tobacco growers has hinged on the felicitous public representation of them as plighted family farmers, disgruntled but harmless. Media accounts of the Duke case, saturated with racial codes and assumptions, recuperated an image of innocence in what was perceived as yet another case of a multicultural assault on white masculinity and its supposedly harmless proclivities. Left out of the media's focus on the unfair loss of personal innocence and potential loss of access to the American Dream for the students—their lives and families were said to be ruined, job chances, friendships, political ambitions all gone—was a serious look at the dangerous moral world of entitlement on campuses and the double standard where hypersexual whiteness undergoes less scrutiny, is sometimes authorized, and can be protected by significant economic and legal resources compared to sex work. Media accounts did not place the event within the deeper context of historical sexual violence involving white men and black women in the South or the historical failures of the

Figure C.2. A farmer and his son in a Wilson County tobacco warehouse, early 1940s. Photo by an unknown *Wilson Daily Times* photographer. Reproduced with permission from the *Wilson Daily Times*.

legal system to attend to racialized sexual violence and control (Leonard 2007). And this brings us back to tobacco.

Even if an individual did not sexually assault a person from the other side of Durham, does this individual have a non-relation to the systems of economic production that helped segregate the town and sustain the inequities that define it, systems that therefore partly or indirectly contribute to the clustering of sex work, substance abuse, and poverty that already made the accuser herself seem guilty? Is the individual who is not guilty of committing a crime but benefits from structures of race, class, and gender privilege that allow entry into a topnotch university and, from the beginning, have put lives on totally different paths, ensuring that this individual who may at some point feel victimized or aggrieved will nonetheless never have to engage in sex work, innocent?

The act of apology has tremendous social and economic currency. Public apologies about personal indiscretions are everywhere. Apologies are also made by governments and religious and other institutions for complicities in major misadventures. To what extent are such apologies efforts to sincerely redress the enduring legacies of these burdens or efforts to reconcile fragmented populations and damaged public images through rearticulated imagined communities, social solidarities, and expressed good intentions? Philosophers of apology have typically idealized a pure form of apology that can be effective in healing political and social antagonisms. For example, friends can apologize to one another to make up for grievances or wrongdoing. Doctors can apologize to patients when a procedure gets complicated. Philosophers and psychologists argue that the therapeutic qualities of apology depend on the speech act's sincerity. A felicitous utterance must reflect the intentionality of the speaking subject as someone who really means it. However, the effectiveness and meaning of an apology also rest on the actions that an individual takes in the future to rectify a situation or demonstrate that a wrongdoing will not be repeated (see Lazare 2005).

Policy efforts to redress the conditions that come out of slavery have not challenged the fundamental notion that the nation itself is innocent. Instead the nation is seemingly marred only by the indiscretions of antiquated ways of thinking, erstwhile commitments to racial supremacy and the pleasures of subjugation, or brutal realities now repackaged as historical artifacts. If the meaning of an apology rests on future actions to rectify or redress a wrongdoing, then what kinds of public policies are needed in the United States to address the legacies of slavery? What would it mean for a nation to eschew frequent reconstructive surgery and admit to being a sorry state? What biblical passages (e.g., Proverbs 16:9, "Better to be lowly in spirit and among the oppressed than to share plunder with the proud," or Romans 3:23, "For all have sinned") are chauvinistically defied in the "no apology" politics? Would Jesus be into this politics of national innocence and the punitive policies that define a supposedly Christian agenda? What policies would stem from a project of recognizing and validating—not ignoring or dispelling—the realities of misery and conflict caused by tobacco and other modern things? What if the Face of the nation circulating throughout the society, propped up and propagated on so many levels and in so many ways, were not a fantasy future American defined by innocence but rather a belabored ordinary one, embedded and complicit in the history of the present?

Bibliography

Abrams, Douglas Carl
  1992   *Conservative Constraints: North Carolina and the New Deal*. Jackson: University of Mississippi Press.
Agamben, Giorgio
  2000   *Means without End: Notes on Politics*. Minneapolis: University of Minnesota Press.
  2005   *The Time that Remains: A Commentary on the Letter to the Romans*. Stanford, CA: Stanford University Press.
Agee, James, and Walker Evans
  1941   *Let Us Now Praise Famous Men*. Boston, MA: Houghton Mifflin.
Agricultural Missions Incorporated
  2000   *Report on the Mt. Olive Pickle Boycott by the Farm Labor Organizing Committee and Migrant Farm Worker Conditions in North Carolina and in the United States*. National Council of the Churches of Christ in the USA.
Algeo, Katie
  2002   Tobacco in Transition: Issues Facing Burley Growers and Communities. *North Carolina Geographer* 10:29–34.
Altman, David G.
  1995   A View from the Fields. *North Carolina Medical Journal* 56 (1): 37–38.
Altman, David G., Douglas W. Devine, George Howard, and Hal Hamilton
  1996   Tobacco Farmers and Diversification: Opportunities and Barriers. *Tobacco Control* 5:192–98.
  1997   Tobacco Farming and Public Health: Attitudes of the General Public and Farmers. *Journal of Social Issues* 53 (1): 113–28.
  1998   Predictors of Crop Diversification: A Survey of Tobacco Farmers in North Carolina. *Tobacco Control* 7:376–82.
  2000   Churches, Tobacco Farmers, and Community Sustainability: Insights from the Tobacco South. *Journal of Community Psychology* 28 (2): 151–68.
Amigo, M. F.
  2010   Small Bodies, Large Contribution: Children's Work in the Tobacco Plantations of Lombok, Indonesia. *Asia Pacific Journal of Anthropology* 11:34–51.
Anderson, Benedict
  1983   *Imagined Communities: Reflections on the Origin and Spread of Nationalism*. London: Verso.
Anderson, Eric
  1981   *Race and Politics in North Carolina, 1872–1901: The Black Second*. Baton Rouge: Louisiana State University Press.
Andrews, Jesse
  2003   *Thirteen Month Crop: One Year in the Life of a Piedmont Virginia Tobacco Farm*. Durham, NC: Center for Documentary Studies.

Appadurai, Arjun, ed.
  1986   *The Social Life of Things: Commodities in Cultural Perspective.* Cambridge: Cambridge University Press.
Appadurai, Arjun
  1990   Disjuncture and Difference in the Global Cultural Economy. *Public Culture* 2 (2): 1–24.
  1996   *Modernity at Large: Cultural Dimensions of Globalization.* Minneapolis: University of Minnesota Press.
Applbaum, Kalman
  2006   Pharmaceutical Marketing and the Invention of the Medical Consumer. Speaking of Medicine. *PLoS Medicine* 3 (4): e189.
Arcury, Thomas A., and Sara A. Quandt
  2007a   Delivery of Health Services to Migrant and Seasonal Farmworkers. *Annual Review of Public Health* 28:345–63.
  2007b   Health and Social Impacts of Tobacco Production. *Journal of Agromedicine* 11 (3–4): 71–81.
Arcury, Thomas A., Sara A. Quandt, and John S. Preisser
  2001   Measuring Occupational Illness Incidence and Prevalence in a Difficult to Study Population: Green Tobacco Sickness among Latino Farmworkers in North Carolina. *Journal of Epidemiology and Community Health* 55 (11): 818–24.
Arcury, Thomas A., Sara A. Quandt, John S. Preisser, John T. Bernert, Deborah Norton, and Joanna Wang
  2003   High Levels of Transdermal Nicotine Exposure Produce Green Tobacco Sickness in Latino Farmworkers. *Nicotine & Tobacco Research* 5 (3): 315–22.
Arcury, Thomas A., Sara A. Quandt, John S. Preisser, and Deborah Norton
  2001   The Incidence of Green Tobacco Sickness among Latino Farmworkers. *Journal of Occupational and Environmental Medicine* 43 (7): 601–9.
Arcury, Thomas A., Sara A. Quandt, and Gregory B. Russell
  2002   Pesticide Safety among Farmworkers: Perceived Risk and Perceived Control as Factors Reflecting Environmental Justice. *Environmental Justice* 110 (supplement 2): 233–39.
Arcury, Thomas A., Sara A. Quandt, and Samuel Simmons
  2002   Farmer Health Beliefs about an Occupational Illness that Affects Farmworkers: The Case of Green Tobacco Sickness. *Journal of Agricultural Safety and Health* 9 (1): 33–45.
Averill, Thomas
  1939a   Farmers Again Urged Slow Down Marketing. *Wilson Daily Times,* October 26, 1.
  1939b   Imperial Holds Key to the Tobacco Situation. *Wilson Daily Times,* September 12, 1.
Badger, Anthony
  1980   *Prosperity Road: The New Deal, Tobacco, and North Carolina.* Chapel Hill: University of North Carolina Press.

Badiou, Alain
   2003   *Saint Paul: The Foundation of Universalism*. Ray Brassier, trans. Stanford, CA: Stanford University Press.
Baer, Hans A., Merrill Singer, and Ida Susser
   2004   *Medical Anthropology and the World System*. 2nd ed. Westport, CT: Praeger.
Balbach, Edith D., Elizabeth A. Smith, and Ruth E. Malone
   2006   How the Health Belief Model Helps the Tobacco Industry: Individuals, Choice, and "Information." *Tobacco Control* 15 (supplement 4): 37–43.
Ballin, Scott D.
   2010   *Preliminary Comments Concerning Risk and Benefits of Long-Term Use of Nicotine Replacement Products: The Need for a More Rational, Coherent and Comprehensive Tobacco, Nicotine and Alternative Products Regulatory System*. Washington, DC: Alliance for Health, Economic, and Agriculture Development.
Barlett, Peggy
   1993   *American Dreams, Rural Realities: Family Farms in Crisis*. Chapel Hill: University of North Carolina Press.
Barnoya, Joaquin, and Stanton A. Glantz
   2006a Cardiovascular Effects of Secondhand Smoke Help Explain the Benefits of Smoke-Free Legislation on Heart Disease Burden. *Journal of Cardiovascular Nursing* 21 (6): 457–62.
   2006b The Tobacco Industry's Worldwide ETS Consultants Project: European and Asian Components. *European Journal of Public Health* 16 (1): 69–77.
Barry, Andrew, Thomas Osborne, and Nikolas Rose, eds.
   1996   *Foucault and Political Reason: Liberalism, Neo-Liberalism, and Rationalities of Government*. Chicago: University of Chicago Press.
Barthes, Roland
   1972   *Mythologies*. Annette Lavers, trans. New York: Hill and Wang.
Bayer, Ronald, and Jennifer Stuber
   2006   Tobacco Control, Stigma, and Public Health: Rethinking the Relations. *American Journal of Public Health* 96 (1): 47–50.
Bazemore, P. E.
   2003   "I Played By the Rules, and I Lost": The Fight for Racial Equality in the North Carolina Agricultural Extension Service. Kieran Taylor, ed. *Southern Voices* (Winter): 66–72.
Beach, Robert H., Alison Snow Jones, and Janet A. Tooze
   2008   Tobacco Farmer Interest and Success in Income Diversification. *Journal of Agricultural and Applied Economics* 40 (1): 53–71.
Beard, Aaron
   2004   Buyout Passes House. *Wilson Daily Times*, October 8.
Beauford, E. Yvonne, H. Max Miller, and Melvin E. Walker, Jr.
   1984   Effects of the Changing Structure of Agriculture on Nonwhite Farming in the US, the South, and Georgia: 1954–1978. *Sociological Spectrum* 4 (4): 405–20.

Beck, Ulrich
  1992   *Risk Society: Towards a New Modernity*. London: Sage.
Benjamin, Walter
  1999   A Small History of the Photograph. In *Walter Benjamin: Selected Writings*,
          vol. 1, Marcus Bullock and Michael W. Jennings, eds. Cambridge: Belknap.
Benson, Peter
  2004   Nothing to See Hear. *Anthropological Quarterly* 77 (3): 435–67.
  2005   Rooting Culture: Nostalgia, Urban Revitalization, and the Abivalence
          of Community at the Ballpark. *City & Society* 17 (1):93–125.
  2008a El Campo: Faciality and Structural Violence in Farm Labor Camps.
          Cultural Anthropology 23 (4): 589–629.
  2008b Good Clean Tobacco: Philip Morris, Biocapitalism, and the Social
          Course of Stigma in North Carolina. *American Ethnologist* 35 (3):357–79.
  2010a Giants in the Fields: Agribusiness and Farm Labor Politics in the
          United States. *Anthropology of Work Review* 31 (2): 54–70.
  2010b Safe Cigarettes. *Dialectical Anthropology* 34 (1): 49–56.
Benson, Peter, Edward F. Fischer, and Kedron Thomas
  2008   Resocializing Suffering: Neoliberalism, Accusation, and the Sociopo-
          litical Context of Guatemala's New Violence. *Latin American Perspectives*
          35 (5): 38–58.
Benson, Peter, and Stuart Kirsch
  2010   Capitalism and the Politics of Resignation. *Current Anthropology* 51
          (4): 459–86.
Benson, Peter, and Kevin Lewis O'Neill
  2007   Facing Risk: Levinas, Ethnography, and Ethics. *Anthropology of Con-
          sciousness* 18 (2): 29–55.
Berlant, Lauren
  1997   *The Queen of America Goes to Washington City: Essays on Sex and
          Citizenship*. Durham, NC: Duke University Press.
Bettcher, Douglas W., Derek Yach, and G. Emmanuel Guindon
  2000   Global Trade and Health: Key Linkages and Future Challenges. *Bul-
          letin of the World Health Organization* 78 (4): 521–34.
Biehl, João
  2004   Life of the Mind: The Interface of Psychopharmaceuticals, Domestic
          Economies, and Social Abandonment. *American Ethnologist* 31 (4): 475–
          96.
  2007   Pharmaceuticalization: AIDS Treatment and Global Health Politics.
          Anthropological Quarterly 80 (4): 1083–1126.
Biener, Lois
  2002   Anti-Tobacco Advertisements by Massachusetts and Philip Morris:
          What Teenagers Think. *Tobacco Control* 11 (supplement 2): 43–46.
Billings, Dwight
  1979   *Planters and the Making of a "New South": Class, Politics, and Devel-
          opment in North Carolina, 1885–1900*. Chapel Hill: University of North
          Carolina Press.
Bivens, Matt
  1990   Tobacco Is Still King in Wilson. *Wilson Daily Times*, September 26, 1
          and 6.

Black, Peter W.
  1984   The Anthropology of Tobacco Use: Ethnographic Data and Theoretical Issues. *Journal of Anthropological Research* 40 (4): 475–503.
Black, Earl, and Merle Black
  2002   *The Rise of Southern Republicans.* Cambridge, MA: Harvard University Press.
Blackwell, Gordon W.
  1934   The Displaced Tenant Farm Family in North Carolina. *Social Forces* 13:65–73.
Bletzer, Keith V.
  2004   Open Towns and Manipulated Indebtedness among Agricultural Workers in the New South. *American Ethnologist* 31 (4): 530–51.
Bolliger, C. T.
  2000   Practical Experiences in Smoking Reduction and Cessation. *Addiction* 95 (supplement 1): 19–24.
Bourdieu, Pierre, Alain Accardo, Gabrielle Balazs, Stéphane Beaud, François Bonvin, Emmanuel Bourdieu, Philippe Bourgois, Sylvain Broccolichi, Patrick Champagne, Rosine Christin, Jean-Pierre Faguer, et al.
  2000   *The Weight of the World: Social Suffering in Contemporary Society.* Stanford, CA: Stanford University Press.
Bourgois, Philippe
  1996   *In Search of Respect: Selling Crack in El Barrio.* Cambridge: Cambridge University Press.
Boyd, William, and Michael Watts
  1997   Agro-Industrial Just-in-Time: The Chicken Industry and Postwar Amercan Capitalism. In *Globalising Food: Agrarian Questions and Global Restruturing*, David Goodman and Michael J. Watts, eds., 192–225. London: Routledge.
Brandt, Allan M.
  1990   The Cigarette, Risk, and American Culture. *Daedalus* 119:155–76.
  2007   *The Cigarette Century: The Rise, Fall, and Deadly Persistence of the Product that Defined America.* New York: Basic Books.
Brandt, Allan M., and Paul Rozin
  1997   Introduction. In *Morality and Health*, Allan M. Brandt and Paul Rozin, eds., 1–11. London: Routledge.
Breen, T. H.
  1985   *Tobacco Culture: The Mentality of the Great Tidewater Planters on the Eve of Revolution.* Princeton: Princeton University Press.
Broadway, Bill
  2003   Churches Back Boycotts over Migrant Workers. *Washington Post*, November 22, B9.
Brown, A. Blake
  2005   U.S. Tobacco Growers: Now and into the Future. Paper presented at the Tobacco Quota Buyout Impacts Workshop, Washington, DC, September 20.
Brown, A. Blake, William M. Snell, and Kelly Tiller
  1999   The Changing Political Environment for Tobacco. Paper presented at the annual meeting of the Southern Agricultural Economics Association, Memphis, TN, January 30–February 3.

Brown, Blake, and Tomislav Vukina
   2001   Provision of Incentives in Agricultural Contracts: The Case of Flue-Cured Tobacco. Manuscript, Department of Agricultural and Resource Economics, North Carolina State University.
Brown, Valerie J.
   2003   Tobacco's Profit, Workers' Loss? *Environmental Health Perspectives* 111:284–287.
Brown, Wendy
   1995   *States of Injury: Power and Freedom in Late Modernity.* Princeton: Princeton University Press.
Bryan, William H.
   1999   Organizers Pick Wrong Target, Use Harsh Tactics in Mt. Olive Pickle Boycott. *News and Observer* (Raleigh), April 13, 10.
Buck-Morss, Susan
   1977   *The Origin of Negative Dialectics: Theodor W. Adorno, Walter Benjamin, and the Frankfurt Institute.* New York: Free Press.
Butler, Judith
   2005   *Giving an Account of Oneself.* New York: Fordham University Press.
Capehart, Thomas C., Jr.
   2002   Is There a Tobacco Quota Buyout in the Future? *Agricultural Outlook* (August): 10–13. Economic Research Service. Washington, DC: United States Department of Agriculture.
   2004a   The Changing Tobacco User's Dollar. TBS 257-01. Economic Research Service. Washington, DC: United States Department of Agriculture.
   2004b   Trends in U.S. Tobacco Farming. TBS-257-02. Economic Research Service. Washington, DC: United States Department of Agriculture.
   2004c   U.S. Tobacco Import Update. TBS-2003-01. Economic Research Service. Washington, DC: United States Department of Agriculture.
Castro, Arachu and Paul Farmer
   2005   *Understanding and Addressing AIDS-Related Stigma: From Anthropological Theory to Clinical Practice in Haiti.* American Journal of Public Health 95 (1): 53–59
Chakrabarty, Dipesh
   2002   *Habitations of Modernity: Essays in the Wake of Subaltern Studies.* Chicago: University of Chicago Press.
Chapman, Simon
   1994   Tobacco and Deforestation in the Developing World. *Tobacco Control* 3:191–93.
   2003   Harm Reduction. *Tobacco Control* 12:341.
Chapman, Simon, and Jonathan Liberman
   2005   Ensuring Smokers Are Adequately Informed: Reflections on Consumer Rights, Manufacturer Responsibilities, and Policy Implications. *Tobacco Control* 14 (supplement 2): 8–13.
Chávez, Leo R.
   1992   *Shadowed Lives: Undocumented Immigrants in American Society.* Fort Worth, TX: Harcourt, Brace, and Jovanovich.
   2001   *Covering Immigration: Popular Images and the Politics of the Nation.* Berkeley: University of California Press.

Chibnik, Michael, ed.
   1987   *Farm Work and Fieldwork: American Agriculture in Anthropological Perspective*. Ithaca, NY: Cornell University Press.
Cleveland, David A.
   1998   Balancing on a Planet: Toward an Agricultural Anthropology for the Twenty-First Century. *Human Ecology* 26 (2): 323–40.
Cobb, James C.
   1992   *The Most Southern Place on Earth: The Mississippi Delta and the Roots of Regional Identity*. New York: Oxford University Press.
Cochrane, Willard W.
   1993   *The Development of American Agriculture: A Historical Analysis*. 2nd ed. Minneapolis: University of Minnesota Press.
Collins, Kristin
   2003   Hopes Run Dry for Farmers. *News and Observer* (Raleigh), March 20, B1.
   2004   Mt. Olive Pickle Boycott Will End with Labor Pact. *News and Observer* (Raleigh), September 16, 1.
Comaroff, Jean, and John L. Comaroff
   2000   Millennial Capitalism: First Thoughts on a Second Coming. *Public Culture* 12:291–343.
Coontz, Stephanie
   1988   *The Social Origins of Private Life: A History of American Families*. London: Verso.
Cooperation Centre for Scientific Research Relative to Tobacco
   2005   Guide No. 3: Good Agricultural Practices (GAP) Guidelines. http://www.coresta.org/Guides/Guide-No3-GAP_Feb05.pdf.
Copeland, Libby
   2003   A Deere in the Headlights. *Washington Post*, March 19, C1.
Coronil, Fernando
   2000   Toward a Critique of Globalcentrism: Speculations on Capitalism's Nature. *Public Culture* 12 (2): 351–74.
Courtemanche, Charles, and Art Carden
   2011   Supersizing Supercenters? The Impact of Wal-Mart Supercenters on Body Mass Index and Obesity. *Journal of Urban Economics* 69 (2): 165–81.
Cowan, Gloria, Livier Martinez, and Stephanie Mendiola
   1997   Predictors of Attitudes toward Illegal Latino Immigrants. *Hispanic Journal of Behavioral Sciences* 19 (4): 403–15.
Crews, Harry
   1978   *Childhood: The Biography of a Place*. Athens: University of Georgia Press.
Crustinger, Martin
   2004   Supporters of FDA. *Wilson Daily Times*, October 9, 2004.
Cummings, K. Michael, Anthony Brown, and Clifford E. Douglas
   2006   Consumer Acceptable Risk: How Cigarette Companies Have Responded to Accusations that Their Products Are Defective. *Tobacco Control* 15 (supplement 4): 84–89.
Daniel, Pete
   1972   *Shadow of Slavery: Peonage in the South, 1901–1969*. Urbana: University of Illinois Press.

1986   *Breaking the Land: The Transformation of Cotton, Tobacco, and Rice Cultures since 1880.* Urbana: University of Illinois Press.

Darling, Marsha Jean
1982   The Growth and Decline of the Afro-American Family Farm in Warren County, North Carolina, 1910–1960. Ph.D. diss., Duke University, Durham, North Carolina.

Das, Veena
1995   *Critical Events: An Anthropological Perspective on Contemporary India.* Oxford: Oxford University Press.

Deacon, Roger
2000   Theory as Practice: Foucault's Concept of Problematization. *Telos* 118:127–42.

De Certeau, Michel
1984   *The Practice of Everyday Life.* Steven F. Rendall, trans. Berkeley: University of California Press.

De Genova, Nicholas
2002   Migrant "Illegality" and Deportability in Everyday Life. *Annual Review of Anthropology* 31:419–47.
2005   *Working the Boundaries: Race, Space, and Illegality in Mexican Chicago.* Durham, NC: Duke University Press.
2006   Latino and Asian Racial Formations at the Frontiers of U.S. Nationalism. Introduction to *Racial Transformations: Latinos and Asians Remaking the United States.* Nicholas De Genova, ed., 1–22. Durham, NC: Duke University Press.

Deleuze, Gilles
1988   *Foucault.* Seán Hand, trans. Minneapolis: University of Minnesota Press.

Deleuze, Gilles, and Félix Guattari
1987   *A Thousand Plateaus: Capitalism and Schizophrenia.* Brian Massumi, trans. Minneapolis: University of Minnesota Press.

Delgado-Wise, Raul, and Himberto Marquez Covarrubias
2006   *The Reshaping of Mexican Labor Exports under NAFTA: Paradoxes and Challenges.* Zacatecas: Universidad de Zacatecas, Red Internacional de Migración y Desarollo.

Derrida, Jacques
1995   *The Gift of Death.* David Wills, trans. Chicago: University of Chicago Press.

Dickens, Charles
1874   *American Notes and Pictures from Italy.* London: Chapman & Hall.

Dimitri, Carolyn
2003   Contracting in Tobacco? Contracts Revisited. TBS-254-01. Economic Research Service. Washington, DC: United States Department of Agriculture.

Dixon, Richard D., Roger C. Lowery, Diane E. Levy, and Kenneth F. Ferraro
1991   Self-Interest and Public Opinion toward Smoking Policies: A Replication and Extension. *Public Opinion Quarterly* 55:241–54.

Dohlman, Erik, Linda Foreman, and Michelle Da Pra
    2009   The Post-Buyout Experience: Peanut and Tobacco Sectors Adapt to
        Policy Reform. *ERS Report Summary.* Economic Research Service. U.S.
        Department of Agriculture, Washington, DC.
Douglas, Mary
    2002   *Purity and Danger.* London: Routledge.
Dudley, Kathryn Marie
    1996   The Problem of Community in Rural America. *Culture & Agriculture*
        18 (2): 47–57.
    2000   *Debt and Dispossession: Farm Loss in America's Heartland.* Chicago:
        University of Chicago Press.
Dumit, Joseph
    2002   Drugs for Life. *Molecular Interventions* 2:124–27.
Durrenberger, E. Paul, and Kendall M. Thu
    1996   The Industrialization of Swine Production in the United States: An
        Overview. *Culture & Agriculture* 18 (1): 19–22.
    1997   Signals, Systems, and Environment in Industrial Food Production.
        Journal of Political Ecology 4:27–39.
Early, Julie, Stephen W. Davis, Sara A. Quandt, Pamela Rao, Beverly M. Snively,
    and Thomas A. Arcury
    2006   Housing Characteristics of Farmworker Families in North Carolina.
        Journal of Immigrant and Minority Health 8 (2): 173–84.
East Carolina University Regional Development Institute
    1999   *Hispanic Economic Impact Study: An Eastern North Carolina Analy-
        sis.* Raleigh: East Carolina University Regional Development Institute and
        Catholic Social Ministries Diocese of Raleigh.
Efroymson, Debra, Saifuddin Ahmed, Joy Townsend, Syed Mahbubul Alam, Amit
    Ranjan Dey, Ranjit Saha, Biplob Dhar, Aminul Islam Sujon, et al.
    2001   Hungry for Tobacco: An Analysis of the Economic Impact of Tobacco
        Consumption on the Poor in Bangladesh. *Tobacco Control* 10:212–17.
Eichelberger, Laura
    2007   SARS and New York's Chinatown: The Politics of Risk and Blame
        during an Epidemic of Fear. *Social Science and Medicine* 65 (6): 1284–95.
Environmental Working Group
    2004   Obstruction of Justice. Environmental Working Group. website http://
        www.ewg.org/reports/blackfarmers.
Fabian, Johannes
    1983   *Time and the Other: How Anthropology Makes Its Object.* New York:
        Columbia University Press.
Fahrenthold, David A., and Allan Lengel
    2003   Patience Paid Off. *Washington Post*, March 20, B1.
Fairchild, Amy, and James Colgrove
    2004   Out of the Ashes: The Life, Death, and Rebirth of the "Safer" Cigarette
        in the United States. *American Journal of Public Health* 94 (2): 192–204.
Faludi, Susan
    1999   *Stiffed: The Betrayal of the American Man.* New York: William
        Morrow.

Faria, Neice Müller Xavier, Cesar Gomes Victora, Stela Nazareth Meneghel, Lenine Alves de Carvalho, and João Werner Falk
   2006   Suicide Rates in the State of Rio Grande do Sul, Brazil: Association with Socioeconomic, Cultural, and Agricultural Factors. *Cadernos Saúde Pública, Rio de Janeiro* 22 (12): 2611-21.

Faris, Clint
   1963   Adult Farmer. *Wilson Daily Times*, January 10, 1 and 2.

Farm Labor Organizing Committee (FLOC)
   2008   Campaign. Farm Labor Organizing Committee (FLOC), website. http://www.floc.com/RJR%20Campaign.htm.

Farmer, Paul
   1992   *AIDS and Accusation: Haiti and the Geography of Blame.* Berkeley: University of California Press.
   2004   An Anthropology of Structural Violence. *Current Anthropology* 45 (3): 305–25.

Farmer, Paul, Bruce Nizeye, Sara Stulac, and Salmaan Keshavjee
   2006   Structural Violence and Clinical Medicine. *PLoS Medicine* 3 (10): e449, doi:10.1371/journal.pmed.0030449.

Farrelly, Matthew C., C. G. Healton, K. C. Davis, P. Messeri, J. C. Hersey, and M. L. Haviland
   2002   Getting to the Truth: Evaluating National Tobacco Countermarketing Campaigns. *American Journal of Public Health* 92 (6): 901–07.

Ferguson, James
   1994   *The Anti-Politics Machine: "Development," Depoliticization, and Bureaucratic Power in Lesotho.* Minneapolis: University of Minnesota Press.
   2006   *Global Shadows: Africa in the Neoliberal World Order.* Durham, NC: Duke University Press.

Fields, Barbara J.
   1982   Ideology and Race in American History. In *Region, Race, and Reconstruction: Essays in Honor of C. Vann Wooward*, J. Morgan Kousser and James M. McPherson, eds., 143–77. Oxford: Oxford University Press.

Finger, William R., ed.
   1981   The Tobacco Industry in Transition: Policies for the 1980s. North Carolina Center for Public Policy Research, Inc.

Fishman, J. A., H. Allison, S. B. Knowles, B. A. Fishburn, T. A. Woollery, W. T. Marx, D. M. Shelton, C. G. Husten , and M. P. Eriksen
   1998   State Laws on Tobacco Control: United States. Centers for Disease Control and Prevention. *Morbidity and Mortality Weekly Report* 48 (3): 21–40.

Fitzgerald, Deborah
   2003   *Every Farm a Factory: The Industrial Ideal in American Agriculture.* New Haven, CT: Yale University Press.

Fitzgerald, Eddie
   1996   USDA Hikes Quota. *Wilson Daily Times*, December 20, 1 and 2.
   1997a   County Will Feel Loss. *Wilson Daily Times*, December 30, 1 and 2.
   1997b   County Farmers Coexist. *Wilson Daily Times*, March 10, 1 and 2.
   2003a   Leaf Firm Opposes Farmers. *Wilson Daily Times*, October 11.
   2003b   Tobacco Growers Anxious. *Wilson Daily Times*, January 18.

2004   Tobacco Buyout a "Miracle" for Local Farmers. *Wilson Daily Times,* October 30.

Flowers, Linda
1990   *Throwed Away: The Failures of Progress in Eastern North Carolina.* Knoxville: University of Tennessee Press.

Foreman, Linda F.
2006   Tobacco Production Costs and Returns in 2004. TBS-260-01. Economic Research Service. Washington, DC: United States Department of Agriculture.

Foucault, Michel
1979   *Discipline and Punish: The Birth of the Prison.* Alan Sheridan, trans. New York: Vintage.
1980   *The History of Sexuality.* Vol. 1. Robert Hurley, trans. New York: Vintage.
1984   Right of Death and Power over Life. In *The Foucault Reader,* Paul Rabinow, trans., 258–272. New York: Pantheon Books.
1985   *Discourse and Truth: The Problematization of Parrhesia.* J. Pearson, ed. Evanston: Northwestern University Press.
1991   Governmentality. In *The Foucault Effect: Studies in Governmentality,* Graham Burchell, Colin Gordon, and Peter Miller, eds., 87–104. Chicago: University of Chicago Press.
1996   Clarifications on the Question of Power. In *Foucault Live: Collected Interviews, 1961–1984,* S. Lotringer, ed., 255–263. New York: Semiotexte.
1997a   Polemics, Politics and Problematizations. In *Ethics: Subjectivity and Truth,* vol. 1, Lydia Davis, trans., 111–20. New York: New Press.
1997b   The Birth of Biopolitics. In *Ethics: Subjectivity and Truth,* Paul Rabinow, ed., 75–80. New York: New Press.

Franklin, Sarah, and Margaret M. Lock, eds.
2003   *Remaking Life and Death: Toward an Anthropology of the Biosciences.* Santa Fe, NM: School of American Research Press.

Friedman, Lissy S.
2007   Philip Morris's Website and Television Commercials Use New Language to Mislead the Public into Believing It Has Changed Its Stance on Smoking and Disease. *Tobacco Control* 16 (6): e9.

Gardner, Bruce L.
2002   *American Agriculture in the Twentieth Century: How It Flourished and What It Cost.* Cambridge, MA: Harvard University Press.

Gaventa, John
1998   The Political Economy of Land Tenure: Appalachia and the Southeast. In *Who Owns America? Social Conflict over Property Rights,* Harvey M. Jacobs, ed., 227–44. Madison: University of Wisconsin Press.

Geist, Helmut
1999   Global Assessment of Deforestation Related to Tobacco Farming. *Tobacco Control* 8:18–28.

Geist, Helmut J., K. Chang, V. Etges, J. M. Abdallah
2009   Tobacco Growers at the Crossroads: Towards a Comparison of Diversification and Ecosystem Impacts. *Land Use Policy* 26 (4): 1066–79.

Gentry, Amanda L., Joseph G. Grzywacz, Sara A. Quandt, Stephen W. Davis, and
    Thomas A. Arcury
    2007   Housing Quality among North Carolina Farmworker Families. *Journal of Agricultural Safety and Health* 13 (3): 323–37.
Gilbert, Jess, Gwen Sharp, and M. Sindy Felin
    2001   *The Decline (and Revival?) of Black Farmers and Rural Landowners: A Review of the Research Literature*. Madison: Land Tenure Center, University of Wisconsin at Madison.
Gilman, Sander
    2001   *Making the Body Beautiful: A Cultural History of Aesthetic Surgery*. Princeton: Princeton University Press.
Ginapp, Kristol Bradley
    2003   Jim "USDA" Crow: Symptomatic Discrimination in Agriculture. *Drake Journal of Agricultural Law* 237 (8): 237–54.
Ginsburg, Allen
    1956   *Howl and Other Poems*. San Francisco: City Lights Books.
Givel, Michael
    2007   FDA Legislation. *Tobacco Control* 16:217–18.
Glantz, Stanton A., John Slade, Lisa A. Bero, Peter Hanauer, and Deborah E. Barnes, eds.
    1996   *The Cigarette Papers*. Berkeley: University of California Press.
Gledhill, John
    1998   The Mexican Contribution to Restructuring U.S. Capitalism. *Critique of Anthropology* 18 (3): 279–96.
Goffman, Erving
    1963   *Stigma: Notes on the Management of Spoiled Identity*. New York: Prentice-Hall.
Good, Byron, and Mary-Jo DelVecchio Good
    1994   In the Subjunctive Mode: Epilepsy Narratives in Turkey. *Social Science and Medicine* 38:855–62.
Goodman, Jordan
    1993   *Tobacco in History: The Cultures of Dependence*. New York: Routledge.
Gordon, Colin
    1991   Governmental Rationality: An Introduction. In *The Foucault Effect: Studies in Governmentality*, Graham Burchell, Colin Gordon, and Peter Miller, eds., 1–51. Chicago: University of Chicago Press.
Graham, Jim
    1971   Tobacco Edition. *Wilson Daily Times*, August 27, 15.
Green, Elna C.
    1999   Introduction. In *Before the New Deal: Social Welfare in the South, 1830–1930*, Elna C. Green, ed., vii–xxvi. Athens: University of Georgia Press.
Green, Gary P.
    1987   Class and Class Interests in Agriculture: Support for the New Deal Farm Programs among Tobacco Producers. *Sociological Quarterly* 28 (4): 559–74.

Greenhouse, Carol J., Barbara Yngvesson, and David M. Engel
 1994 *Law and Community in Three American Towns*. Ithaca, NY: Cornell University Press.
Griffith, David
 2009a The Moral Economy of Tobacco. *American Anthropologist* 111 (4): 432–42.
 2009b Unions without Borders: Organizing and Enlightening Immigrant Farm Workers. *Anthropology of Work Review* 30 (2): 54–66.
Griffith, David, and Ed Kissam
 1994 *Working Poor: Farmworkers in the United States*. Philadelphia: Temple University Press.
Grim, Valerie
 1995 The Politics of Inclusion: Black Farmers and the Quest for Agribusiness Participation, 1945–1990s. *Agricultural History* 69 (2): 257–71.
 1996 Black Participation in the Farmers Home Administration and Agricultural Stabilization and Conservation Service, 1964–1990. *Agricultural History* 70 (2): 321–36.
Gudeman, Stephen
 2001 *The Anthropology of Economy: Community, Market, and Culture*. London: Blackwell.
Hahamovitch, Cindy
 1997 *The Fruits of Their Labor: Atlantic Coast Farmworkers and the Making of Migrant Poverty, 1870–1945*. Chapel Hill: University of North Carolina Press.
Hall, Stuart, and David Held
 1989 Citizens and Citizenship. In *New Times: The Changing Face of Politics in the 1990s*, Stuart Hall and M. Jacques, eds., 172–88. London: Verso.
Hart, John Fraser, Ennis L. Chestang
 1978 Rural Revolution in East Carolina. *Geographical Review* 68 (4): 435–58.
Harvey, David
 2005 *A Brief History of Neoliberalism*. Oxford: Oxford University Press.
Hatsukami, Dorothy K., Jack E. Henningfield, and Michael Kotlyar
 2004 Harm Reduction Approaches to Reducing Tobacco-Related Mortality. *Annual Review of Public Health* 25:377–95.
Heath, Shirley Brice
 1983 *Ways with Words: Language, Life and Work in Communities and Classrooms*. Cambridge: Cambridge University Press.
Heffernan, William D., and Douglas H. Constance
 1994 Transnational Corporations and the Globalization of the Food System. In *From Columbus to ConAgra: The Globalization of Agriculture and Food*, Alessandro Bonanno et al., eds., 29–51. Lawrence: University of Kansas Press.
Herzfeld, Michael
 1992 *The Social Production of Indifference*. Oxford: Berg.
Hillier, Bill and Julienne Hanson
 1984 *The Social Logic of Space*. Cambridge: Cambridge University Press.

Hirschhorn, Norbert
   2004   Corporate Social Responsibility and the Tobacco Industry: Hope or
   Hype? *Tobacco Control* 13:447–53.
Holden, Christopher
   2002   Bitter Harvest: Housing Conditions of Migrant and Seasonal Farm-
   workers. In *The Human Cost of Food: Farmworkers' Lives, Labor, and
   Advocacy*, Charles D. Thompson, Jr., and Melinda F. Wiggins, eds., 169–93.
   Austin: University of Texas Press.
Holland, Dorothy, Donald M. Nonini, Catherine Lutz, Lesley Bartlett, Marla
   Frederick-McGlathery, Thaddeus C. Guldbrandsen, and Enrique G. Murillo, Jr.
   2007   *Local Democracy under Siege: Activism, Public Interests, and Private
   Politics*. New York: New York University Press.
Hollander, Gail M.
   2006   "Subject to Control": Shifting Geographies of Race and Labour in U.S.
   Sugar Agroindustry, 1930–1950. *Cultural Geographies* 13:266–92.
Holmes, William L.
   2004   Burr Votes Down FDA. *Wilson Daily Times*, October 6.
Hsu, Spenser S.
   2001   Davis's Bill on Tobacco Is Criticized; Philip Morris Stands to Benefit,
   Foes Say. *Washington Post*, June 22, sec. B.
Huffman, Wallace E.
   1981   Black-White Human Capital Differences: Impact on Agricultural Pro-
   ductivity in the U.S. South. *American Economic Review* 71 (1): 94–107.
Hyatt, George, Jr.
   1963   Extension. *Wilson Daily Times*, August 16.
Institute of Medicine
   2001   *Clearing the Smoke: The Science Base for Tobacco Harm Reduction*.
   Washington, DC: Institute of Medicine.
Jacoby, Mary
   2003   Closed Streets. *St. Petersburg Times*, March 19, 12.
Jernigan, Connie H.
   1985   Farmers Could Lose Profits. *Wilson Daily Times*, January 14, 6B.
Jones, Alison Snow, W. David Austin, Robert H. Beach, and David G. Altman
   2007   Funding of North Carolina Tobacco Control Programs through the
   Master Settlement Agreement. *American Journal of Public Health* 97 (1):
   36–44.
   2008   Tobacco Farmers and Tobacco Manufacturers: Implications for Tobacco Control in Tobacco-Growing Developing Countries. *Journal of Public
   Health Policy* 29 (4): 406–23.
Jones, Hezekiah, S.
   1994   Federal Agriculture Policies: Do Black Farm Operators Benefit? *Review of Black Political Economy* 22 (4): 25–50.
Jones, Lu Ann
   1986   Interview with Clifton Tomlinson, December 29, in Wilson, North Carolina. Series 1, Sub-series 1e, Box 14, Folder 9. Southern Agriculture Oral
   History Project Records, 1986–91. Washington, DC: National Museum of
   American History.

2002   *Mama Learned Us to Work: Farm Women in the New South*. Chapel Hill: University of North Carolina Press.

Joseph, Miranda

2002   *Against the Romance of Community*. Minneapolis: University of Minnesota Press.

Jubera, Drew

2003   Standoff Ends, but Not Farmers' Plight. *Atlanta Journal-Constitution*, March 20, B1.

Kasarda, John D., and James H. Johnson, Jr.

2006   The Economic Impact of the Hispanic Population of the State of North Carolina. Chapel Hill: Frank Hawkins Kenan Institute of Private Enterprise.

Katz, Michael B.

1986   *In the Shadow of the Poorhouse: A Social History of Welfare in America*. New York: Basic Books.

1989   *The Undeserving Poor: From the War on Poverty to the War on Welfare*. New York: Pantheon Books.

Kendall, Debbi

1985a   Tobacco Market Ends. *Wilson Daily Times*, October 29, 1 and 11.

1985b   Even the Best Farmers. *Wilson Daily Times*, October 3, 1 and 6.

Keown, Alex

2003a   Buyout Prospects Dimmer. *Wilson Daily Times*, November 14.

2003b   Burr Defends His Position on Buyout. *Wilson Daily Times*, October 17.

2004a   Burr on Negotiation. *Wilson Daily Times*, September 30.

2004b   Buyout in Final Stages. *Wilson Daily Times*, October 7.

Kessler, David A.

2001   *A Question of Intent: A Great American Battle with a Deadly Industry*. New York: Public Affairs.

Kingsolver, Ann, ed.

2001   *NAFTA Stories: Fears and Hopes in Mexico and the United States*. Boulder, CO: Lynne Reinner.

Kingsolver, Ann

2007   Farmers and Farmworkers: Two Centuries of Strategic Alterity in Kentucky's Tobacco Fields. *Critique of Anthropology* 27 (1): 87–102.

2011   *Tobacco Town Futures: Global Encounters in Rural Kentucky*. Long Grove, IL: Waveland Press.

Kirby, Jack Temple

1987   *Rural Worlds Lost: The American South, 1920–1960*. Baton Rouge: Louisiana State University Press.

Kleinman, Arthur

1986   *Social Origins of Distress and Disease: Depression, Neurasthenia, and Pain in Modern China*. New Haven, CT: Yale University Press.

1999   Experience and Its Moral Modes: Culture, Human Conditions, and Disorder. In *The Tanner Lectures on Human Values*, vol. 20, G. B. Peterson, ed., 357–420. Salt Lake City: University of Utah Press.

2006   *What Really Matters: Living a Moral Life amidst Uncertainty and Danger.* Oxford: Oxford University Press.

Kleinman, Arthur, and Peter Benson
2006   Anthropology in the Clinic: The Cultural Competency Problem and How to Fix It. *PLoS Medicine* 3 (10): e294.

Kleinman, Arthur, Veena Das, and Margaret Lock, eds.
1997   *Social Suffering.* Berkeley: University of California Press.

Kleinman, Arthur, Wen-Zhi Wang, Shi-Chuo Li, Xiu-Ming Cheng, Xiu-Ying Dai, Kun-Tun Li, and Joan Kleinman
1995   The Social Course of Epilepsy: Chronic Illness as Social Experience in Interior China. *Social Science and Medicine* 40 (10): 1319–30.

Kluger, Richard
1996   *Ashes to Ashes: America's Hundred-Year Cigarette War, the Public Health, and the Unabashed Triumph of Philip Morris.* New York: Alfred A. Knopf.

Kohrman, Matthew
2004   Should I Quit? Tobacco, Fraught Identity, and the Risks of Governmentality in Urban China. *Urban Anthropology* 33 (2–4): 211–45.
2008   Smoking among Doctors: Governmentality, Embodiment, and the Diversion of Blame in Contemporary China. *Medical Anthropology* 27 (1): 9–42.

Kohrman, Matthew, and Peter Benson
2011   Tobacco. *Annual Review of Anthropology* 40. In press.

Korstad, Robert Rodgers
2003   *Civil Rights Unionism: Tobacco Workers and the Struggle for Democracy in the Mid-Twentieth-Century South.* Chapel Hill: University of North Carolina Press.

Kosky, Jeffery L.
2001   *Levinas and the Philosophy of Religion.* Bloomington: Indiana University Press.

Kulikoff, Allan
1986   *Tobacco and Slaves: The Development of Southern Cultures in the Chesapeake, 1680–1800.* Chapel Hill: University of North Carolina Press.

Kusow, Abdi M.
2004   Contesting Stigma: On Goffman's Assumptions of Normative Order. *Symbolic Interaction* 27 (2): 179–97.

LaFey, Laura
1986a   No Smoking Rare. *Wilson Daily Times*, August 9, 1986, 1.
1986b   Farm Downturn. *Wilson Daily Times*, January 3, 2.

Lamm, Wayne
1955a   Colored Farm Families. *Wilson Daily Times*, June 30, 1 and 2.
1955b   Wilson County Progresses. *Wilson Daily Times*, August 19, 11.

Lamont, Michele
2000   *The Dignity of Working Men: Morality and the Boundaries of Race, Class, and Immigration.* Cambridge, MA: Harvard University Press.

Landon, Charles E.
    1934   The Tobacco Growing Industry of North Carolina. *Economic Geography* 10 (3): 239–54.
Larson, Alice C.
    2000   *Migrant and Seasonal Farmworker Enumeration Profiles Study: North Carolina*. Washington, DC: Migrant Health Program, Bureau of Primary Health Care, Health Resources and Services Administration.
Layton, Lyndsey
    2009   Senate Passes Bill to Let FDA Regulate Tobacco. *Washington Post*, June 12.
Lazare, Aaron
    2005   *On Apology*. Oxford: Oxford University Press.
Lazzarato, Maurizio
    2002   From Biopower to Biopolitics. *Pli: Warwick Journal of Philosophy* 13:112–25.
Lee, Sing, Marcus Y. L. Chiu, Adley Tsang, Helena Chui, and Arthur Kleinman
    2006   Stigmatizing Experience and Structural Discrimination Associated with the Treatment of Schizophrenia in Hong Kong. *Social Science and Medicine* 62 (7): 1685–96.
Lehman, Charlie
    1981a   Farmers Pleased. *Wilson Daily Times*, February 19, 1 and 2.
    1981b   Wilson County Farmers Lobby. *Wilson Daily Times*, February 18, 1 and 2.
    1982a   Tobacco Program Faces Change. *Wilson Daily Times*, April 16, 1 and 8.
    1982b   Is American Leaf Losing. *Wilson Daily Times*, August 20, 1982, 1 and 6
    1982c   In 1982 Do or Die. *Wilson Daily Times*, April 22, 1 and 12.
Leonard, David J.
    2007   Innocent until Proven Innocent: In Defense of Duke Lacrosse and White Power (and Against Menacing Black Student-Athletes, a Black Stripper, Activists, and the Jewish Media). *Journal of Sport and Social Issues* 31 (1): 25–44.
Leonnig, Carol D.
    2003   Farmer Found Guilty in Mall Standoff. *Washington Post*, September 27, B1.
    2004a   Farmer's Future in Judge's Hands. *Washington Post*, March 3, B1.
    2004b   Man Gets Six-Year Term for DC Tractor Standoff. *Washington Post*, June 24, B1.
Leonnig, Carol D., and Allan Lengel
    2004   Mall Standoff Farmer Freed. *Washington Post*, July 2, B1.
Leonnig, Carol D., and Neely Tucker
    2004   U.S. Judge Cuts Farmer's Sentence in Mall Standoff. *Washington Post*, July 1, A1.
Levinas, Emmanuel
    1969   *Totality and Infinity: An Essay on Exteriority*. Alphonso Lingis, trans. Pittsburgh: Duquesne University Press.

1981   *Otherwise than Being, or Beyond Essence*. Alphonso Lingis, trans. Pittsburgh: Duquesne University Press.

1988   Useless Suffering. In *The Provocation of Levinas*, Richard Cohen, trans. Robert Bernasconi and David Wood, eds., 156–67. London: Routledge.

1998   *Entre Nous: On Thinking-of-the-Other*. Michael B. Smith and Barbara Harshav, trans. New York: Columbia University Press.

2000   *God, Death, and Time*. Bettina Bergo, trans. Stanford, CA: Stanford University Press.

Lewis, Bill

1963a   Delayed. *Wilson Daily Times*, July 15, 9.

1963b   Tobacco. *Wilson Daily Times*, May 13, 13.

Lillard, Margaret

2004   Democrats See GOP Scheme. *Wilson Daily Times*, October 1.

Lingis, Alphonso

1994   *Foreign Bodies*. London: Routledge.

1998   *The Imperative*. Bloomington: Indiana University Press.

Link, Bruce G., and Jo C. Phelan

2001   Conceptualizing Stigma. *Annual Review of Sociology* 27:363–85.

2006   Stigma and its Public Health Implications. *Lancet* 367 (9509): 528–29.

Lipsitz, George

1995   The Possessive Investment in Whiteness: Racialized Social Democracy and the "White" Problem in American Studies. *American Quarterly* 47 (3): 369–87.

2006   Learning from New Orleans: The Social Warrant of Hostile Privatism and Competitive Consumer Citizenship. *Cultural Anthropology* 21 (3): 451–68.

Lochlann Jain, Sarah S.

2004   "Come up to the Kool Taste": African American Upward Mobility and the Semiotics of Menthols. *Public Culture* 15 (2): 295–322.

Low, Setha M.

2003   *Behind the Gates: Life, Security, and the Pursuit of Happiness in Fortress America*. London: Routledge.

Lowitt, Richard, and Maurine Beasely, eds.

1983   *One Third of a Nation: Lorena Hickok Reports on the Great Depression*. Urbana: University of Illinois Press.

Major, Brenda, and Laurie T. O'Brien

2005   The Social Psychology of Stigma. *Annual Review of Psychology* 56:393–421.

Malone, Ruth E.

2007   Working to Make a Disease. *Tobacco Control* 16:361–62.

Mann, Charles Kellogg

1975   *Tobacco: The Ants and the Elephants*. Salt Lake City, UT: Olympus.

Massey, Douglas S., Jorge Durand, and Nolan J. Malone

2003   *Beyond Smoke and Mirrors: Mexican Immigration in an Era of Economic Integration*. New York: Russell Sage Foundation.

Massey, Douglas S., Rafael Alarcón, Jorge Durand, and Humberto González
    1987   *Return to Aztlán: The Social Process of International Migration from Western Mexico.* Berkeley: University of California Press.
Martin, Andrew
    2004   Loan Discrimination Policies Thinned Ranks of Minority Farmers, Organizations Claim. *Chicago Tribune,* August 15.
Martin, Vernon
    1955   Saratoga Winner. *Wilson Daily Times,* June 16, 1 and 6.
Marx, Karl
    1972   *The Eighteenth Brumaire of Louis Bonaparte.* In *Marx/Engels Reader,* Robert C. Tucker, ed., 594–617. New York: Norton.
Massumi, Brian
    1992   *A User's Guide to Capitalism and Schizophrenia: Deviations from Deleuze and Guattari.* Minneapolis: University of Minnesota Press.
Matthews, Scott L.
    1999   Farm Tenancy and Race in the Tobacco Culture of Wilson County, North Carolina, 1865–1992. Master's thesis, Guilford College.
McAdams, Robert C.
    1996   The Tobacco Culture of Wilson County, North Carolina. Ph.D. diss., University of Tennessee, Knoxville.
McDaniel, Patricia A., and Ruth E. Malone
    2005   Understanding Philip Morris's Pursuit of U.S. Government Regulation of Tobacco. *Tobacco Control* 14:193–200.
McDaniel, Patricia A., Elizabeth A. Smith, and Ruth E. Malone
    2006   Philip Morris's Project Sunrise: Weakening Tobacco Control by Working with It. *Tobacco Control* 15:215–23.
McKinney, Charles Wesley, Jr.
    2003   "Our People Began to Press for Greater Freedom": The Black Freedom Struggle in Wilson, North Carolina, 1945–1970. Ph.D. diss., Duke University, Durham, North Carolina.
Merleau-Ponty, Maurice
    2002   *Phenomenology of Perception.* Colin Smith, trans. London: Routledge.
Mintz, Sidney W.
    1985   *Sweetness and Power: The Place of Sugar in Modern History.* New York: Viking.
Mitchell, Thomas W.
    2000   *From Reconstruction to Deconstruction: Undermining Black Land Ownership, Political Independence, and Community through Partition Sales of Tenancies in Common.* Madison: Land Tenure Center, University of Wisconsin at Madison.
Montopoli, Brian
    2009   Tobacco Bill's Big Winner: Philip Morris? CBS News, June 11. http://www.cbsnews.com/blogs2009/06/11/business/ecowatch/entry5081439.shtml.
Mooneyham, Scott
    2004   Tobacco Buyout Bill Puts Squeeze on Richard Burr. *Wilson Daily Times,* October 1.

Morgan, Philip D.
    1998   *Slave Counterpoint: Black Culture in the Eighteenth-Century Chesa-peake and Lowcountry*. Chapel Hill: University of North Carolina Press.
Murdock, S. H., and F. L. Leistritz, eds.
    1988   *The Farm Financial Crisis*. Boulder, CO: Westview Press.
Murray, C. J. L., S. C. Kulkarni, C. Michaud, N. Tomijima, M. T. Bulzacchelli, T. J. Iandiorio, and M. Ezzati
    2006   Eight Americas: Investigating Mortality Disparities across Races, Counties, and Race-Counties in the United States. *PLoS Medicine* 3 (9): e260.
Myers, Matthew L.
    2004   Opposition in Search of a Rationale: The Case for Food and Drug Administration Regulation. *Tobacco Control* 13:441–43.
Nader, Laura
    1997   Controlling Processes: Tracing the Dynamic Components of Power. *Current Anthropology* 38 (5): 711–38.
Nakamura, David
    2003   N.C. Man Made Trip of Last Resort. *Washington Post*, March 19, A6.
Nakamura, David, and Allan Lengel
    2003a   Tractor Driver in Standoff with Police on Mall. *Washington Post*, March 18, B1.
    2003b   Farmer Says He'll Give Up Thursday if He Gets Respect. *Washington Post*, March 19, A1.
Nakamura, David, and Michael D. Shear
    2003   Unhappy Man Grabs the Spotlight. *Washington Post*, March 20, B1.
National Institute for Tobacco-Free Kids
    1999   *False Friends: The US Cigarette Companies' Betrayal of American Tobacco Farmers*. Washington, DC: National Institute for Tobacco-Free Kids.
    2001   *Golden Leaf, Barren Harvest: The Costs of Tobacco Farming*. Washington, DC: National Institute for Tobacco-Free Kids.
    2003a   Major Issues and Questions Raised Regarding FDA Legislation. http://www.tobaccofreekids.org/research/factsheets/pdf/0189.pdf.
    2003b   Tobacco Bill Negotiations Failed Due to Loopholes. http://www.tobaccofreekids.org/Script/DisplayPressRelease. php3?Display=696&zoom_highlight=loopholes.
    2005a   The Toll of Tobacco in the Tobacco Growing States. http://www.tobaccofreekids.org/research/factsheets/pdf/0278.pdf.
    2005b   Why the FDA Should Regulate Tobacco Products. http://www.tobacco freekids.org/research/factsheets/pdf/0187.pdf.
    2007   Federal Tobacco-Caused Health Costs and Revenues. http://www.tobaccofreekids.org/research/factsheets/pdf/0108.pdf.
    2010a   Smoke-Free Laws Do Not Harm Business at Restaurants and Bars. http://tobaccofreekids.org/research/factsheets/pdf/0144.pdf.
    2010b   Toll of Tobacco in the United States of America. http://www.tobacco freekids.org/research/factsheets/pdf/0072.pdf.

2011   Key State-Specific Tobacco-Related Data and Rankings. http://www
        .tobaccofreekids.org/research/factsheets/pdf/0176.pdf.
Nations, Marilyn K., Geison Vasconcelos Lira, and Ana Maria Fontenelle Catrib
    2009   Stigma, Deforming Metaphors and Patients' Moral Experience of Mul-
        tibacillary Leprosy in Sobral, Ceará State, Brazil. *Cadernos Saúde Pública,
        Rio de Janeiro* 25 (6): 1215–24.
Newman, Katherine S.
    1988   *Falling from Grace: Downward Mobility in the Age of Affluence.*
        Berkeley: University of California Press.
    1993   *Declining Fortunes: The Withering of the American Dream.* New
        York: Basic Books.
New York Times
    2004   Restitution for Black Farmers. July 27.
    2009   Tobacco Regulation, at Last. June 11.
Nichter, Mark
    2003   Smoking: What Does Culture Have to Do with It? *Addiction* 98
        (supplement 1): 139–45.
Nichter, Mark, and Elizabeth Cartwright
    1991   Saving the Children for the Tobacco Industry. *Medical Anthropology
        Quarterly* 5:236–56.
Nisbet, Lynn
    1939   Sustain Test Farm Set-Up. *Wilson Daily Times,* March 16, 2.
North Carolina Department of Labor
    2008   Introduction to Migrant Housing Inspections in North Carolina. Ra-
        leigh: Agricultural Safety and Health Bureau, Division of Occupational
        Safety and Health.
North Carolina Farmworker Institute
    2007   Facts about North Carolina Farmworkers. Raleigh: North Carolina
        Farmworker Health Program, Office of Rural Health and Community
        Care, North Carolina Department of Health and Human Services.
Omi, Michael, and Howard Winant
    1994   *Racial Formation in the United States: From the 1960s to the 1990s.*
        New York: Routledge.
Ong, Aihwa
    2003   *Buddha Is Hiding: Refugees, Citizenship, the New America.* Berkeley:
        University of California Press.
    2006   *Neoliberalism as Exception: Mutations in Citizenship and Sovereignty.*
        Durham, NC: Duke University Press.
Ong, Aihwa, and Stephen J. Collier, eds.
    2005   *Global Assemblages: Technology, Politics, and Ethics.* Oxford:
        Blackwell.
Orlandi, Lorraine
    2005   Fox's Immigration Comments Backfire. *Seattle Times,* May 16, A7.
Ortiz, Fernando
    1995   *Cuban Counterpoint: Tobacco and Sugar.* Durham, NC: Duke Uni-
        versity Press.

Ortner, Sherry
    2003   *New Jersey Dreaming: Capital, Culture, and the Class of '58*. Durham, NC: Duke University Press.

Otañez, Marty G. and Stanton A. Glantz
    2011   Social Responsibility in Tobacco Production? Tobacco Companies' Use of Green Supply Chains to Obscure the Real Costs of Tobacco Farming. *Tobacco Control* doi:10.1136/tc.2010.039537.

Otañez, Marty G., Hadii Mamudu, and Stanton A. Glantz
    2007   Global Leaf Companies Control the Tobacco Market in Malawi. *Tobacco Control* 16:261–69.

    2009   Tobacco Companies' Use of Developing Countries' Economic Reliance on Tobacco to Lobby Against Global Tobacco Control: The Case of Malawi. *American Journal of Public Health* 99:1759.

Otañez, Marty G., M. E. Muggli, R. D. Hurt, and Stanton A. Glantz
    2006   Eliminating Child Labour in Malawi: A British American Tobacco Corporate Responsibility Project to Sidestep Tobacco Labour Exploitation. *Tobacco Control* 15 (3): 224–30.

Oxfam America
    2004   *Like Machines in the Field: Workers without Rights in American Agriculture*. Boston, MA: Oxfam America.

Parrish, Steven
    2007   FDA Authority Over Tobacco Products Offers Healthy Future. *Richmond Times Dispatch*, February 25, E1.

Patton, Janet
    2007   Bills Would Let FDA Regulate Tobacco. *Lexington Herald-Leader*, January 28, A1.

Peters, Pauline
    1993   Transforming Land Rights: State Policy and Local Practice in Malawi. Paper presented at the Program in Agrarian Studies, Yale University, New Haven, CT, February 19.

Petryna, Adriana
    1999   *Life Exposed: Biological Citizens after Chernobyl*. Princeton: Princeton University Press.

    2005   Ethical Variability: Drug Development and Globalizing Clinical Trials. *American Ethnologist* 32 (2): 183–97.

Philip Morris USA
    2001   FDA Regulation of Cigarettes, June 27, 2001. Bates No. 2085626863/6868. Legacy Tobacco Documents Library, University of California, San Francisco. http://legacy.library.ucsf.edu/tid/byf31c00.

    2007a   Philip Morris USA online. http://www.philipmorrisusa.com/en/home.asp.

    2007b   Smoking and Health Issues. Philip Morris USA. http://www.philipmorrisusa.com/en/health_issues/?source=home_fca1.

    2007c   Tobacco Farmer Partnering Program. Philip Morris USA. http://www.philipmorrisusa.com/en/ourinitiatives/suppliers_guidelines_programs/tobacco_farmer_partneringprogram.asp.

2008a   About Us. Philip Morris USA. http://www.philipmorrisusa.com/en/ about_us/our_people/diversity_organizational_engagement/default.

2008b   Cigarette Litter Prevention. Philip Morris USA. http://www.philip morrisusa.com/en/our_initiatives/reducing_environmental_impact/cigarette_ litter_prevention.asp.

2008c   FDA Regulation of Tobacco Products. Philip Morris USA. http:// www.philipmorrisusa.com/en/legislation_regulation/fda/regulation_tobacco _products.

2008d   Reduced Harm. Philip Morris USA. http://www.philipmorrisusa. com/en/our_initiatives/reduced_harm.

2008e   Tobacco Farmer Partnering Program. Philip Morris USA. http://phil- ipmorrisusa.com/en/our_initiatives/business_partners/tobacco_farmer_ partnering_program.

2010   Helping Reduce Underage Tobacco Use. Philip Morris USA. http:// www.philipmorrisusa.com/en/cms/Responsibility/Helping_Nav/Helping_ Reduce_Underage_Tobacco_Use/default.aspx?src=top_nav.

Pierce, John P.
2002   Harm Reduction or Harm Maintenance? *Nicotine & Tobacco Research* (supplement): 53–54.

Polanyi, Karl
1957   The Economy as Instituted Process. In *Trade and Market in the Early Empires: Economies in History and Theory*, Karl Polanyi, Conrad M. Arensberg, and Harry W. Pearson, eds. Glencoe, IL: Free Press.

Pollay, R. W., and T. Dewhirst
2002   The Dark Side of Marketing Seemingly "Light" Cigarettes: Successful Images and Failed Fact. *Tobacco Control* 11:18–31.

Pottier, Johan
1999   *Anthropology of Food: The Social Dynamics of Food Security*. Cambridge: Polity Press.

Proctor, Robert N.
2001   Tobacco and the Global Lung Cancer Epidemic. *Nature Reviews Cancer* 1 (1): 82–86.

Pulliam, Daniel
2003   North Carolinian Disrupts Washington Traffic with Tractor. *States News Service*, March 18.

Quandt, Sara A., Thomas A. Arcury, Colin K. Austin, and Rosa M. Saavedra
1998   Farmworker and Farmer Perceptions of Farmworker Agricultural Chemical Exposure in North Carolina. *Human Organization* 57 (3): 359–68.

Quandt, Sara A., Thomas A. Arcury, John S. Preisser, Deborah Norton, and Colin Austin
2000   Migrant Farmworkers and Green Tobacco Sickness: New Issues for an Understudied Disease. *American Journal of Industrial Medicine* 37 (3): 307–15.

Rabinow, Paul
1996   *Essays on the Anthropology of Reason*. Princeton: Princeton University Press.

2003   *Anthropos Today: Reflections on Modern Equipment.* Princeton: Princeton University Press.

Ramírez-Ferrero, Eric
2005   *Troubled Fields: Men, Emotions, and the Crisis in American Farming.* New York: Columbia University Press.

Rao, Pamela, Thomas A. Arcury, Sara A. Quandt, and Alicia Doran
2004   North Carolina Growers' and Extension Agents' Perceptions of Latino Farmworker Pesticide Exposure. *Human Organization* 63 (2): 151–61.

Reddy, Gayatri
2005   Geographies of Contagion: Hijras, Kothis, and the Politics of Sexual Marginality in Hyderabad. *Anthropology and Medicine* 12 (3): 255–70.

Reif, L. L.
1987   Farm Structure, Industry Structure, and Socioeconomic Conditions in the United States. *Rural Sociology* 52:462–82.

Rhoades, Robert E.
1984   *Breaking New Ground.* Lima, Peru: International Potato Center.

Rice, David
1999   Tobacco Firms Push Direct Contracts. *Richmond Times Dispatch*, December 7, C8.

R. J. Reynolds Tobacco Company
1978a   Tobacco Still King in North Carolina. Tobacco Documents Online. http://tobaccodocuments.org/rjr/500184801-4816.html.
1978b   R. J. Reynolds Industries 1978 Annual Report. Tobacco Documents Online. http://tobaccodocuments.org/rjr/500433812-3879_D1.html.
1979   R. J. Reynolds "Pride in Tobacco" Dinners. Bates Number 03532441/ 2442. Legacy Tobacco Documents Library. http://legacy.library.ucsf.edu/ tid/kdb81e00.
1982   "Pride in Tobacco" Expansion Proposal. Tobacco Documents Online. http://tobaccodocuments.org/rjr/503772203-2216.html.
1984   Pride in Tobacco, Newsline. Bates Number TIMN0175950/5951. Legacy Tobacco Documents Library. http://legacy.library.ucsf.edu/tid/ yoh82f00/pdf.

Rosaldo, Renato
1997   Cultural Citizenship, Inequality, and Multiculturalism. In *Latino Cultural Citizenship: Claiming Identity, Space and Politics*, William V. Flores and Rina Benmayor, eds., 27–38. Boston, MA: Beacon Press.

Rose, Nikolas
2007   *The Politics of Life Itself: Biomedicine, Power, and Subjectivity in the Twenty-First Century.* Princeton: Princeton University Press.

Rosen, James
2002   "Cookie Jar" Approach to Tobacco Fund. *News and Observer* (Raleigh), November 23.

Rothenberg, Daniel
1998   *With These Hands: The Hidden World of Migrant Farmworkers Today.* New York: Harcourt Brace.

Ryan, Joan
    2002   High-Nicotine Tobacco Smells Like Money. *San Francisco Chronicle*, December 1, D4.

Sandalow, Marc
    2003   Hussein Defiant. *San Francisco Chronicle*, March 19, A1.

Sapolsky, Robert
    2005   Sick of Poverty. *Scientific American*, November, 93–99.

Saul, Stephanie
    2008a   Bill to Regulate Tobacco as a Drug Is Approved by a House Committee. *New York Times*, April 3, C3.
    2008b   Black Lawmakers Seek Restrictions on Menthol Cigarettes. *New York Times*, July 1.

Schell, Greg
    2002   Farmworker Exceptionalism under the Law: How the Legal System Contributes to Farmworker Poverty and Powerlessness. In *The Human Cost of Food: Farmworkers' Lives, Labor, and Advocacy*, Charles D. Thompson, Jr., and Melissa F. Wiggins, eds., 139–66. Austin: University of Texas Press.

Scheper-Hughes, Nancy
    1992   *Death without Weeping: The Violence of Everyday Life in Brazil.* Berkeley: University of California Press.

Schreiner, Bruce
    2010   Farmers' Tobacco Contracts Cut. *News and Observer* (Raleigh), May 20.

Schutz, Alfred
    1967   *The Phenomenology of the Social World.* Frederick Lehnert Walsh, trans. Evanston, IL: Northwestern University Press.

Schweninger, Loren
    1989   A Vanishing Breed: Black Farm Owners in the South, 1651–1982. *Agricultural History* 63 (3): 41–57.

Scott, James C.
    1985   *Weapons of the Weak: Everyday Forms of Peasant Resistance.* New Haven, CT: Yale University Press.
    1998   *Seeing Like a State: How Certain Schemes to Improve the Human Condition Have Failed.* New Haven, CT: Yale University Press.

Shatenstein, Stan
    2004   Food and Drug Administration Regulation of Tobacco Products: Introduction. *Tobacco Control* 13:438.

Shields, P. G.
    2002   Tobacco Smoking, Harm Reduction, and Biomarkers. *Journal of the National Cancer Institute* 94:1435–44.

Shifflett, Crandall A.
    1982   *Patronage and Poverty in the Tobacco South: Louisa Country, Virginia, 1860–1900.* Knoxville: University of Tennessee Press.

Shiffman, S., J. G. Gitchell, K. E. Warner, J. Slade, J. E. Henningfield, and J. M. Pinney
    2001 Tobacco Harm Reduction: Conceptual Structure and Nomenclature for Analysis and Research. *Nicotine & Tobacco Research* 4 (2): 113–29.

Shreiner, Bruce
    2004   Study Bashes Tobacco Buyout. *Wilson Daily Times*, June 22.
Sider, Gerald
    1986   *Culture and Class in Anthropology and History: A Newfoundland Il-
            lustration*. Cambridge: Cambridge University Press.
    2006   The Production of Race, Locality, and State: An Anthropology. *An-
            thropologica* 48 (2): 247–63.
Siegel, Frederick F.
    1987   *The Roots of Southern Distinctiveness: Tobacco and Society in Dan-
            ville, Virginia, 1780–1865*. Chapel Hill: University of North Carolina Press.
Siegel, Michael
    2004   Food and Drug Administration Regulation of Tobacco: Snatching
            Defeat from the Jaws of Victory. *Tobacco Control* 13:439–41.
Simpson, David
    2008   Malaysia: Tough New Warnings. *Tobacco Control* 17:368–71.
Singer, Merrill
    2006   *The Face of Structural Violence: Life History of a Street Drug Addict*.
            Prospect Heights, IL: Waveland Press.
Smail, John
    1994   *The Origins of Middle-Class Culture: Halifax, Yorkshire, 1660–1780*.
            Ithaca, NY: Cornell University Press.
Smith, Elizabeth A., and Ruth E. Malone
    2003a   Altria Means Tobacco: Philip Morris's Identity Crisis. *American Jour-
            nal of Public Health* 93 (4): 553–56.
    2003b   Thinking the "Unthinkable": Why Philip Morris Considered Quit-
            ting. *Tobacco Control* 12:208–13.
Smith-Nonini, Sandy
    1999   *Uprooting Injustice: A Report on Working Conditions for North Car-
            olina Farmworkers and the Farm Labor Organizing Committee's Mt. Olive
            Initiative*. Durham, NC: Institute for Southern Studies.
    2005   Federally Sponsored Mexican Migrants in the Transnational South. In
            The American South in a Global World, J. L. Peacock, H. L. Watson, and
            C. R. Matthews, eds., 59–79. Chapel Hill: University of North Carolina
            Press.
Snell, William M.
    2004   Tobacco Quota Buyout: Implications for Kentucky's Tobacco Economy.
            Department of Agricultual Econoics, University of Kentucky. http://www.ca
            .uky.edu/cmspubsclass/files/lpowers/buyout/04nov_implications.pdf.
Snell, William M., Laura Powers, and Greg Halich
    2008   Tobacco Economics in the Post-Buyout Era. In *The 2008 Kentucky
            Tobacco Production Guide*, Kenny Seebold and Bob Pearce, eds., 4–6.
            Lexington: College of Agriculture, University of Kentucky.
Spellman, C. L.
    1947   Elm City: A Negro Community in Action. Unpublished manuscript,
            Rural Education, Florida A&M College.
Stair, Margaret J.
    2004   Burr Will Accept FDA. *Wilson Daily Times*, September 20.

Stebbins, Kenyon R.
   2001   Going Like Gangbusters: Transnational Tobacco Companies "Making a Killing" in South America. *Medical Anthropology Quarterly* 15 (2): 147–70.
Stephenson, Joan
   2000   A "Safer" Cigarette? Prove It, Say Critics. *Journal of the American Medical Association* 283:2507–8.
Stewart, George C.
   1983   Net Fund. *Wilson Daily Times*, January 1, 6B.
Stewart, Kathleen
   1988   Nostalgia: A Polemic. *Cultural Anthropology* 3 (3): 227–41.
   1996   *A Space on the Side of the Road: Cultural Poetics in an "Other" America*. Princeton: Princeton University Press.
   2000   Real American Dreams (Can Be Nightmares). In *Cultural Studies and Political Theory*, Jodi Dean, ed., 243–57. Ithaca, NY: Cornell University Press.
   2002   Scenes of Life/Kentucky Mountains. *Public Culture* 14 (2): 349–60.
   2005   Trauma Time: A Still Life. In *Histories of the Future*, Daniel Rosenberg and Susan Harding, eds., 321–40. Durham, NC: Duke University Press.
   2007   *Ordinary Affects*. Durham, NC: Duke University Press.
Stolberg, Sheryl Gay
   2011   Wal-Mart Shifts Strategy to Promote Healthy Foods. *New York Times*, January 20.
Storper, Michael
   2000   Lived Effects of the Contemporary Economy: Globalization, Inequality, and Consumer Society. *Public Culture* 12 (2): 375–409.
Strasser, A. A., K. Z. Tang, M. D. Tuller, and J. N. Cappella
   2008   PREP Advertisement Features Affect Smokers' Beliefs Regarding Potential Harm. *Tobacco Control* 17 (1): 32–38.
Stratton, Kathleen, Padma Shetty, Robert Wallace, and Stuart Bondurant
   2001   Clearing the Smoke: The Science Base for Tobacco Harm Reduction. *Tobacco Control* 10:189–95.
Striffler, Steve
   2005   We're All Mexicans Here: Poultry Processing, Latino Migration, and the Transformation of Class in the South. In *The American South in a Global World*, J. L. Peacock, H. L. Watson, and C. R. Matthews, eds., 152–65. Chapel Hill: University of North Carolina Press.
Sullivan, Sarah, and Stanton A. Glantz
   2010   The Changing Role of Agriculture in Tobacco Control Policymaking: A South Carolina Case Study. *Social Science & Medicine* 71 (8): 1527–34.
Sullivan, Sarah, Richard L. Barnes, and Stanton A. Glantz
   2009   *Shifting Attitudes Towards Tobacco Control in Tobacco Country Tobacco Industry Political Influence and Tobaco Policy Making in South Carolina*. Center for Tobacco Control Rsearch and Education.

Sunder Rajan, Kaushik
    2006   *Biocapital: The Constitution of Postgenomic Life.* Durham, NC: Duke
        University Press.
Swanson, Mark A.
    2001   No Substitute for Tobacco: The Search for Farm Diversification in
        Appalachian Kentucky. Ph.D. diss., University of Florida, Gainesville.
Szczypka, Glen, Melanie A. Wakefield, Sherry Emery, Yvonne M. Terry-McElrath,
    Brian R. Flay, and Frank J. Chaloupka
    2007   Working to Make an Image: An Analysis of Three Philip Morris
        Corporate Media Campaigns. *Tobacco Control* 16:344–350.
Taussig, Michael T.
    1983   *The Devil and Commodity Fetishism in South America.* Chapel Hill:
        University of North Carolina Press.
    1987   *Shamanism, Colonialism, and the Wild Man: A Study in Terror and
        Healing.* Chicago: University of Chicago Press.
    1999   *Defacement: Public Secrecy and the Labor of the Negative.* Stanford,
        CA: Stanford University Press.
Teater, Robin
    1982   Allotment Holders Relieved. *Wilson Daily Times*, July 19, 8.
Thomas, John G.
    1939   Wilsonia. *Wilson Daily Times*, October 23, 7.
Thompson, Charles D., Jr.
    2002a   Introduction. In *The Human Cost of Food: Farmworkers' Lives,
        Labor, and Advocacy*, Charles D. Thompson, Jr., and Melissa F. Wiggins,
        eds., 2–20. Austin: University of Texas Press.
    2002b   Layers of Loss: Migrants, Small Farmers, and Agribusiness. In *The
        Human Cost of Food: Farmworkers' Lives, Labor, and Advocacy*, Charles
        D. Thompson, Jr., and Melissa F. Wiggins, eds., 55–86. Austin: University
        of Texas Press.
Thompson, Charles D., Jr., and Melissa F. Wiggins, eds.
    2002   *The Human Cost of Food: Farmworkers' Lives, Labor, and Advocacy.*
        Austin: University of Texas Press.
Thrasher, J. F., J. Niederdeppe, M. C. Farrelly, K. C. Davis, K. M. Ribisl, and
    M. L. Haviland
    2004   The Impact of Anti-Tobacco Industry Prevention Messages in Tobac-
        co Producing Regions: Evidence from the US Truth Campaign. *Tobacco
        Control* 13:283.
Thu, Kendall
    2001   Agriculture, the Environment, and Sources of State Ideology and
        Power. *Culture & Agriculture* 23 (1): 1–7.
Tiller, Kelly, William Snell, and Blake Brown
    2007   Tobacco Policy. In *The 2007 Farm Bill: Policy Options and Conse-
        quences*, Joe Outlaw, ed., 1–5. Oak Brook, IL: Farm Foundation.
Tilley, Nannie May
    1948   *The Bright Tobacco Industry, 1860–1929.* Chapel Hill: University of
        North Carolina Press.

Tobacco Institute
  1988   Press Release, July 29. Legacy Tobacco Documents Library. http://
       legacy.library.ucsf.edu/tid/jpf92100.
Toussaint, W. D., and Dale M. Hoover
  1962   The Lease and Transfer Program in Prospectus. *Flue-Cured Tobacco
       Farmer* 2:14–15.
Trouillot, Michel-Rolph
  1991   Anthropology and the Savage Slot: The Poetics and Politics of Other-
       ness. In *Recapturing Anthropology: Working in the Present*, Richard Fox,
       ed., 17–44. Santa Fe, NM: School of American Research.
  2001   The Anthropology of the State: Close Encounters of a Deceptive Kind.
       Current Anthropology 42 (1): 125–38.
  2003   *Global Transformations: Anthropology and the Modern World*. New
       York: Palgrave.
Tucker, Neely
  2003   Farmer Deemed Fit for Trial. *Washington Post*, March 22, B3.
Unger, Jennifer B., et al.
  2003   Exploring the Cultural Context of Tobacco Use: A Transdisciplinary
       Framework. *Nicotine & Tobacco Research* 5 (6): 101–7.
U.S. Centers for Disease Control
  1996   Recall of Philip Morris Cigarettes, May 1995–March 1996. *Morbidity
       and Mortality Weekly* 45 (12): 251–54.
U.S. Department of Agriculture
  1997   *Civil Rights at the United States Department of Agriculture*. Washing-
       ton, DC: United States Department of Agriculture.
  1998   *A Time to Act: A Report on the USDA National Commission on Small
       Farms*. Washington, DC: United States Department of Agriculture.
  2001   *Tobacco at a Crossroad: A Call for Action; Final Report of the Presi-
       dent's Commission on Improving Economic Opportunity in Communities
       Dependent on Tobacco Production While Protecting Public Health*. Wash-
       ington, DC: United States Department of Agriculture.
Valentine, Patrick M.
  2002   *The Rise of a Southern Town: Wilson, North Carolina, 1849–1920*.
       Baltimore, MD: Gateway Press.
Villarejo, Don
  2003   The Health of U.S. Hired Farm Workers. *Annual Review of Public
       Health* 24:175–93.
Wagner, J.
  1999   Group Aims to Rejuvenate Rural Areas. *News and Observer* (Raleigh),
       July 2.
Wakefield, Melanie, Glen Szczypka, Yvonne Terry-McElrath, Sherry Emery, Brian
     Flay, Frank Chaloupka, and Henry Saffe
  2003   Mixed Messages on Tobacco: Comparative Exposure to Public Health,
       Tobacco Company–and Pharmaceutical Company–Sponsored Tobacco-
       Related Television Campaigns in the United States, 1999–2003. *Addiction*
       100:1875–83.

Wakefield, Melanie, Kim McLeod, and Cheryl L. Perry
  2006 "Stay Away from Them until You're Old Enough to Make a Decision":
    Tobacco Company Testimony about Youth Smoking Initiation. *Tobacco Control* 15 (supplement 4): 44–53.
Waldby, Catherine
  2000 *The Visible Human Project: Informatic Bodies and Posthuman Medicine*. London: Routledge.
Wall Street Journal
  2009 Washington's Marlboro Men: Congress Loves Big Tobacco Enough to Regulate It. June 13.
Weber, Max
  1958 *The Protestant Work Ethic and the Spirit of Capitalism*. Talcott Parsons, trans. New York: Scribner.
Welch, William M.
  1981 What Will Happen If Tobacco Program Scrapped by Congress? *Wilson Daily Times*, August 7, 6.
Welker, Marina A.
  2009 "Corporate Security Begins in the Community": Mining, the Corporate Social Responsibility Industry, and Environmental Advocacy in Indonesia. *Cultural Anthropology* 24 (1): 142–79.
Wells, Miriam J.
  1996 *Strawberry Fields: Politics, Class, and Work in California Agriculture*. Ithaca, NY: Cornell University Press.
West, Cornel
  1999 The Ignoble Paradox of Modernity. In *The Cornel West Reader*, 51–54. New York: Basic Civitas Books.
  2008 *Hope on a Tightrope: Words and Wisdom*. New York: Hay House.
White, Larry C.
  1988 *Merchants of Death: The American Tobacco Industry*. New York: William Morrow.
Williams, Raymond
  1977 *Marxism and Literature*. Oxford: Oxford University Press.
Wilson Advance
  1896 [Title Unknown.] November 12.
Wilson Daily Times
  1896a Farm Papers. May 22, 3.
  1896b Why the Farmer Should Be Educated. May 15, 7.
  1897 Word with Southern Farmers. June 2, 7.
  1939a Selling Tobacco Too Rapidly. September 10, 4.
  1939b Marketing Tobacco Too Fast. October 24, 4.
  1955 Wilson County Farm. February 11, 9.
  1961 Bill Lewis Says. November 20, 17.
  1963 Farm Practices. January 4, 1 and 3.
  1981 Leaf Loan Not a Subsidy. February 24, 4.
  1982 Tobacco Problems Mount. November 23, 4.
  1983a Another Tobacco Fight. February 18, 4.
  1983b Rose Answers Helms' Criticism. February 17, 1.

1983c   Helms Wrote Letters. May 26, 1 and 6.
1983d   Helms Says He Was Only Trying. May 27, 1 and 12.
1983e   Helms Says Subcommittee. June 2, 1.
1985a   No Agreement Made. January 30, 1.
1985b   Slim Chances for Leaf. May 17, 4.
1985c   Leaf Plan Raising Doubts. July 3, 1 and 10.
1985d   Reynolds Rejects. July 10, 1 and 6.
1985e   Rose Says Bailout Plan Victory for Companies. June 10, 1 and 12.
1985f   Rose Wants Stabilization to Operate. July 27, 1 and 2.
1985g   Helms Tobacco Plan Meeting Opposition. October 17, 1 and 10.
1985h   Leaf Program Agreement. December 14, 1.
1985i   Rose Says Bailout Plan Victory for Companies. June 10, 1 and 12.
1986a   Reply to FmHA. January 15, 4.
1986b   Cash Flow Needed. January 17, 4.
1989a   Attacks on Tobacco Hypocritical. February 23, 4.
1989b   Greensboro's Smoking Ordinance. November 16.
1989c   New Law Should Lead to Migrant Housing Improvements. September 4, 1 and 8.
1989d   Inspector. November 1, 1 and 12.
1992   Dozens of Illegal Aliens. June 24, 1.
1997a   Leaf Quotas May Be Cut. December 1, 1 and 2.
1997b   Tobacco Quota Decline Will Hurt. December 4, 8
2001a   Buyout Would Disrupt Economy. May 14.
2001b   Growers Seem to Favor Buyout. May 30.
2002   Tobacco Cuts Touch All. December 20.
2003   Buyout Proposal Riles Tobacco Makers. August 6.
2004a   Farmers Urged to Maintain Pressure for Tobacco Buyout. June 12.
2004b   Tobacco Buyout Unlikely This Year. March 15.
2004c   House Passes Tobacco Buyout. June 18.
2004d   Tobacco Bill Has Become a Big Handout. July 3.
2004e   Farmers Want Quota Buyout. April 19.
2004f   Invest Buyout Revenue in Local Jobs. July 13.
2004g   Growers Praise Buyout Move. June 7.
2004h   Ads Show Unity for Buyout. August 28.
2004i   FDA Control is Excuse. September 17.
2004j   Fellow Friends of Tobacco. November 2.
2005   No Rush to Sign Up For Buyout. March 14.
Wilson, Richard, David F. Duncan, and Thomas Nicholson
    2004   Public Attitudes toward Smoking Bans in a Tobacco-Producing County. *Southern Medical Journal* 97 (7): 645–50.
Winters, Donald L.
    1998   Agriculture in the Post–World War II South. In *The Rural South since World War II*, R. Douglas Hurt, ed., 8–27. Baton Rouge: Louisiana State University Press.
Wolf, Eric
    1982   *Europe and the People without History*. Berkeley: University of California Press.

Womach, Jasper
    2003   *U.S. Tobacco Production, Consumption, and Export Trends.* Washington, DC: Congressional Research Service.
    2004a   *Tobacco-Related Programs and Activities of the U.S. Department of Agriculture: Operation and Cost.* Washington, DC: Congressional Research Service.
    2004b   *Tobacco Farmer Assistance.* Washington, DC: Congressional Research Service.
    2004c   *Tobacco Quota Buyout Proposals in the 108th Congress.* Washington, DC: Congressional Research Service.
Wood, Phillip J.
    1986   *Southern Capitalism: The Political Economy of North Carolina, 1880–1980.* Durham, NC: Duke University Press.
World Bank
    1999   *Curbing the Epidemic: Governments and the Economics of Tobacco Control.* Washington, DC: World Bank.
World Health Organization
    2004   Tobacco and Poverty. World Health Organization website. http://www.emro.who.int/TFI/wntd2004/kit-part2.htm.
    2008a   *WHO Report on the Global Tobacco Epidemic, 2008: The MPOWER Package.* Geneva: World Health Organization.
    2008b   Study Group. World Health Organization website. http://www.who.int/gb/fctc/PDF/cop3/FCTC_COP3_11-en.pdf.
    2009   Framework Convention. World Health Organization website. http://www.who.int/fctc/en.
Wright, Gavin
    1986   *Old South, New South: Revolutions in the Southern Economy since the Civil War.* New York: Basic Books.
Yach, Derek
    2005   Injecting Greater Urgency into Global Tobacco Control. *Tobacco Control* 14 (3): 145–48.
Yach, Derek, and Douglas Bettcher
    2000   Globalisation of Tobacco Industry Influence and New Global Responses. *Tobacco Control* 9:206–16.
Yang, Lawrence Hsin, Arthur Kleinman, Bruce G. Link, Jo C. Phelan, Sing Lee, and Byron Good
    2007   Culture and Stigma: Adding Moral Experience to Stigma Theory. *Social Science and Medicine* 64 (7): 1524–35.
Žižek, Slavoj
    1989   *The Sublime Object of Ideology.* New York: Verso.
Zuckerbrod, Nancy
    2004a   Opposition to Tobacco Buyout. *Wilson Daily Times,* July 26.
    2004b   More Jobs Expected in South. *Wilson Daily Times,* October 14.
    2004c   Antismoking Groups Decry Buyout Legislation. *Wilson Daily Times,* October 8.

Index

Italicized page numbers indicate illustrations, figures and maps.